THE
SEXUALLY
OPPRESSED

ALSO BY HARVEY L. GOCHROS

Human Sexuality and Social Work
(edited with LeRoy G. Shultz)

Planned Behavior Change
(with Joel Fischer)

Handbook of Behavior Therapy with Sexual Problems: Vols. I & II
(edited with Joel Fischer)

BY JEAN S. GOCHROS

What Do You Say After You Clear Your Throat:
A Practical Guide to Sex Education

THE
SEXUALLY
OPPRESSED

Edited
and with Introductions by

Harvey L. & Jean S. Gochros

ASSOCIATION PRESS

NEW YORK

HN
57
.S48

International Standard Book Number: 0-8096-1915-6
Library of Congress Catalog Card Number: 76-49051

Library of Congress Cataloging in Publication Data
The sexually oppressed.

Includes bibliographies.
1. Discrimination—United States.   I. Gochros, Harvey L.
II. Gochros, Jean S. [DNLM: 1. Sex.   2. Minority groups.
3. Aged.   4. Women.   5. Homosexuality.
6. Handicapped.   7. Human rights.   HO64   S518]
HN57.S48   301.41'7973
ISBN 0-8096-1915-6

Printed in the United States of America
Designed by The Etheredges

We have found it impossible to give our support to conventional morality or to approve highly of the means by which society attempts to arrange the practical problems of sexuality in life. We can demonstrate with ease that what the world calls its code of morals demands more sacrifice than it is worth, and that its behavior is neither dictated by honesty nor instituted with wisdom.

SIGMUND FREUD
A General Introduction to Psychoanalysis
(*1920, pp. 376–377*)

This book is dedicated to
the oppressed who fight back,
and to those who fight beside them.

THE EDITORS

HARVEY L. GOCHROS, D.S.W., is professor of social work and Director of the Social Work Institute for the Study of Sex, University of Hawaii. He has conducted numerous workshops on human sexuality throughout the United States and has authored a number of articles and papers on social work education with sex-related problems. His books include *Human Sexuality and Social Work, Planned Behavior Change,* and the *Handbook of Behavior Therapy with Sexual Problems.* He wrote the article on "'Human Sexuality" which appears in the new (17th) edition of *The Encyclopedia of Social Work.*

JEAN S. GOCHROS, M.S.W., is a social worker in private practice specializing in family and sexual counseling in Honolulu, Hawaii. She is the author of many articles in the lay and professional literature. Her articles "From a Family Counselor's Notebook" appear in the *American Baby Magazine.* She has conducted numerous workshops and classes in human sexuality in Hawaii and on the mainland. She is currently completing a book on sex education for parents and teachers.

CONTENTS

II. THE YOUNG AND THE OLD

III. WOMEN

IV. THE HOMOSEXUALLY ORIENTED

CONTENTS

FOREWORD

Lester A. Kirkendall
Professor Emeritus of Family Life
at Oregon State University
and cofounder of SIECUS
(Sex Information and Education Council
of the United States)

In this time of continuing concern for minority groups who have been denied their rights, the Gochroses have added other hitherto ignored groups. Their oppressed groups, however, are not a particular segment of the population; rather, they are based on the use, or more specifically the denial, of the opportunity to enjoy and experience the satisfactions associated with the universal human impulse—the sexual. As these sexually oppressed are broken into groups some will be known to most readers: adolescents, the aged, blacks, homosexuals, women. Not so well known are some of the others—the poor, the imprisoned, the mentally disabled, the terminally ill, the Asian American, the asexual individual.

One realizes, of course, that at some time or another every person feels oppressed, or at least deprived of some sexual experience he would have enjoyed. However, this deprivation is something very different from the prevailing attitude that sexual expression is only for the young; that any interest in or sexual expression beyond forty or fifty years of age labels one as a dirty-minded oldster. Still another example of oppression includes homosexuals, who have few places to meet partners, who are often harassed and persecuted, and whose sexual acts need to be protected by consenting-adult laws. The mentally retarded and the physically handicapped are oppressed by the reticence which prevents both professional and nonprofessional people from speaking openly and explicitly about sexual matters and by the lack of the necessarily specialized knowledge required even if the readiness were there. It is obvious, then, that oppression comes in many forms and manifests itself in many ways.

One ray of hope, however, comes from the oppressed minorities themselves. Certain groups are demanding that the hampering restrictions they have experienced be removed; that they be accorded the freedom that other more liberated groups now have. This has resulted in several of the liberation movements which have attracted much attention and drastically changed the climate in the past several years. Gay Liberation, Women's Liberation, and the not-so-thoroughly organized, yet needed, Men's Liberation Movement are examples. The contribution made by these groups goes beyond the physical, copulatory aspects of sex, and attacks stereotypes, points out contradictions in psychosexual development, indicates available options, and spots sources of anxiety. The Gochroses note this development. But even if these movements have altered public views to some extent, more help is needed.

The Gochroses are social workers, and so their book is addressed, at least in part, to their peers; but I think it has a vastly wider audience. I hope it will be read by the average citizen, who will bring a particular frame of mind to its reading. Certainly many of the oppressions which are portrayed will exist and be maintained so long as various cultural support systems are retained. Thus I hope the citizen readers will think of themselves as activists who have their work mapped out for them. As voters who influence public opinion, as members of school boards, city councils, hospitals or retirement homes, as persons whose views influence others—these citizen readers have a contribution to make, and one which they should be asked to make.

This will certainly not be easy, for, as the Gochroses and their contributors point out, some of these attitudes and regulatory arrangements have deep historical roots. And here we arrive at a point where all of us, bar none, are oppressed—oppressed by the prevailing climate of opinion which everywhere prevents us from speaking openly, honestly and straightforwardly about our own sexuality. Until we can discard this repressiveness, our aid to the sexually oppressed about whom this book is written will indeed be much less effective than we should like it to be.

PREFACE

This book was written out of our concern about what we considered to be an unjust aspect of the contemporary sexual scene. Some time ago we had begun to realize the profound effect that the sexual revolution has had on many people, by enabling them to enjoy sexual expression with more choice of the manner in which they meet their sexual needs. At the same time, however, we were beginning to see some disparities: there were many people belonging to such groups as the aged, the homosexually oriented, the disabled, and the retarded, whose needs were still being unjustly and unnecessarily ignored, and often curtailed, by the general public and even by many of the supposedly professional helpers.

We realized, of course, that these groups are not equally oppressed, and that individuals within such groups encounter varying degrees of oppression. Indeed, there are many who might not feel oppressed at all. But, still, it seemed to us that these groups had, in varying degrees, been bypassed in the general rush toward sexual freedom.

We were particularly concerned that workshops, classes, and books for professionals in the area of human sexuality often gave only minimal attention, if any, to the unique needs, problems, and concerns of these groups. Perhaps more important, they offered no useful direction to professional helpers choosing to work with these oppressed groups. In our own practice and teaching of professionals, we then began to place more and more emphasis on these groups, despite the fact that many of our students initially seemed interested only in the sexuality of healthy, intelligent, verbal, attractive, and heterosexual young adults. We noted with pleasure, however, that when students were once exposed to the concerns of these overlooked groups, there was an increase in their interest, concern, and commitment to working with those we call "the sexually oppressed."

As we ourselves continued to learn more and more about the problems faced by these sexually oppressed groups, we became increasingly anxious to reach more people. Eventually we began to plan a book that would deal with the broad range of these problems and bring them to the attention of others, as well as presenting solutions already under way, and perhaps suggesting some new ones.

It was our hope that this book would be useful to professionals in such fields as medicine, law, social work, psychology, and education, and also that it would be of interest and help not only to the families and friends of sexually oppressed individuals but also to the oppressed themselves and to the lay public as well. We soon ran into two major problems in planning the book, however.

First, which oppressed groups should we include? As we proceeded to talk with others and to read articles and books on sex-related problems, we quickly learned that sexually oppressed groups are legion in our society; indeed, including virtually everyone but the New York Jets and Robert Redford. It became obvious that we certainly couldn't cover all of them.

Second. We had to find and select the authors. We were pleased to learn as we progressed with planning the book that an ever-growing number of practitioners and researchers are dealing directly and assertively with the sexual problems of these under-served groups who have for so long been ignored.

In choosing the oppressed groups, we felt that the size of the group should not be the major criterion, for the size of any group should not solely determine its rights and certainly does not determine its needs. Thus asexual women or aging gay men may indeed comprise a relatively small number of people, but still we must address ourselves to their concerns. We therefore decided on using, flexibly, three criteria for selecting the limited number of groups we could fit into a reasonably sized volume.

1. Groups already generally recognized as sexually oppressed were obviously appropriate to our book, even though they might be beginning to receive attention from the community as a whole. The homosexually oriented population is one such example.

2. Smaller, less obvious sexually oppressed groups whose needs and rights are still generally overlooked, such as prisoners and the terminally ill.

3. Those who are members of more than one sexually oppressed group and therefore have their problems compounded. Thus black widows encounter not only the oppression of women but also of blacks and widows; while aging gay men encounter not only the prejudices against homosexuality but also the prejudice against the aged—the burden of being old in a youth-oriented culture.

We tried to include representative groups from all these categories. Some of our choices were serendipitous; for example, at a workshop we were giving on sexual oppression, Lois Jaffe commented that there was one group that was almost always the last-thought-of when talking about sex—the dying. She made a convincing argument that dying persons do indeed have sexual needs and problems that have been ignored. Hence, we included them in our book.

Of course space did not permit our including all the groups we would have liked to include. There can be no question, for example, that transsexuals are oppressed or that the blind have significant problems to overcome in order to achieve a rewarding sex life. Perhaps even our omissions, however, will lead our readers to think of the many other groups who comprise the great mass of the sexually oppressed.

Selecting our contributors was only slightly less difficult than selecting our topics. We wanted original material written especially for this book by knowledgeable people who had firsthand experience in working with and understanding oppressed groups. Wherever possible, we preferred authors who were themselves members of these groups and who might thus be able to speak from personal experience. Over the years, we have had the opportunity to hear, and often meet, people who have taken the initiative in developing educational programs and clinical services for particular oppressed groups. We were fortunate in being able to convince many of them to become contributors to this book.

The reader will also note that a significant number of our contributors are (as we are) social workers. This is not by accident. The social work profession has long concerned itself with problems of oppression in general; and sexual oppression (although not always defined in these terms) in particular. While there are experts in many fields who share this concern and are quite knowledgeable, we feel that social workers bring a unique perspective to social problems, because they share a common conviction as to the dignity and worth of all people, along with an understanding and appreciation of cultural and socioeconomic influences on behavior. Social workers have borrowed freely from the knowledge bases of many professions, unifying them into an overview of people as total beings rather than as sets of walking symptoms of either biological, psychological or societal pathology. Hence social workers may be as concerned with legislation and social action as they are with individual problems, behaviors, and clinical interventions. Sexual problems are seen as part and parcel of other problems, and help in any one area may be useless without understanding and help in the individual's total life situation.

Furthermore, social workers are in a position continually to see at first hand the problems that people face, to explore various ways of helping them solve these problems, and to be acutely aware of the gaps in society's services to these people. At the same time, however, social workers belong to the society in which they live, share in its biases and blind spots, and often overlook problems which are outside their immediate area of specialization. It would seem logical, then, that they should share their experience, knowledge, and perspective with one another, with the general public and with those in allied professions.

It is our hope that this book will call attention to problems, raise questions, suggest solutions, and in general stimulate further comment and research. If it does that, perhaps it will serve as a small step toward reducing sexual oppression and creating a climate in which people having diverse backgrounds and needs can find greater fulfillment through their sexual expression.

HARVEY AND JEAN GOCHROS

Honolulu, Hawaii
August 1976

ACKNOWLEDGMENTS

An anthology of original writings involves a great deal of work by many people besides the editors. Without the help of those we now mention, this book could never have been completed, and our appreciation is far greater than our words can convey.

We first want to express our profound gratitude to the dedicated educators, practitioners and scholars who wrote these chapters. Many of them are pioneers in championing the sexual needs and rights of oppressed and under-served groups.

We also want to thank our many friends and colleagues who suggested oppressed groups we had not recognized, who helped us locate the right authors for our topics, and who encouraged us and acted as readers for segments of the book.

We want to note the help of two ardent feminists, Wanita Willinger and Susan Gochros, who gave both encouragement and time, but who never let their convictions interfere with sound judgment in their critiques.

Our special thanks go to Robert Roy Wright of Association Press, who has been at all times the enthusiastic, sensible, and helpful publisher's representative that all authors hope for, but rarely get.

Lester Kirkendall is a veritable pioneer in the area of understanding the interplay of the individual and society in sexual matters. He was therefore a logical choice to write our foreword and we were honored that he accepted our invitation to do so.

Louise Young and Susan Sakimoto certainly deserve our thanks and appreciation for their hard work, which has included not only typing but also retyping our last-minute revisions, often at breakneck speed.

Our thanks, too, go to our children, David and Susan, who not only gave us direct help, but who also put up with occasional parental-editorial squabbles and a good many McDonald suppers.

We especially wish to express our affection and deep appreciation to our good friend, Joel Fischer, of the University of Hawaii School of Social Work, for the unstinting gift of his time and thought, for his excellent editorial counsel, his support, and his ability to push us into action whenever we became discouraged or bogged down.

Finally, our appreciation goes to our many students, clients, colleagues and friends who shared their experiences with us in order that we might share them with others.

INTRODUCTION: WHO ARE THE SEXUALLY OPPRESSED?

Much of the excitement and controversy over the sexual revolution has abated in the last few years. There is no longer even a major debate over whether that revolution has indeed occurred. In place of the sensationalism and ballyhoo of the Sixties, there is a steady stream of events in the Seventies which seem to consolidate the sexual revolution in our daily lives. Recently, these events have come with some regularity, and often from unlikely places:

— the President's wife publicly acknowledges the possibility that her daughter might have an affair, and that if that were to happen, she would calmly discuss it with her daughter.

— a best-selling book presents a cookbook approach to sexual joy;

— the Supreme Court upholds the right of any woman to terminate an unwanted pregnancy, with her physician's approval;

— the American Psychiatric Association votes the "disease" label for homosexuality out of existence, as an Air Force sergeant fights for his right to remain in the service despite his open acknowledgment of his homosexuality, and a Massachusetts state legislator is elected despite (and perhaps, for some people, on the basis of) her homosexuality;

— popular TV series treat transsexualism, rape, and abortion with sensitivity and honesty, and at least implicitly allow their heroes and heroines to be sexually active, both in and out of marriage;

— an increasing number of states remove prohibitions of adultery, fornication, homosexual behavior and other adult consensual sexual behaviors from their law books, and some lower the age of sexual consent to as young as fourteen.

What has led to these extraordinary events? Here we find a common thread that connects them all, and, indeed, a common factor which is largely responsible for their occurrence: People are slowly but steadily accepting the idea that reproduction and sexuality are not inevitably bound together, and that they may be treated and accepted separately.

Sexuality in its fullest sense obviously involves much more than its reproductive potential. Otherwise, humans would have evolved as did other mammals—to be sexually interested in one another only at those points in the female's cycle at which she is likely to become pregnant. Instead, humans have nonseasonal sexuality. Their sexuality involves many nonreproductive elements, some of which are difficult to define or measure. Sexuality can include the satisfaction of skin hunger, the enjoyment of physical contact, and stimulation of one's body either by one's self or with a partner. It can include the release of tension that orgasm can bring, and it can include intense emotional intimacy and desire for closeness with a particular person. It can include the expression of one's sense of maleness or femaleness to those in the individual's environment. In short, sexuality can be many things unrelated to reproduction.

This is a relatively new idea. Throughout history the strength of any society has been directly related to how many children were born and cared for. Therefore, each society, through its laws, religion, mores, and other pressures and reinforcements, has funneled the sexual drive and its associated pleasures into heterosexual intercourse within semipermanent relationships. In other words, an almost universal rule controlling sexual behavior has evolved. This is known as "The Reproductive Bias." This rule states that the only acceptable (normal, natural, beautiful, legal, healthy, mature, Christian, desirable, and so on) sexual behavior is that behavior between adults that could lead to a socially approved pregnancy. In essence, this rule limited sex to young (but not too young), healthy (both mentally and physically), intelligent, rich, white, and beautiful heterosexual couples. We refer to these people as "The Sexual Elite."

The sexual elite is best exemplified by the idealized hero and heroine of the film *Love Story*. In that film the hero is a young and handsome law student and the heroine is a young and beautiful music student. They fall in love immediately, engage in premarital intercourse primarily as an expression of their love, and subsequently marry. She uses four-letter words, but, underneath it all, is a nice girl who would not dream of marital infidelity. They have a great deal of fun and never stop loving each other until she dies an elegant death. Neither seems to feel much love or affection for anyone else except her father, who is sweet but passive. One is led to speculate that the hero is always potent, the heroine always achieves multiple sequential orgasms, and that they never need Kleenex. They seem to consider genital-to-genital intercourse in the missionary position culminating in simultaneous orgasms the logical and normal conclusion to every sexual activity that occurs 2.7 times a week immediately following Johnny Carson. This is obviously a stereotype of the sexual elite that is maintained by the white middle class. There are, of course, sexual spectrums in other American subcultures. The ideal sexual model varies from group to group, place to place, and time to time.

The sexually elite, however, are not without their problems: even the *Love Story* image presented above implies that the reproductive bias limits not only who may engage in sexual behavior but also indicates what sexual behavior is acceptable. Hence, even the elite are taught that sexuality is essentially equivalent to "doing it"—especially for the man. "It" involves getting a willing partner, achieving and maintaining an erection, inserting the erect penis into her vagina and, after an appropriate interval, ejaculating. After all, this *is* the surest way of creating a pregnancy. At a relatively early age, the adolescent is set on this road of seeking "it" and doing "it" in pair relationships. Even in marriage, sex is often equated with "it." Alternatives to genital intercourse (*i.e.*, stroking, fondling, oral or anal contact, self-stimulation, and so on) are often seen as either cumbersome, effete, or sick, and, at best, merely a prelude (*i.e.*, "foreplay") to the "real thing." Masturbation as either a supplement or an alternative to intercourse provokes considerable anxiety among many of the elite. It clearly violates the reproductive taboo in that one can neither become nor make anyone else pregnant through masturbation (unless one has fantastic aim!). And many teen-agers have been led to believe that while intercourse without marriage may sometimes be tolerable, contraception (which involves "premeditated sex") isn't. Such a paradox can prove catastrophic. Certainly then, the reproductive bias limits and restricts the range of potential sexual expressions and joys of those in the sexual elite.

There are, however, a large number of men and women whose sexual behavior, for one reason or another, could not possibly lead to a socially approved pregnancy. Their needs, therefore, have at best been ignored, and at worst have been prevented from expression. To a greater or lesser degree, we—*i.e.*, significant segments of society—have considered it unlikely, impossible, or undesirable for many of these diverse groups of people to enjoy their sexuality. These groups include adolescents with strong—perhaps the strongest of all—sexual needs, and whose range of sexually acceptable behavior is circumscribed but increasingly vague; the old, who have been exhorted to "act their age" which means to be sexless; the imprisoned, who in our society are supposed to relinquish their sexuality as a punishment for their crimes; the homosexually oriented, perhaps the most oppressed because they can't even make each other pregnant; the handicapped (such as the paraplegic and the blind), whose physical condition allegedly prevents them from assuming the regular roles associated with sexual fulfillment; the mentally retarded, who go through life not smart enough to be permitted sexual fulfillment; unmarried adults, whose sexual needs are rejected or ignored by society, despite the Playboy image of the happy swinger; women, who have come a long way but still suffer from sexual ambivalence; and the poor, who have almost everything against them as far as sex goes, from poor nutrition and crowded housing to restrictive welfare laws.

Many of those in the helping professions did—and to some extent, still do—go along with these restrictions. Those working with the aged, the homosexual, the imprisoned, the handicapped, the adolescent, and so on, have rarely perceived their sexual needs and desires as legitimate and something to be assertively supported. All too often the sex-related needs of such groups have been considered as pathology to be suppressed or "cured."

The dramatic changes we have seen recently in sexual behavior and attitudes have resulted both from the greater acceptance of a basic human right to be different, and the diminution of the Reproductive Bias. As world population has increased to the point of suffocation, the idea has spread that unlimited reproduction, even within marriage, is not necessary or even productive for society as a whole. Indeed, the strength of any given society may now be measured not by the degree to which it reproduces itself, but rather by the degree to which it limits itself. As this reality spreads, sexuality increasingly becomes freed of its reproductive imperative. Contraception and even abortion technology enables such a separation. Once sexuality is separated from its reproductive consequences, a wider range of previously prohibited behaviors is permitted to occur. Nonreproductive sexual expression, (such as masturbation and homosexual behavior) becomes more permissible, other parts of the body besides the genitals come into view as sexual areas, women are allowed to have other goals and functions besides being sexual objects and baby machines, men need not constantly assert their *machismo*, and groups formerly excluded from sexual expression are now allowed it.

Revolutions do not occur simply because an oppressed group realizes it is oppressed. Rather, oppressed groups seek radical change in their situation when they see that because of changing environmental conditions such changes are within their reach. We have now entered an era in which it will be possible for people, very different from one another in their general characteristics, to maintain their differences and yet derive mutual joy from their common humanness.

We are just beginning this era, however, and the reproductive bias still pervades much of our thinking, causing professionals and citizens alike to overlook the needs of many groups, and to actively deny the fulfillment of some. Indeed, the fact that society as a whole is being freed from dysfunctional sexual repression, while particular segments of society are bypassed by the sexual revolution, constitutes true sexual oppression. We are barely beginning to recognize the needs and rights of women, homosexuals, the aged, the retarded, and others. As changes have begun, there also has been a backlash of considerable indignation and vehement opposition to these changes. Liberal laws that have been passed (such as the right to abortion) are in a tenuous position and could well be revoked, and oppressive laws concerning adult consensual sexual behavior could be reinstated, depending upon the political power in charge at any given time, and the degree of public pressure. Witness, for example the recent Supreme Court decision upholding Virginia's sodomy law.

Furthermore, many in the helping professions have subscribed to the notion that sex is a luxury; that compared to the other problems encountered in contemporary America, it is almost a frivolous diversion. Who can consider sexual deprivation seriously, it is asked, in light of the monumental social problems of racism, sexism, and poverty? It is difficult, if not pointless, to measure or compare degrees of pain and suffering, however. The presence of one form of oppression does not negate the presence—or virulence—of another. The World Health Organization has defined *health* as "the state of optimal social and physical well-being and not merely the absence of disease." Sexuality, at base, is the ultimate expression of this well-being. Its expression, in forms in which there are no victims, can enrich and give greater meaning to the life of all people.

I.
SOCIAL
AND
HISTORICAL
PERSPECTIVES

Sexual oppression can best be understood as a product of the social control of individual sexual expression. Most sexual behaviors are learned, and every society, to a greater or lesser extent, shapes and controls the form of expression of biological sex drives.

Because social needs vary from time to time and place to place, there are relatively few sexual behaviors that are universal. As a result of this shaping, a range of acceptable and even encouraged sexual behaviors emerges at any particular time in any particular social reference group. This spectrum of acceptable behaviors shifts over time: formerly forbidden behaviors become more permissible, while formerly approved behaviors may be rejected. In white, college-educated urban American society, for example, premarital sex, oral-genital sexual contact, and adult masturbation are becoming more widely acceptable, while the ideal of permanent marital fidelity and sexual romanticism is becoming weaker.

At any one time, in any social reference group, however, this sexual spectrum determines who can *have sex, who* must *have it, and who* must not *have it. The spectrum also determines when they should begin, in what form, and when they should stop; it determines the age, sex, number and characteristics of acceptable sexual partners; where, when and under what circumstances sexual activities should occur; and which sex-*

ual acts are condoned, involving which parts of the body, and in coitus, which positions.

These proscriptions are maintained in many obvious and other more subtle ways: religious edicts, laws, folklore and myths, the lyrics of songs, poetry, public opinion, edicts from "professionals," tradition communicated by parents and family, and, perhaps most significantly, the ridicule or fear of ridicule from friends and peers.

There are few aspects of culture about which people tend to be as ethnocentric as sexual behavior. Most societies have little tolerance for individuals who exhibit culturally defined deviant sexual behaviors either in other cultures or at home. Even today the vast majority of states still have laws which enforce concepts of sexual morality, including those situations in which there is no clear victim of the sexual behavior.

In this introductory section of our book, two articles are presented to provide a background for understanding contemporary sexual oppression. Haeberle traces the historical development of our current sexual values in a number of areas through significant epochs from Biblical times to contemporary America; while Kirk reviews the concept of deviance as it applies to the social control of sexual behavior.

CHAPTER 1

HISTORICAL ROOTS OF SEXUAL OPPRESSION*

Erwin J. Haeberle

In the eighteenth century a philosopher allegedly told one of his opponents: "I disagree with what you say, but will defend to the death your right to say it." This noble maxim perfectly summarizes the spirit of an enlightened age which struggled to free itself from intellectual and moral bondage, and which, for the first time in human history, proclaimed universal liberty, equality, and brotherhood. This same spirit also guided our Founding Fathers when, in the Constitution of the United States, they guaranteed every citizen freedom of speech, of religion, and of the press.

In the meantime these freedoms have found advocates in many other parts of the world. Over the last two hundred years the ideals of tolerance, individualism, self-determination, and personal privacy have been incorporated into the laws of most modern nations. Indeed, our own century has seen a "Universal Declaration of Human Rights" in which all member states of the United Nations pledge their support for these ideals. Thus, at least in theory, the liberation of the human race seems almost complete.

* The interested reader is referred to the author's forthcoming book, *The Sex Atlas*, to be published by Seabury Press. The material on which this chapter is based will appear there in a greatly revised and expanded form.

[3]

Alas, we all know that in actual practice things are much less encouraging. Officially, governments may very well subscribe to the famous maxim of that enlightened philosopher, but unofficially many of them still treat all dissent as treason. As a matter of fact, in spite of their libertarian rhetoric, some modern states are more oppressive than were the worst medieval kingdoms.

All of this is, of course, quite obvious and therefore does not warrant any further discussion here. However, it is not often realized that even in the most tolerant Western countries the tolerance does not extend equally to all spheres of human life. Most notably two kinds of behavior continue to suffer irrational and often severe restrictions: the use of drugs and sexual activity. No public official is yet willing to say: "I disapprove of the drugs you take, but will defend to the death your right to take them" or "I disapprove of your sexual interests, but will defend to the death your right to pursue them." Such pronouncements would be considered scandalous and irresponsible by most citizens. Drugs and sex remain the great taboos of our civilization.

Actually, in recent times drugs and sex have also begun to be feared by many formerly permissive societies which have been subject to Western influence. It is therefore hardly surprising to find that the celebrated "Universal Declaration of Human Rights" says nothing about people's right to control their own bodies. The document only cites the "right to marry and to found a family" and to choose one's marriage partner freely (Article 16). There is no mention of a right to sex education or sexual fulfillment, the right to free choice of a sexual partner or type of sexual activity, a right to contraception or abortion. Nor is this merely an oversight. Unfortunately, there is little doubt that even today the General Assembly of the United Nations would overwhelmingly reject any official declaration which dared to affirm these rights. Too many member states still consider sex legitimate only within marriage and for the purpose of procreation.

However, it should be well understood that societies which make procreation the only permissible function of sex thereby implicitly condemn most actual human sexual behavior as abnormal or deviant. Thus, solitary masturbation, sex play among children, adolescent sexual experiments, premarital and non-coital forms of marital intercourse, homosexual activity, sexual contact with animals, sex after the menopause—all of these and many other harmless forms of sexual behavior come to be seen as heretical practices which have to be suppressed. This suppression, in turn, creates a universal feeling of guilt and anxiety. Furthermore, since the suppression can never be complete, the development of a sexual double standard and widespread hypocrisy is virtually inevitable. In short, narrow sexual dogmatism always leads to social conflict and a great deal of human misery.

THE "REPRODUCTIVE BIAS"

The nature of sex is by no means as limited or as obvious as many people believe. There have been primitive peoples on this planet who were quite unaware of any connection between sex and procreation. They assumed that a spirit entered the female body, where it then grew into a child. Thus, for them, sex was simply a joyful experience in its own right. We also know that in the past many advanced civilizations considered the pleasure of sexual intercourse at least as important as the possibly resulting pregnancies. We therefore have to conclude that the restriction of human sexual capacities to the single task of producing children is not a natural necessity, but the result of a very specific cultural development.

What are the causes of this development? Over the years, many writers have wrestled with this question and have provided quite different answers. In 1884 Friedrich Engels, in *The Origin of the Family, Private Property and the State*, linked sexual oppression to oppressive economic conditions. In 1930 Sigmund Freud, in *Civilization and Its Discontents*, explained sexual frustration as the inevitable price of human progress. In 1932 Wilhelm Reich traced "The Imposition of Sexual Morality" and ascribed all modern sexual problems to the emergence of a patriarchal family structure.

However, these and other theories, while pervasive in many details, remained highly speculative and were eventually contradicted by newer anthropological findings. When, in *Patterns of Sexual Behavior* (1951), Clellan S. Ford and Frank A. Beach compared 191 different societies, they found no direct correlation between cultural advancement and sexual oppression. Restrictive, semirestrictive, and permissive sexual attitudes could be documented for both primitive and civilized peoples. In short, as of now, the mystery is still unsolved.

Nevertheless, a great deal has been learned from the existing limited inquiries. The deeper causes of sexual oppression may still escape us, but there is no longer any uncertainty about its effects on our own particular culture. We also have gained some insight into the growth of Western asceticism and sexual negativism. Thus, it has now become possible to illuminate certain important aspects of the problem. We can only hope that future research will fill in the missing parts of the puzzle. In the present short article we shall have to limit ourselves to a few historical observations.

SEXUAL MORALITY AND RELIGIOUS BELIEF

The moral values of our Western civilization can be derived from three main sources: the world of classical Greece and Rome, the Christian Church, and, through it, the cultural heritage of ancient Israel. This means, among other things, that many of our present attitudes (including sexual attitudes) are rooted in a far distant past, and that, at least initially, they were not based on rational considerations.

We have to remember that in all ancient societies moral questions were decided on strictly religious grounds. People knew good from bad and right from wrong because they had learned the difference from some superhuman authority. Thus, all of their norms, standards, customs, and laws were a direct expression of their religious beliefs. Indeed, for many thousands of years every law of nature and society was, in some sense, a religious law. The spirits, the gods, or God ruled not only the natural, but also the social world. They wanted human beings to behave in a certain way and promptly punished any disobedience. The laws, therefore, practically enforced themselves.

The earliest known sex laws were no exception to this rule. Originally, there was no difference between sin and crime. Sexual offenders were both sinners and criminals, and their punishment was certain. Where human law enforcement was necessary, it simply carried out divine orders. In accordance with this general view, the first great lawgivers of the ancient world therefore claimed to be mere instruments of a higher will. Hammurabi received his laws from the Sun-god; Moses was given the Ten Commandments by Yahweh on Mount Sinai; Mohammed had the Koran dictated to him by the archangel Gabriel.

Naturally, these and various other "divinely inspired" legal codes differed rather widely from each other, especially in regard to sexual behavior. We also know that even some of Yahweh's sexual commandments changed or reversed themselves in the course of time (for example, see Genesis 38:8–10 and Leviticus 20:21). Still, when we compare the first historical attempts at sex legislation, we also find that they had at least one thing in common: they all covered both social and religious offenses. Sexual behavior was punished not only when it caused harm to other human beings, but also when it merely showed disbelief. Indeed, the latter offense usually carried a harsher penalty than the former. People were much more afraid of divine displeasure than of any personal injury. By the same token, sexual heretics could never claim to be socially harmless. Even if they endangered nobody in particular, they still posed an indirect threat to the community. Their very existence insulted God and invited his retribution. Therefore they could not be tolerated. Their persecution was a religious duty, and any measure taken against them was justified.

ANCIENT GREECE AND ROME

While this basic approach was shared by all ancient cultures, the precise definition of sexual orthodoxy or heresy depended, of course, on their specific religious dogmas. The ancient Mediterranean cultures were, on the whole, rather tolerant in sexual matters. In classical Greece, for example, sex was seen as an elementary life force, and all sexual impulses were therefore accepted as basically good. In fact, various gods and goddesses of fertility, beauty, and sexual pleasure were worshipped in special temples or on special occasions, often with orgiastic rites. The Greeks also believed that virtually all of their gods led vigorous and varied sex lives. Therefore they considered it only proper for mortals to follow this divine example. The Greeks thought so little of sexual abstinence that their language did not even have a special word for "chastity." Instead, they devoted themselves to what they called *hedone, i.e.* sensual pleasure in all its manifestations. However, the hedonism of ancient Greece was by no means a prescription for sexual license, self-indulgence, or unbridled lust. Rather it was a cheerful enjoyment of life, a grateful appreciation of the human body and especially of its sexual functions. Pleasure was not divorced from reason, but always in harmony with it. The body was never punished or starved for the sake of the soul. Since the Greeks had only the most shadowy notion of a life after death, they felt obliged to live every moment on this earth to the fullest.

Greece was, of course, a male-dominated society, and, during its golden age, the ideal of beauty was male. Although men usually felt obliged to marry and raise a family, they sought little romantic involvement with their wives. Their most noble sentiments and passionate feelings were reserved for homosexual relationships before and outside of marriage. Here, again, they found support in their religion. Gods like Zeus and Apollo and demigods like Hercules were believed to have fallen in love with beautiful young men. There can be no doubt that for many Greeks these exalted models were a constant source of inspiration.

In classical Greece love and sexual desire were personified in the youthful, powerful, and unpredictable god Eros. He took possession of human beings according to his whim, and any resistance would have been not only sacrilegious but hopeless. All forms of love were of divine origin and had to be respected. This basic belief explains why the Greeks were quite nonjudgmental in their sexual attitudes, and why there was no organized persecution of sexual heresy. Where certain gods or goddesses were offended by a particular human action, they themselves sought to punish the offender, although sometimes he could win protection from rival deities. At any rate, most of our modern, more unusual manifestations of human sexuality were virtually unknown. For instance, pain and pleasure were rarely associated, and thus sexual cruelty, "bondage and discipline," and other such practices had no chance to develop.

In this latter respect, Greece stood in sharp contrast to Rome where, especially in imperial days, sexual cruelty and brutality was fairly widespread. Eventually, sex among the Romans became more crude, coarse, and vulgar than it had been among the Greeks. However, apart from certain eccentricities of the rich, even in Rome the general attitude toward sex was still reasonable and realistic.

In Rome, as in Greece, the religious beliefs originally reflected the values of an agrarian society. Farmers prayed mostly for large families, increased cattle herds, and good harvests, and the oldest religious ceremonies were fertility rites. Naturally, in the course of time many of these rites were changed and refined, but even the urban Rome of the emperors still saw various orgiastic religious celebrations and sexually licentious festivals. Fields and gardens were protected by statues of the fertility god Priapus displaying an enormous erect penis. Artistic representations of male sex organs were also carried in procession and worn in the form of jewelry as good-luck charms.

Like the Greeks, the Romans never regarded sex and procreation as inseparable, but accepted all types of sexual activity as divinely inspired and therefore good. Indeed, with the expansion of their empire into areas dominated by Greek culture the Romans directly adopted many Greek customs and beliefs. Thus, the Greek deities Eros and Aphrodite also were worshipped in Rome as Amor and Venus. As in Greece, homosexual relationships were considered normal and natural although they were rarely seen as superior, idealistic or noble. On the whole, the Roman approach to sex was rather direct, prosaic, and practical.

As may be gathered from these few general observations, the cultures of both Greece and Rome were sex-positive and, by our present standards, rather permissive. Children, adolescents, and old people, as well as homosexuals and persons with specialized sexual interests were not prevented from finding sexual satisfaction, but were encouraged to express themselves freely. Hermaphrodites often inspired respect and awe; transsexuals were allowed to follow their "calling." In sum, many forms of sexual oppression which concern us today simply did not exist.

Still, it would be a mistake to assume that sexual freedom was total. First of all, as we indicated earlier, women were treated as "the inferior sex" throughout most of classical Greece. They usually received no education and remained confined to the house, where they were expected to bear and raise children. In contrast to their sons and husbands, they enjoyed no sexual privileges outside the marital bed. They had no political rights and did not take part in public affairs. It was relatively late in

Roman history that women became somewhat more emancipated and achieved some measure of self-determination.

The second largest group of sexually oppressed people was, of course, created and maintained by the institution of slavery. Slaves were the property of their masters and therefore subject to all forms of sexual abuse and exploitation. In Greece there were, at times, certain laws which prohibited sexual contact between free men and male slaves, but these laws expressed not so much a protective attitude toward the slave as a high regard for the male homosexual relationship which was not to be degraded by the choice of an unworthy love object. Needless to say, female slaves were held in even lower esteem.

ANCIENT ISRAEL

The oppressed status of slaves and women is well documented for all ancient Mediterranean and Near Eastern societies and was, as may be expected, characteristic of life in ancient Israel, whose history, customs, laws, and religious beliefs are carefully and extensively recorded in the Bible. Thus, in most Western countries where the Bible is still widely read, the general population knows more about the Israelites than about any other ancient people. Because of this, we can restrict ourselves to a very brief sketch here.

In contrast to their polytheistic neighbors, the Israelites believed in only one God, Yahweh, the creator and ruler of the world. He had given them his law through Moses; therefore they felt obliged to live according to his commandments and to reject all foreign influences. For the people of Israel the main purpose of sex was procreation. Men and women had the duty to "be fruitful and multiply" (Genesis 1: 28), and there was no greater blessing than a large family. Therefore, when Yahweh decided to reward Abraham, He told him: "I will indeed bless you, and I will multiply your descendants as the stars of the heavens and as the sand which is on the seashore" (Genesis 22: 17). By the same token, sexual abstinence was not only offensive in the eyes of the Lord, but also betrayed an antisocial attitude. As a matter of fact, a person who chose not to have children was regarded as little better than one who shed blood.

Various biblical passages (among them the sexually explicit "Song of Songs") make it quite clear that the Israelites thought highly of sexual pleasure. Sex was considered a normal part of a healthy life, and it was a virtue to enjoy sex. In accordance with this view, newlywed couples were entitled to an extended honeymoon: "When a man is newly married, he shall not go out with the army or be charged with any business; he shall be free at home for a year, to be happy with his wife whom he has taken" (Deuteronomy 24: 5).

On the other hand, neither men nor women were encouraged to display their nude bodies. Nudity was generally regarded as shameful and embarrassing. For instance, an adulterous woman was publicly stripped naked by her husband as an act of humiliation. Numerous customs and regulations tried to prevent even the involuntary exposure of sex organs. (In later times a Jew who exercised in a Greek gymnasium was assumed to have betrayed his faith.)

Nevertheless, the ancient Israelites can hardly be said to have been prudish or puritanical. In most respects their approach to sex was positive. However, because of their strong emphasis on reproduction, coitus was the only acceptable form of sexual expression. All nonreproductive sex (including sexual self-stimulation) was considered unnatural, i.e., contrary to the will of God. Homosexual intercourse and sexual contact with animals were even punished by death (Leviticus 20: 13 and 15).

It is important to remember the religious basis of this sexual intolerance. At a time when the Israelites fought for their national and religious survival, they were surrounded by peoples who worshipped numerous gods and idols, and who usually made all types of sexual activity part of that worship. Indeed, we know from the Book of Kings and from the denunciations of the prophets that at times even the Israelites themselves had male and female prostitutes attached to the temple in Jerusalem and to various local shrines. However, for the sake of monotheistic purity, this sacred prostitution, along with all other polytheistic customs, was eventually eliminated from the nation's life. Thus, people began to associate nonreproductive sex with idolatry and to treat it as a major religious offense. Still, within the relatively narrow framework of marital coitus, sexual pleasure remained well recognized and was actually encouraged. It was only late in Israel's history that certain peripheral and extremist sects, such as the Essenes, developed strictly ascetic ideals. This sexual asceticism was never representative of Jewish culture as a whole.

THE EARLY CHRISTIANS

Unfortunately, at the time of Jesus not only Jewish sects but also various pagan cults had begun to preach sex-negative doctrines. In many parts of the Roman Empire philosophers and spiritual leaders renounced all sexual pleasure, declared the human body to be impure and demanded that it be neglected, mistreated, and even starved, for the sake of the pure soul. Jesus himself, however, does not seem to have subscribed to such notions, but, rather, followed the more traditional, sexually positive, Jewish teachings. Very little is actually known about his views on specific sexual issues. He remained a chaste celibate himself, but never praised or condemned the sexual urge as such. In practice, his attitude towards sexual outcasts was compassionate and forgiving (Luke 7: 36–50; John 8: 1–11).

Human sexuality is discussed in more detail by Paul, one of the earliest and most energetic of the Christian missionaries. Paul, who had not been among Jesus' personal disciples, was apparently influenced by some of the more negative sexual philosophies of his time. His strong condemnation of homosexual behavior can, of course, be explained as traditionally Jewish (Rom. 1: 26–27; I Cor. 7: 38). However, he goes far beyond this tradition when he sees sexual desire itself as a rather deplorable weakness. Indeed, in clear opposition to Jewish doctrine, he declares celibacy to be superior to marriage (I Cor. 7: 8–9; I Cor. 7: 38).

This ascetic approach to sex was soon developed further by stern and somber Christian scholars such as Tertullian, Jerome, and Augustine. All of these so-called "Fathers of the Church" had a low opinion of sensual pleasure. Augustine, a brilliant thinker and writer, proved to be especially influential. He was born and later died in Northern Africa, but he spent his middle years in Italy, where his thinking was shaped by certain of the fashionable ascetic beliefs and philosophies then current. During his youth and early manhood he had led a relatively active sex life, but after his conversion to Christianity he came to see sex as shameful and degrading. In his opinion, the involuntary bodily responses during sexual intercourse were embarrassing signs of enslavement to the flesh. They proved that human beings were not masters of their own bodies as God had intended them to be. Instead, the sin of Adam and Eve had robbed them and all their descendants of the proper self-control, and thus they were given over to *concupiscence*—lustful desire which seeks self-satisfaction at all cost. A new Christian life therefore demanded strict repression of such lust. Marriage in itself was not evil because it allowed the spouses to employ their base desires in the noble service of procreation. Still, somehow every sexual act, even between husband and wife, remained tainted, and every child born as a result of such an act needed the cleansing power of baptism. Even then the unfortunate disposition toward lust, inherited from Adam and Eve, remained.

Augustine's association of sex with original sin and guilt had a lasting and unfortunate effect on later Christian thinkers. It has to be understood, however, that the entire intellectual and moral climate of the early church was inimical to any cultivation of the senses. The first Christians believed that the end of the world was imminent, and even when it failed to arrive their general outlook on life remained gloomy and ascetic. Virginity, total abstinence, and systematic neglect of the body were considered marks of virtue. Monks and hermits were praised and admired for their relentless fasting and their fight against sexual temptation. Even self-castration was considered a moral act. Finally, when Christianity became the Roman state religion, these negative views found expression in the criminal code. The Christian emperors Theodosius (390 A.D.) and Justinian (538 and 544 A.D.) passed draconic laws condemning certain sexual practices as relics of paganism. The Code of Justinian, which survived for nearly a thousand years in the Byzantine (i.e., East Roman) Empire, was especially intolerant of sexual heresy.

For example, Justinian declared that heathen abominations like homosexual intercourse and sexual contact with animals cried out for God's punishment by famine, flood, drought, storm, and earthquake, and that the state therefore had the solemn duty to protect the land by executing all such offenders. The execution consisted of burning at the stake or live burial, often preceded by torture and mutilation. Thus, shortly after the Christians had escaped from their own persecution, they began the persecution of others.

MEDIEVAL CHRISTIAN DOCTRINES

As the Christian church spread and flourished throughout Europe, this early extreme asceticism gave way to a more lenient attitude. Indeed, many members of the clergy themselves married and had families, a custom which prevailed well into the Middle Ages, when it was officially abolished by church leaders. In the course of time, the jurisdiction over sexual offenses shifted from secular to ecclesiastical courts which now assumed the right to try all matters related to the salvation of souls. (In certain cases, however, the defendant's body was handed over to government authorities for punishment.)

Medieval church policy towards sexual behavior is well documented in "penitentials," i.e., books written for the guidance of confessors and providing long lists of sins together with the appropriate penance. In general, these penitentials show little tolerance of heretical sexual behavior or even of a vigorous normal marital sex life. Indeed, noncoital forms of sexual intercourse between husband and wife were prohibited altogether, and coitus itself was severely restricted. For example, coitus was forbidden for three days after the wedding, during a woman's menstrual period, during her pregnancy, and for several weeks after childbirth. Coitus was also prohibited on Thursdays (Jesus' arrest), Fridays (Jesus' crucifixion), and Sundays (Jesus' resurrection), as well as during official periods of fasting (forty days before Easter, Pentecost, and Christmas). Menstruating women were not allowed to enter the church. Fornication demanded a penance for up to one year, adultery for up to seven years. Masturbation and involuntary orgasm during sleep were treated somewhat more leniently. On the other hand, homosexual acts and sexual contact with animals could require a penance of twenty-two years to life. (The severe penance imposed for these latter "abominations" reflected, of course, the original harsh Jewish doctrine as recorded in the Book of Leviticus. However, in a deeply ironic turn of history, this doctrine was now used against the Jews themselves. Medieval theologians declared that a Christian's sexual contact with a Jew or Moslem was nothing more than unnatural intercourse with an animal "inasmuch such persons in the eyes of the law and our holy faith differ in no wise from beasts.") Penitents usually were expected to dress in a white sheet and to appear barefooted and bareheaded at the church door. They had to carry a heavy candle and march down the aisle to the front of the congregation where they made a public confession. Finally, after several weeks or even years, when the terms of their penance had been fulfilled, they were given a written certificate. Offenders who either refused to confess their sins or failed to do the prescribed penance were excommunicated.

For many centuries Christian sexual doctrines remained irrational and repressive. It was only later, when Thomas Aquinas and his followers gained a wider influence in the church, that a more balanced view began to prevail. Thomas, the greatest medieval theologian, made a serious effort to approach the subject of sex in a systematic and logical manner. His basic assumption was this: It is the "nature" of human sexual intercourse to lead to the procreation of children. Therefore, any sexual activity that does not serve this ultimate end is "unnatural," *i.e.*, contrary to the will of God and sinful. The rest of Thomas' sexual philosophy followed from this premise. "Natural" sexual activity took place only for the "right" purpose, with the "right" partner, and in the "right" way (*i.e.*, for the purpose of procreation, with the marriage partner, and by means of coitus). Sexual acts were "unnatural" and sinful to the degree in which they deviated from this triple moral standard. The greatest offense against nature was committed when the wrong purpose (for example, mere sexual pleasure) was sought with the wrong partner (for example, a partner of the same sex) in the wrong way (for example, by means of oral or anal intercourse). Similarly, sexual contact with animals and sexual self-stimulation were very grave sins. Somewhat less sinful was coitus with a wrong partner of the opposite sex, such as in rape, adultery, and incest. By the same token, simple "natural" fornication was only a minor transgression as long as it did not lead to pregnancy. In this latter case, however, it became a serious "unnatural" act, because the child was illegitimate and would lack a father's care and attention.

Unlike Augustine, Thomas did not see the "right" sexual activity, *i.e.*, marital coitus, as tainted by concupiscence. He merely regretted that it involved a loss of rational control. Thus, generally speaking, Thomas had a moderating influence on theological thinking about sex. Nevertheless, even for him sexual abstinence remained morally superior to marriage.

FROM RELIGIOUS HERESY
TO SECULAR CRIME

So far, we have concentrated on the religious aspect of sexual morality, because in the ancient and medieval world religion was indeed the most important moral force. But actual human behavior also has always been influenced by other factors. Moral values, even when they are defined in religious terms, are often developed, changed, or abandoned in response to purely external, secular events. Rising or falling birth rates, technological changes, contact with foreign cultures, wars, natural disasters, or epidemic diseases—any or all of these can deeply affect sexual attitudes. Indeed, with the end of the static medieval world period and the dawn of the modern age, these external factors acquired an ever-increasing importance. At the same time, the church began to lose much of its former influence and the state eagerly and openly assumed the role of moral guardian.

SEXUAL ATTITUDES IN THE MIDDLE AGES

In regard to sex, medieval moralists were hardly tolerant or affirmative. They showed little concern for human happiness here on earth, but rather encouraged the mortification of the flesh for the sake of a pure afterlife. In their opinion, physical pleasure was, at best, unimportant, and, at worst, corrupting. It diverted the soul from the straight path toward heaven. Thus, one can easily assume that the Middle Ages were a period of austerity, cheerlessness, and unrelenting asceticism. For several reasons, however, such an impression would be wrong.

First, we have to remember that in actual practice the medieval world was not as uniform as the official moral doctrines seem to imply. There were vast differences between countries and even between regions of the same country. City dwellers lived by different values than did farmers, and feudal lords had different sexual mores from their serfs. Furthermore, in spite of its great influence, the church did not have an iron grip on every citizen. Pre-Christian sexual customs and attitudes persisted in many areas for a very long time. Under the circumstances, theologians tended to be more rigoristic than they might have been otherwise. Thus, a certain gap between the ideal and the real was always taken for granted. Also, the general living conditions were still so unrefined that there was not much room for sexual delicacy. The majority of the population lived in the countryside close to nature. Many people, in fact, shared their houses with their cattle. Families were used to sleeping together in the same room, often in the same bed. Neither the highest nor the lowest classes enjoyed much personal privacy, but there was no squeamishness or embarrassment about the natural bodily functions. Nudity as such was not a moral issue. Inns and hostels expected their guests to sleep together with strangers of both sexes. A person refusing to share his bed or to take off his clothes would have been suspected of being diseased or disfigured. Public nudity was common in bathhouses, which were a favorite social gathering places for men and women of all ages. That there was also a great deal of vigorous sexual activity is well documented by writers such as Chaucer and Boccaccio. In short, compared to our own time, people were remarkably uninhibited.

Still, for the modern observer, the most surprising aspect of sexual life in the Middle Ages is perhaps the general attitude toward children. It is often believed today that infant sexuality was discovered for the first time by Sigmund Freud in our century, and that before him children were always considered "pure" and "asexual" creatures. Actually, however, the taboo against childhood sex play is only a few hundred years old. In ancient and medieval Europe alike, the sexual interests of children were well recognized. Indeed, mothers, grandmothers and nurses were accustomed to masturbating small children in order to put them to sleep or keep them quiet. Until boys and girls were able to reproduce, they were not closely supervised, and remained free of sexual restrictions. Furthermore, nobody made any effort to determine a person's exact age. Children often did not know how old they were, and neither did their parents. As soon as a girl had her first menstruation, she was believed ready for marriage.

These traditional customs began to change only with the arrival of our modern age. Technological progress, increasing specialization of labor, growth of the cities, and the gradual transition to a capitalist economic system produced a new way of life. The churches started to keep accurate birth registers. Age differences became more important, as did the efficient use of time and the strict observation of schedules. Between the sixteenth and the eighteenth centuries, childhood began to be perceived as a separate phase of life with special needs of its own. Religious orders founded the first exclusive schools for the young. And people began to create fashions, books, games, and toys that were "suitable for children."

It should be noted, however, that in many parts of Europe the older, less protective view persisted for a long time. This view is exemplified by one of the earliest children's books, the *Colloquia Familiaria* by Erasmus of Rotterdam. Erasmus wrote the *Colloquia* in 1522 for his six-year-old godson "in order to teach him good Latin and to educate him for the world." The text deals with all sorts of domestic experiences and problems, including sexual ones. There are detailed and very frank discussions of sexual desire, sexual pleasure, and sexual intercourse, conception, pregnancy, birth, marriage, divorce, prostitution, and venereal disease. The language is straightforward and sometimes even humorous. Sex appears as a natural and pleasant part of life which must be approached with understanding and common sense.

THE EMERGENCE OF THE BOURGEOIS

Over the next two hundred years, the old realistic frankness disappeared from all educational literature—eventually to be considered inappropriate even for adults. The epidemic spread of syphilis in the sixteenth and seventeenth centuries and the rise of the middle class produced a new, largely negative attitude toward the human body. The former intimacy was now rejected as uncivilized and unhealthy. People no longer ate from the same dish or drank from the common mug. Instead of using their fingers to eat with, they began to use knives and forks. The wealthy started to wear special sleeping clothes or nightgowns. Privacy became a growing concern. The bed was removed from the living room and hidden in a separate bedroom. The bathhouses were closed, recreational swimming in lakes and rivers became sexually segregated until, finally, public bathing in the nude was prohibited altogether. In other words, the former open acceptance of the body and its functions gradually turned into prudery. At the same time, there was a growing awareness of generational differences. Children became more "childlike," and adults more "serious." To be an adult now meant to be able to control oneself, to submit to a greater degree of discipline than ever before. The modern age with its emphasis on efficiency and performance demanded a great deal of self-control from each individual. People could no longer afford to follow their impulses, and they became very sensitive about their spontaneous physical reactions. Open coughing, sneezing, yawning, belching, and farting, which had been considered healthy and natural, were now unacceptable in polite society. The organs of excretion as well as the sex organs began to be seen as disgusting and dirty, and in the end their very existence became a shameful secret.

Obviously, these social developments were bound to lead to new kinds and degrees of sexual oppression. Moreover, in the course of time, the older sexual taboos grew much stronger than they had ever been before. They were no longer seen as mere external prohibitions, but became increasingly internalized by ever larger segments of the population. The rising middle class was "inner-directed," self-motivated, and highly scrupulous. Its outlook on life was sober, its philosophy practical, and its morality stern.

The new "solid citizen," or "bourgeois," was of course the herald of our own age. When we now study his familiar figure, we realize that his growing sexual oppression involved other factors besides traditional religious beliefs. Before we turn to a closer examination of these factors, however, we should perhaps take a brief final look at the further history of Christian sexual doctrines.

PROTESTANTISM AND PURITANISM

The Protestant Reformation of the sixteenth century divided the once unified church of Western Europe and gave birth to numerous new Christian churches, sects, and movements. Luther and Calvin, the first important Protestant leaders, rejected the supremacy of the pope along with various other Catholic dogmas, but in regard to sex they retained most of the then-established attitudes. However, they did attack the custom of clerical celibacy and the glorification of sexual abstinence. Luther, himself a former monk, set an example by marrying a former nun, and Calvin also felt obliged to marry in order to lead a more regular and productive life. Both considered women to be necessary, if subservient, companions for men. Calvin in particular saw the role of wife as that of a lifelong close associate of the husband. She was to be more than just a bearer of his children. By the same token, marriage was not simply a means of producing and educating offspring, but also was a social institution for the natural benefit of the partners. Sexual pleasure in marriage was therefore moral and proper, provided it did not degenerate into excessive passion or sheer lust. In most other respects the early Protestant views on sex remained firmly medieval. Not only were women still denied equal religious, social, and sexual status with men, but the old intolerance for all sexual nonconformists was reconfirmed.

Calvin's theology had a great influence on the English Puritans for whom the Reformation under Henry VIII had not gone far enough, and who eventually seized power under Oliver Cromwell. Henry, as the head of the English church, had already taken over some of the ecclesiastical jurisdiction and turned various religious offenses into secular crimes. Thus, homosexual acts and sexual contact with animals, which before had required only penance, had begun to be punished as felonies. Offenders were executed and all their possessions confiscated. The Puritans were even more severe and greatly intensified the persecution of sexual heretics. Cromwell himself never tired of demanding more zeal on the part of prosecutors. In 1650 Parliament passed the so-called Puritan Act "for the suppression of the abominable and crying sins of incest, adultery, and fornication, wherewith this land is much defiled and Almighty God highly displeased." Thus, the religious basis of Puritan sex legislation was made unmistakably clear. The prescribed penalties were the same as those used in biblical times. For instance, just as in ancient Israel, adultery was punished by death.

Though the Puritan rule soon came to an end in England, it experienced a second flowering in America. The Puritan colonies of New England were, in fact, totalitarian religious states. Most of their sex laws were based on the laws of Moses. The Massachusetts colony, for instance, directly copied the Old Testament when it passed legislation demanding death for adultery, homosexual acts, and sexual contact with animals. Fornication posed a rather difficult problem, because the ancient Iraelites had never condemned it as such. Nevertheless, Christians had, over the centuries, learned to regard it as a grave sin. The Puritans eventually developed their own approach and specified various forms and degrees of punishment. Fornicators could be enjoined to marry, they could be fined, or they could be pilloried and publicly whipped as a warning to others. Sometimes all three penalties were combined. In later times it also became customary to force fornicators to wear the letter "V" (for Vncleanness) conspicuously displayed on their clothing. When the death penalty for adultery was finally abolished, offenders were stigmatized with the letters "AD" or simply "A." (Nathaniel Hawthorne's novel *The Scarlet Letter* tells of this.) In spite of these strict laws and harsh penalties, however, complete sexual conformity was never achieved. Many contemporary reports leave no doubt that illegitimate births were frequent and that homosexual behavior was fairly widespread. This latter fact is, of course, hardly surprising, since the community concentrated its efforts on the prevention of all nonmarital heterosexual contact.

On the whole, it is difficult to avoid the judgment that the Puritan culture was among the sexually most oppressive that have ever existed anywhere. Occasional outbursts of mass hysteria, such as in the Salem witch trials, undoubtedly had sexual overtones and prove that the Puritan sexual morality had become unrealistic, fanatical, and destructive. Fortunately, in the following centuries this rigid culture became increasingly diluted by the growing tide of new immigrants with a more liberal heritage.

THE RELIGIOUS ORIGIN OF AMERICAN SEX LEGISLATION

The current sex laws in most states of the United States still follow the Puritan model. As the American population moved westward across the continent, the New England penal codes were simply carried along and copied in every new state. Most settlers were content with preserving the legal traditions to which they had been accustomed on the East Coast. Unlike the inhabitants of the Old World, they were not interested in new legal theories or fundamental reforms. Western and Southern Europe had, in the early nineteenth century, liberalized their sex laws at the command of Napoleon I. The Napoleonic code, which practically legalized all consensual sex between adults in private, had an influence reaching well beyond the French national borders. It was either adopted or used as a model in Italy, Spain, Portugal, Belgium, the Netherlands, and all of Latin America. Thus, most of the world's Catholic countries entered the new Industrial Age with a sensible minimum of modern sex legislation, while the Protestant countries of Central Europe and North America remained tied to the past, with most of their ancient and medieval sex laws preserved intact. The only real change was a gradual reduction of penalties. For example, while adultery continued to be a crime in Massachusetts, the death penalty was relatively soon replaced with a public whipping, a fine, and imprisonment. Then the whipping was omitted, leaving the fine and the prison term on the books. Finally, even these reduced penalties were considered too harsh. However, instead of repealing the law, the authorities simply ceased to enforce it.

At the present time the majority of states in the United States still retain a host of laws against socially harmless, but heretical sexual behavior. Thus, "fornication," "cohabitation," "seduction," "adultery," "lewd and lascivious conduct," "sodomy," "bestiality," and similar ancient sins are still treated as modern crimes.

The fact that these and other sexual acts may be performed by consenting partners in private does not make them permissible in the eyes of the law. In short, now as before, legislators try to impose purely religious taboos on the population. Some state penal codes even admit the religious character of certain sex crimes by calling them "crimes against nature." However, the "nature" which the law endeavors to protect here is not the nature of the natural sciences, but rather an archaic concept of "God's natural order." Modern scientific findings stand in sharp contrast to the philosophy expressed in these laws. As a result, most authorities on sexual matters today find themselves in a position where, for reasons of therapy, they have to counsel the public to engage in practices that are legally "against nature" and therefore crimes.

It goes without saying that these absurd, obsolete, and probably unconstitutional laws can no longer be equally enforced today. They are enforced only periodically and selectively against certain individuals or groups who offer themselves as convenient scapegoats for various social disasters or mistaken policies. This kind of official hypocrisy, in turn, leads to blackmail, bribery, and the corruption of law-enforcement officials. It also produces widespread contempt for the entire legal system.

THE SINNER AS MENTAL PATIENT

There is no question that the old Puritan laws against victimless sex crimes are irrational and invite all sorts of abuses. Nevertheless, today they may not even be the most dangerous and unjust instruments of sexual oppression in America because, in addition to their traditional sex laws, a number of states now also have special laws allowing the commitment and forced psychiatric treatment of sexual offenders. These states declare certain offenders to be sexual psychopaths in need of a cure. Consequently, such offenders, who otherwise would perhaps receive only a suspended sentence or serve a short prison term, can be committed to a mental hospital for an indefinite period or for the rest of their lives. In some states they may even be committed without a trial. Strangely enough, these curious laws were enacted in the name of science, although there was, and is, no scientific evidence to support the assumptions on which they are based. Indeed, the very term "sexual psychopath" is unscientific and does not correspond to any particular disease constellation recognized by psychiatrists today. Thus, one and the same person may be legally considered sick in one state and healthy in another. Unsound and unfair as they are, these laws remain on the books because they give an uninformed general public the illusion of preventing socially harmful sexual behavior. However, current diagnostic techniques are incapable of distinguishing between potentially dangerous offenders and those who are not dangerous. At any rate, only a very few sex offenders are violent. Furthermore, sex offenders are less likely to repeat their crimes than are other types of offenders. Finally, there is little evidence that forced psychiatric treatment is an effective tool of rehabilitation.

For the average layman today it is, of course, the concept of "sexual psychopathology" more than that of "heresy" or "wickedness" which explains nonconformist sexual behavior. After all, in most other spheres of life religious explanations have been replaced by scientific ones, and by now the habit of calling sexual deviants "sick" instead of "evil" already has a long and respectable history of its own.

THE MYTH OF MASTURBATORY INSANITY

Paradoxically, it was the Age of Enlightenment which laid the foundation for many of the later, irrational and oppressive sickness theories of sexual deviance. We mentioned earlier that the end of the medieval world, the transition to a capitalist economic system, and the rise of the middle class produced a new, rather negative attitude toward the human body and its natural functions. For the bourgeois, the body was, above all, a machine, an instrument of labor which had to function in the most regular and profitable manner. Inefficiency, idleness, and waste, which had been of little concern to the ancient and medieval mind, now became the supreme vices. The new supreme virtues, on the other hand, were discipline, thrift, punctuality, and sobriety. The feudal lords had decorated their coats of arms with unicorns, eagles, bears, and lions, but the middle class preferred more stolid heraldic animals: the hardworking ox, the useful sheep, the diligent ant, and the industrious bee. Not only business but also pleasure had to be judged by practical standards. Thus, sexual activity was permissible only so long as it produced children and thereby increased the labor force. Pure sensuality without purpose was subversive and dangerous.

As we explained before, in the two centuries after the Reformation the middle class developed a new, protective attitude toward the young. First childhood and then adolescence began to emerge as special innocent periods in a person's life. These periods had to be spent wisely in preparation of a productive adult career. Youthful excesses had to be curbed, youthful energy had to be saved, and youthful strength had to be preserved at all cost. Finally, in the early eighteenth century, the bourgeois twin anxieties—a general loss of discipline and the corruption of youth—combined to create a new, terrifying menace: "masturbatory insanity."

Masturbation had, of course, long been condemned as sinful by Jews and Christians alike, because it subverted the procreative purpose of man's sexual faculties. Still, throughout the Middle Ages, very little attention had been paid to this sin. The loss of male semen was always deplored, but this problem was largely seen as a moral one. At any rate, women and children did not produce any semen and therefore had no great feelings of guilt about masturbation. They simply thought of it as a way of relieving physical irritations, comparable to scratching.

In 1710, however, an anonymous pamphlet appeared in England under the title *Onania, or the Heinous Sin of Self-Pollution and all its Frightful Consequences in Both Sexes, Considered with Spiritual and Physical Advice*. The author, Bekker, was a former clergyman turned quack who offered his readers some frightening theories about the dangers of wasting semen and overheating the blood. He called this behavior *onania* in reference to Onan, a biblical character who was punished by God for practicing the withdrawal method of contraception (Genesis 38:8–10). Unfortunately, Bekker's absurd ideas and his misleading term soon found wide acceptance. The pamphlet was quickly translated into several European languages and eventually went through more than eighty editions.

In 1760 a respected Swiss physician by the name of Tissot published an even more influential book entitled *Onanism, or a Treatise upon the*

Disorders Produced by Masturbation. The author claimed that masturbation was not only a sin and a crime but also that it was directly
responsible for many serious diseases, such as "consumption, deterioration of eyesight, disorders of digestion, impotence . . . and insanity."
Tissot's success was spectacular. He was widely quoted as the greatest
authority on the subject of masturbation and was universally praised as a
benefactor of mankind. Within a few decades, his views became official
medical doctrine. Physicians all over the Western world began to find
masturbation at the root of almost every physical problem.

By 1812, when Benjamin Rush, "the father of American Psychiatry,"
published his *Medical Inquiries and Observations upon the Diseases of
the Mind,* the harmful effects of masturbation were taken for granted
everywhere, and the number of effects had greatly increased. According
to Rush, onanism caused not only insanity but also "seminal weakness,
impotence, dysury, tabes dorsalis, pulmonary consumption, dyspepsia,
dimness of sight, vertigo, epilepsy, hypochondriasis, loss of memory,
manalgia, fatuity, and death."

As these examples indicate, the first modern fighters against the so-
called evils of masturbation were physicians, and their arguments were
mostly medical. Very soon, however, they found themselves supported by
"enlightened" educators who feared for the "moral health" of their students. On the other hand, the churches at first showed little interest in
joining the crusade. Some clergymen pointed out, for example, that they
could not find a single reference to masturbation in the Holy Scriptures,
and that they were therefore unable to condemn it. It seemed that the
only solution was a new, much broader interpretation of the biblical
commandment against adultery. In the long run, however, this procedure
could easily make matters worse. It would require a great deal of detailed
sex education, and particularly the young and innocent would suddenly
have to be told about sins of which they had never even heard before.
Moreover, the exact definition of masturbation appeared far from easy.
After all, the term had first been applied only to adult males. The notion
that women and children also masturbated was new. Indeed, it is evident
from the anti-masturbation pamphlets of the time that their authors had
great difficulty explaining to the public what exactly they were talking
about. Nevertheless, after some initial reluctance, even the clergy became
"progressive" enough to recognize the dangers of masturbation, and soon
everybody was convinced that these dangers demanded the most drastic
and extraordinary measures of protection.

Naturally, this meant that young people were in particularly serious
danger. If they succumbed to the vice in their early years, they could
never reach a healthy adulthood. Thus, parents risked the very lives of
their sons and daughters by ignoring the practice. Medical experts found

that among the "pampered" children of the rich, the vast majority already masturbated to excess, most notably between the excitable ages of 6 and 12. (These are the very same years that were later believed to constitute the "latency period.") The future of these unfortunates offered no hope. Needless to say, this ideology soon led to the most bizarre educational practices and to elaborately cruel "treatments" at the hands of psychiatric authorities. In the nineteenth century, these authorities found that the insanity caused by masturbation was of an especially disagreeable kind. As explained in 1867 by Henry Maudsley, the greatest British psychiatrist of his time, it was "characterized by . . . extreme perversion of feeling and corresponding derangement of thought in early stages, and later by failure of intelligence, nocturnal hallucinations, and suicidal and homicidal propensities." In other words, masturbators were mad potential killers, and thus it seemed only prudent to have them locked up in an asylum.

"PSYCHOPATHIA SEXUALIS"

Actually, in the first half of the nineteenth century, masturbation had become one of the most important causes of madness: Self-abuse slowly but surely destroyed the brain. At the same time, however, the habit itself was also an expression of some inherited psychological weakness. That is to say, masturbators were born sick and then could hardly help aggravating their sorry condition. In 1843 a Russian physician named Kaan published a book under the title *Psychopathia Sexualis* (Sexual Sickness of the Mind) which explained this double jeopardy of masturbation. (More than 40 years later, the Austrian psychiatrist von Krafft-Ebing used the same book title for a new study of unconventional sexual behavior.) According to Kaan, nearly all human beings were afflicted with a certain "phantasia morbosa" (sick imagination) which predisposed them toward sensual excess. It took only the accident of a faulty diet, a soft mattress, tight clothing, or even mere idleness to trigger the inevitable chain of events. In addition to this dismal theory, Kaan also offered a first list of other, comparatively minor, sexual "aberrations," such as love of boys, homosexual mutual masturbation, violation of corpses, coitus with animals, and sexual contact with statues. This short list of sexual mental diseases was, of course, soon expanded by other psychiatrists. Indeed, the ever-growing number of new aberrations eventually reduced the once all-important disease of masturbation to the second rank. Nevertheless, Kaan's belief in the possible heredity of sexual deviance retained its appeal and was, in fact, strengthened in subsequent years.

Before we turn to these further "scientific" developments, however, we should perhaps briefly comment on the concept of "sexual psychopathology" itself. Quite obviously, in the beginning it was nothing more than the secular version of an old religious dogma. It is hardly a coincidence that Kaan's sexual "aberrations" are virtually identical with the "abominations" of the Bible. Moreover, the parallel of his inherited "phantasia morbosa" to Augustine's "concupiscence" is striking. In short, science, as the new religion, was still preoccupied with strengthening the old sexual taboos.

THE FEAR OF DEGENERACY

The traditional religious bias was further strengthened when, in 1857, the French psychiatrist Morel turned to the concept of *"dégénérescence"* for the explanation of madness. Morel, who earlier in his life had pursued theological studies, came to the conclusion that progressive degeneracy was the cause of most physical and mental illnesses. The first man (whom the Bible had called "Adam") had been of a healthy "primitive type." However, after his nature had become corrupted at some early date, man found himself subjected to weakening external and internal influences. As a result, today we no longer see the original perfect primitive type, but various imperfect human races as well as a great number of degenerates. These degenerates usually suffer from hereditary sexual perversions and are destined to die out.

In the course of time Morel's theory came to be seen as too openly biblical by many of his colleagues, and was recast in more fashionable secular terms. It began to be assumed that degeneracy could appear in the course of an otherwise progressive evolutionary process. Still, degenerates retained their basic characteristics, and they, together with their offspring, were inevitably doomed. These ideas were further popularized by great nineteenth century dramatists like Ibsen and Hauptmann, who described the effects of degeneracy in the most depressing detail. Indeed, novelist Emile Zola presented the "natural and social history" of a whole family, the Rougon-Macquarts, as a case of hereditary progressive decay. The notion of an inborn pathological disposition toward madness and sexual deviance continued to dominate psychiatric thinking up to the time of Sigmund Freud, who finally replaced it with the concept of a traumatic (and largely unconscious) individual life history.

In this context it should be remembered that the nineteenth century also laid the "scientific" foundations of modern racism. The term "degeneracy" was easily applied to entire social or ethnic groups which were unpopular for some reason or another and which could now be labeled as biologically inferior. Needless to say, such labeling also always implied the charge of sexual perversion. The logical implications of racism, in turn, led to eugenic policies, *i.e.*, official attempts to improve the biological health of the population by preventing the breeding of degenerates.

On the other hand, it was felt that the superior races did not breed enough. There was a widespread fear that, sooner or later, the whole of mankind might become degenerate and die out. (This fear seems especially grotesque today when one looks at the population curve between 1800 and 1900.) At any rate, growing racial pride, nationalism, and a rapidly expanding industry prompted many governments to demand a population increase. Procreation was again confirmed as the only correct goal of sexual intercourse.

VICTORIAN SEXUAL POLICIES

In the early nineteenth century at least, married couples had still been able to obtain some realistic sexual information. In France, for example, the Revolution of 1789 and the Napoleonic reforms had produced a certain amount of sexual freedom. A variety of serious marriage manuals were published which took a rather reasonable attitude toward sex and also described various methods of contraception. These books were not always scientifically correct (some important facts about human reproduction had not been discovered), but at least they tried to be helpful. Furthermore, around the middle of the century, new technical processes made the mass production of condoms possible. As a result, more and more people began to plan the size of their families. The Christian churches were, of course, aware of all this, but took no official stand on the matter. Even most of the Catholic bishops preferred to remain silent, and instructed their priests not to upset parishioners who acted in good faith. It was only later, when the fear of degeneracy began to spread, that the churches became more outspoken. Pastoral letters began to extoll the virtues of hardship and the blessings of a large, industrious family. The biblical injunction to be fruitful and multiply was re-emphasized, and contraception was condemned as contrary to the will of God and the national interest. Finally, politicians and clergy were joined by various civic groups which feared for the very survival of civilization, and which called for a Christian crusade against contraception and other immoral practices.

In the United States the most successful of these new crusaders was Anthony Comstock (1844–1915), the secretary of the New York Society for the Suppression of Vice. With his slogan "Morals, not Art or Literature," he set out to prevent the use of contraceptives and the dissemination of sexual knowledge. By intense lobbying efforts he persuaded Congress in 1873 to pass the so-called Comstock Act, which made it a felony to mail any obscene, lewd, or lascivious book, pamphlet, picture, writing, paper, or other publication of an indecent character. Comstock himself was made a special agent of the U.S. Post Office. This gave him the long-coveted right to open other people's mail, and soon he was able to establish a veritable reign of puritanical terror.

There is no doubt that a zealot like Comstock could not have gained his immense power in a healthy and free society. As we have seen, however, in the second half of the nineteenth century most Western nations were gripped by an unprecedented prudery. Ignorance and hypocrisy carried the day, and thus many hard-won civil liberties were surrendered. The phenomenon is also known as Victorianism, after the English Queen Victoria, who reigned in this period. Sexual repression was international, however, and England and the United States were neither better nor worse than other countries.

Today we can see that the Victorian fears about sex were based on a particularly "modern" mixture of pseudoscientific and religious beliefs. The two systems of belief mutually reinforced each other. It seems, however, that the men of science, and especially psychiatrists, had a much more ascetic outlook than the men of the church. At least in the beginning the church was a rather reluctant ally in the fight for mental health and the racial improvement of mankind. Nevertheless, over the years many clergymen embraced these secular values and even incorporated them into their own doctrines. Ironically, when science later freed itself from its narrow views, certain church leaders were unable to do likewise. For them, the Victorian sexual ideology had become part of the gospel.

MODERN SEX RESEARCH AND
SEXUAL LIBERATION

At the end of the Victorian era psychiatry and medicine had begun to develop a more critical spirit. Early twentieth-century researchers like Freud, Ellis, Bloch, and Hirschfeld increasingly questioned the traditional moral assumptions and turned their attention to the victims of sexual oppression. Some of this oppression was lifted when the First World War shook the foundations of bourgeois culture. In 1936 Wilhelm Reich, the most radical of the new psychiatrists, described the accelerating social change in a book titled *The Sexual Revolution*. The Second World War produced even greater upheavals in Europe and North America. New empirical sex research on a grand scale replaced the traditional vague speculations. First Kinsey, and then Masters and Johnson revealed many of the remaining secrets of human sexual behavior. The old Victorian prudery finally was dying.

Or was it? As we observed at the beginning of this historical survey, the actual sexual policies of most modern nations still express the "reproductive bias" of former times. People who use their sexual faculties for the purpose of mere pleasure are still regarded as heretics in many parts of the world. When they are not directly threatened by the law, they are nevertheless despised, ridiculed, and harassed. In short, they are still oppressed in the name of some higher social good. This social good may be described in religious, scientific, or openly political terms, but its sexually inhibiting effect is the same: The individual still does not have the universal human right to pursue his personal, perhaps idiosyncratic, sexual interests even if they do not harm anyone.

As we enter the third century after the American Revolution, however, there is some hope that at least in the United States, much of the traditional sexual oppression will soon end. The various American sexual rights movements have made significant gains in recent years, and their eventual success seems likely. This success, if and when it finally comes, will be largely due to an enlightened libertarian spirit and a farsighted political constitution which to this day provides for free and unhindered expression.

REFERENCES AND RECOMMENDED READINGS

BARNETT, WALTER. *Sexual Freedom and the Constitution.* Albuquerque: University of New Mexico Press, 1973.
   A thorough and comprehensive legal attack on the American "sodomy" laws, providing, among other things, a detailed discussion of their history and social function.

HAEBERLE, ERWIN J. *The Sex Atlas,* New York: The Seabury Press, 1977.
   A popular illustrated textbook covering all aspects of human sexuality; including the history of sexual oppression in Western civilization.

HORKHEIMER, MAX. "Authority and the Family." In *Critical Theory.* New York: The Seabury Press, 1972.
   The classic essay on the sexually oppressive role of the family in Western civilization.

MARCUSE, HERBERT. *Eros and Civilization.* Boston: Beacon Press, 1966.
   An essay on the causes of sexual oppression, combining Marxian and Freudian theories.

SZASZ, THOMAS S. *The Manufacture of Madness.* New York: Delta Books, 1971.
   A historical survey comparing the social role of the Inquisition with that of modern Institutional Psychiatry.

YOUNG, WAYLAND. *Eros Denied.* New York: Grove Press, 1964.
   A short history of sexual oppression in Europe from ancient to modern times, offering many illuminating anecdotes and examples.

CHAPTER 2

SOCIETY AND SEXUAL DEVIANCE

Stuart A. Kirk

Human sexual behavior has always generated a considerable amount of interest and even controversy. It is at once hidden but ubiquitous, a private pursuit but a public concern, a harbinger of both ecstasy and anguish. It is a subject deeply rooted in biology, psychology, sociology and mythology. It is basic to social life, yet problematic to society. (It is basic because it provides for a society's continuance; it is problematic because it is uniquely an intense individual drive that is not inherently social.) Any topic of such great social and personal significance is likely to have a history strewn with myths, superstitions, and complex social regulations.

It is sexuality's social importance that makes its regulation seem so essential and the violation of those regulations so threatening. Few areas of social behavior are so rich in intricacies, so elusive in rationale, and so imbedded in morality as is sexual behavior. Ironically, it is this concern, perhaps overconcern, for the propriety and structure of sexual conduct that makes it such a fertile field for deviation.

This paper analyzes sexual deviance from a sociological perspective, with particular attention to some of those who may be considered as sexually oppressed. A general framework in which to view deviant behavior is outlined and applied to deviance of a sexual nature in order to shed some light on the social situation of the sexually oppressed.

SOCIAL DEVIANCE

The traditional view of social deviance focused upon certain individual acts which violated the normative expectations of a group; those acts were thought to be distinct and easily distinguishable from normal behavior. The study of deviance addressed the question of what biological, psychological or social factors impinged upon the individual to produce unconventional behavior. Thus, questions thought worth pursuing focused narrowly on deviant individuals, their personal histories, personalities, motivations, and attitudes. Virtually overlooked were the social context of the deviance and the social processes involved in its definition, detection, and control.

This oversight, or bias, has fortunately been corrected in the last decade by a cadré of sociologists and others who have steadfastly refused to be content with the conventional views of social deviance and have effectively refocused the analysis of deviance (for an excellent overview, see Schur, 1971; Sagarin, 1975). One of the earliest influential statements was Becker (1963: p. 91):

> . . . *social groups create deviance by making the rules whose infraction constitutes deviance*, and by applying these rules to particular people and labeling them as outsiders. From this point of view, deviance is *not* a quality of the act the person commits, but rather a consequence of the application by others of rules and sanctions to an "offender." The deviant is one to whom that label has successfully been applied; deviant behavior is behavior that people so label. (Italics in original)

This statement and similar ones by many investigators (Erikson, 1964; Kitsuse, 1962; Lemert, 1951) highlighted the relativity of that which is considered deviant by emphasizing that deviance involves not only the behavior of the individual but also the creation of norms or rules, their selective application, and the social reaction of a variety of control agents. Deviance was seen as the result of the interaction of deviants and control agents and as fundamentally part of a social process rather than an individual condition.

The consequences of taking such a stance toward deviance were dramatic. No longer were research questions concerned only with, or even seriously with, the psychosocial history of the individual but instead they were focused on the social contingencies that elicited reactions from others (Kirk, 1972). Thus, attention has increasingly turned to the nature of the rules, their application and consequences.

A sizable and popular sociological sub-specialty involves the study of deviance. Within that academic arena, one can find discussions of hobos and hookers, alcoholics and addicts, crooks and crazies, radicals and retardates, and an assortment of fellow outsiders. Among that diversity, however, there are some common characteristics that justify analysis of an otherwise heterogeneous collection of individuals. These characteristics constitute a working definition of deviance. Perhaps the most refined definition available is Schur's [1971: p. 24]:

> Human behavior is deviant *to the extent that* it comes to be viewed as involving a *personally discreditable* departure from a group's normative expectations, *and* it *elicits* interpersonal or collective reactions that serve to "isolate," "treat," "correct," or "punish" *individuals* engaged in such behavior. (Italics in original)

With the slight modification suggested by Sagarin [1975: p. 9] that the definition be expanded to include human beings as well as human behavior, the definition encompasses the crucial unifying dimensions of deviance. First, deviance does not reside solely in the violation of normative expectations, but also in the extent to which such behavior elicits negative sanctions or reactions from others; second, deviance is evident to the extent that it involves personally discreditable characteristics or behaviors. Deviance is not simply the commission of a norm violation, but is also an inference that others make about the character of the norm violator who is often viewed to be morally weak, sinister, and inferior—in short, he is stigmatized. And third, to be deviant, the person must be the target of some attempts to change him, whether those interventions have the label of treatment, rehabilitation, correction or punishment [Schur, 1971].

Violating a social norm makes one vulnerable to being discredited—to being stigmatized—if the existence of the violations is known to others. Stigma may result from three different types of conditions [Goffman, 1963]: 1. It may occur with abominations of the body—the various physical deformities—which violate our expectations about human normality. 2. It may stem from character blemishes which are usually inferred from one's behavior when one is perceived as mentally ill, alcoholic, homosexual, suicidal, or as having propensities to engage in unsavory activities. 3. There is a broad class of discrediting attributes that might be viewed as tribal stigma, those disvalued traits associated with one's race, religion, ethnicity, and national citizenship which are in disfavor among a dominant group. What those who are stigmatized have in common, if nothing else, is that they are viewed as something less than human, less worthy of our respect and consideration, and less entitled to the resources and opportunities of the society. They become the object, at best, of our pity, benign neglect, or supposedly benevolent social interventions; they become the socially oppressed in our midst.

Stigma, then, can either result from certain *behaviors* which are viewed as discrediting or it can be associated with certain *bodily conditions* and *social statuses* that are disvalued within a social group. Although all deviants, by definition, are stigmatized, not all conditions that are stigmatized are instances of deviance. For example, members of minority racial groups are often stigmatized, but they are not the target of treatment or rehabilitation solely by virtue of their racial characteristics. It is known, however, that in some instances being of a disfavored racial or ethnic group may make one more vulnerable to deviant labeling.

SEXUAL DEVIANCE

It is nowhere as clear as in the area of sexual behavior that deviance lies in large measure in the eye of the beholder. There are very few forms of sexual behavior that have not been at certain times and places staunchly prohibited, and at other times and places just as rigorously prescribed. Sexuality and the control of sexual behavior are fundamental for any society, not only because of the communal need to reproduce a population but also because sexuality can be integrated with important social institutions—the family, religion, the economy (Davis, 1971). Freud (1961), for example, viewed sexual drives as so important and basic to human life that the existence of civilization required that sexuality be controlled and channeled.

Virtually no one views sexuality as a trivial or insignificant social concern. But sexual behavior is not just important to a society collectively, it is also a part of everyone's personal experience. Sexual drives are something with which everyone must contend, as with our needs for food and shelter. Our sexual drives, however, can be expressed in an infinite variety of forms which every society attempts to structure and regulate. No society is without such regulations, nor is it likely that such a society could even exist, except in the fantasies of sexual anarchists. Conversely, it is impossible to completely regulate all sexual conduct of all citizens; the sex drive is too constant, too universal, and too subject to idiosyncratic and surreptitious satisfaction. All societies attempt to strike some balance between regulation and license and to integrate such regulation with important social institutions. Thus, every society creates its own world of sexual normalcy and sexual deviation. What constitutes sexual deviance, just as what constitutes general social deviance, is that which is effectively labeled as such.

We might begin to formulate an answer, inductively, to the question of what is sexual deviance by examining types of sexual behavior that are usually considered, in this time and place, to constitute sexual deviation. In the 1971 *Encyclopedia of Social Work*, a paper on sexual deviance discusses the following: pornography, masturbation, fetishes, exhibition-ism, peepism, bestiality, rape, incest, child molestation, prostitution, premarital sex, postmarital sex, extramarital sex, and homosexuality (Bell, 1971). A best-selling textbook on the sociology of deviant behavior in-cludes discussions of the following forms of sexual deviance: premarital sex relations, nudity, prostitution, co-marital sex (swingers), pornogra-phy, and homosexual behavior (Clinard, 1974). Finally, that comprehen-sive catalogue of normative social violations, the American Psychiatric Association's *Diagnostic and Statistical Manual* (1968), lists the follow-ing sexual deviations: homosexuality (which was recently and contro-versially dropped by the APA as a psychiatric illness), fetishism, voyeurism, sadism and masochism. What can we make of such listings? Do these forms of behavior have anything in common? What connection can be made between such diverse characters as the literature buff whose discerning tastes run to volumes found at the local "adult" bookstore and the raincoated purveyor of visual surprises? Or between the woman who provides sexual favors for a modest fee and volleyball players at a "nature camp"? Needless to say, instructive typologies are difficult to find or create, indicating that caution should be taken in studying "sexual devi-ance." These behaviors range for example from those that are widespread in the population and might be considered "normal deviance" (*e.g.*, masturbation and premarital sexual relations) to those that are relatively uncommon (*e.g.*, incest); they encompass those that are only mildly disapproved of by the society (*e.g.*, adultery) and those that evoke con-demnation (*e.g.*, male homosexuality); they include those behaviors that are essentially individual and private (*e.g.*, fetishes) and those that are highly social in organization (*e.g.*, prostitution).

SEXUAL DEVIANCE AS STATUS VIOLATIONS

Perhaps nowhere is "deviance" as divorced from the actual behavior per se and as associated with attributes of the individual as with sexual deviance. Labeling thievery, murder, alcoholism, and schizophrenia gen-erally is not contingent upon the individual's age, sex or marital status, but is almost always in response to some alleged behavior the person pursues. This is not so with much sexual deviance. For example, oral-genital sexual behavior between an adult male and female would usually not elicit stern condemnation, but the same behavior—say, fellatio—between two adult males most certainly would (and does). This ten-dency for sexual deviance to be closely contingent on the attributes of the individual or characteristics of the sexual object and not simply on the behavior itself would apply to fetishes, exhibitionism (almost always only applicable to males), bestiality, incest, child molestation, prostitution, premarital and extramarital sex, homosexuality, nudity, and transvestitism.

This observation that sexual deviance is not closely associated with the actual behavior in which the individual engages, but rather with the person's status and the status of the sexual partner (object) suggests that much sexual deviance may be viewed as status offenses, *i.e.*, violations of the norms governing one's position in the social order. Many of the norms that govern or attempt to govern sexual behavior are tied to particular social statuses, most importantly to those of sex, age and kinship, but also in a less obvious way to those of race, socioeconomic position, and what might be called human status. Each of these is briefly described below.

KINSHIP STATUS

Incest, premarital and extramarital sex, and prostitution involve violating norms that govern the kinship relationships required for acceptable sexual relations between persons. Sexual relations with close blood relatives (father, mother, son, daughter, brother, sister or other close relative) are proscribed. Acceptable sexual relations are to occur between a couple who are married either legally in a formal ceremony or through a common-law relationship. Sexual relations between unmarried adults, although relatively common and not severely punished, generally are discouraged.

AGE

Sexual behavior is restricted to those who are deemed not too young to understand nor too old to care, and between persons of a similar age. Thus children, adolescents and the elderly have fewer social supports for their sexual interests than do young adults and those persons in middle age. Similarly, sexual relations between adults of substantially different ages usually results in reactions of suspicion and distaste. Of course, one of the most sternly enforced norms prohibits sexual activity between adults and children, heterosexual activity which would be quite acceptable if both partners were adults.

SEXUAL STATUS

Perhaps the most distinctive of the status-related norms is that one which legitimizes sexual relationships only between two people of the opposite sex. Homosexual behavior, although slowly being decriminalized in many states, is viewed with disgust, discomfort or fear by a large majority of the population (Clinard, 1974: p. 547). It is also one of the types of behavior that the public readily associates as "deviant" (Simmons, 1965) and one of the forms where even one instance of the behavior is translated into an identity, *i.e.*, one who occasionally engages in homosexual behavior becomes a homosexual.

SOCIOECONOMIC STATUS

Although our society does not have a rigid caste system, there are inter-class barriers which regulate both dating and mating (Davis, 1971). Though a wealthy upper-class young woman who proposes to marry an unskilled laborer may not normally be seen as deviant or be the subject of organized attempts at rehabilitation, it is not at all unlikely that such a budding romance would evoke neighborly disapproval and family anguish at the possibility of such an ill-conceived union. Certainly, there must be a number of upper-class young adults whose proposed interclass marriages land them, with family assistance of course, on the psychiatrist's couch or on a plane bound for a European vacation. Violation of interclass sexual norms has always made good Hollywood melodrama.

RACIAL STATUS

In a segregated and racist society, sex, like other goods and services, is regulated according to one's racial status. In our society, this does not so much pertain to different norms for each racial group (although there may be such differences) as it does to interracial marriage and sexual relations. Interracial premarital sexual relations and marriage, although rarely showing up on lists of social deviance (see Sagarin 1975: p. 260), is disvalued by many people and in the recent past was illegal in many states. No doubt some of the overt resistance to racially integrated schooling stems from parental fears that interracial sexual barriers will be weakened and that their sons or daughters may become intimate with those of the wrong color.

HUMAN STATUS

Put simply, sexual behavior is only condoned when it is directed toward other humans. Sexual relations with animals (bestiality) or sexual arousal and gratification through the use of inanimate objects (fetishes) is clearly suspect as a form of deviance. Likewise, sexual relations with or between persons who are viewed as somewhat less than fully human are discouraged. For example, those who have severe mental or physical handicaps are seen as inappropriate sexual partners.

Thus, norms governing sexual behavior in the society are closely tied to the status characteristics of the individuals (objects) involved, and the violation of these status norms—especially those of age, sex, and kinship —often is labeled as sexual deviance and confers upon the labelee a stigma, not simply for what he did, but because of who he is.

THE SEXUALLY OPPRESSED

Not all social statuses are socially equal. Even with the egalitarian ethos, some status characteristics are favored. In our society, the most highly valued status is to be male, white, adult, married, and of upper social class. As Goffman says (1963: p. 128): ". . . in an important sense there is only one complete unblushing male in America: a young, married, white, urban, northern, heterosexual Protestant father of college education, fully employed, of good complexion, weight, and height, and a recent record in sports." Everyone else is to some extent, at least at moments, made to feel unworthy, incomplete, inferior, and to that extent stigmatized.

Similarly, the preferred form of sexual behavior is equally narrow: genital-to-genital intercourse in the missionary position between an able-bodied married male and female. Deviations from that prescription, if publicly known, cause social concern if not outright hostility. Thus, those who engage in sexual behavior with persons to whom they are not married, objects that are not human or not of the opposite sex, in positions that are unconventional or involve orifices or organs other than the genitals, become sexually suspect. It is in this sense that those who voluntarily engage in homosexuality, prostitution, premarital and extramarital sex, bestiality, exhibitionism, and fetishism, may be considered as sexual deviants by virtue of their sexual behavior vis-à-vis their statuses.

There are members of the sexually oppressed, however, who are not oppressed primarily for their sexual preferences, but who encounter sexual oppression by virtue of their nonsexual stigmatizing attributes. These are persons who are social deviants first, and only secondarily sexual deviants. Here are people in double jeopardy who are socially discredited and, by virtue of that stigma, are viewed as unworthy of, uninterested in, or unable to engage in, meaningful sexual relationships. They are the retarded, the mentally ill, the disabled, the institutionalized, the imprisoned, and the aged; deviant individuals who are viewed as less than fully human and who therefore are often denied any gratifying, socially sanctioned sexual expression. Consequently, sexual behavior among such oppressed peoples constitutes a double risk. They are socially oppressed in the first place for nonsexual reasons, and, as a consequence, are often forced into what is viewed as sexual deviance as well. For example, an institutionalized person, whether in a state hospital, correctional facility, or in a health-care facility such as a nursing home, and even though placed there for reasons quite apart from his sexual behavior, usually is denied access to conventional sexual objects (spouse, a person of the opposite sex, etc.) and finds that he must engage in illicit sexual liaisons for gratification. Frequently, their caretakers are ignorant of institutionalized persons' sexual needs and fail to provide legitimate sexual opportunities for them. More serious, perhaps, is the tendency among professional helpers to view unconventional sexual expression as pathological, as symptomatic of personality problems, and as further evidence that treatment is needed. Rehabilitation, then, may attempt to discourage sexual expression among these people, rather than provide meaningful opportunities for it.

There is evidence, however, that the sexually oppressed are beginning to demand greater freedom, especially those who have been considered deviant for engaging in sexual behavior among consenting adults. Both homosexuals and prostitutes, for example, have publicly organized to resist attempts at further regulation and oppression. Similarly, institutionalized people, most notably prisoners, are becoming much more vocal about their rights, and it may be expected that sexual rights will emerge as one of their issues.

CONCLUSION

Sexual behavior is too important to go unregulated, yet too personal and varied to lend itself readily to total control, except perhaps in some totalitarian nightmare of a society. There are, in fact, a multitude of sexual improprieties committed daily. The task for human service professionals is, first, to promote rational and humane social policies and attitudes regarding sexual behavior; and, secondly, to make provision for the sexual needs of those who currently have been oppressed by virtue of their style of sexual expression. Although there are certainly sexual norms that one may want to continue to enforce, such as those prohibiting incest, pedophilia, and rape, there are many others which have long outlived any important social function they may once have had and therefore they deserve to be lifted from the shoulders of the sexually oppressed.

REFERENCES AND RECOMMENDED READINGS

American Psychiatric Association. *Diagnostic and Statistical Manual of Mental Disorders.* 2nd edition. Washington, D.C.: American Psychiatric Association, 1968.

BECKER, HOWARD S. *Outsiders: Studies in the Sociology of Deviance.* New York: Free Press, 1963.

BELL, ROBERT R. "Sexual Deviance," in *Encyclopedia of Social Work*. New York: National Association of Social Workers, 1971.

CLINARD, MARSHALL B. *Sociology of Deviant Behavior*. 4th edition. New York: Holt, Rinehart and Winston, 1974.

DAVIS, KINGSLEY, "Sexual Behavior." In *Contemporary Social Problems*, 3rd edition, edited by Robert K. Merton and Robert Nisbet. New York: Harcourt, Brace, Jovanovich, 1971, pp. 313–360.

ERIKSON, KAI. "Notes on the Sociology of Deviance," In *The Other Side: Perspectives on Deviance*, edited by H. S. Becker. New York: Free Press, 1964, pp. 9–21.

FREUD, SIGMUND. *Civilization and Its Discontents*. New York: W. W. Norton, 1961.

GOFFMAN, ERVING. *Stigma: Notes on the Management of Spoiled Identity*. Englewood Cliffs, N.J.: Prentice-Hall, 1963.

KIRK, STUART A. "Clients as Outsiders: Theoretical Approaches to Deviance," in *Social Work*, 17(2) (1972), pp. 24–32.

KITSUSE, JOHN. "Societal Reaction to Deviant Behavior: Problems of Theory and Method." *Social Problems*, Vol. 9 (Winter, 1962), pp. 247–256.

LEMERT, EDWIN. *Social Pathology*. New York: McGraw-Hill, 1951.

SAGARIN, EDWARD. *Deviants and Deviance: An Introduction to the Study of Disvalued People and Behavior*. New York: Praeger, 1975.

SCHUR, EDWIN M. *Labeling Deviant Behavior: Its Sociological Implications*. New York: Harper and Row, 1971.

SIMMONS, J. L. "Public Stereotypes of Deviants." *Social Problems*, Vol. 13 (1965), pp. 223–232.

II.
THE YOUNG
AND
THE OLD

Sex is for the young . . . but not too young. At least, that is the basic value of much of contemporary society. Again, we have been led to associate sexual behavior, especially the sexual act, with socially responsible reproduction. Neither the very young nor the old should reproduce, we feel, therefore there's something wrong with their engaging in sexual activity.

Many reasons have been offered as to why young people should not have sex. Sex is still seen by many persons as being intrinsically evil—a necessary evil for adults, but not for children, who are innocent, and therefore are, and should remain, sexless. In fact, children have become the symbol of sexual innocence. Therefore, if you don't want to deal with the troublesome sexuality of people who are aged, institutionalized, handicapped or ill, all you have to do is think of them, and treat them, as children.

Furthermore, we say, responsible sexual relationships require maturity of both participants. Children and adolescents, by definition, lack maturity; therefore sexuality must be hazardous to their health and well-being. This is reasonable enough if we are clear as to what maturity is, and if we are convinced that adults are necessarily "mature" or at least make wise sexual decisions, and that adolescents are necessarily incapable of making such decisions. Furthermore, even if intercourse is deemed hazardous for adolescents, how openly and even willingly do we offer and support other forms of sexual pleasure and expression? The needs and problems associated with adolescent sexuality along with some changes in current thinking about adolescent sexuality itself are the subject of Larry Lister's chapter. As he points out, the oppression of adolescents is particularly unfortunate since it has such a negative effect on their subsequent adulthood, and creates a cyclic effect on future generations.

At the other end of the life spectrum are the aged. Their child-producing years are over. Often they have, by popular standards, lost their sexual attractiveness, if not their stamina and good health. For many of them, growing old gracefully does not include sexual activity. The sexual attitudes of many of them were established in an era when sexual information was limited and not openly discussed. Many women were taught that sex was a pleasure for men but only a duty for women, and that this duty was completed when the childbearing years came to an end. Indeed, for many aging men and women, who for a variety of reasons have never enjoyed their sexuality, the onset of aging with the concomitant termination of sexual obligations to their marital partners is met with relief. Sexiness is not an expectation for the aged as it is for the young. Society labels the aging man who retains a vigorous interest in sexual expression a "dirty old man"—certainly neither a compliment nor a reinforcement for his continued sexual expression. Often the wives of such men, who share society's view that sex is for the young, respond to their husbands' hopeful sexual overtures by testily saying, "For heaven's sake, act your age!"

The termination of sexual activity with aging should be a choice of the aged. To feel forced into unsatisfying sexual activity by coercion of a spouse or by aggressively liberal public opinion which orders that everyone must enjoy sex is itself oppressive. It can be hoped, however, that people—including old people—can make informed choices about their own sexual behavior. It is unfortunate that most sex education efforts are directed to the young. The aging (and that includes those in their thirties and up) could profit from understanding the physiological and psychological changes that occur with aging, and how they can integrate these changes in their own lives.

Some aging persons are more constricted than others in making these choices. Those aged men and women who are confined to nursing homes and other institutions are often deprived of choices—and perhaps of almost any form of sexual expression. While the percentage of aged people confined to such institutions is small, they still constitute a sizable group of sexually oppressed people who are often overlooked. Mona Wasow and Martin Loeb, in their article on the aged, review the sexual problems of the aged in general as well as reviewing their research on the sexual problems of those living in nursing homes.

CHAPTER 3

ADOLESCENTS

Larry Lister

The dictionary defines *oppression* as "unjust or cruel exercise of authority or power" and "a sense of heaviness—in the body or mind" (Webster, 1973). In other words, oppression can be viewed as either actions from outside sources working against an individual (or a collective of individuals) or as the responses within individuals to forces which produce "a sense of heaviness." By these criteria; adolescents can be considered a sexually oppressed group, since they do have what is too frequently an unjust authority exercised toward them by parents, peers, and society in general. And, as reflected in their own current slang, they certainly do frequently feel "heavy."

It is our purpose in this paper to discuss the sources of this oppression, to discuss the ways in which these oppressive experiences cause the adolescent to feel "heavy," and to describe current attempts to modify some of society's oppressive actions. It should be noted at the outset that these remarks are directed mainly toward the more common features of sexual oppression of contemporary adolescents in our wider American culture, for we know that historically many other cultures have neither been sexually oppressive nor have they created an adolescent period which is as extensive and as complex as has evolved in our society in the past fifty or so years. And, indeed, within our own society there are still various segments where the expression of sexuality runs counter to the dominant pattern, either to greater extremes of repressiveness or to attitudes of much greater permissiveness.

SOME SOURCES OF OPPRESSION

The exercise of authority over the sexual conduct of adolescents occurs at various levels throughout society. Only a few of the sources of oppression will be discussed here, though they are the ones which have an overpowering influence.

SOCIETY'S CONFLICT

American society expresses rather extreme conflicts over basic sexual values. The sexual attitudes of people have not generally been consistent with their sexual practices. That the public does not want this inconsistency pointed out was well illustrated by the publicity given Betty Ford's televised remarks in the summer of 1975 that she "wouldn't be surprised" if her unmarried 18-year-old daughter came to her and said, "I'm having an affair." The well-publicized reaction of the public to this statement was probably actually due less to any real surprise that an 18-year-old might have an affair than to the fact that a prominent public figure would *acknowledge* this probability. The reaction to this statement by the President's wife seems to indicate the degree to which our society wishes to retain a puritan public morality in spite of more permissive private behavior indicated by the fact that over two-thirds of the men and over one-half of the women in this country have premarital coitus.*

The conflict between the public attitude and the private behavior is created on many societal levels. For example, the news media strongly influence the dissemination of role expectations to the public, with adolescents being one of the most importantly influenced groups, due partly to the fact that adolescence is the period in life when identity is being consolidated. Thus, what is the teen-age girl to decide when she encounters in the daily newspaper the juxtaposition of a news item about the ordination of women priests with an ad for car batteries which is dominated by a woman in a bathing suit? Not only are these confusing messages to the developing young woman, but they indicate to young men that on the one hand women should be treated with equality yet on the other hand they should "light your fire" (or at least start your engine)! When looked at from this perspective, we should not be surprised at an increase in rape statistics.

---

* It is important to note, however, that this "permissiveness" does not connote a casual or promiscuous sexuality, since about one-half of the women, for example, who have premarital coitus eventually marry their sexual partner.

Not only does society's conflict produce confused expectations for the sexual behavior of adolescents but it also produces inconsistent and stereotypical policies and programs for the adolescents whose sexual behavior has created problems. It is generally assumed, for example, that a teen-age pregnancy for the middle-class girl is strongly condemned and a source of tremendous guilt, while for the lower-class girl such a pregnancy is more within the routine of things. Whether true or not, the resources available to girls from these differing strata can be greatly dissimilar, with the middle-class girl encouraged to terminate her pregnancy quietly and continue her education, while the lower-class girl is processed for AFDC and given an appointment at the county hospital's prenatal clinic. In spite of the revolution in abortion services, such services are still not universally available to the poor.

SOCIETY'S ONE-SIDED MESSAGE

It is a form of oppression when a natural and universal human function is simply suppressed or when acceptable channels for its expression are not made known. In spite of sex education in the schools and an enormous amount of literature available on the subject, the message communicated to adolescents is often that of the dangers and difficulties to be encountered with their sexuality rather than with the pleasures and choices. This in no way should be interpreted to mean that because there has been much repression of sexuality in our society the antidote must be sexual license. What is meant is that our society has not been able to deal with the bio-social reality of sexuality in any way comparable to, for example, the bio-social reality of hunger. Whereas with hunger, our culture has been fairly well able to give people permission to eat, and at the same time communicate which foods are healthy and which eating habits are constructive, we have been less able to be positively assertive about which adolescent sex practices are constructive. Most adolescents have to use a process of elimination of all the sex activities which are labeled as dangerous or potentially harmful in order to arrive at some personal sex ethic. When all the prohibited activities are eliminated, it would appear that adolescent boys are primarily left with "nocturnal emissions," since these are presumably about the only outlet over which males have no control, and, similarly, girls are left with nothing.

Actually are there not many more options for adolescents which can be socially sanctioned and which do not have to be problematic? Would not a positive approach to teen-age sexuality deal in a constructive way with masturbation, for example? Rather than viewing masturbation as heedless self-indulgence signifying a waste of energy and power, as has tended to be the traditional underlying attitude in our society, would not a positive approach view the activity as a way to release sexual tension and as a substitute for intercourse? Actually, as stated by Salzman (1974: p. 190), masturbation "is an effective means of relieving anxiety. In fact, it is more frequently used for this purpose than to provide an outlet for frustrated sexual needs." Evidence is also available to the effect that women who masturbated before marriage achieve orgasm more frequently during the first year of marriage than those who did not (Kinsey, Pomeroy & Gebhard, 1953).

What about petting? Practically all adolescents pet in various ways. How much they pet might be indicated by a recent survey which found that almost 60 per cent of a sample of college women had been involved in heavy petting (genital stimulation while in an unclothed state) while they were still in high school (McCary, 1973). Petting to this extent is usually not carried out with a casual partner and yet for the majority of teen-agers this experience is accompanied by feelings of guilt. This is not to suggest that all teen-agers should feel compelled to pet heavily; for those who prefer other outlets or who are comfortable in abstaining, that should be an acceptable position. But for those who are into heavy petting with a partner for whom there is mutual respect, why need they feel guilt? Part of the reason is the oppression by omission on the part of a society which resists giving permission for responsible sex among teen-agers.

One of the reasons for society's oppressive attitude regarding petting is the fear, or belief, that such intimacy will naturally be only a step removed from intercourse. Of course it is true that teen-agers rarely make a lockstep progression from a kiss to coitus; heavy petting will usually be an activity along this continuum, however; so many adults feel that holding the line at minimal involvement will prevent the intensive intimacy of intercourse. However much justification there is for this position, a more expansive approach might advocate the education of adolescents to how arousal occurs, how arousal may be avoided, and how, once aroused, there may be an acceptable satiation.

Certainly one fact which seems to be going for the adult educator today is the franker and more open communication which exists among today's youth. Because of this greater openness, it is possible for a teen-age girl to clearly say she is not interested in going "too far" with her date, rather than having to nonverbally manipulate an evening's activity so as not to find herself a reluctant contortionist in the back seat of her date's car at the end of the evening.

Actually, the adults' fear of adolescents' sexual intercourse is often based on the belief that each act of sexual intimacy between teen-agers will lead only to more intensive involvement. This fear reflects a belief on the adult's part that youths are really uncontrollably impulsive and that once they are sexually knowledgeable, they will be insatiable in further pursuing and deepening that knowledge. The gradual accretion of intimacy, of course, can occur, but some interesting data of Simon and Gagnon (1972: p. 472) indicate that this process may evolve differently for male and female, since "the male suitor frequently becomes emotionally involved with his partner and correspondingly less interested in engaging in sexual activity with her, and the female, whose appreciation of the genuineness of her suitor's affection allows her to feel that sexual activity is now both legitimate and desirable, becomes more interested in engaging in sexual activity with him." What appears to be involved in this process is that the male, socially conditioned to try to "get all he can from the girl as early as he can," finds, sometimes to his own surprise, that real intimacy begins to evolve, causing him to shift from an exploitative to a more protective orientation toward the girl. Thus, it should be possible to clarify to adolescents—and, more specifically, to the adults who are responsible for their socialization—that boys, once aroused, are not coital "gluttons" any more than are girls, but that girls, when they have "gone all the way," have often done so with a real sense of attachment and commitment.

A word should be said about teen-age homosexuality, since feelings or experiences of a homosexual nature can be an area of confusion and concern to adolescents, to say nothing of their parents and society in general. When defined in terms of having experienced orgasm through sex activity with a member of the same sex, the Kinsey studies found that more than one-third of males and nearly one-fifth of females have had at least one homosexual experience by the time they are adults [Kinsey *et al.* (1953) and Kinsey, A. C., Pomeroy, W. B. and Martin, C. E. (1948)]. If thoughts, inclinations or fantasies of a homosexual nature are added to the definition, then probably a majority of adolescents have had some type of homosexual experience at one time or another.

It should be recognized, however, that homosexual experiences can be problematical for two groups of teenagers: (1) those who are basically on a heterosexual course, but who are confused or worried about what seems to them a path toward interest in the same sex, and (2) the other, smaller number of youths who are just beginning to recognize that they will be basically homosexual in orientation in their adulthood. Society, through the schools and other channels of information, could do more than is presently done to reassure the first group of adolescents that their experiences are transitory and not a source of shame or disgust and to make it possible for the second group to continue the process of forming a satisfying self-concept, free from the burden of self-loathing which too frequently has resulted from our society's responses to homosexuality.

PARENTS' OPPRESSION

Many, if not most, adolescents are decidedly oppressed by their own parents. The reasons are numerous and in many cases specific to individual families, so that all of them cannot possibly be catalogued here. However, several common reasons for parental oppression will be briefly discussed:

1. *Parental fear.* As touched upon already in regard to society in general, parents fear the potential power which sex has to motivate their adolescents. Out of fear of how stimulating and exciting sex activity will be to their teenager, the parents feel that the more they can hold the line on the experiencing of sexuality, the less it will take hold of their child. Thus, many parents set early limits on hours for dating, make sure the kid is up early in the morning and at some kind of work, and otherwise try to program the adolescent's activities in such a way that the youth will not turn to the pleasures of his own—or another's—body.

2. *Parental discomfort and ignorance. Ignorance* is a strong word, but it is too often a fact that parents know little about sexuality in general and even less about positive aspects of adolescent sex behavior. According to Gadpaille (1974), "The majority of youngsters are no better off than their parents with regard to accurate sex information or healthful sexual attitudes." But where differences exist, Gadpaille feels that it is with "increased knowledge among the young." If they could only talk to each other, the parents could learn much from their adolescents and the adolescents *could also learn* from the parents. Often, however, the parents are not able to even talk of their sexuality with each other, much less comfortably discuss the subject with their offspring.

3. *Parental dissatisfaction with their own sexuality.* The preceding reason for oppression logically gives rise to the issue of the parents' own sexuality. With so many married couples having renounced the excitement and gratification in their own relationship, how are they to deal in any but a cautionary or prohibitive way with the emerging sexuality of their teenagers? For example, how is the nonorgasmic mother going to look at the possibility for pleasure through sexuality on the part of her daughter? How is the bureaucratically controlled father, who has sex on schedule, going to feel about a sensuous son? How are two parents who undress in the dark going to respond to their daughter's uninhibited lack of a bra? As adolescence is considered a period of crisis for the youth, so it must also be viewed in crisis terms for the parents. In fact, one of the felicitous outcomes of the adolescent period of their children *can be* the rejuvenation of the sex lives of the parents, whose own sexuality comes up for review as they necessarily deal with sexual issues which their

children's stage of life forces upon them. The empty nest needn't contain two dried-up old birds; in fact, if the parents "get it together" between themselves, this will make the process of child emancipation not one of loss, but one of new gains between the parents. In the numerous ways in which the parents' gratification with each other is therefore observable, it lifts the often subtle—and oppressive—sense of responsibility which is so often placed on the children for holding their parents' marriage together.

4. *Parental irresponsibility.* This can also be a form of oppression. Some parents simply disavow any responsibility for guiding their young, repressing the issue entirely or else rationalizing that it is now the domain of school and church, and that these institutions know more and better than they about the subject. While sex education is indeed part of the responsibility of these other socializing institutions, at least one study has shown that the majority of adolescents would prefer that their sex education come from their parents, though in fact less than one-half of the girls or the boys received it from their mothers, far fewer boys received it from their fathers, and, interestingly in the case of girls, hardly a girl had any sex education from her father (Gagnon, 1965). This whole subject of sex education is obviously an area of confusion and disagreement among both parents and professionals, with some professionals pointing out that "to try and discuss total sexuality with one's own adolescent children is indeed not only an impossibility but often a profound mistake" (Curry, 1974: p. 23). Evidence suggests that when responsibility for sex education is shared between parents, school and church, and if these sources are both accurate and comfortable with the subject, then the teenager's curiosity is satisfied. While, on the other hand, the teenager's excitement, curiosity and sex desires are increased when information is given only by peers, sex cartoons, and similar sources (Kirkendall, 1970: pp. 30–32).

One other aspect of parental irresponsibility should also be noted, and this is with regard to the pseudoliberated parents who avow a quite complete sexual permissiveness in connection with their children. When fully honest and consistent on the part of loving parents, this attitude does not interfere with the development of secure and nonpromiscuous youth. Unfortunately, in our society, in too many cases the ultraliberated attitude masks the parents' need to defy society's norms, with their kids performing as pawns. It is irresponsible conduct if these parents do not provide ample opportunity for their adolescents to know what are the general attitudes of society toward sex and give their kids the chance to exercise some choice in their adherence to these societal standards, even when these choices are more "conservative" than are those of the parents.

A variation of the above militantly liberal parents is the male parent who believes himself permissive "because that is where society is now at" or "because intellectually it is right." This is the parent who, for example, sets no time deadline for his daughter to come in at night, but who—when she strolls in at 4 A.M.—becomes enraged and calls her a "whore." A parent in such serious conflict has placed his child in an impossible double-bind, but fortunately such a parent is often eagerly accessible to professional help.

THE PEER GROUP

Finally, to complete the discussion of some of the sources of oppression, there is the pressure from the adolescent's own peer group. For example: a boy who is in serious conflict about his own identity is pressured by his more secure friends into mutual masturbation; the girl whose "closet virgin" friends urge her to have intercourse with her current casual boyfriend; the boy who sets up the vulnerable girl for sex on the first date and who never phones again (but his friends do); the handicapped or "different" kid who never even has the opportunity to "get a bad reputation." Since the peer group is so vital to the whole sense of identity of the adolescent, the myriad forms of oppression which emanate from this source can be as devastating as any we have mentioned. Fortunately, many of today's youth tend to devaluate hypocrisy and to accept individuality much more than previous generations did, but they still are left to cope with the severe strains which attend the actual implementation of their often lofty ethics.*

SOME TRADITIONAL AREAS OF SOCIETAL OPPRESSION

Because of conflicts and ambivalence at various levels of our society regarding adolescent sexuality, there arise a number of social problems which directly relate to adolescent sexual behavior. Over the years our society has attempted to cope with these problems in various ways with limited success. Given the basic conflict about sexuality, it has not been possible to prevent some adolescent sexual problems from occurring in the first place, so that emphasis has usually been on residual policies and programs. A slightly new emphasis is currently being manifested, this emphasis being placed on the rights of minors and, hopefully, offering some possibilities for primary, as well as secondary and tertiary, prevention. In the following section we will briefly discuss some of these current developments as they relate to contraception, abortion, and pregnancy of unmarried teenagers.

Contraception. With a fairly high proportion of teenagers having

---

* For an unnecessarily pessimistic discussion of the problems encountered by the older adolescent, see Herbert Hendin, "The Revolt Against Love, Sexual Warfare on the Campus," *Harper's Magazine*, August 1975, pp. 20–27.

intercourse* (Newman, 1975: p. 195), it follows that contraceptive information and methods should be made available and widely utilized. Family planning services are currently available throughout most of the country, with these services receiving Federal funding and being dispensed through Office of Economic Opportunity (O.E.O.) programs, Planned Parenthood affiliates, churches, philanthropic foundations, and numerous other sources. That these services are being increasingly utilized by younger people is illustrated by the fact that in the second quarter of 1972, 44 per cent of new patients enrolling at Planned Parenthood clinics were under age 20, representing an increase of 6 per cent over 1971 (Amer. Journal of Public Health, 1973: p. 285).

In spite of wide availability and the high rate of utilization by the under-20 group, however, a recent study found that "more than 75 per cent of the sexually active teenage girls never, or only occasionally, used contraception" (Amer. Journal of Public Health, 1973: p. 286). The methods used were often withdrawal, condoms or douching. While many of the reasons for non-use of contraceptives have to do with the attitudes of the adolescents themselves, other reasons relate to laws of the various states.

According to a report in late 1973, two-thirds of the states would not permit the unmarried, newly pregnant minor under age 18 who was living at home to consent to her own contraceptive counseling (Amer. Journal of Public Health, 1973: p. 286). Such restrictions have traditionally been based on the desire of the state to protect the influence of the parents over their minor children and to attempt to limit teenage sex activity. Recent court decisions in several states have challenged these questionable assumptions, however, so that it now is possible for minors to have greater access to contraceptives. For example, while California still does not permit sale of condoms in vending machines, a new law eliminates the old requirement that condoms be sold by licensed pharmacists only (*Family Planning, Population Reporter*, 1974).

Unwed pregnancy. The pregnant teenager has long been a source of great concern to society. In 1968, the illegitimacy rate of non-wed births per 1,000 unmarried females 15 to 19 years of age was 19.8 (McCary, 1973: p. 447). In 1973, total births to girls under 19 years of age were over 600,000, with the majority of these conceived out of wedlock (Ambrose, 1975: p. 10). One solution to a teenage pregnancy is of course marriage, but statistics indicate that about 50 per cent of these marriages will terminate in divorce within five years (Maddock, 1973: p. 333), and even if they endure, "these couples rarely manage to catch up educationally or economically with couples similar in background except for the

* The 1973 survey indicated that among white females, 30 per cent were non-virgins by age 15 and 57 per cent by age 19.

premarital pregnancy" (Juhasz, 1974: p. 270). For the young unmarried mother who keeps her child, compared with older women, "there was a higher incidence of complications in pregnancy, more caesarean sections, more premature births, and more neonatal and maternal mortality" (Juhasz, 1974: p. 268).

Teenage unwed pregnancy qualifies as a social problem—more than just a sexual problem—on several bases, not the least of which are the interpersonal needs of the unwed mother herself. Contrary to what would be assumed, these girls are generally neither promiscuous (nor even sexually sophisticated), nor are they particularly gratified in intercourse. It is a sad commentary that the very girls who are, to society, the most obviously sexually active, should seem "almost unaware of it [their sex drive] as part of their lives. Most of the girls found intercourse to be either disgusting or only tolerable" (Schaffer & Pine, 1972: pp. 519–20). Sex, for these girls, was an attempt at relating and being connected to another person; it was a social, and not a sexual need.

Far from helping her to get better connected with people, society's usual response to the pregnant adolescent has been to sequester and isolate her, albeit frequently in the company of other pregnant girls. Nowhere has this isolation been accomplished more completely than in the schools. "Traditionally, most pregnant students have been expelled or quietly excluded from school" (Ambrose, 1975: p. 10). Such oppressive practices by the schools have characteristically been based on unwritten policies which were never systematically challenged until recently.

The 1972 Education Amendments to Title IX now mandate that "sex discrimination be eliminated in Federally assisted education programs" (Ambrose, 1975: p. 11). With enforcement handled through the Office for Civil Rights of the U.S. Department of Health, Education and Welfare (DHEW), schools will no longer be able to deny school participation to a pregnant teen-ager. While schools could continue to offer separate classes to pregnant students, no student could be required to attend them or to have to receive her education through home tutoring. With the threat of withdrawal of Federal funds, the schools should begin to move in the direction of less exclusionary practices against pregnant teen-agers. As this occurs, there should be some possibility for many pregnant adolescents to continue their education. Their inability to do so in the past has unfortunately relegated many of them to permanent second-class citizenship.

Abortion. This remains a highly controversial public issue, and especially so with regard to unmarried adolescents. With adequately informed and responsible teen-agers who have been given access to sex information so that they can make sound choices regarding their sex conduct and who (if they are having intercourse) have had access to birth control measures, abortion should not be necessary for any but a small number. The facts reveal, unfortunately, that the actual situation is not ideal as stated above, but that nearly one-quarter of the *legal* abortions between July 1970 and June 1971 were performed on women who were less than 20 years of age! (Amer. Journal of Public Health, 1973: p. 285). While there are many medical and moral justifications for the anti-abortion position, it is a fact that the U.S. Supreme Court decision in the case of Roe *vs* Wade in January 1973 declared that all states must make abortions available. As of early 1975, however, only 31 states had passed laws in compliance with the Supreme Court ruling (NASW, 1975).

Even as the states comply with the Supreme Court ruling, there are still issues to be resolved regarding the rights of minors to these services. These issues involve not just the appropriateness of abortion, but the whole question of a minor's ability to consent to medical care without parental involvement. Many states require parental consent for abortions to minors, while other states are now dealing with this issue by passing facilitative laws, such as that passed in the District of Columbia in August of 1974 which specifies that a minor of any age may consent to medical services, including abortion, with the minor responsible for payment. In this law, no physician or health facility is *required* to treat the minor, but they *are* obligated to refer the minor to another facility if they do not offer treatment (*Family Planning, Population Reporter*, 1974: p. 86).

As in the instance of teen-age contraception already mentioned, an issue in the dispute regarding abortion laws is that of preserving the family unit and maintaining parental authority. A judgment in the state of Washington rejected this argument on the basis that "parental control is already largely lost in the case of a minor seeking an abortion" and that "consideration of parental rights must include recognition that the pregnant girl is on the verge of being a parent herself." In fact, in that same decision, the judge wrote that "prima facie, the constitutional rights of minors, including the right to privacy, are coextensive with those of adults" (*Family Planning, Population Reporter*, 1975: p. 3).

CONCLUSIONS

Are adolescents a sexually oppressed group? Unquestionably they are, as are many other segments of our society if considered in respect to the discrepancy between their potential for sexual fulfillment and their ability to express themselves sexually. With adolescents—and, indeed, younger children—there is so much opportunity for society to create sexual attitudes and behavior that will bring happiness and security in adulthood, that it seems particularly unfortunate for the oppressive forces to continue unabated. Since so many levels of our society have an input into the oppression, it could seem that nothing short of radical social change could provide the antidote. It would be unfortunate if the content of this paper left only that impression, however, for—aside from, or in spite of, the oppressive forces touched upon in this presentation—both adolescents and adults do have opportunities and choices available to them to help fulfill and even enhance their sexual potential.

The helping professions should be one obvious source of assistance to adolescents, as well as society in general, in helping us arrive at a nonoppressive sexual ethic. In order to do so, the professionals must arm themselves with information about the reality of sex in modern society, including a knowledge of the stereotypes and false assumptions as well as the actual sex practices. Such information is necessary not only for helping troubled adolescents and their parents at the level of clinical intervention but also for adequate dissemination of sex information through the schools, churches, and other socializing institutions of society. Obviously, too, the laws and public policies which relate to sexual conduct of youth are changing; thus the professionals need not only to familiarize themselves with these changes in their own communities but also they should develop an informed opinion to use in helping initiate and support the still further changes which are needed.

Adolescents do grow and most of them become mature and responsible adults. There is no inherent reason why—when *they* become the adult attitude and policy setters—they should need to take an oppressive stance in regard to the succeeding generation of teen-agers. No reason, that is, unless their own adolescent sexual experiences were so fraught with conflict, guilt and turmoil that they feel compelled to impose these same conditions on their offspring.

REFERENCES AND RECOMMENDED READINGS

AMBROSE, LINDA. "Discrimination Persists Against Pregnant Students Remaining in School." In *Family Planning, Population Reporter*, Vol. 4, No. 1 (February 1975).

CURRY, MARCIA. In *Medical Aspects of Human Sexuality*, Vol. 8, No. 9 (September 1974).

Editorial, *American Journal of Public Health*, Vol. 63, No. 4 (April 1973), p. 285.

Family Planning, Population Reporter, Vol. 4, No. 1 (February 1975), p. 3.

———, Vol. 3, No. 5 (October 1974), p. 86.

———, Vol. 3, No. 6 (December 1974), p. 121.

GADPAILLE, WARREN J. In *Medical Aspects of Human Sexuality*, Vol. 8, No. 10 (October 1974).

GAGNON, JOHN H. "Sexuality and Sexual Learning in the Child." *Psychiatry*, Vol. 28 (1965).

HENDIN, HERBERT. "The Revolt Against Love, Sexual Warfare on the Campus." *Harper's Magazine*, August 1975, pp. 20–27.

JUHASU, ANNE MC CREARY. "The Unmarried Adolescent Parent." In *Adolescence*, Vol. 9, No. 34 (Summer 1974), p. 270.

KINSEY, A. C., W. B. POMEROY, C. E. MARTIN. *Sexual Behavior in the Human Male*. Philadelphia: Saunders, 1948.

————, and PH. H. GEBHARD. *Sexual Behavior in the Human Female*. Philadelphia: Saunders, 1953.

KIRKENDALL, LESTER. "Does Sex Education Arouse Unwholesome Curiosity?" In *Sex in the Childhood Years: Expert Guidance for Parents, Counselors and Teachers*, edited by Isadore Rubin and Lester Kirkendall. New York: Association Press, 1970.

MADDOCK, JAMES W. "Sex in Adolescence: Its Meaning and Its Future." In *Adolescence*, Vol. 8, No. 31 (Fall, 1973).

NEWMAN, BARBARA and PHILIP NEWMAN. *Development Through Life: A Psycho-Social Approach*. Homewood, Illinois: Dorsey Press, 1975.

"Proposed Policy Statement on Abortion Services" prepared by Western Coalition for the National Association of Social Workers Delegate Assembly, June 1975.

SALZMAN, LEON. "Masturbation in Disturbed Adolescents." *Medical Aspects of Human Sexuality*, Vol. 8, No. 9 (September 1974).

SCHAFFER, CAROLE and FRED PINE. "Pregnancy, Abortion and the Developmental Tasks of Adolescence." In *Journal of the American Academy of Child Psychiatry*, Vol. 11, No. 3 (July 1972), pp. 519–20.

SIMON, WILLIAM and JOHN H. GAGNON. "On Psychological Development." In *Developmental Psychology: A Book of Readings*, edited by William R. Loaft. Hinsdale; Ill.: The Dryden Press, Inc., 1972.

CHAPTER 4

THE AGED*

Mona Wasow and Martin B. Loeb

The sexual needs of the elderly are generally misunderstood, stereotyped, and/or ignored. Younger and healthier people tend to believe that sexual desire and activity normally cease with old age. Those elderly individuals who do show an interest in sexuality are regarded as moral perverts or liars (Pfeiffer, 1969; Lewin, 1965). Thus, an honest look at what society expects of the older person is unsettling, because society expects grand-parently, nonsexual, nonphysical beings sitting contentedly in rocking chairs while reviewing the past. Reality, however, reveals that this is only an illusion. Older people have physical, social, emotional and sexual needs just as do the rest of the population.

In addition, many elderly persons are denied a normal sexual outlet through widowhood, physical disability or nursing home confinement. They retain, however, their normal desire for the warmth and comfort of bodily contact. Older women are often able to satisfy some of this need by cuddling infants and children. Older men who attempt to do the same may be branded as "dirty old men." Whiskin (1970) points out that

* With Stephen Buttenhof, Joanne Halter, Joan Lerman, Mary Ellen McMeen, Noah Rosenberg, Sheera Strick, and Janet Thaxton. D. Richard Green, M.S.S.A., Statistical Consultant. Sponsored by The Faye McBeath Institute on Aging and Adult Life, University of Wisconsin, Madison, Wisconsin.

society tends to overreact to the geriatric sex offender, who tends to be involved mainly in exhibitionism or fondling without harming the child.

One explanation of the problem of geriatric sex offenders is that unrelieved sexual desire, when it builds up too long, may break out unconsciously in deviant behavior. Thus, when intimacy is denied the older person, inappropriate sexual expression may reflect the human hunger for touching and closeness (Berkey, 1971; Weinberg, 1971).

SELF-CONCEPT AND PSYCHOLOGICAL MAKE-UP

Older people often find that aging—with its shift in roles, physical well-being, and status—requires a new adjustment of one's self-concept. One must worry not only about establishing an appropriate identity but also about becoming dependent on others (Thompson, 1965). Many elderly people tend to focus on the deterioration that inevitably accompanies old age and ignore the "full range of possibilities available to them" (Rosenfelt, 1965).

Sexual roles become confused in the minds of many elderly persons, who must deal with societal misconceptions and their own lessening physical functioning simultaneously. Worries about sexual performance and attractiveness creep in. Some men think intercourse and the subsequent emission of semen are debilitating and may hasten old age and death. Many women view menopause as the end of female sexuality (Rubin, 1965). Women may complain that their husbands have lost interest in marriage both physically and psychologically (Lief, 1968). The aging man who finds he can no longer get quick erections may become frightened that he is losing his sexual functioning. To avoid failure, he avoids his wife. A vicious circle develops when the wife interprets her husband's lack of sexuality as either rejection of herself or normal for his age. In either case the fear of failure produces enough anxiety to actually bring about the loss of sexual powers in the aging male (Masters and Johnson, 1970).

Yet the maintenance of a satisfying intimate relationship is closely associated with mental health and vitality in one's older years. Because many elderly people have lost their marital partners, sexual outlets are denied them. Men find replacing intimate partners easier to do than women since the number of elderly women exceeds that of elderly men. In addition, elderly women are denied the cultural perogative of men to socialize with younger members of the opposite sex. May/December marriages are tolerated, even smiled upon, only when the bride is the younger mate. Noncoital relief of sexual tensions through masturbation unfortunately tends to produce guilt and anxiety in men and women reared prior to our current period of comparative sexual enlightenment

(Felstein, 1970). Many older people fear that their sexual interests and activities are abnormal and suffer feelings of shame in secret (Eaid, 1972).

Love, affection and sex can be vital, rewarding experiences in the life of any individual, regardless of age. In the past few years, research in the area of human sexuality has produced a vast amount of information and new ideas. The focus, however, primarily has been on the young, even though it is recognized that the elderly continue to have sexual and affectional needs and desires. These needs and desires include sexual intercourse, touching, holding, masturbating; as well as any and all feelings and acts that make the person feel good. This need for close, warm, physical and emotional contact is an integral part of every human being's make-up and does not have to diminish with age. Sexuality in the aging really hasn't been given the attention it deserves.

The elderly often find themselves in a setting that offers little or no encouragement to express their sexuality. Sometimes they are embarrassed to admit to their children or friends that they have sexual interests "at their age." One of the problems in this area of sexuality and aging is that older individuals themselves accept the myths of a "sexless old age." Many were raised in a puritanical environment which stressed that sex was basically for reproduction. Of course people raised in that milieu often discovered for themselves that sex was also pleasurable! But there was stress and fear attached to sex: fear of pregnancy, fear of venereal disease, false shame, feelings of guilt, and a consciousness of sin. For women, especially, this anxiety about sex was often at a very high pitch, which tended to impair the enjoyment of their sex role.

Sexuality can be a healthy and fulfilling part of an older person's life. There are, however, physiological changes that do take place. These are natural changes, however, and are not so drastic as they are often thought to be. It is assumed by too many people that at a certain age—say, in their 60's or even earlier—individuals lose their sexual interest and capacity. More and more men and women are realizing this just isn't so, and that they need not lose their sexual interest or ability. Given reasonable health, they are able to function sexually into their 70's and 80's. There is, of course, a natural slowing down of the entire body, sexual activities included, but they don't stop.

COMMON PROBLEMS OF AGING MEN

There are several basic physical changes that are to be expected in men as they grow older. These changes do not have to affect sexual ability or satisfaction, however, nor do they signal the onset of impotency. Since his hormone levels are higher and the man is more rested in the morning, it is true that sexual activity may be easier for him at that time. There also is a widely prevalent idea that sexual intercourse will tend to speed the aging process. This notion has been disproved time and time again, and is far from the truth. Here are the actual changes that may be expected:

1. The erection may become less hard.

2. The ability to postpone ejaculation for a longer period of time usually increases.

3. It may take longer to achieve an erection and ejaculation.

4. Orgasm may be less intense and the semen release less forceful.

5. It may be longer before a second erection is possible.

Men who are experiencing difficulty in getting an erection may find helpful the technique called the "stuffing technique." This is just what it says: The man (or his partner) can take the penis when it's still not very hard or erect, and stuff it right into the vagina. Usually, within a few seconds to a minute, the penis becomes hard enough for sexual intercourse.

COMMON PROBLEMS OF THE AGING WOMAN

Women also experience a slowing-down process, along with physical changes that may affect, but need not stop, sexual feelings, activities and satisfactions. Most changes in women occur at menopause; yet these changes mark only the end of childbearing, and in some women this may be the beginning of a pleasant time for sex without the fear of pregnancy.

Many of the physical changes in women are the results of lowered hormone levels. They may include:

1. A thinning of the vaginal walls which can cause irritation during intercourse.

2. Less lubrication (wetness) in the vagina which can also make sexual intercourse uncomfortable.

3. The contractions experienced during orgasm sometimes become uncomfortable.

4. A longer time may be needed to become excited.

5. The orgasm itself may be somewhat shorter or less strong than it used to be.

The discomfort caused by the thinning of the vaginal walls and less lubrication can be easily remedied by using a vaginal jelly or cream, such as K-Y jelly.

The changes discussed above may affect some people and not others, may take place at a different age for different individuals, and may show up in varying degrees. But again, they need not stop sexual interest or activity.

Experts on aging agree there is a gradual decline of sexual activity for both males and females with advancing age (Masters and Johnson, 1970; Christenson, 1965; Verwoerdt, Pfeiffer and Wang, 1969; Rubin, 1966), with the incidence of sexual activity approaching zero by the late 80's (Verwoerdt, 1969). Studies also point out, however, that sexual activity is not a rarity in men past 80 (Pfeiffer, 1969; Rubin, 1966). Understandably, age is not the only variable which influences sexual activity. The amount of sexual activity for both men and women can be influenced by such factors as *a*) availability of a willing and able partner, *b*) physical health, *c*) mental health, and *d*) availability of privacy. Masters and Johnson stress the importance of continuing regular sexual relations in order to maintain sexual capacity and performance, especially for the aged. Unfortunately, the slowing-down process is often misunderstood and sexual activity may be forsaken completely, instead of being adjusted to the tempo of change.

In the past, physicians as well as lay people often took it for granted that the older male coronary patient was threatened by the physical exertion required for sexual intercourse. Recent medical studies show that the effects of intercourse on postcoronary and coronary-prone individuals do not appear to present unusual danger (Hellerstein, 1969; Trumble, 1970). Likewise, many males with quite advanced pulmonary diseases, including chronic bronchitis, asthma and emphysema, are capable of active and satisfying sexual relationships (Koss, 1972). Similarly, Alex Finkle (1967) found that a major concern of male patients who are faced with the possibility of prostatectomy is their fear of loss of sexual potency. His studies of men before and after prostatectomy, however, showed that the majority were potent preoperatively and retained that potency after the operation. Postoperative sexual functioning may well be determined by the surgical procedure involved.

While the aging male is often confronted with heart and respiratory problems, the aging female must contend not only with the possibility of gynecological surgery, but also with menopause. Not unlike the aging male, the aging female may fear that her sexual desire or performance will be altered. This fear may often be strong enough to cause profound psychiatric disturbances (Hollander, 1969). The fact is, however, that alterations in sexual reactions are infrequent after gynecological surgery if patients are emotionally stable and have been adequately prepared (Huffman, 1969; Drellich, 1967), and that only a small number of women have any physical problems as a result of menopause (Masters and Johnson, 1970; Rubin, 1966). Furthermore, although doctors are becoming increasingly cautious about its use, many problems resulting from menopause are correctable through hormone replacement (Rubin, 1966; Kaufman, 1967; Sturgis, 1969; Michael, 1970).

The point to be made here is that contrary to the myth that sex is

only for the young, the aging couple is capable of enjoying a full, rewarding sex life even when confronted with major medical problems. In fact,
such sexual relationships are not only physically possible but also may be
physically and emotionally beneficial. There are times when sexual activity may be both therapeutic and preventive medicine. There is some
evidence, for example, that sex activity helps arthritis, probably because
of adrenal gland production of cortisone. The sexual act itself is a form of
physical activity, helping people to stay in good physical condition. It
also helps to reduce tensions, which are both physical and psychological
(Felstein, 1970). A study done in San Francisco found that elderly people are still interested in sex, but confused, and eager for information
(Feigenbaum, Lowenthal and Trierg, 1967).

THE AGING IN NURSING HOMES

Until now, we have discussed the sexuality of elderly persons in general,
but when we focus on elderly persons confined to nursing homes we find
that the literature dealing directly with their sexuality is almost nonexistent. As Felstein (1970) has pointed out, research in this area is not
popular among those who pass out the grants. And Pfeiffer (1969) further notes that aged subjects are difficult to recruit for studies on sexuality. Their relatives, too, can be a problem, especially when they insist that
participants withdraw from "such foolishness."

Many articles on aspects of nursing home life have failed to mention
sexuality at all (Dominick, Greenblatt and Stotsky, 1968; Miller, 1965;
Savitz, 1967; Berkman and Rehr, 1972; Farrar, Ryder, Blenkner, 1964).
Several did point out, however, that the drastic change in role relationships forced upon the new nursing-home resident and his significant
others coupled with the strangeness of unfamiliar surroundings can result
in "emotional malnutrition" (Farrar, et al., 1964). The new patient frequently cannot find new satisfactory roles within the nursing home itself.
Dominick (1968) reports that the best-adjusted elderly inmates had special friends within the home and maintained positive, rewarding interpersonal relationships there.

The nursing-home resident who has sexual needs is truly a member
of a forgotten and neglected population. In his study on sexually deprived individuals, Barton (1972) is concerned with the effects caused by
the denial of sexual expression on institutionalized people, but fails to
mention the nursing-home resident as part of his population. Is this oversight? We wonder. Is it part of a societal belief that once a person has
reached the age and physical state where confinement in a nursing home
is necessary, he no longer has a need for sex?

Most nursing homes are geared for institutional efficiency and to serve the desires of the families of the patients there. Victor Kassel (1974) has been outspoken in describing the plight of the typical resident: "Most nursing-home operators simply don't allow sexual relations between patients, either because of their own middle-class morality or because of their fear of causing a moral uproar in the community, particularly among the patients' families." In addition, both the medical and behavioral professions' reluctance to treat the aging for sexual dysfunction perpetuates the problem (Masters and Johnson, 1970).

Unfortunately, professionals who deal with nursing-home residents are often reluctant to discuss sexual matters. The myth that sick people or older people should not, or do not, have sexual desires often makes it difficult for either physician or patient to mention the subject (Fond and Orferer, 1967). Nurses, who sometimes receive sexual overtures from their elderly male patients, often hold stereotypic views about aging sexuality that reinforce the "dirty old men" image. It is obvious that many improvements must be made in the curricula of schools involved in the helping professions—especially medicine, social work, nursing and psychology—so that the sexual needs of the elderly will be understood, coped with, and, hopefully, accommodated (Pease, 1974). Indeed, Masters and Johnson (1970) have said: "The disinclination of the medical and behavioral professions to treat the aging population for sexual dysfunction has been a major disservice perpetuated by those professions upon the general problem."

In reviewing the literature, we were able to discern three different approaches: The first is that which assumes the potentiality for sexual activity throughout the life span. Masters and Johnson in particular have been able to convince us that although there is a decrease in the potentiality for sexual activity as one grows older, any cessation of this activity —given reasonable health—is likely to be caused by social and psychological factors rather than biological. Secondly, based on this knowledge, there is another theme in the literature that discusses sexuality as being good for people, and out of this there have been manufactured a multitude of "ought-to's." Thirdly, there is the area of empirical research, and one finds very little about this, especially concerning institutions and nursing homes. That is what the remainder of this chapter will be about. What we found out as to what actually goes on in nursing homes.

SEXUALITY IN NURSING HOMES

In studying sexuality in nursing homes, we concentrated largely on a nursing-home population from rural Wisconsin. So far as we know, the sexuality of a nursing-home population had never been looked at in any formal study. We formulated an interview schedule which focused on attitudes, knowledge, and actual sexual activity, factual data, and demographic information.

We went in with an expectation that the residents would indicate that sex is not for the aged. We asked the residents two questions in this area: (1) Should a person your age have sex? (2) Should older people be allowed to have sex? Regarding the first question, we found that 38 per cent of the men and 52 per cent of the women felt that sex was not for someone of their years. When asked if older people should be allowed to have sex, however, almost 81 per cent of the men and 75 per cent of the women said Yes.

Another expectation of ours was that men enjoy and feel they need sex more than women or, to put it another way, that evidence of a double standard would be found. When asked if sex was different for men and women, more of the men (50%) than women (30.45%) agreed that there was a difference, while almost 39 per cent of the women did not know. A very few felt that it depends on the particular person. Compared to women, three times as many men thought that unmarried people should be allowed to enjoy sexual activity. Conversely, compared to men twice as many women overtly opposed any sexual behavior of the unmarried. We cannot say with any certainty if the respondents interpreted "unmarried" to mean both sexes or just one sex, so the results are unclear in this regard.

A further expectation we had was that the residents would not view masturbation as "normal." An open-ended question was used here, i.e., "There are a lot of different ideas about masturbation. What are yours?" Five categories of response were used, which basically broke down into positive and negative. Half of the men felt it was "normal" or "OK." Over 60 per cent of the women viewed masturbation in a negative light as compared to some 42 per cent of the men. No other area of questioning evoked so much discomfort, embarrassment, and denial as did this one. Because this finding is inconsistent with what the literature tells us about masturbation (that probably close to 100 per cent of the population masturbates at one time or another), we doubt the validity of our data on masturbation.

The residents were asked why they had given up sexual intercourse. The most commonly given reasons were "have no partner" or "poor health." In this section, the feelings and attitudes of many of the women residents can be generalized from this not atypical response: "Lost interest—seems like filth to me." Many women were not interested in sexual behavior because of what they had been taught in the puritan context. They used any excuse for stopping sexual activity. Almost 28 per cent of the women claimed to have lost interest in sex and over 15 per cent of the men stated they could not perform.

We also asked the residents if they felt sexually attractive. Masters and Johnson feel that this is an important variable in one's level of sexual activity. It is possible that the residents' dominant feeling of being sexually unattractive plays a role in their lack of sexual activity. Fifty-eight per cent of the men and 78 per cent of the women said they no longer felt sexually attractive.

In the section on factual knowledge, the results show a general lack of knowledge about sex, with women scoring dramatically lower than the men. Nobody scored over 70 per cent on this section. By sex, however, almost 58 per cent of the men scored 50 per cent or higher as opposed to some 33 per cent of the women. Taking that a little further, close to 20 per cent of the men, but less than 3 per cent of the women had a score of 70 per cent correct answers.

In this area we also did a correlation between the attitude toward, and knowledge of, sex. The findings, when broken down, made it clear that the higher knowledge scores corresponded with a permissive attitude, while low factual knowledge was indicative of a restrictive attitude.

INTERVIEWING STAFFS OF NURSING HOMES

We were familiar with the dictum of Dr. Edward Tyler (1974): "Health care professionals familiar with nursing-home patients have observed the adaptive capabilities of the senile and the invalid when the expression of sexual behavior is not suppressed by the professional staff." After due consideration we decided to interview the staffs of the local nursing homes.

During the pretesting of our questionnaire an occasional resident interviewee expressed hostility toward a nursing-home staff member who had denied him the opportunity to express sexuality. We subsequently considered it mandatory that obtaining a dynamic overview of sexual standards and activity within the nursing homes would require administering the questionnaire to all staff members (administrators, direct service workers, and maintenance help). Were the society taboos on sexual expression among the aged similarly prevalent among nursing-home staff? We hypothesized Yes, and initially predicted that staff attitudes would indicate that they as a group would be in favor of strict controls on the nature and level of sexual expression among residents.

As compiled, our data did *not* support our preliminary expectation. The staff indicated unanimously that the elderly should be allowed to have freedom of sexual expression. We were surprised, but upon further analysis we found that perhaps there were certain elements in our data which gave credence to our initial contention. It was easy for staff to approve of sexual activity among the aged in society in general, but they gave little support for such expressions among residents in their respective nursing homes. Several comments made by staff members of different homes illustrated the existence of physical and/or mental repression of sexual expression by the elderly as a result of staff behavior. For example, one service worker related: "One couple was caught visiting each other late at night. The administrator put them on separate wings and forbade this type of activity in the future. He did not want this kind of stuff going on in his home. It would be bad publicity if it got to the public."

A staff aide related: "One couple who weren't married left here because the administration wouldn't allow them to share a room."

Not one staff member indicated that the nursing home allowed sexual activity of any kind among residents. Not one staff member spoke of the possibility for progressive change being effected in this area in that home. Thus, despite expressed enthusiasm among staff for possible positive change, there was minimal evidence to indicate that inmates' sexual expression was being supported and encouraged at their respective nursing homes.

DISCUSSION: NURSING HOME AGED

It is our firm belief that the elderly nursing-home resident, if physically able, is capable of enjoying some sexual life. It is unfortunate that this natural desire for sexual expression has been frustrated by social mores. These mores categorize expressed sexuality among senior citizens as being deviant and immoral. Despite the obvious inhumane nature of these rules, they have had a significant negative impact upon the thought and activity of nursing-home staff and residents. As illustrated in our findings, the elderly enthusiastically supported sexual expression among age peers, yet they themselves reported no active participation in sex for a variety of reasons. Staff exhibited no real interest in changing the traditional institutional environment of their respective homes to facilitate the assurance of needed privacy for residents.

It is essential that administrators recognize the present denial of sexual freedom in their homes and begin to openly confront this issue. Few staff can boast that they have a comprehensive understanding of human sexuality. Even fewer nursing-home employees can profess to an understanding of the particular problems of the elderly and sexuality.

We strongly recommend the development of in-service training programs to explore the sexuality of the aging. We consider it important that such study opportunities be made available to agency staff members at some time during their employment at the home. Staff should be encouraged to supply input into this process and to seek out advice or consultation when a question arises. This training would hopefully educate staff to the substantial inaccuracies prevalent in the societal image of the abnormal senior citizen who deviously searches for the sexual outlet. Staff members would then be less prone to deny the sexual expression of residents. They could be trained to answer the questions of residents and to encourage the elderly in their repressed desires to be physically loved and cared for.

It is of primary importance to involve those individuals presently approaching their "golden years" in sex education classes. An active, satisfying sex life in middle age is the best predictor known today for a long and satisfying sex life in old age. Perhaps such sex education classes can serve to alleviate the multitude of sexual frustrations experienced by senior citizens.

We consider it important that future research should concentrate on developing programs designed to improve the over-all quality of life for senior citizens living in and out of nursing homes. There is an urgent need for specific programs to conscientiously confront the pertinent issues of loneliness and personal isolation experienced by nursing home residents. Allowing sexual expression is an essential component but not the sole ingredient in this programming.

Professionals working with the aged—be they medical personnel, social workers, aides, or whatever—need a better understanding of human sexuality, in order to be able to effectively bring about positive changes in institutional policy regarding the sexuality of nursing-home residents. Myths need to be replaced with facts, with professionals feeling more comfortable with their own sexuality. They need to view sexuality in the aged as a good thing rather than something to be eliminated. Indeed, sex counseling services both within and without nursing homes should be equipped to provide information that can alleviate some of the normal concerns of the elderly regarding their own sexual functioning.

If we are going to confine the elderly in nursing homes, we must be responsible for structuring an environment which doesn't add to the special problems of the aging process. At present most homes for the aged assume that the elderly are sexless: there are no provisions for privacy, men and women are segregated, conjugal visits are seldom provided for, and nursing-home staff become anxious when confronted with any expression of sexuality by the residents. Their being aged and dying is not sufficient reason to deny to them what joys of affection and sensuality are possible.

CONCLUSION

The nursing-home sex syndrome is a somewhat extreme example of the sexual problems of the aged. It is clear that many men and women long past three score and ten are sexually able (some are sexually interested, while others have been convinced that sex is no longer their right or responsibility).

Let us look at other, less extreme, situations. There are many old people who live independent lives. They have houses, apartments, mobile homes or live in retirement centers. Most of these old men and women are widows or widowers—the ratio is about 2 to 1 after age 70. These people living alone often have fond memories of their earlier married life. They are, however, oppressed by their own values and by the strictures of their children and grandchildren, most of whom feel that sex in old age is both immoral and/or impossible. Some of these old people, however, manage to overcome the cultural and situational difficulties. For some, the Social Security Act makes marriage expensive; it is much more realistic to "shack up" as they say in St. Petersburg. Marriage or any other living arrangement may not have as much sex in it as it does have a function in differentiating roles in the daily round of living ("I'll cook if you take out the garbage"). At best this is not a solution to the general problem because it must be remembered that there are twice as many women as men. The fact is that some sort of communal living may be appropriate for the elderly where some men and more women share the household tasks, and there sexual relationships are possible while other roles are shared.

Think of the old parent who lives with one of her children. From a sexual point of view, the nursing home may be better. At least there would be people of the opposite sex around.

Many old people live satisfactory lives in rooming houses and hotels. These generally are the unfamilied elderly. For some of the old men there are prostitutes who cater to them, but the women have few such opportunities. However, these older people may be the most sexually free of all.

To be old is to be sexually oppressed—first the old values inhibit, then the younger generation disapproves, and finally society sets up formal barriers to accessibility of sexual partners. Sexual behavior for the aged—though not physiologically impossible, nor affectionately dismissable—is culturally and psychologically restricted. We should be actively spreading the news around that sexuality for the aged is a good thing for those who want it!

REFERENCES AND RECOMMENDED READINGS

BARTON, DAVID. "Sexually Deprived Individuals," *Medical Aspects of Human Sexuality*, Vol. 6, No. 2 (Feb. 1972), p. 88.

BENNETT, R. G. "Distinguishing Characteristics of the Aging From a Sociological

Viewpoint," *Journal of the American Geriatric Society*, 16(12) (1968), pp. 127–35.

BERKEY, BARRY. "Psychiatric Sequelae of Sexual Deprivation," *Medical Aspects of Human Sexuality*, Oct. 1971.

BERKMAN, B. G., and H. REHR. "Social Needs of the Hospitalized Elderly: A Classification," *Social Work* 17(4) (1972), pp. 80–88.

CARMIN, MICHAEL, HERMAN KANTOR and HERBERT SHORE. "Further Psychometric Evaluation of Older Women—The Effect of Estrogen Administration," *Journal of Gerontology*, Vol. 25, No. 4 (Oct. 1970), pp. 337–41.

CHRISTENSON, C., and J. GAGNON. "Sexual Behavior in a Group of Older Women," *Journal of Gerontology*, Vol. 20 (1965), pp. 351–356.

DALY, MICHAEL JOSEPH. "Sexual Attitudes in Menopausal and Post Menopausal Women," *Medical Aspects of Human Sexuality*, Vol. II, No. 5 (May 1968), pp. 48–53.

DOMINICK, J. R., D. L. GREENBLATT and B. A. STOTSKY. "The Adjustment of Aged Persons in Nursing Homes." The Patients Report, *Journal of the American Geriatric Society*, 16(1) (1968), pp. 63–77.

DRELLICH, M. D. "Sex After Hysterectomy," *Medical Aspects of Human Sexuality*, Vol. 1, No. 3 (Nov. 1967), pp. 62–64.

EAID, C. R. M. "Sex Counselling for Your Geriatric Patients," *Canadian Family Physician*, Dec. 1972: pp. 58–60.

FARRAR, M., M. B. RYDER and M. BLENKNER. "Social Work Responsibility in Nursing Home Care," *Social Casework* 45(9) (1964), pp. 527–533.

FEIGENBAUM, ELLIOTT M., MARJORIE FISKE LOWENTHAL and MELLA L. TRIERG. "Sexual Attitudes in the Elderly," University of California School of Medicine, San Francisco, *Geriatric Focus*, Vol. 5, No. 20 (Jan. 1, 1967).

FELSTEIN, IVOR. *Sex and the Longer Life*. London: Allen Lane, The Penguin Press, 1970.

FINKEL, ALEX L. "The Relationship of Sexual Habits to Benign Proptatic Hypertrophy," *Medical Aspects of Human Sexuality*, Vol. 1, No. 2 (Oct. 1967), pp. 24–25.

———. "Sex After Proptatectomy," *Medical Aspects of Human Sexuality*, Vol. II, No. 3 (Mar. 1968), pp. 40–41.

FOND, AMASA, and ALEXANDER ORFINER. "Sexual Behavior and the Chronically Ill Patient," *Medical Aspects of Sexuality*, Vol. 1, No. 2 (Oct. 1967), pp. 51–61.

FRIEDFELD, LOUIS. "Geriatrics, Medicine and Rehabilitation," *Journal of the American Medical Assn.*, Feb. 18, 1961.

GORDON, S. K., and W. E. VINACKE. "Self- and Ideal Self-Concepts and Dependency in Aged Persons Residing in Institutions," *Journal of Gerontology*, 26(3) (1971), pp. 337–43.

HAVEN, CLAYTON and MARJORIE F. LOWENTHAL. "Interaction and Adaptation: Intimacy as a Critical Variable," *American Sociological Review*, 33(1) (1968), pp. 20–30.

HELLERSTEIN, M. D. "Sexual Activity and the Postcoronary Patient," *Medical Aspects of Human Sexuality*, Vol. III, No. 3 (March 1969), pp. 70–96.

HOLLENDER, MARC. "Hysterectomy and Feelings of Feminity," *Medical Aspects of Human Sexuality*, Vol. III, No. 7 (July 1969), pp. 6–15.

HUFFMAN, JOHN. "Sexual Reactions After Gynecologic Surgery," *Medical Aspects of Human Sexuality*, Vol. III, No. 2 (Nov. 1969), pp. 48–57.

KAHN, EDWIN and CHARLES FISHER. "Amount of REM Sleep Erection in the Healthy Aged," *Psychophysiology*, 5(2) (1968), p. 226.

KAPLAN, HELEN S. "Sexual Patterns at Different Ages," *Medical Aspects of Human Sexuality*, June 1971, p. 10.

KAPP, IRVING. "Sex in Chronic Obstructive Pulmonary Disease," *Medical Aspects of Human Sexuality*, Vol. 6, No. 2 (Feb. 1972), p. 33.

KAUFMAN, SHERWIN A. *The Ageless Woman—Menopause, Hormones and the Quest for Youth*. Englewood Cliffs, N.J.: Prentice-Hall, Inc., 1967.

KORDEL, LELORD. *How to Keep Your Youthful Vitality After Forty*. New York: G. P. Putnam's Sons, 1969.

KOSBERG, JORDAN J. "The Nursing Home—A Social Work Paradox," *Social Work* 18(2) (1973), pp. 104–110.

LEVITON, DAN. "The Significance of Sexuality as a Deterrent to Suicide Among the Aged," *Journal of Death and Dying*, Vol. 4, No. 2 (Summer 1973), pp. 163–173.

LEWIN, S. "Some Comments on the Distribution of Narcissistic and Object Libido in the Aged," *International Journal of Psychoanalysis*, 46(2) (1965), pp. 200–207.

LIEF, HAROLD. "Roundtable Sex After Fifty," *Medical Aspects of Human Sexuality*, Vol. II, No. 1 (Jan. 1968), pp. 41–47.

MASTERS, WILLIAM H., and VIRGINIA E. JOHNSON. *Human Sexual Inadequacy*. Boston, Little, Brown and Company, 1970.

————. *Human Sexual Response*, Boston, Little, Brown and Company, 1966.

MILLER, M. B. "Physical, Emotional and Social Rehabilitation in a Nursing Home Population," *Journal of the American Geriatrics Society*, 13 (12) (1965), pp. 176–185.

NEWMAN, GUSTAVE, and CLAUDE NICHOLS. "Study of Those Aged 60–80 in a North Carolina Community." (Survey made over 7-year period.) *Journal of American Medical Assn.*, May, 1960.

PEARSON, MANUEL. "Middle-Aged Crises," *Medical Aspects of Human Sexuality*. Vol. II, No. 8 (Aug. 1968), pp. 6–13.

PEASE, RUTH A. "Sexuality in the Aging Male," *The Gerontologist*, Vol. 14, No. 2 (April, 1974), pp. 153–157.

PFEIFFER, ERIC. "Geriatric Sex Behavior," *Medical Aspects of Human Sexuality*, Vol. III, No. 7 (July 1969), pp. 19–28.

————, A. VERWOERDT and H. S. WANG. "Normal and Abnormal Sex Behavior in Aging," *Geriatric Focus*, Vol. 7, No. 13, (July-Aug., 1968).

————. "Sexual Behavior in Senescence," *Geriatrics*, Feb. 1969.

ROSENFELT, R. H. "The Elderly Mystique," *Journal of Social Issues*, 21(4) (1965), pp. 33–43.

RUBIN, I. *Sexual Life After Sixty*. New York: Basic Books, 1966.

SAVITZ, H. A. "Humanizing Institutional Care for the Aged," *Journal of the American Geriatric Society*, 15(2) (1967), pp. 203-10.

STURGIS, SOMERS. "Hormone Therapy in the Menopause: Indications and Contraindications," *Medical Aspects of Human Sexuality*, Vol. III, No. 5 (1969), pp. 69–75.

THOMPSON, P. W. "Understanding the Aged," *Journal of the American Geriatric Society*, 13(10) (1965), pp. 893–899.

TRUMBLE, GEORGE. "The Coital Coronary," *Medical Aspects of Human Sexuality*, Vol. IV, No. 5 (May 1970), pp. 64–69.

TYLER, EDWARD. "Sex and Medical Illness." In *Comprehensive Textbook of Psychiatry*. 2nd edition. Baltimore: Williams and Wilkins, 1974.

WEINBERG, JACK. "Sexuality in Later Life," *Medical Aspects of Human Sexuality*, April 1971.

WHISKIN, FREDERICK. "The Geriatric Sex Offender," *Medical Aspects of Human Sexuality*, Vol. IV, No. 4 (April 1970), pp. 125–29.

III.
WOMEN

Despite the fact that women comprise more than half of our population, they have problems that put them clearly in the category of the oppressed. Neither the women's liberation movement nor the sexual revolution has eradicated their problems, which, indeed, have either increased or been replaced with new ones.

In this section, Gochros discusses the problems of women in transition, relating common elements of all minority groups in a transition period to the specific problems facing women today.

As noted earlier, our society's "reproductive bias" results in either overlooking or suppressing sexual behavior that is purely sensual or that occurs between people unable or not wishing to have children. Myra Johnson takes this idea one step farther by noting that we view women who do not actively engage in sexual activity with men as neurotic and repressed. She suggests that we as a society fail to recognize, much less respect, the many women who either have no sexual desire or who prefer to satisfy that desire only through self-stimulation. Whether or not one agrees with her assessment of such women (and some may not) is almost irrelevant. Unless they themselves perceive a problem for which they wish help, their "problem" is merely society's unwillingness to recognize and accept them.

Although men are sometimes victims of coercive sexual advances, assault and rape (especially in correctional institutions), "victimization" is primarily a problem for women. Both legal and social-emotional problems accruing from victimization have become of increasing concern in our society today. We are faced with complex dilemmas in safeguarding the rights of victim and aggressor alike; in giving adequate preventive instruction to children; and in mitigating the harmful effects after a person becomes a victim. *Schultz provides insights and information which strip away the pervasive hysteria usually associated with such problems, allowing for more rational and useful interventions.*

Many women's problems are compounded by racial and cultural factors: Gossett shows an understanding of all widows, as she points out the particular problems facing those who are black and who have been bypassed by our society's changing sexual attitudes. Her discussion not only highlights the need for more effective answers to racism and poverty but it also brings forward questions in new areas: How does the church in black culture serve to create problems and/or provide solutions? How can we enable poverty-stricken women who have turned to a fundamentalist church for emotional aid to reap the benefits of the sexual revolution without bringing them into conflict with the church that sustains them? How can existing programs be made more relevant to their needs? And, finally, do cultural elements make the needs of black women unique or are their problems basically universal?

CHAPTER 5

WOMEN—
MINORITY
IN
TRANSITION

Jean S. Gochros

So much has been said and written lately about the oppression of women that to merely repeat the Germaine Greers and the Gloria Steinems would seem pointless. Indeed, many people now say, "What do women want? Things are changing! The job market is opening up, few men today insist on their wives staying chained to the house, and women are recognized as having sexual needs and rights both in and out of marriage. With labor-saving devices, unless they choose to work (and many don't), they sit around, well taken care of, bored, and able to play bridge all day. So where's the oppression? Perhaps men are really the oppressed sex!" In some ways they are right. But such comments stem from failure to grasp the nature of either sex's oppression, the nature of a revolutionary movement, or the nature of the problems faced when an oppressed group seeks and obtains beginning change, putting itself in the position of "minority in transition."

The term "minority" is used here in a sociological sense rather than a numerical one. While sociologists differ in their definitions, and women do not fit into every category of the strictest ones, there seems to be agreement that women do hold most of the important attributes of a "minority group": *i.e.*, they belong to a social group occupying a position of lower status in the larger society to which they belong; because of

certain physical or cultural characteristics, they are subjected to prejudice, ridicule, and discrimination at the hands of the dominant ("majority") group; and they form a self-conscious social group which has
both an esprit de corps and a sense of self-hatred (Wirth, L. in Linton,
R., 1945, p. 347; Hacker, H., 1951).

PROBLEMS

Women's problems today are real! True discrimination is so well documented as to need no comment here. But the most devastating problems
are often so subtle that they almost defy analysis. Here we face a dilemma: many of the problems and solutions discussed will seem to be
political or economic rather than sexual. But women are a unique minority in that they are defined totally by their sexuality. With the retarded,
homosexuals, and so on, it is relatively easy to differentiate between
sexual oppression per se and economic or political oppression that is
either rooted in or extended to sexual behavior. With women, however,
every problem (indeed, every act, problematic or not) is to some extent
defined by their gender and how society characterizes the qualities and
defines the roles of that gender.

Hence, women's sexual problems are to some extent a product of
economic and political oppression, and, conversely, political or economic
solutions can greatly, if only indirectly, affect sexual freedom. In sum,
then, the combination of strictly sexual, political and economic problems
adds up to difficulties with role and sexual identity, self-esteem, and the
kind of ease with sexuality that permits real use of women's so-called
sexual liberation. These difficulties are compounded by the nature of a
revolutionary movement and the reactions to it.

To initiate change, any oppressed group must engage in certain
activities. It must establish need, gather support, and create a common
cause and identity. To do this, it must "rub raw the sores of discontent"
(Alinsky, quoted in Silberman, 1965), establishing focal points, rallying
cries, symbols and slogans.

For blacks, "last hired and first fired" was a slogan focusing on a
particular problem; "we shall overcome," the "black salute," and "black is
beautiful" were all techniques for creating a common bond and raising
self-image. For women, bra burning, the use of Ms., and insistence on
such terms as "chairperson" have served the same purpose. What happens when a minority begins to assert itself is quite interesting. The
oppressor has four options: 1. He can say, "I'm not a bigot, I'm right!
You're inferior and should be kept in your place." (Not many in recent
years have outspokenly taken this stance.) 2. He can say, "You're right!
I'll change immediately!" But it is virtually impossible for either a society

or the individuals within it, no matter how good their intentions, to immediately abolish discrimination and prejudice merely by declaring victory and going home. It is doubtful whether any adult can ever completely rid himself of attitudes integrated into his total being and receiving continual reinforcement. 3. He can say, "You're right *up to a point*," make a few changes in good faith, and then say, "Now stop fussing at me; the problem is solved." 4. He can say, "You're right, I'll change," and assume that this has solved the problem.

These last two have happened with many revolutionary movements. Most citizens (including many of the victimized persons themselves) have recognized the need for, and have made, token changes, but they are then left with a residue of feelings that strongly resist true elimination of oppression, and that are harder to deal with than honest bigotry.

How do we as a society handle the radicals in our midst? In various ways: by outright repression (usually used when other techniques fail); by denial and projection; by obtusely refusing to understand the techniques and symbols and misreading the entire meaning of the revolution; by using condescending tokenism, humor (or rather, ridicule), and "reason" to subtly diminish the validity of the complaints and the self-esteem of the complainant. And also by co-option—exploiting the cause for their own gratification.

With the black liberation movement we heard:

"Why call themselves black? What will that change? But if that's what they want, I'll go along—makes no difference to me."

"Don't they realize Rome wasn't built in a day? That you have to be qualified to get good jobs? What do they want, anyhow? Why aren't they more reasonable?"

With the women's liberation movement, the same comments were made, and the combination of obtuse misreading, humor, and condescension abounds:

"Out with the girls, eh? Gee, too bad. Wish I were oppressed!"

"Bra burning? How funny! Don't they know that bralessness doesn't make them liberated? It only makes them floppy!"

"MIZZZ—sounds like a lady bee. But if that's what they want, I'll go along with the gag."

Ridiculous suggestions are made:

"Well, if you wanna be liberated, why not let me sit around while *you* move the piano?"

> "You think you got a hard life? Okay, I'll stay home for a week and you come to my office and do my job. Let's see how well you handle it!"

Humor and reason are the oppressed person's worst enemies. There is no defense against humor. The victim has only two choices: to laugh at an admittedly funny caricature, thereby admitting how ridiculous she has been, or to become angry, knowing full well that she will appear a poor sport, humorless and unreasonable.

> "C'mon, be reasonable! If you don't care for the kids, who will? Not me, I'm the major breadwinner, remember?"

> "You can work or you can stay home. But you can't do both. Why aren't you more reasonable?"

> "Be reasonable. I'm glad for you to take a job, but either you don't apply or you aren't qualified. And education costs money. Come up with a solution, and I'll agree. All I ask is that you be reasonable about it!"

Again there is no defense: the victim can either admit defeat (since the problem posed is often one that has no immediate easy solution), or adamantly reject "reason" as a relevant process. Blacks long ago recognized that "reason" led nowhere, and that changes were made only in response to unreasonable demands for "equality NOW."

Unfortunately, no matter which group is victimized, such responses on the part of the oppressor lead to confusion, depression, heightened sensitivity bordering on paranoia, and both self-hatred and increased anger toward the oppressing group. But if reason is refused, positions harden and rigid polarization occurs, leading, indeed, to open battle of wills rather than cooperative efforts to understand problems and reach solutions.

The difficulty with "reason" is that while the logic is usually unassailable, it solves nothing for the victim. And when positions harden, while the society does in fact creep slowly (albeit reluctantly) toward change, during the process many individuals find themselves caught in some classic double binds.

Being a "minority in transition" is almost worse than being merely oppressed, for it means giving up the secondary gains of oppression before they have been replaced with anything better. Liberation is obtained in principle, but is far from being a reality.

For women this is true in many ways. Women were once tied to the nursery, to the kitchen, and, for their husbands' satisfaction only, to the bedroom. If their life was less than happy, however, it was at least simple and unconfusing and often allowed for such pleasantries as *kaffeklatsch-*

ing, lunching, and such hobbies as bridge, flower arranging, knitting, and so on. "Women's Lib" has not made those pleasantries less pleasant (or less necessary to preserve mental health); it has merely extended the range of choices in those areas.

Grandma was a slave to the washboard and the ironing board, and one would hardly have wished to trade places with her. But have labor-saving devices really left women with nothing to do? For some, perhaps. But as leisuretime has increased, so have expectations. In grandma's day, people wore only two changes of clothing a week instead of two or three a day. Grandma was expected to turn out merely an adequate basic meal. And all but the poorest housewives had servants (even if those servants were their own children). Further, one suspects that the reason grandma never complained about sexual demands was that when her husband had only himself to consider, intercourse may have not held much gratification for her, but it probably took very little time.

Today's woman has basic problems in logistics as well as in competence. If married (and middle class), she is expected to be intelligent and well read (but not too controversial), a gourmet cook, partial bread-winner, errand runner (since she has either no job or one that is seen as of less importance than her husband's. Hence her time is filled quickly with little chores that she is considered "free" to do). She is further expected to be a skilled hobbyist, entertainer and possibly helpmate with her husband's business associates, Playboy bunny (yet not *too* sexy), housekeeper and mother (meaning psychologist, nurse, Cub Scout den mother, and chauffeur for children who are now catered to rather than being the helpers). She must be completely competent in all the endeavors, and the myths that abound (and which women themselves perpetuate rather than risk criticism or embarrassment) suggest that if she is really a true woman, she will maintain these roles with equanimity, efficiency, and cheerfulness.

Unfortunately, even when all these skills are possible in one person, Women's Lib has not yet produced a day with more than twenty-four hours. Yet her failure to live up to these expectations often results in depression: acute postpartum, acute menopausal, and chronic in-between. And if the woman is told magnanimously to give up something, it is seldom the cleaning of the kitchen floor that must be eliminated, but rather the benefits of both the traditional role and the new range of possibilities. A choice? That she has! But it is seldom a choice between the activities she likes versus those she dislikes, but rather between those she has learned to like.

Are jobs and education really available? Sometimes. But wives, at least, often receive double messages: "Work at the office, but don't let it interfere with home"; and conversely, "Being a housewife or engaging in jobs outside of an office is important, but it is not 'work.' " And with a constant barrage of such subtle ego-deflating messages, women often approach both jobseeking and education with considerable trepidation, especially if they have left the work or education arena for a time in order to care for their children.

Often women remain caught between the hard line of the true male chauvinists and the hard line of the militant Women's Libbers who insist that not only do they have the *right* to be "liberated" but they also have the *obligation*! They feel ashamed and guilty when they like any (or all) part(s) of their traditional roles, yet resent more than ever the newly recognized symptoms of oppression. Often they are trapped into an un-happy marriage not because their husbands are deliberately chaining them, but because their own fears, lack of skills, or financial problems hold them back, with their husbands unknowingly aiding and abetting such chaining.

Recently I was counseling a young couple with four children. Al-though they had originally decided amicably on a divorce, the wife had neither the job training nor financial resources she would need. Her husband could not afford the alimony she was demanding. So, with some bitterness on both parts, the two felt forced to try to patch up the mar-riage. But the wife still felt utterly dependent. Any job she could get would hardly pay enough to cover costs. Education, which she wanted, would take at least four years to bring her any earning power, and, furthermore, she was finding it difficult to even determine her field of interest. Was she unreasonable? She certainly was—in many ways. Her husband, with all his faults, was sympathetic to her plight and trying desperately to meet her needs. During one interview he agreed to grant her small sums of money that she could save in order to enhance her independence. He pointed out his generosity here, since he knew that it could conceivably backfire on him (in about ten years), but this was his "gift" to prove his concern and sincerity in not wanting a "chained" wife.

A few minutes later, in casual conversation, I commented that seeing the bind they were both in because of finances, I could appreciate a recent suggestion that newlyweds should take out divorce insurance just as they take out life and medical insurance. His former statements sud-denly forgotten, the husband turned red with anger. "Now just a min-ute!" he exploded, "I believe in Women's Lib and all that, but *divorce insurance*? That does it! You women are going too damned far!"

Such underlying attitudes as this can hardly help but find their way into the bedroom; the husband, in this instance, had been sure that sex was the one really satisfactory area of their marriage. But it later turned out that the woman had the same grievances about his attitudes toward sex as she had in other areas, was extremely dissatisfied, and had merely focused initially on other more urgent matters.

In sexual relationships, women again find that today's transition stage of liberation presents difficulties and double binds. Today's woman and the men she knows pay lip service to "sexual liberation," but still hold values and inhibitions from the past that may prevent her from really enjoying her new freedom.

If she follows her husband's admission of an extramarital affair with one of her own, she is apt to learn that while his excursion was merely a male's right to give in to temptation, her affair was a violation of all that is sacred. If she refuses his amorous advances, today's husband verbally recognizes her right to do so. But when this is explored in counseling, it often turns out that he is acting so hurt that the wife finally gives in out of her own sense of guilt. She may no longer easily plead she is "sick" or "tired," but neither can she easily say "No."

Not only is she "allowed" orgasm today but both she and her husband now gauge her femininity (and his prowess) by it. She must achieve at least one orgasm per session or risk the label of "frigid." Frequently, women ask me, "How do I convince my partner that failure to have an orgasm is not a personal affront to him? There are times when I am satisfied without one; *he's* the one who gets angry."

Lack of knowledge is oppressive. Given a bit of information, men now are more than willing to pay attention to women's sexual needs. But their techniques are often still faulty, often dictated by male "experts," and women are often still too uninformed, too ruled by the male expert's opinion of what they want, too cowed by their partners' defensiveness, or too guilt-ridden to communicate effectively what will please them. These problems place them in new double binds.

For example, the male assumption that if he likes a certain rhythm or stroke she will too, often makes for techniques that turn her off instead of on. Women are now being told to communicate their needs and desires more clearly. But some women have reported that in trying to do so, they become trapped by the fact that their physiological responses are both variable and highly dependent upon minute variations in their partner's touch; hence, when they do try to communicate their needs, they are faced with an accusation of being contradictory (which they readily admit), mechanical, or forcing the male into a passive, submissive role. Partly out of frustration and partly out of true compassion for the man's confusion, some of these women have given up on orgasm, rather than destroy the total relationship.

Part of the problem here is the insistence on orgasm as proof of success in sex, with women trying desperately to achieve it (thereby reducing their chances) and sometimes trying as much for the male's sake as for their own, and the still widespread belief that only "vaginal" orgasm is proper orgasm, and that such activities as oral sex, manual stimulation to orgasm, and self-stimulation are either improper or merely forerunners for the real thing (*i.e.*, orgasm during intercourse).

Freud started out as an early liberator of women, but his theories about female sexuality eventually made him an oppressor. It took Masters and Johnson to dispel the myth of the vaginal orgasm, although many women already knew full well that clitoral stimulation produced orgasm, and were merely afraid to say so. Now our new experts are in danger of becoming gods. If they decree that women can enjoy a variety of positions (or especially enjoy one position in particular) women who don't are made to feel abnormal. If the expert (backed up by the porno flicks) suggests that women truly enjoying sex often wiggle and groan a lot, then the woman who doesn't is assumed to be passive and bored. If a woman experiences sensations that are not yet corroborated by experts, she is assumed to be incorrect, and presumably will wait twenty years for another expert to declare her feelings valid, rather than speak up and risk the label of "neurotic."

Such new problems suggest that we still have much to learn about female sexuality, and that for a variety of reasons, the women who can best help us are prevented from doing so.

Attitudes toward dress bring on another double bind: if a woman dresses sexily, she is seen as provocative and asking for rape. If she does not, she is seen as masculine and hostile. Trying to gauge when "sexy" stops being "nice" and starts being "cheap" is a difficult task, especially for teen-agers.

A common problem in marriage occurs when for some reason intercourse is not possible. While masturbation has long been fairly acceptable for men (under certain conditions), there is still a common belief that it is either immoral, neurotic, or (during marriage) disloyal for women. During an absence from the husband, women are much more guilt-ridden than men about self-stimulation, fantasy, or even any recognition that their sexual needs remain unmet. For wives of traveling salesmen, conventioneers, and military men, for example, such problems often reach crisis dimensions, especially when it is assumed (and often true) that their husbands will be having affairs and are apt to return home enamored with their out-of-town companions.

Co-option becomes a frequent technique in the sexual area, with women now feeling guilty if they do not wish for "liberation." A number of women have related to me variations on the same theme—either being tricked into seeing the movie *Deep Throat* or being rushed home immediately after seeing it, with the statement, "Okay, if Linda Lovelace can do it, so can you!" The resentful women had either refused an activity they might have enjoyed (though, incidentally, that movie, so hailed as a Women's Lib movie, focuses solely on activity that will please a man, since the woman's clitoris is definitely *not* in her throat) or else had felt too guilty and "abnormal" to refuse what they really did not want.

Are younger single women free from such problems? Not quite, despite our myths to the contrary. True, they are more able to hold honest discussions about sexual activity with their dates, to feel less guilt about saying Yes, and to have their No accepted. But they still wrestle with the social mores of the past as opposed to the dictums of the present, and they are more apt to have to do such wrestling at an earlier age, with fewer guidelines to help them. Parents still feel a duty to help their sons achieve manhood via the bed, while preserving their daughters' virginity for marriage; yet torn by their own conflicts, they often deny the honest discussion, education and value giving that will help their daughters to either say No or to prepare for the realities of sexual activity.

Teen-agers have been freed, but part of that freedom is to engage in the locker-room bravado that was once a male prerogative. "Is it better to be 'with it' and lose respect or 'goody good' and lose popularity?" This is an age-old question, but the new myth that "everybody does it" is both freeing and coercive.

One fourteen-year-old told me:

"My boyfriend says that while he tries with everyone, he respects me for saying No. He's not mad at me, but he wants a relationship that includes intercourse. So he's stopped asking me out."

Another pretty teenager reported:

"I feel trapped when I wait for a bus and the guys start whistling and making comments. If I ignore them, get mad or turn my back, they get angry and then I *really* get hassled. But if I joke and go along with the gag, it encourages them. They think I like it. I can't win!"

Co-option enters in here, too. "What do you mean you won't go to bed with me? I thought you were liberated!" employs the name of liberation. But the game of exploitation remains the same.

When it comes to contraception or protection against VD, the single woman is again in a bind. Many women do not or cannot use the pill or the I.U.D. To carry around a diaphragm is both inconvenient and a signed invitation to their dates. To ask a boy to use a condom is unthinkable for many teenagers (and even to some adults), while to ask it for protection against VD is seen not only as inconsiderate, but also as an insult.

An emerging issue is one of coercion in providing contraceptives, sterilization, or abortion to the poor, black, and retarded. Society's concern here is proper! But the only solutions supplied so far seem to be legal measures to prevent the retarded from getting such help when needed, for Federal funds to be removed from such agencies as Planned Parenthood, and for the Federal and state governments to refuse financial aid to individuals wishing such medical help. Our society has see-sawed back and forth for years between *denying* women protection against *their* unwanted pregnancies, and *forcing* them to protect society from *its* unwanted pregnancies. Either extreme is oppressive.

Older single women have many of the problems already mentioned, compounded by the fact that few men are attracted to them, and that society tends to look a bit askance at the idea of grandma engaging in sexual relationships outside marriage.

These, then, are a few (and only a few) of the many problems women still face. Much of this discussion has been more applicable to women in middle-class circumstances than to those in the lower class, who are even more oppressed. The results are confusion, anger, low self-esteem, and unsatisfactory, guilt-ridden sexual relationships. Liberation seems just around the corner, but for many, if not most women, it is ephemeral and unattainable.

SOLUTIONS

Unfortunately, it is always easier to state problems than to solve them. But there already are some solutions, ranging from small ones designed to help individuals, to those larger ones that will inevitably require changes in our fundamental institutions.

Solutions already under way are found in changing marriage contracts, women's (and men's) "rap," or "consciousness-raising," groups, and in workshops designed to foster self-awareness and self-acceptance, along with understanding and communication between the sexes. Many counselors (social workers, psychologists, and so on) are using such groups as useful adjuncts to individual or couple therapy, and are finding that even sexual problems are often treated better in groups that do not focus on such difficulties as symptoms of neurosis, but instead view them as a logical outcome of society's illogical ideas about sex. Similarly, therapists are beginning to abandon outmoded Freudian diagnoses of "inability to accept female role" in favor of acting as catalysts for real listening, appraisal and problem-solving, and helping women to assert themselves both individually and through social action groups. (Brown and Hellinger, 1975). Such changes are long overdue and need to be increased.

Sex education in schools should be ongoing from early grades through high school and college, and should devote more attention to such problems rather than focusing mainly on biology. Teen-agers especially need more opportunity to discuss the pleasures, responsibilities and problems of sexual activity, under informed leadership, in nonsegregated groups. As a teen-age boy once said to me following such a workshop:

> "Thanks! We got the facts okay in school, but our teachers never talked to us about rights or how to play fair. . . . In fact, they never talked to us about . . . anything! I never realized that girls were as scared as I was, or that they had rights and needs; I just thought about proving myself by getting them into bed!"

All those in the helping professions, but perhaps especially social workers, whose profession is steeped in concern for the oppressed, can and should be participating actively in such programs.

Marital partners not only can but are beginning to appraise their needs more honestly, and to make contracts providing greater satisfaction for each. For example, household tasks are divided according to skills and interests rather than sex, with mutually disliked chores being shared equally, and with lists so detailed as to distinguish between cake baking and salad making or fixing faucets and hanging pictures. This limits the number of disliked chores to a minimum for each person and allows time for each to pursue other interests. And parents can inculcate such non-sexist attitudes in children and provide more honest information and values regarding sex.

Sexually "open" marriage contracts are becoming more common. But it is equally important to make them at the beginning, to be specific about the rules, and to be sensitive to feelings when a contract is changed during a marriage: many wives still find it difficult to take advantage of the supposed freedom that their husbands suddenly suggest. They feel coerced and abandoned, and suspect (often with good reason) that the male is merely using "co-option" to rationalize infidelity that he would have engaged in, anyhow. (Of course, husbands can also be the victims in such situations.) At any rate, professional helpers such as social workers, psychologists, and so on, can be extremely helpful to couples contemplating such arrangements.

Perhaps one difficulty in finding an adequate solution is that, as we have seen, any solution creates new problems. We have either used our recognition of that fact as an excuse to delay change or have denied it, attempting to solve those problems with outmoded answers. This has often been true with problems of education and race relations, and it has also often been true with women's problems. However, more creative approaches can be sought.

For example, one reason even qualified women often refuse jobs is that full or even part-time work pre-empts the time that they may both need and want for child care, housework and recreational activity. Part-time jobs are helpful for some, but for many they only mean full-time work with little pay.

What women often need much more in a job is flexibility: the ability to meet the crisis of a child's illness or school problems, time to prepare for the entertaining expected of them after work, and yes, even time for relaxation during the day. For this they need not the set, long hours based on a forty-hour week, but jobs assigned by task, whereby they can devote as little or as much time per day or week as they can realistically give.

It seems ironic that in a society rife with educational, economic, social, medical, and emotional problems, qualified professionals are sitting at home merely because they cannot manage a full workweek or even a full day (Hillman, Raskin, & Kaplan, 1975). But they might easily manage one or two classes, patients or clients. Furthermore, untrained women also have skills. They too could easily teach or help a few people at a time, for a limited amount of hours (and often do it better than the professional). They could and should get paid for their work.

Would such a system produce problems? Certainly! Perhaps other alternatives would be better or perhaps solutions to those new problems could be found. A typical male (seldom female) reaction to such an idea, however, has been one of contempt:

"That's ridiculous! Idealistic! It would involve a total change of our labor system. And men don't work that way. You women just want the fun part of jobs, and none of the drudgery. Don't you think we want time off for play, too? Don't we have the same needs and rights?"

The answer to their question is obvious: *Yes.* If women would benefit from such a system, so would men, who have—inadvertently indeed—oppressed themselves in many ways (though their reaction suggests that they prefer the oppression of the office to any liberation giving them more time to share even a part of the oppression of the home). Our system of labor may have fitted the old male-dominated world, but may not so well serve our more modern and complex society. Recently a few innovative companies, recognizing that fact, have initiated programs whereby employees choose their own shifts according to their own personalities, family needs at a given time, and life-styles. While such programs are still young, they seem to have created greater satisfaction on and off the job, for both employer and employee, male and female alike (Irwin, 1975). And it may be anticipated that the ability to choose shifts may automatically help many working husbands and wives to find time for a sexual relationship now absent because their working hours conflict.

Again, some of these solutions may seem more related to economic problems than to sexual ones. But, as is frequently pointed out, sex is not merely a matter of genitals, but also of mind; the two areas are interrelated, and we cannot solve problems in one without dealing with problems in the other.

In the end, it is incumbent upon all of us to recognize that neither the women's liberation movement nor its rigid "unreasonable" cries have created sexual oppression (as many would have us believe), and that it polarizes only as a technique to overcome unreasonable responses to pleas for help. It is doubtful that even the most militant woman would wish change to mean merely a turnabout of who is on top and who is on bottom (no double entendre intended). It is time to realize that much work is ahead before women are truly liberated sexually or in any other way, and that until they are, we are all oppressed!

REFERENCES AND RECOMMENDED READINGS

ALINSKY, SAUL, as quoted in Silberman, C., *Crisis in Black and White.* New York: Vintage Books, p. 220.

BENGIS, I. *Combat in the Erogenous Zone.* New York: Knopf, 1972.

BROVERMAN, I., D. BROVERMAN, and F. CLARKSON. "Sex Role Stereotypes: A Current Appraisal," *Journal of Social Issues,* 28, (1972).

BROWN & HELLINGER. "Therapists' Attitudes Toward Women," *Social Work Journal,* July 1975, pp. 266–27.

BURTON, G. *I'm Running Away From Home But I'm Not Allowed to Cross the Street.* Pittsburgh: Know, Inc., 1974.

CLINEBELL, C. *Meet Me in the Middle.* New York: Harper & Row, 1973.

DELL'OLIO, A. "The Sexual Revolution Wasn't Our War." In *The First Ms Reader.* New York: Warner Paperback Library, 1973.

GREER, G. *The Female Eunuch,* New York: McGraw-Hill, 1971.

HACKER, HELEN, "Women as a Minority Group," *Social Forces* 30 (Oct. 1951).

HILLMAN, RASKIN, & KAPLAN. "Preventing Professional Death at an Early Age," *Social Work Journal,* July, 1975, pp. 325–327.

IRWIN, T., "Flexible Working Hours to Match Your Lifestyle," *Parade,* Jan. 5, 1975.

MILLETT, K. *Sexual Politics,* Garden City, N.Y.: Doubleday, 1970.

O'NEILL, N., and G. O'NEILL. *Open Marriage: A New Life Style for Couples.* New York: M. Evans & Co., 1972.

WIRTH, LOUIS, "The Problems of Minority Groups." In *The Science of Man in the World Crisis,* ed. R. Linton, New York: Columbia University Press, 1945.

CHAPTER 6

BLACK
WIDOWS

Ruth R. Gossett

The civil rights movement of the Sixties has continued into the Seventies in more subtle forms and has refocused attention on the demands of women and, to some extent, away from the issues and concerns of blacks. This has provided the impetus for a plethora of literature on women and the black movement. However, the black woman outside the constellation of the family has been given little attention. There is a growing minority of women who are widowed and who, because they are not old, cannot be subsumed under the category of the aged. The issue of young widows has been ignored.

Eric Hoffer (1954) has observed:

> Death would have no terror were it to come a month from now, a week or even a day, but not tomorrow. For death has but one terror, that it has no tomorrow.

The terror of death has been removed for the deceased. Terror remains for the survivors—the terror not of death, but of life and what it holds for those who remain. The loss of a husband can be accompanied by a number of other losses. Those losses may include, but not be limited to, loss of status, financial security, companionship, sexual partner, and the father of her children. These are problems for all women, regardless of race, but the black woman's problems are further compounded by the significantly limited population of available black males (Jackson, 1970). In 1971 the black male's life expectancy at birth was 61.2 years as compared with 68.3 years for white males. During the period between 1971 and 1973, the age-specific death rate for black males between the ages of 15 and 45 increased. (U.S. Census Data, 1970). This increase is attributed to the increase in fatal accidents and homicides; heart disease, neoplasms, cancer and hypertension continue to be ranked as major contributors to the death rate of black males. The 15 to 45 age group presents a large percentage of the "never-married" and "recently marrieds," which tends to highlight the early age at which black women are likely to become widowed.

The availability issue, according to Staples (1973), is further intensified by the tendency of white females to pursue black males, while white males rarely pursue black females. United States census data indicate that the median age of the black widow is 39 years. Among this group, a large number are either unemployed or underemployed and are responsible for the financial and emotional support and guidance of two or more minor children. (U.S. Census 1970). These statistics depict an alarming situation which requires investigation in order to determine what, if any, impact early widowhood has on the black woman, including her sexual life.

BACKGROUND

The removal of the institution of marriage from some women, no matter what their color, is a traumatic experience, since marriage is considered to be the only setting for lawful or moral sexuality. Malinowski (1962) suggests that marriage determines even extra-connubial liberties, defines intra-and inter-familial relationships, status, and imposes economic cooperation. It is frequently concluded in a public and solemn manner, thereby receiving as a sacrament the blessings of religion, and as a rite the good auspices of magic.

Marriage represents somewhat of an individual crisis which frequently requires the acquisition of new roles, new responsibilities and new skills. Parkes (1972) suggests that in addition to marriage being an important contract in human societies, it also implies the most delicate and difficult adjustment of a passionate and emotional relationship. It involves the cohabitation of male and female perennially attached and in many ways forever incompatible (Parkes, 1972). The transition from the role of wife to that of widow carries a new burden. Apart from the grief that accompanies widowhood, stigma (loss of status) and deprivation (absence of a necessary person) are also major factors.

Many experiences of a black widow are similar to those of other unattached black women. The widow's uniqueness lies in the fact that she had no choice in how she would live this portion of her life. She chose marriage as her way of life, as compared with those who in most instances had some input into decisions to remain single or to end dysfunctional marriages. Death eliminates the opportunity for decisions. In this she also shares many experiences with her white counterpart. However, the black experience, which includes the paucity of black male partners and the younger age at which black men die, contributes significantly to the uniqueness of the group.

This presentation does not presume to explore all of the variables which affect the sexual behavior of young black widows. It is, however, an attempt to enhance our understanding of their sexual behavior and identify the gaps in knowledge which will require further inquiry.

The specific aims are to:

— explore the economic constraints which affect the sexuality of black widows,

— examine some methods of sexual readjustment,

— suggest some strategies of intervention that will be helpful to black women in coping with sexuality in widowhood.

The illustrative materials utilized for this presentation have been drawn from preliminary unstructured inquiries over a twelve-month period with a selected number of black women widowed before the age of fifty-five and at the time of the interview still unmarried. Other than the age and the widowed status, the only other criterion for participation was self-identification as black. Although the respondents resided in several metropolitan areas, most of the data were collected in an Upstate New York city. The groups interviewed classified themselves as either poor or middle class. (Those women who referred to themselves as *poor* indicated that this category related to source and amount of income received, *i.e.*, service professions which included, but were not limited to, domestics, migrant workers, babysitters, and so on. At no time did any woman refer to herself as lower-class.) The paucity of material is noteworthy: research on the sexual behavior of youthful black widows could not be isolated through the Educational Research Information Center, the Federal Government retrieval system nor through manual library review. Information available on widowhood in general can be located in gerontology literature which focuses on the problems of aged widows, and can be used to supplement this presentation.

ECONOMIC CONSTRAINTS

Many of the economic issues which create problems for the youthful black widow have their roots in the black experience in American society which relegates blacks to lower income and educational levels than other groups. These lower levels limit the income which comes into the black family, frequently requiring both the husband and wife to work in order to maintain the family. This situation, interfaced with the early age at which black men die, represents a severe financial crisis for the young widow. The resolution of the financial crisis will have an impact on her ability to establish and maintain satisfactory sexual relationships later.

The major economic issues identified by these women as having major impact on their sexuality were (1) insufficient money or other financial resources with which to maintain themselves and their families and (2) the low income of black men who were potential sexual partners. This, in turn, related to the position of the family on the economic ladder at the time of death. Often these families were only in the beginning stages of establishing themselves financially and had not amassed any assets on which long-term maintenance could be based.

In most instances there was little insurance over and above what was required to meet funeral and burial expenses. There were very few homes that had paid-up mortgages. Those widows who did not have mortgage insurance frequently lost their homes. In most cases earnings from employment and income from survivors' benefits were insufficient to meet the family's daily needs. There were few who had any substantial savings.

This lack of resources continued over a span of years in some cases. Many of the women who were under the age of fifty-five when their husbands died had young children, some of whom were less than a year old. From necessity, therefore, child maintenance had to be projected to span one or more decades.

Since money matters were issues that had to be clarified early, *i.e.*, seeking employment, increasing incomes through other means and/or establishing eligibility for public assistance, the constraints of living for an extended period of time with insufficient funds were major concerns. Some of these constraints were lack of visibility, lack of privacy, diminished social contacts, and problems related to finding a partner of similar financial status.

Mrs. O (26 years old) complained of lack of visibility because of her financial situation. The family had no insurance and she is heavily in debt. "I had to borrow money to pay for the funeral and burial expenses. Since I could not afford the bills, I let the car go. We had discussed insurance before his death, but we thought there was plenty of time. The reason there is no man in my life is because I seldom go out except with the children. You can't meet any men that way. There are some single men in the neighborhood; however, they don't have any more than I have. Even if I had somewhere to go, I wouldn't have anything to wear."

Place and time for coitus are governed by practical considerations. Sexual activities usually take place in the privacy of one's bedroom. This is the American way, and becomes one of the forms of social control over sexual activity. The most appropriate times appear to be those times when there are no other obligations, when there is no work to be done, when the children are away or asleep. For many black women, economic problems make privacy impossible.

> Mrs. P (aged 40) stated that the lack of privacy, the expectations of the children, and her desire to be an appropriate role model are very restric- tive. Her living quarters are small because her limited income prohibits relocating in large quarters, and attempts at sexual union are difficult: "How can I tell my fifteen-year-old daughter not to have sex with boys if she sees me at home in the next room in bed with a man? I also have four other kids. You can't find a sitter in order to go off and sleep with a man. After my husband was dead a few years, I tried to keep company with a man. It didn't work out, so I don't bother any more. It's too frustrating!"

Since life-styles were established prior to the death of the husbands, those women with middle-class orientation appeared to have different problems. There was a strong desire on their part to maintain the upward mobility that was in process when interrupted by death.

> Mrs. H is fully employed as a semiprofessional and plans to send their four children to college. Mortgage insurance paid off the mortgage and life insurance provided them with some other monies. However, there was not enough for college for the children *and* for social life. She stated, "I had two problems—lack of money around which to plan my and the children's future and decreased social contacts. I liked parties and being with people, but could no longer afford to entertain. I felt guilty about going out with people and always having to watch my pennies. I finally stopped being asked. You don't meet new people if you are always at home."

The financial situation even works against some young widows who have no children and consider themselves financially secure. Their ex- pectations of sexual partners include the expectation that the man will be in the same financial bracket they are in, or better. They tend to reject those men who have either financial problems or a lot of other respon- sibilities. That is when they run head-on into the real-life situation that if black men are generally scarce, black men who are professionals or rich are even scarcer.

> Mrs. B (age 40), a high-school teacher, lives alone in the home she and her husband were buying prior to his death. She would not consider an

affair with someone who could not take her to nice places, or assure her of a permanent relationship. She is looking for a professional person: "He must be a good companion as well as sexual partner." She acknowledged no sexual relationships since her husband's death. "I can't leave the city to go where there might be a wider selection because this is where my job is . . ."

In summary, the economic situations which interfere with sexual activity between youthful black widows and black men are not only questions of the source and amount of *her* income but also those of the prospective partner. These conditions, combined with past experiences (frequently those that relate to marital relationships which some widows wish to either replicate or forget), provide most widows with little opportunity for sexual relationships. From necessity many black widows are required to severely modify their sexual behavior more consistently and more frequently than almost any other groups.

Most societies have recognized the importance of coitus for adults (and the constraints placed on it outside the institution of marriage) and have built into their cultures sex roles for widows which may be assumed with dignity. American society, however, has identified no specific role for widows. Becoming a widow relegates the woman, regardless of her age, to a position of relative sexual deprivation. She is no longer a never married woman, seeking for the first time the hallmark of social approval. Nor is she a wife with accompanying roles and responsibilities. She is thus outside the sanctions and controls established for sexual behavior, and must establish her own guidelines.

Masters and Johnson (1970) suggest that if sexual function is honored as a natural process, but sublimated deliberately for sufficient and valued reasons, a high degree of tolerance to sexual tension may exist with grace and without distortion. On the other hand, however, if sexual function is unrealized because of a natural development which has put it aside or held it in abeyance without sustaining expectations, the result may be unfulfillment.

Forms of sexual gratification and modification are not only subject to personal preferences but are also frequently controlled to some extent by religious beliefs and cultural mores. The need to adjust sexual behavior is also related to community and family perceptions of sexual behavior, the individual's perceptions of appropriate sexual behavior and comfort with one's own sexuality.

Mrs. Q (age 36), widowed for two years, commented, "Since my husband died, the neighbors keep their eyes on me. I used to have men visitors sometimes. I had a male friend who lived with his sister. We had no place to meet except at my place. The neighbors started to talking and it got back to my children that I was a loose woman. This disturbed them and so I broke off the relationship."

Mrs. D stated, "I had a male friend once. We couldn't visit and have sex at my home because of the children. We couldn't go to his place because he was living with another woman. I wouldn't go to a hotel or motel because only prostitutes use those places, unless you're out of town. He stopped seeing me and found someone else who didn't care what people thought of her."

This appeared to be a recurring theme throughout these discussions, and there were even more-deep-seated concerns about what constituted appropriate sexual behavior:

Mrs. Z (age 28) has been widowed for three years. She is childless and lives alone in an apartment house where there are a number of single persons living. She observed, "I am always anxious about what is expected sexually any more. I have never known any other man. My husband and I were childhood sweethearts. . . . I had been seeing this man socially for a few weeks and I decided to invite him for dinner. We were having a good time. We had a few drinks and started some sex play. I was beginning to feel good, so he insisted on oral genital manipulation. I panicked. He got angry and turned off. I haven't been that close to anyone else since then—that was about six months ago. I understand that anything is acceptable nowadays. Maybe one day . . ."

Staples (1973) notes that sexual satisfactions other than coitus are considered forms of perversion by the black community; therefore, oral sex and homosexuality tend to occur less frequently in the black community than in other isolated groups. The growing societal acceptance of such forms of sexual behavior, however, continues to be a source of anxiety and is compounded by insecurity about appropriate and acceptable forms of sexual behavior. This does not mean that black widows have not experienced and will never practice these forms of sexual activity. It does mean they may be less likely to discuss such activity, however, because of the perceived feelings of the black community, and may feel more guilt.

Another major problem area is related to black women's feelings about the behavior of black males and how this affects them. Some of the younger women tend to be more concerned about permanent relationships with a romantic love attachment than are the older women. They verbally deny that black males are sexually superior, but there appears to be some confusion which they find difficult to explain. Staples (1973) states that there may be some reality to the black male's virility-cult status. This status is based on the number of women with whom one male is able to have sexual relationships. Thus sexual conquest becomes strongly identified with masculinity and is a symbol of manhood. The discrepancy between rhetoric and reality can be explained by the kind of image black men wish to sustain. While the gap between talk and action may be large, black women do suffer the consequences.

> Mrs. D stated, "My husband was one of those men who could not keep his hands off other women. We would go out together and before I knew it he would have some woman in a corner. It was embarrassing to go out in the street, since everybody knew who he was sleeping with but me. He was a good provider and took care of the home, however, so I put up with him. I guess I'll eventually trust somebody else, but not yet . . ."

Another option available to most women seems to be less available to black women, since it tends to be defined by the black community as a perversion. Although a few widows do acknowledge infrequent masturbation, they tend to find it unsatisfactory in producing orgasm. A small group acknowledge utilization of masturbating devices, also with little satisfaction.

Sublimation seemed to be the major way of handling sexual needs, and the most common forms tend to be child care, church activities and platonic friendships.

Child care and concern for children appeared the most frequent form of sexual diversion. This concern and care is expanded to include children of relatives, neighbors, and friends of their own children.

> Mrs. N (age 32) works a night shift so that she can be home with the children during the day. She stated, "My house is always full of children. This keeps my children occupied and gives me a chance to get some rest even though I can't sleep. I take the neighbors' children on our outings and often let them stay overnight. I stay tired and don't think about having men with the children around."

Many older children tend to use and be used by widowed mothers, particularly if they have developed a pattern over most of their lives of getting and giving full attention to and from each other.

> Mrs. P (age 56) was widowed at the age of 30. Her sons were small, and she went on public assistance to support them. Now she is proud that they all have good jobs. She stated, "The first thing they did was to take me off relief and buy me a house. Two of them are still at home and I care for them just like they were babies. I do all the cooking, laundering, everything. They don't need wives and I don't need men. I didn't have none to

raise them and I don't need them now. There is so much to do that I stay busy all of the time. The middle one got married, but he and his wife have separated. He has his own apartment, but I keep his two children. I'm not an active church member; I enjoy doing for my children more."

The black church plays an important role in the lives of many widows, especially those who are older and no longer have children at home and those who are childless. The black church is a humanizing one, taking into account the social, economic and political aspects of the world. It frequently provides an avenue for restoration of the usefulness which is lost when a mate dies. Although it supports the community's sex behavior codes, it does not insist on strict adherence. There is no punishment for breach of the behavioral codes. It further permits individuals to participate on their own level and within their own scope of commitment.

Mrs. W (age 60) was not very involved in the church before her husband died. But, she says, "Now I spend most of my spare time doing church work. I have found a place in my church. I visit the sick, even stay over sometimes with them. I cook for church dinners every week, and do anything else I can do there. I have not had a man since my husband died, but I don't miss sex."

There further seems to be a strong belief that through faith one will not suffer from lack of sex. One widow at the initial interview suggested, "Just say that God will take care of everything. He took away the need for sex when he took my husband."

Another form of sexual modification that tends to occur frequently among the better educated is platonic relationships interspersed with periodic love affairs:

Mrs. R (age 42) has two children, is a college professor, and lives in a home that is heavily mortgaged. She reported, "I have a number of male friends. Some of them are married, but some are available. I manage to maintain a platonic relationship with them. Most of the time I am satisfied with that kind of arrangement, since it provides some affection and affiliation without the commitment that sexual relationships often involve. I travel a lot and have occasional affairs, but they do not last very long. I am frequently lonely, but I believe that I am relatively content. I believe that I have made a good adjustment. When I am depressed, I change the scenery, take a trip, have an affair, and go back to work. I enjoy my job and I manage to stay busy."

Conversely, some other women deliberately avoid both men and high-contact sources (*i.e.*, places where men are likely to congregate), choosing instead reading, television, and drinking. Alcohol tends to be very popular; in some instances, alcohol abuse was reported.

SUGGESTED STRATEGIES FOR INTERVENTION

There are no experiences in the early socialization process that prepare women for widowhood. In fact, most societies socialize their female young into the role of wife and mother. This phenomenon precludes the possibility of having stored knowledge or information that can be recalled to help women adjust to widowhood. The community and helping professionals (social workers, ministers, and so on) might well offer services aimed at prevention of problems through advance planning and discussion.

Grief associated with the loss of any endeared person can be accompanied by a host of physical and psychological symptoms, but the loss of a mate is also frequently accompanied by the deterioration of social interactions. Therefore, symptoms tend to be intensified, to occur more frequently, and to be of longer duration. There is a strong possibility that the intensity of symptoms is related to the roles into which one is socialized and the deterioration of social contacts without anticipatory sustaining supports.

Erikson (1963) discusses the general state of trust which implies that one not only learns to rely on the sameness and continuity of outside providers but also may consider oneself trustworthy enough so that providers will need not be on their guard. Although Erikson's statement is postulated in terms of the development of basic trust in infancy, there are parallels for widowhood. The absence of experience places a widow in the type of situation where basic trust in others as well as in herself must be re-established.

In many instances some of the previous roles and relationships will only be slightly altered; those of mother, daughter, wage earner, and so on. In those cases, it is important that the values that sustain these roles and the values which form the basis for the new roles coexist with a minimum of conflict. Family counseling and crisis intervention can be helpful here.

Since young black women are more likely to be involved with the home and peer married groups, they are less likely to have affiliations with social clubs, organizations or other agencies which could be a source of assistance and which could become the socializing agent. They are therefore likely to have to take the first step and, in essence, the person who is to be socialized becomes the socializing agent. Professionals could more actively reach out in offering help. It is extremely important that the young black widow should not become disengaged from the social scene either because of her attitude or because of her perceptions about the attitudes of others.

In addition to the need for major changes on a societal level which would extend the life expectancy of black males, there is also the need for a process of socialization into widowhood. This process involves an adjustment to widowhood and may require the development of new skills, value reorientation and the establishment of new roles. Families, friends and those in the helping professions such as social work, the ministry, and so on, can and should aid in this process. Caseworkers, for instance, might help the widow redefine goals, develop new social and vocational skills that can enhance self-esteem as well as financial status and that may affect sexual attitudes and behaviors.

Discussion groups, consciousness-raising groups, workshops on sexuality, and so on, have begun to flourish for white middle-class (and often married) women. These need to be made more available to (and more pertinent to the needs of) black widows, helping such women to increase their sexual options with less guilt. But it almost goes without saying that helping professionals leading such groups need sensitivity to cultural values and to the additional problem of being black in America.

Social isolation is the major condition which separates young black widows from social situations where they are most likely to meet prospective sexual partners. Professionals should aid in providing opportunities to meet men and test out new roles and relationships in a supportive and nonthreatening environment. These environments would function as the socializing agency, and personal contacts in these environments would function as the socializing agent. These agents might well be kinship and friendship groups, socially oriented or task-oriented groups. They also might well be individuals internal or external to the group.

Social service agents and departments should be keenly aware of the need to modify services to meet the needs of those (including widows) who need help after working hours. (Most accidents and homicides, which acutely affect black people, occur after the traditional working hours.) There is a need to have information available at that point so that resources can be easily identified when needed.

In most instances, sexual dysfunction that results from prolonged sexual anxiety, abstinence and social disengagement can be avoided through alert socializing agents. When useful, referral should be made to appropriate agencies. There are a number of psychotherapeutic techniques geared to treatment of women, which can prove to be effective with black widows, so long as the therapist considers the black experience in their application. (Franks, 1974) Of paramount importance is an awareness that the reality behind the phrase in the wedding rite, ". . . 'Til death do us part . . ." indeed arrives early for black women.

REFERENCES AND RECOMMENDED READINGS

BERNARD, JESSIE. *Marriage and Family Among Negroes.* Englewood Cliffs, N. J.: Prentice-Hall, Inc., 1966.

CADE, TONI. *The Black Woman.* New York: New American Library, 1970.

ERIKSON, ERIK H. *Childhood and Society.* New York: W. W. Norton & Co., Inc., 1963.

FRANKS, VIOLET, and VASANTI BURTLE, eds. *Women in Therapy.* New York: Brunner/Mazel Publishers, 1974.

GORNICK, VIVIAN, and BARBARA K. MORAN, eds. *Woman in Sexist Society.* New York: New American Library, 1971.

HARTMAN, WILLIAM E., and MARILYN A. FITHIAN. *Treatment of Sexual Dysfunction.* New York: Jason Aronson, 1974.

HOFFER, ERIC. *The Passionate State of Mind.* Harper and Row, 1954.

JACKSON, JACQUELINE. "But Where Are the Men?" *Black Scholar* (1970).

LADNER, JOYCE A. *Tomorrow's Tomorrow.* New York: Doubleday & Co., Inc., 1971; Anchor Books, 1972.

LOPATA, HELENA ZNANIECKI. *Widowhood in an American City.* Cambridge, Mass.: Schenkman Publishing Co., Inc., 1973.

MALINOWSKI, BRONISLAW. *Sex, Culture, and Myth.* New York: Harcourt, Brace and World, Inc., 1962.

MASTERS, WILLIAM H. and VIRGINIA E. JOHNSON. *Human Sexual Inadequacy.* Boston: Little, Brown and Company, 1970.

PARKES, COLIN MURRAY. *Bereavement.* New York: International Universities Press, Inc., 1972.

STAPLES, ROBERT. *The Black Woman in America.* Chicago: Nelson Hall Publishers, 1973.

U.S. Bureau of the Census. *United States Census Data, 1970.* Washington, D.C.: Government Printing Office, 1970.

U.S. Department of Commerce, Social and Economic Statistics Administration. *Current Population Reports: Special Studies, P-23, No. 50.* Washington, D.C.: Bureau of the Census—Government Printing Office, July 1974.

CHAPTER 7

ASEXUAL AND AUTOEROTIC WOMEN: TWO INVISIBLE GROUPS

Myra T. Johnson

> *No more fiendish punishment could be devised, were such a thing physically possible, than that one should be turned loose in society and remain absolutely unnoticed by all the members thereof.*
>
> WILLIAM JAMES
> *Psychology*

The term *asexual* is rarely used in scientific literature on human sexuality. When the word is recorded, its meaning is usually left vague, with its definitions ranging from "unexpressed" sexuality to "absence of sexual desire" due to "loss of the sex glands" or to psychiatric disorder (Johnson and Belzer, 1973: p. 90; Hinsie and Campbell, 1970: p. 66). In current popular usage it often carries a pejorative connotation, as here:

> The least interesting character, of course, is Joan, a kind of *asexual* coathanger on which to hang the banner of Marxist conversion. Joan's personality is not nearly so important as her manipulated goodness. (*Boston After Dark*, Feb. 25, 1975: p. 6) (Italic added)

This connotation of "manipulated goodness" is also evoked by such synonyms as *celibate, chaste* and *virgin*—all of which are identified, historically, with religious principles. *Webster's Seventh New Collegiate Dictionary* (1963), for example, includes "abstention by vow from marriage" in its definitions of *celibate*, describes a *chaste* person as "refraining from acts or even thoughts or desires that are not virginal or not sanctioned by marriage vows," and defines a *virgin* as "an unmarried woman devoted to religion."

These various definitions suggest that people are *restrained* from sexual relations with others either by physical or psychological damage or by devotion to certain religious tenets. The implication being, of course, that if it were not for these constraints, sexual interaction would occur. There appear to be few really appropriate words in the English language to describe the individual who, regardless of physical or emotional condition, actual sexual history, and marital status or ideological orientation, seems to *prefer* not to engage in sexual activity. Oppressed by a consensus that they are nonexistent, these are the "unnoticed" who in this article are called "asexual"—by default.

FUNCTIONS AND OPPRESSION

The term *oppression* often suggests an unfair and discriminatory distribution of rights and resources to the observable detriment of some. Oppressiveness can also be subtle and indirect, however, the result of inegalitarian principles and dynamics insidiously molding the attitudes of societal members (Halleck, 1971: p. 22; Gil, 1973: p. 5). Women are acknowledged as constituting one of the most consistently oppressed groups in history, both directly and indirectly (Kopp, 1972: p. 33). According to the newly developing Function/Activity Theory of women's oppression, the essence of oppression lies in the assignment of certain functions as "natural" or "fitting" for women. "Child-bearer," "child-rearer," "personal servant to the male," and "sex object" are cited as among the most significant of these functions (Kearon and Mehrof, 1971: pp. 71–72). While recognizing societal oppression of asexual men,[1] the focus here is on the subtle oppression of those women who, because of asexual feelings, have avoided, refused or have not enjoyed the functions women have traditionally been obligated to perform.

1. The oppression of asexual men in contemporary American society is illustrated by Perry Deane Young's remark in *Ms* Magazine (March, 1975) that Vietnam served as an escape hatch for some men from "back home . . . where men and women were expected to move in couples." "Any sort of eccentricity (in sexual or other behavior) was tolerated in Vietnam so long as one behaved properly in combat. This allowed for those loners who wanted nothing to do with any kind of sex involving another person" (p. 116). The same sort of oppression applies to women, but combat is not usually available as a solution for them.

THE ASEXUAL WOMAN AS ASCETIC

At one point in history the woman who rejected "sex-object" and "child-bearer" functions was lauded. A theoretical concept of sexual asceticism is said to have developed among Greek thinkers who seemed to view woman as evil and inferior and who saw salvation from the flesh for her through catharsis and Platonic love.[2] Some scholars believe that this Greek trend preceded and influenced the position eventually adopted by early Christian groups (Bullough, 1974: pp. 107–108). The consensus among many early spokesmen of Christianity, Gnosticism, Manicheanism and similar sects seemed to be that a woman, otherwise viewed as wicked, might become more like a man, and thereby gain salvation, if she elected a life of celibacy and asceticism (Bullough, 1974: pp. 97–120).

Rather than freeing a group of women from designated female functions, this ideal of virginal womanhood seems to have assigned additional prescriptions which oppressed almost everyone. Today, many people continue to protest the centuries of negative impact this doctrine has had on vast numbers of women considered inferior for engaging in sexual relations with others:

> For centuries, women have (believed) that . . . it is unforgivable for (them) to show even the slightest signs of sexual proclivity. Only in the last decade or two have women freed themselves of this irrationality. (*Glamour*, March, 1974)

The woman who may have gravitated toward this life-style because she really felt asexual also seems to have been oppressed. Her asexuality was apparently considered a religious duty. To surmount the sins of her gender, she was expected to live in poverty, fasting, meditating, seldom speaking, and in general making herself unnoticed. (Bullough, 1974: pp. 118–119)

THE ASEXUAL WOMAN AS NEUROTIC

Historical changes in dominant definitions of reality seem to have transformed the asexual woman from a self-disciplined ascetic, to be awed, to a repressed neurotic, to be "cured."

2. Pythagoras is reported to have identified women with the "unlimited principle" of "badness" and "darkness." He seemed to believe that the soul could be saved only through catharsis, which was achieved, in part, by avoiding sexual consummation. While Plato is said to have indicated in his *Timaeus* that women needed men sexually, (Bullough, 1974: pp. 60–61) he later developed the concept of Platonic love. According to this idea, happiness apparently could only be gained through "sacred," or non-physical, love (Bullough, 1974: pp. 107–108).

A young virgin suffering from acute nervousness due to repressed desires paid a visit to a highly recommended psychiatrist. The doctor took one look at the voluptuous maiden and lost all his professional objectivity. "Take off your clothes", he ordered, scarcely able to disguise the lust in his voice. "Now lie down on this couch. Now close your eyes and very slowly spell the word *bedroom*."

She began, "B—E—D—R—*Oh!*—Ohhhhhhhhhh—Mmmmmmmmmmm-mmm."

She was cured. (*Playboy's Complete Book of Party Jokes*, 1972: p. 115)

Researchers of modern psychiatric literature have identified a trend to term any sexual behavior which violates traditional reproductive morality or which seems dysfunctional to the family as abnormal, disorganized or immature (Sprey, 1972: p. 88; Halleck, 1971: pp. 104–105). Redlich and Freeman's authoritative *Theory and Practice of Psychiatry* (1966), for example, labels those "patterns of sexual behavior that predominantly and habitually satisfy other sexual needs than those gratified by normal coitus" as sexual deviations or perversions (p. 384).

This psychiatric consensus oppresses not only asexual women but also all the women who avoid, or are dissatisfied with, their "naturally assigned" functions. Women who engage in pre- or extra-marital sexual relations, prostitutes, lesbian and bisexual women could all be construed as violating "reproductive, family-oriented morality." Of all these violators, however, asexual women seem to be the most invisible. Rarely conceded a unique identity by therapists, professional agreement seems to hold that really asexual women simply do not exist.

A review of the Psychological and Sociological Abstracts for the past ten years, for instance, uncovers almost no articles directly concerning women who prefer not to have sex with others. Those articles which do mention such women seem to explain their behavior in terms of "Victorianism," "premarital chastity," "religious vows" or "repressed homosexuality." The possibility that some women might freely prefer an asexual life-style is seldom examined.

THE AUTOEROTIC WOMAN

While the asexual woman, who has no sexual desires at all, is almost completely unrecognized, the autoerotic woman, who recognizes such desires but prefers to satisfy them alone, is similarly dismissed.

The construction of the nonexistence of truly autoerotic women is illustrated by a look at some of the literature on masturbation. Masturbation has been defined in Hinsie and Campbell's *Psychiatric Dictionary* as:

... psychologically normal during adolescence and to some extent even in adulthood when gratification of a physical emotional relationship with a member of the opposite sex is impossible. (Hinsie and Campbell, 1970: p. 453)

This definition not only seems to imply that masturbation is psychologically abnormal, if an adult continues to prefer it exclusively when heterosexual relations are available but it also suggests the abnormality of homosexual people. This determination of what is abnormal can be interpreted as politically powerful in terms of maintenance of conventional mores. It seems to pressure the asexual woman to construct her identity *out* of the social order and *out* of reality.

Therapy with the adult woman who enjoys autoerotic stimulation and prefers not to have sex with others therefore often includes aiding her to develop more mature methods of achieving satisfaction (Brooks, 1967: pp. 820–823; Halleck, 1971: pp. 104–105).[3] In other words:

> Children who are told over and over that they are liars or thieves become liars or thieves. People who are told over and over that they are crazy become crazy. If you are told over and over that you are a being who has profound sexual needs the odds are very good that you will discover that you do. Particularly when other outlets are forbidden or discouraged. Particularly when it is emphasized that those who do *not* feel these needs are frigid, neurotic, sexually maladjusted (which for a woman means *essentially* maladjusted) dried up, barren, to be pitied. (Densmore, 1971: p. 58)

Excess consensus about the sinfulness of sexual interaction has had an oppressive impact on the lives of generations of women. Many women who always stimulate themselves autoerotically or who never engage in any form of sexual activity may be suppressing strong desires.[4] New oppression seems to lie, however, in excess psychiatric consensus that

3. The fantasies which often accompany masturbation have sometimes been used as evidence that those whose total sexual outlet consists of autostimulation are repressed. Masturbation is seen as having an "interpersonal quality . . . in which . . . wishes regarding relationships with another can be fulfilled" (Koff, 1972: p. 55). While this is undoubtedly true for many people, it is popularly acknowledged that many others entertain fantasies involving exotic settings and unusual circumstances which they never intend to actually act out:

> "Anything goes in fantasy. It's a healthy out for desires you'd *never* act on. So feel free! Fantasize whatever pleases you (lesbianism, group sex, fetishism, voyeurism, exhibitionism)—you'll soon be floating into another hazy realm." *Cosmopolitan Love Guide*, 1972: pp. 54–55)

4. Kinsey's research indicated that while masturbation was the most important sexual outlet for the unmarried females in his sample; about 2 per cent of the women studied said they had never recognized sexual arousal under any conditions. (Kinsey, 1953: pp. 512–525)

women who deny their "natural" female functions are just repressed heterosexuals in need of "a good fuck."

ASEXUAL AND AUTOEROTIC WOMEN

During the 1960's the Radical Left advocated egalitarian revolution, but virtually forgot to include women in their plans (Koedt, "Women and the Radical Movement", 1973: pp. 318–321; Willis, 1970: pp. 55–56). Asexual women were similarly ignored by the "sexual revolution" of that same decade.

Fashion magazines, recognized as one barometer of stylish prescription in both clothing and mores, stressed the full sex lives of "liberated" women during this period (Tortora: 1973). By the 1970's, however, a few women readers were writing letters to the editors to protest:

> The tortured, belabored and endless articles on orgasm, intercourse, marital games, premarital sex, how-to-do-it-in-56-different-ways-while-playing-the-castanets and the evaluate-your-orgasm charts which all of you [magazines] seem dedicated to explore . . . (*Glamour*, January, 1974: p. 50)

This writer described herself as "a devoted wife, mother of three, affectionate female who abhors sex." She pleaded:

> Please, would someone mention the fact that life can be beautiful, meaningful, rich and satisfactory with *or without* sex? It is possible to adore your husband and enjoy affection while the act of intercourse holds anything but appeal. (*Ibid.*)

While feeling that her outlook on life was "warm-blooded, knowledgeable and free of restraint," she seemed to believe that her existence dangerously contradicted accepted psychiatric tenets:

> We mustn't breathe a word of opposition, though. We must be all salivating at the sight of the fourposter and if not, seek therapy. (*Ibid.*)

Women sharing similar feelings wrote in support of this possibly asexual woman's statement:

> I wholeheartedly agree with the anonymous "Protest." (Jan.) It is about time that the other side of the coin was shown. (*Glamour*, March, 1974).

> . . . I'm sure there are a lot more women in the world who feel the same way. I, for one, want to congratulate the woman of this article for speaking up for all of us who are either ashamed or afraid to do so. (*Ibid.*)

Other women also began to suggest to the magazine editors that because some women were being overlooked and left out of the revolution, perhaps the sexual liberation they publicized did not exist:

> The cataclysmic change in sexual attitudes in the latter part of the sixties supposedly brought relief to women, burdened for centuries by the hypocritical double standard. Now it seems a new rigidity is developing. A woman is no longer free *not* to have a sex life . . .
>
> This is not a recommendation for a return to the rigid standards of grandma's girlhood nor a put-down of premarital sex. . . . If it was wrong for the self-righteous of the past to condemn a woman who departed from society's cast-iron rule of behavior, it is also wrong for the disciples of today's sexual liberation to downgrade a girl who chooses not to participate.
>
> Because a girl chooses not to have sexual relations does not make her a case for the analyst . . . (Head, 1971: p. 76)
>
> . . . In many ways, sexual freedom is the philosophical toy of the college student. Individuals "discuss" sexual freedom all too often in terms that will serve only to reinforce the choice *they* have made. (*Mademoiselle*, Nov., 1972: p. 224)

Despite publication of these reader protests, however, fashion magazine editorial consensus seems to continue to popularize a consumption-oriented image of the sexually "liberated" woman much like that Una Stannard describes in her "Mask of Beauty":

> The modern woman's liberty to expose her legs and most of her body does not signify women's sexual liberation, but only her obsessive desire to please men. Women are "free" to start wearing padded bras at the age of nine and to spend forty-eight million dollars annually in eye make-up alone. Women are free to be Playboy bunnies or to be topless and bottomless waitresses. Women are not free *not* to be sexy. (Stannard, 1971: p. 192)

Not fitting this popular definition of "liberated," the asexual woman seems to only rarely receive recognition in feature articles or staff written columns.[5] When one recent column did mention "celibate" women, its author's partial motive seemed to be nullification of their "newsworthiness"—their public existence:

> One of the women at the speakout described *her* sexual style as celibacy. And recently I read a newspaper article by a woman who said she and her

5. This statement is based on the author's review of three wide-circulation magazines (*Glamour, Mademoiselle,* and *Seventeen*) from January 1970 through January 1975.

friends believed that celibacy was a "valid sexual alternative." Could this be a trend? If so, what could the media possibly make of this most non-of-non-events? With any luck, not a thing. (Durbin, 1975: p. 24)

THE ASEXUAL AND AUTOEROTIC WOMAN AS POLITICALLY CONSCIOUS

One of the women referred to by the *Mademoiselle* columnist was addressing the Second Annual Conference on Sexuality sponsored by the New York chapter of the National Organization of Women (NOW). Although the columnist's remarks suggest a personal contempt for "celibate" women, the theme of her article revolves around the manufacture of sexual fashion, which she feels was reflected at the conference. Autoeroticism and asexuality, once recommended as a demonstration of religious consciousness, are beginning, in some sectors of the feminist movement, to be recommended as one demonstration of political consciousness.

The origin of this newly developing imperative may partially lie in feminist analysis of a growing body of research about vaginal orgasms. The scientific investigations of Kinsey and also Masters and Johnson exposed the vaginal orgasm as a hoax by indicating that the clitoris, rather than the vagina, functions in producing orgasm. (Koedt, 1973a: 201–203).

On the basis of this evidence, many feminists have evaluated the theory of the "vaginal orgasm" as exploitative in its assumption that only the mature, submissive woman, who accepted her "natural" functions, could enjoy it (Atkinson, 1970: p. 42; Koedt, 1973a: pp. 199-200).

Rejecting the vaginal orgasm as a myth created to ensure female sexual dependence on the male, some feminists recognized clitoral orgasm as opening up sexual options for women (Koedt, 1973a: pp. 204–206; Atkinson, 1970: p. 42; *The Feminists* . . . , 1970: pp. 117–118).

Backed scientifically by new evidence that sex may be an "acquired habit, appetite or even addiction" rather than a "biological force" (Wright, 1972: p. 119), the idea of options may have encouraged some women in the Liberation Movement who feel asexual or autoerotic to talk about their lives. (Densmore, 1971: p. 59)

Other feminists, repulsed by the idea of sexual involvement with men who, they feel, oppress and even despise them, have begun to equate sexual options with political strategy (Bernard, 1972: p. 373):

The moving nucleus of feminism is a gradual accretion of women defining themselves irrevocably as political lesbians, women sexually celibate or asexual or lesbian in the traditional sense of the word, who perceive the bonding of women in every phase of existence as the sine qua non of feminist revolution. (Johnston, 1973)

We must destroy the institution of heterosexual sex which is a manifestation of the male-female role. Since physical pleasure can be achieved in both sexes by autoerotic acts, sex as a social act is psychologically in nature; at present its psychology is dominance-passivity. (*The Feminists* . . ., 1970: pp. 117–118)

In seeking to liberate women, the advocates of these strategies may be inviting yet another tyranny. A consensus which praises women who do not have sex with men as politically conscious might alleviate the oppression of traditionally assigned female functions, but would probably create new oppressive functions. The woman who still wants to have sex with men might function as "scapegoat" and the woman who feels asexual or autosexual might function as a political symbol—her identity still lost in the slogans, and her reality going unnoticed.

CONCLUSION

Asexual and autoerotic women seem seldom to have been accorded the equal right to be different, the equal right to celebrate their unique experiences in the world. For their violation of established female function, they have been oppressed by a societal consensus that they, as free and unique individuals, do not exist. Again and again, their personal experiences have been redefined for them in terms of socially constructed meanings: they are "ascetic," "neurotic," "unliberated," or "politically conscious." Their sexual preferences are explained away in the rhetoric of whatever sexual ideology seems currently to be in vogue.

The assumption that members of certain groups, as a function of their being so identified, need help may be one force in the perpetuation of this kind of consensual redefinition of experience. When women as a group were considered sexually sinful, those women who preferred not to have sexual relations with others were often "helped" in their struggle with evil through religious asceticism. When women as a group came to be viewed as performing important sexual and reproductive functions for men, those women who preferred not to have sexual relations with others were frequently "helped" by therapy in working through their neuroticism. Now that women as a group are beginning to be redefined as "oppressed" in their relationships with men, those women who prefer not to have sexual relations with others are sometimes "helped" in their struggle for "consciousness" through political support.

One possible explanation for this "helping" system might be that because these asexual and autoerotic women are different they must be "consensually redefined," "fitted into" and "understood" in the gestalt of the dominant, or alternative, society in question in order to avoid social upheaval. In this context, religion, therapy and politics might all be viewed as mechanisms of social control useful in maintaining the reality of established ideas against serious challenge.

HELPING ASEXUAL AND AUTOEROTIC WOMEN TO BE THEMSELVES

In the framework of this broad kind of social policy perspective, women who, for a portion or all of their lives, feel asexual or autoerotic may cease to be victims only when people no longer feel a need to conceptualize each other in terms of the "functions" they can perform—when the "sexual is dissolved into the fully personal . . . and . . . sexual ideologies are discarded." (Wright, 1972: p. 121)

Pat allusions to sweeping changes in social structure, however, can sometimes oversimplify the complexity of life. These generalizations can easily become just another way of ignoring the individual uniqueness of human beings; an excuse for not attempting to provide relief for those people now in psychic pain. Black psychiatrists, for example, have angrily cried "racism" against the contentions of some of their colleagues that they cannot effectively treat black patients until the prejudiced attitudes of the society which oppresses them have been altered (Thomas and Sillen, 1972: p. 139). A similar analogy could be made regarding asexual and autoerotic women.

> If you have an alive body, no one can tell you how to experience the world. And no one can tell you what truth is, because you experience it The body does not lie. (Keleman in Braun, 1975: p. 9)

Some of the newest therapies do propose, at least on paper, that the aim of therapy should be to furnish support and insight for the individual's life-style, with acceptance and respect for his or her individuality (Vocations for Social Change, 1975: p. 106; Grimstead and Rennie, 1975: p. 60).

While the power of politics to group and redefine the life experiences of asexual and autoerotic women can be illustrated by a look at some camps of the feminist movement, other feminists interpret feminism as freeing all women to express their sexual uniqueness in an atmosphere of acceptance:

> Sex can be expressed with a woman, with a man, with a group of people, alone, or not practiced at all. (Mander and Rush, 1974: p. 24)

Going unnoticed in society, being told that one doesn't feel what one feels but that, indeed, one feels something else can be a very painful and even debilitating experience for some women. Feminist consciousness-raising sessions and group therapies are beginning, hopefully, to work like this in exploring such problems:

> If a woman continually blames herself for her inadequacies . . . the group works with her to explore what part is her responsibility and what part is imposed on her by society. Thus she is at the same time encouraged to assume responsibility and to relinquish responsibility for the part that is not hers so that she can be freed of that burden and grow. (Mander and Rush, 1974: p. 17)

This can often increase the awareness "that there is in fact nothing wrong with the tormented individual, but a great deal wrong with the social circumstances which limit her life choices" (Grimstad and Rennie, 1975: p. 66).

Some women coming to grips with their longtime feelings that they prefer not to have sex with others—and others who are initially recognizing these feelings after perhaps years of involvement in lesbian or heterosexual activities—may want support in making their transition.

Even autoerotic women may have orgasmic difficulties. In fact, one serious drawback of the Masters and Johnson type of sex therapy for these women is its emphasis on working with couples, thus excluding women who are single, temporarily between sex partners, or autoerotic in orientation (Grimstad and Rennie, 1975: pp. 54–55).

Alfred Kinsey (1953) demonstrated that not everyone has or maintains one exclusive sexual preference throughout an entire lifetime. The woman who has felt asexual or autoerotic and is beginning to feel differently may want support in the transition to another point on the sexual continuum:

> When celibacy no longer feels good we should get out of it—but that's easier said than done. And it feels harder the longer we have been celibate. Coming out of celibacy, we may feel embarrassed by needs that seem insatiable. (Boston Women's Health Book Collective, 1973: p. 44)

It is recognized, of course, that a few women may have very deep and complex difficulties which cannot simply be attributed to society. They may exhibit asexual or autoerotic behavior while really wanting something entirely different or even because of fear of any kind of physical intimacy.

"Helping," therefore, takes on the discriminatory tone that robs women of the truth of individual experiences when it makes them victims of excess consensus, with the underlying assumption being that *all* or *most* asexual or autoerotic women, because of their orientation, *need* help.

If a woman feels that she does want help in any of these areas she should realize that the political biases of therapists, whether conscious or unconscious, frequently influence their work (Halleck, 1971). Thus, she might want to interview prospective therapists to see if she will be able to work with them without having the truth of her life altered to fit another truth.[6]

Before an asexual or autoerotic woman decides on sometimes expensive professional guidance, however, she might first try tapping the strengths within herself. The following is a description of a woman learning to love the appearance of her physical body, but the concept involved could as easily be applied to an asexual or autoerotic woman accepting the uniqueness of her life:

> I stood as though I were proud before I was proud, and then I became proud. (Braun, 1975: p. 16)

REFERENCES AND RECOMMENDED READINGS

ATKINSON, TI-GRACE. "The Institution of Sexual Intercourse." In *Notes from the Second Year: Women's Liberation*, edited by Shulamith Firestone and Anne Koedt. New York: Radical Feminism, 1970.

BERNARD, JESSIE. "Women, Marriage and the Future." In *Intimate Life Styles: Marriage and Its Alternatives*, edited by Joann S. DeLora and Jack R. DeLora. Pacific Palisades, Calif.: Goodyear Publishing Co., Inc., 1972.

Boston After Dark, February 25, 1975, p. 6.

Boston Women's Health Book Collective. *Our Bodies, Our Selves*. New York: Simon and Schuster, 1973.

BRAUN, SAUL, ed. *Catalog of Sexual Consciousness*. New York: Grove Press, Inc., 1975.

BROOKS, PATRICIA A. "Masturbation," *American Journal of Nursing* (1967), pp. 820–823.

BULLOUGH, VERN L. *The Subordinate Sex: A History of Attitudes Toward Women*. Baltimore: Penguin Books, Inc., 1974.

Cosmopolitan's Love Guide. New York: Cosmopolitan Magazine, 1972.

DENSMORE, DANA. "Independence from the Sexual Revolution." In *Notes from the Third Year: Women's Liberation*, edited by Shulamith Firestone and Anne Koedt. New York: Notes from the Second Year, Inc., 1971.

---

6. *Guidelines for Women Seeking Psychotherapy* provides detailed advice on how to select a therapist. It is available from Cleveland Women's Counseling, P.O. Box 18472, Cleveland, Ohio 44118 for 50¢ per copy.

DURBIN, KAREN. "The Intelligent Woman's Guide to Sex," *Mademoiselle* (January 1975), p. 24.

"The Feminists: A Political Organization to Annihilate Sex Roles." In *Notes from the Second Year: Women's Liberation*, edited by Shulamith Firestone and Anne Koedt. New York: Radical Feminism, 1970.

GIL, DAVID G. "Some Thoughts on Political Strategy Toward an Egalitarian, Humanistic, Democratic Social Order." Submitted to the second convention of the New American Movement, DeKalb, Illinois, July 5–8, 1973.

GRIMSTAD, KRISTEN, and SUSAN RENNIE, eds. *The New Woman's Survival Sourcebook*. New York: Alfred A. Knopf, Inc., 1975.

Guidelines for Women Seeking Psychotherapy. Cleveland: Cleveland Women's Counseling Group.

Glamour, March 1974.

HALLECK, SEYMOUR L. *The Politics of Therapy*, New York: Science House, Inc., 1971.

HEAD, MARY E. "Protest: Is There a Place for a Virgin in the Sexual Revolution?" *Glamour* (February 1971), p. 76.

HINSIE, LELAND E., and ROBERT JEAN CAMPBELL. *Psychiatric Dictionary*. Fourth edition. New York: Oxford University Press, 1970.

"In the Mail," *Mademoiselle* (November 1972), p. 224.

JOHNSON, WARREN R., and EDWIN G. BELZER. *Human Sexual Behavior and Sex Education*. Philadelphia: Lea and Febiger, 1973.

JOHNSTON, JILL. *The Village Voice* (June 21, 1973).

KEARON, PAMELA, and BARBARA MEHRHOF. "Prostitution." In *Notes from the Third Year: Women's Liberation*, edited by Shulamith Firestone and Anne Koedt. New York: Notes from the Second Year, Inc., 1971.

KOEDT, ANNE. "The Myth of the Vaginal Orgasm." In *Radical Feminism*, edited by Anne Koedt *et al.* New York: Quadrangle/The New York Times Book Co., 1973a.

———. "Women and the Radical Movement." In *Radical Feminism*, Anne Koedt *et al.*, eds. New York: Quadrangle/The New York Times Book Co., 1973b.

KOPP, SHELDON B. *If You Meet the Buddha on the Road, Kill Him!: The Pilgrimage of Psychotherapy Patients*. Ben Lomond, Calif.: Science and Behavior Books, Inc., 1972.

"Letters: Readers' Opinions," *Glamour* (March, 1974).

Mademoiselle, November 1972, p. 224.

MANDER, ANICA VESEL, and ANNE KENT RUSH. *Feminism as Therapy*. New York: Random House/Book Works, 1974.

Playboy's Complete Book of Party Jokes. Chicago: Playboy Press, 1972.

"Protest: Sex Is Okay But I'd Rather Read," *Glamour* (January 1974), p. 50.

REDLICH, FREDERICK C., and DANIEL X. FREEDMAN. *The Theory and Practice of Psychiatry*. New York: Basic Books, Inc., 1966.

"St. Joan of the Stockyards—Review." *Boston After Dark* (February 25, 1975), Art and Entertainment Section, p. 6.

SPREY, JETSE. "On the Institutionalization of Sexuality." In *Intimate Life Styles: Marriage and Its Alternatives*, edited by Joann S. DeLora and Jack R. DeLora. Pacific Palisades, Calif.: Goodyear Publishing Co., Inc., 1972.

STANNARD, UNA. "The Mask of Beauty." In *Woman in Sexist Society*, edited by Vivian Gornick and Barbara K. Moran. New York: Basic Books, 1971.

The Shorter Bartlett's Familiar Quotations. Christopher Morley and Louella D. Everett, eds. New York: Permabooks, 1961.

THOMAS, ALEXANDER, and SAMUEL SILLEN. *Racism and Psychiatry*. New York: Brunner-Mazel, 1972.

TORTORA, PHYLLIS. "Fashion Magazines Mirror Changing Role of Women," *Journal of Home Economics*, March, 1973, pp. 19–23.

Vocations for Social Change. *People's Yellow Pages* (1976 edition). Cambridge, Mass.: Vocations for Social Change, 1975.

Webster's Seventh New Collegiate Dictionary. Springfield, Mass.: G & C Merriam Company, 1963.

WILLIS, ELLEN. "Women and The Left." In *Notes from the Second Year: Women's Liberation*, edited by Shulamith Firestone and Anne Koedt. New York: Radical Feminism, 1970.

WRIGHT, DEREK. "The New Tyranny of Sexual Liberation." In *Intimate Life Styles: Marriage and Its Alternatives*, edited by Joann S. DeLora and Jack R. DeLora. Pacific Palisades, Calif.: Goodyear Publishing Co., Inc., 1972.

YOUNG, PERRY DEANE. "Some Things I've Wanted to Say," *Ms.* Magazine, March, 1975, pp. 115–120.

CHAPTER 8

SEXUAL
VICTIMS

LeRoy G. Schultz

Perhaps the most direct and ugly instances of sexual oppression occur when direct violence is employed to gain sexual satisfaction against the will of another. There is something uniquely unsettling in civilized man when he sees the sexual self-determination of another abused or stolen— all the more so if physical violence is used or when the victim is an innocent child. Equally at issue is the fact that society's response to sexual oppression has not been rational. In fact, society has neglected its own best interests by basically ignoring the rehabilitation and welfare of both sex victim and sex offender. This report is going to concentrate on two sets of sex victims: the molested child and the raped adult. The remarks will be limited to the victim of heterosexual assault. This is not to imply, however, that homosexual assault is not an equally significant social problem. Though the literature of homosexual rape and assault is sparse, the small quantity at least suggests that the incidence is becoming more visible and has its own related problems. (Feigan, 1974; Olsen, 1974; Scacco, 1975)

THE SEXUALLY ABUSED CHILD

The sexual abuse of children was far more prevalent in the past than it is today. In ancient Rome and Greece, children were considered to be

[110]

legitimate sex objects—particularly young boys. Sexual abuse of children continued until well into the nineteenth century. Servants and teachers were well known as child molesters, and parents were even known to masturbate their own children for various accepted reasons. Routinely, children would share the family bed during intercourse of their parents.

By the eighteenth century, however, parents had begun to inflict severe punishments for childhood sensuality, perhaps to control their own sexual desires toward their children. By the nineteenth century, parents, doctors and others began waging a frenzied campaign against childhood masturbation, threatening to cut off the child's sex organs without anesthesia, telling children that masturbation caused all forms of illness and stunted growth, forcing children to wear chastity belts, and sending children to sanatoria for the control of masturbation. Battering children on discovering them to be masturbating was common. In the late 1800's, our first laws were passed to protect children against sex abuse from parents and other adults. The rationale for such laws is very vague by today's values and was based upon myths and superstitions as well as upon a general ignorance of human sexuality—all of which has been codified into the criminal laws of today.

Our attitudes toward child molestation are also a reflection of American attitudes toward the human sexual response. No matter what adult man may do, it is only when he behaves sexually that church and state use the word *unnatural*. Children are considered at birth to be *unnatural*, i.e., "sexually polymorphous perverse." Society is reluctant to acquaint children and adolescents with their own sexual bodies or to allow sex education of a nonbiological character out of fear of the child's natural sex interest and alleged lack of control by the child. In our schools we accelerate all educational subject matter, but delay sexual awareness until the last moment. The beliefs of most adults about childhood sexuality foster fear and reaction toward sexual molestation which is unfounded and perhaps misdirected.

WHAT IS SEXUAL ABUSE?

Laws against child molestation are vague and ambiguous, while the law against child rape is rather distinct and clear. Both offenses are difficult to prove. For example, there is no agreed-upon definition of *sexual abuse* within or between states. If the sexual offense against the child involves less than intercourse involving the vagina, mouth or anus, definition becomes more difficult. Where does normal affection and fondling end and sexual molestation begin? It is factually difficult to distinguish between appropriate display of affection and other possibly disturbing behavior. Adults have been charged with child molestation when, as teachers, they placed an arm around an injured child following a playground accident, and when, as parents, they employed the child witnessing the "primal scene" as a sex education method. Legislators, lawyers, physicians, social workers, child development specialists, and child advocates all have avoided the question of the difference between normal affection and sexual molestation.

INCIDENCE

There is a noticeable lack of any reliable data on the incidence of sexual victimization of children and adolescents in this country. There is no centralized national or state recording system for sexual offenses against children. Even what little data exist are confusing in that different police jurisdictions use different crime definitions for the same type of sexual event. The lack of reliable incidence figures makes policy formation and implementation of services for victims difficult.

Estimates of the number of cases of sexual abuse of children are 4,000 cases per year in cities, approximately 5,000 cases of incest per year, and approximately 200,000 to 500,000 cases of sexual molestation of children under the age of 14 years (Schultz, 1972: p. 174). Kinsey (1953: p. 117) found that 24 per cent of all females are sexually molested while they are children.

In Washington, D.C., the emergency room of a large hospital reported that 24 per cent of all sexual abuse cases reported to them were of children under the age of 14, and that 30 cases annually were of young males who had been forcibly sodomized (Hayman 1972: p. 92). The Philadelphia General Hospital, which has a rape crisis center, reports that 10 per cent of all rape cases each year are of children under the age of 14 years (Peters, 1975: p. 193). In a recent study of 1,070 rapes, 22 per cent of the victims were under the age of 15 years (Bart, 1975: p. 39).

Girls tend to be molested *before* puberty, at which time they develop inhibitions, and their victimization decreases thereafter. Boys show just the opposite pattern. Their rate of victimization increases *after* they reach puberty, because growing feelings of manhood combined with curiosity may lead them more easily into sex play and resultant seduction.

The recent strengthening of child abuse reporting laws may increase the official incidence and improve the record keeping. For example, Connecticut reported a 200 per cent increase in suspected sex abuse one year after putting teeth in its child abuse reporting laws (Sgroi, 1975: pp. 19–21, 44).

PHYSICAL ASPECTS OF SEXUAL ABUSE

Most sex offenses against children are not of the types that leave any physical evidence. The most common sex offenses against children involve an adult exposing his sex organs to the child, verbal suggestive talk of a sexual nature, touching, fondling or stroking the child's sex organs in a gentle way, or licking and kissing the child and/or his sex organs. Approximately 90 per cent of all sex offenses against children do not result in any violence or physical damage that will be obvious to family members, social workers, teachers, or even examining physicians. (Gagnon, 1965: p. 191). In the remaining 10 per cent of the cases in which penetration or physical violence was involved, there may be sex organ damage such as tearing or rupturing of the vaginal barrel, hymen, or anal sphincter; possible hemorrhage or general body damage such as abrasions, bites or bruises or ligament laceration, venereal disease, vulvitis, and pregnancy depending on age and sex. With parental cooperation, these physical symptoms can be treated promptly and efficiently in any clinic, hospital or properly equipped doctor's office, if properly staffed. The social worker, nurse or doctor may have to discover sexual abuse by recurrent unexplained vulvitis, vaginitis, and anal fissures—all or any of which should raise suspicion. For example, V.D. in a pre-pubertal child is likely to have a sexual cause, whether it occurs in the vagina, anus or mouth. The mouth and throat of the child should be examined for gonococcal tonsillitis, a condition often associated with oral-genital contacts.

Using age-relevant wording, skilled questioning of the child by the social worker may produce an account of child molesting. This should include questions such as:

1. Does mother have a boyfriend living at home?

2. In what bed and room does child sleep in at night? Does child share a bed? If so, with whom?

3. What does the child think has caused her vaginal problem?

If the child indicates molestation, other younger siblings should be examined also, particularly females. If the child acknowledges molestation, one should record her and her mother's statements. Instructions should be given to parents and child to preserve physical evidence, particularly blood, fecal, urine or semen stained clothing, bed coverings, etc., as well as fingernail scrapings if resistance was offered, plus hairs and fibers. In some cases, a photograph of general body damage may be required.

EMOTIONAL ASPECTS OF SEXUAL ABUSE

The emotional effect of victimization upon children has been exaggerated in the earlier literature, partly because of a naive misunderstanding of the role of sexuality in the development of children, partly because of misunderstanding of the average child's adaptive capacity and partly because of a Victorian belief that sex must leave a permanent trauma for the innocent child. Generally, sexual assaults of children do not have an excessively unsettling effect on personality development (Burton, 1968: pp. 87–161) nor a serious effect on his or her later adult adjustment. Psychosocial aftereffects of the sexual offense against the child are not so readily assessed, however, as are the physical effects. Possible negative or traumatic effects are related to the amount of violence employed by the offender, the type and depth of the child's relationship to the offender, and the reaction of the family, society, and significant others to the offense. Immediate reaction in the child may range from simple fright, much like when a child encounters something new and unpleasant, to vomiting, hysteria and panic. Some children will react without fear or guilt, while some may even report the offense as stimulating and erotic.

The child's relationship to the offender is very important in understanding the offense dynamics and effect upon the victim. Most victimized children are seeking out and allowing affectionate behavior from their offenders; many feel kindly and loving toward them, and perhaps have long-term relationships established with them (sometimes over a period of years with a pattern of frequent sexual behavior). This gratification of the child's love needs from her father over a period of time is particularly significant in cases of incest when a daughter will refuse to place criminal charges or to testify against her father for fear of being responsible for parental separation or divorce, and the consequent loss of the father or her love supply by seeing him sentenced to a correctional institution, leading to oedipal guilt. Young female victims are sometimes blamed by their mothers for breaking up the family, particularly when the family was held together by the classic sexual three-way process. The same holds true for the young female adolescent victim who manifests strong resistance to placing charges against her "steady" boyfriend or lover.

In many instances, young victims engaged in behavior that was seductive or affectionate, but were naive about its potential as a sexual stimulus. Once the offense was committed, they felt betrayed, shocked, and had a general negative reaction. Many victims appear dismayed to find, post-offense, that the offenders' behavior was in direct response to cues they gave. The child victim also may feel guilt if she reports some gratification from the offense, being the object of love and attention from an older person whom her family and society suddenly condemn. In the older child, having invited the offense may take one of two directions: *First*, partial involvement in victimogenesis may actually minimize the traumatic aftereffects; *second*, post-offense symptoms may be accentuated as a result of guilt feelings. If the child victim feels she precipitated or helped stimulate the sexual event, she may feel guilty in that society has chosen to prosecute only one-half of the criminal relationship. The young adolescent victim may wonder about her reputation or marriage-ability. If the sexual offense involved considerable physical violence, the victim may display hysteria, shock, or disabling feelings of hostility toward the offender(s) or evince a grieflike reaction. Her self-confidence may disappear as she questions herself as to what she did wrong or what precautions she did not take against victimization. She may fear possible victimization again or question if she will develop a normal interest in sexuality.

By far the greatest potential trauma to the child's personality is caused by society and its institutions, and the victim's parents, as a result of (a) the need of the court to use the child victim for the prosecution of the offender and (b) the need of the victim's parents to prove to themselves, to other family members, to neighbors, and to significant others that the victim was free of any victimogenesis and that they were good parents. Naturally, we expect society to react severely to forced child-adult sex relations, and such interpretation is bound to ensure the unlikelihood of the victim escaping the trauma produced by the definition and interpretation.

In the administration of justice in common law countries, the suspect has the right to trial and to confront and cross-examine those who charge him with an offense. Child trauma occurs as a result of the court's need to have the child victim repeat the details of the sexual offense several times—to police, warrant officers, prosecutors, and finally to a jury of twelve adults, sometimes with the suspected sex offender present. This places what is perhaps in the child's mind a short-lived traumatic event with few permanent consequences, out of all proportion in its importance to him, and forces the child to reorient his ideas toward a confusing adult interpretation of the offense, its new importance, and the victim's role in punishing the offender. Most police, sheriffs, and prosecutors have no training or education in nondamaging methods of interviewing children and tend to use adversary approaches which are appropriate for adults and which are successful in gaining convictions. The suspect's lawyer or defense attorney has the duty of defending his client with every tool at his command, and he may contribute or induce emotional trauma, by attempting in open court to show the victim is incompetent, malicious, seductive, a consenting "Lolita" or has brought false charges for any one of various personal reasons. The dilemma here is the need to protect the child from the potential trauma induced by the court's legal proceedings, but at the same time convicting and rehabilitating the offender. This dilemma can be reduced by using special interrogation methods and professional interviewers (Libai, 1975). If law enforcement agencies and courts cannot eliminate the trauma induced by repeated testifying, then nonreporting of the offense may be the best choice in terms of the child's welfare. In addition, if most American correctional institutions have no effective rehabilitation programs, the rationale for reporting the offense to police is weakened.

It is clear from research on child sex victims that it is not the sexual act per se that creates trauma, but the parent's behavior toward the child victim on discovery of the offense.

The parents may overreact: become hysterical; physically attack the offender in front of the child; physically attack the child victim; berate, belittle or punish the victim; demand, under threats, that the child inform court and police officials that the sex offense was not provoked by the victim; or the parents may even threaten the court officials with reprisals unless the offender is sentenced instantly. As rapidly as possible after the offense, parents will need help in accepting the offense in such a way that horror, panic, and fright are not communicated to the child so as to create trauma where perhaps none existed before.

CONCLUSIONS

1. Probably less than 5 to 10 per cent of all child sex victims are assaulted through physical violence or vaginal/anal penetration, so that physical damage is minimal in most cases. (Gagnon, 1965: p. 191)

2. Most of the children sexually molested, where no violence was employed, were engaging in affection-seeking behavior and did not perceive the offense at the time as traumatic.

3. Guilt in sex victims is fairly absent, but may be engendered by parents, courts, social services and the community *after* the fact.

4. Most sexual assaults do not affect the child's personality development in a negative way, particularly when neither violence nor court appearance occurred.

5. Children who go through the court process and testify in an effort to bring a conviction should be financially compensated by the state for their injury and related costs.

6. Courts should experiment with one-way screens and/or video-taping of children's evidence to prevent or reduce trauma, or else use professional welfare staff to testify in lieu of the child victim where trauma appears likely.

7. If adequate sexual education occurs for children under any auspices in school, family, church or other social organization, sexual victimization may be reduced if it includes important aspects of sexuality and potential victimization. A child has as much right to information about sex as do adults.

8. There appears to be a change coming in this country regarding sex values, coupled with a rising concern for children's rights. At what

age can a child or adolescent give consent to engage in sexual behavior with another child or with an adult? It is becoming more and more difficult for the state and its agencies to determine what is good, sexually, for children. We very seldom ask the children. People are having voluntary sex relations at a younger and younger age. If we can't prove that damage to the child occurs as a result of "child molestation," does society have the right to criminalize it? There is need for considerable research and attitude restructuring here. Demographic studies have indicated that the age of first intercourse or other sexual activity is occurring earlier than it did only a few years ago. Today's thirteen-year-old may simply be the first to combine a biological fact with a sense of individual style. Children need the option of refusing sex with other children and adults. However, children are reared in such a way that they cannot refuse adults. Parents have insisted that children accept all forms of affection from friends and relatives—being picked up, hugged, kissed and squeezed—thus leaving children with little experience in saying No. Children also have little experience in trusting their own reactions to people and in resisting the promise of rewards. They are not informed about sexual matters, do not understand their own sexuality or that of others and thus cannot deal effectively with this problem. We keep children ignorant of sexuality and then worry that they are vulnerable to the sexual advances of others. Public anxiety about child molestation has deprived our children of many dimensions of nonsexual intimacy with parents and other adults who could be important to them. This is the next frontier for child advocates. Age-ism now joins racism and sexism as our oppressor.

9. We will need to train social welfare personnel in order to effectively process child sex victims, from beginning to end, in the least damaging way for society as a whole.

10. Perhaps prevention of sexual abuse and/or the use of children as sex objects might be learned from what adult molesters think of children. "Children give love freely as no adult does." . . . "Children do not compare you to others and children do not expect sexual expertise from you." Perhaps the need to restructure adult sexuality with some of these factors in mind could reduce the use of children as sex objects.

THE ADULT RAPE VICTIM

Current professional interest in the rape problem emerged with the general thrust of the anti-violence movement in America, the sexual evolution in sex communication, the new field of victimology, and the feminist movement's re-emergence. As a social problem, knowledge is in its infancy. Much of the earlier data on rape victims were based on incomplete and poorly developed questionnaires, or were from police reports that did not include factors of victim welfare. Some recent and past studies dealt with theory, usually psychoanalytical, based on poor samples of clinical records of women in treatment or in the hospital emergency room. These studies suggested what the victim *ought* to have experienced according to some particular theory. Most research to date suffers from sample difficulties, biased value or political orientations, and little direct contact with victims.

I am going to attempt to assess the emotional aftermath of rape as reported in the literature, weak as it may be, since it is all we have to go by at this time (Schultz, 1972: pp. 396–405), and suggest some helping roles for social workers and others in the human services agency.

RAPE INCIDENCE

The crime of rape against women is occurring with greater frequency in recent years and now stands at the ratio of 2 women per 1,000 yearly (U.S. Dept. of Justice, 1974: pp. 14–15). Women and girls are increasingly unsafe at home or in the streets because most crimes of violence are committed against women (F.B.I., 1973). From 1967 to 1972 there was an increase of 70 per cent in reported forcible rape in the United States, along with some 49,507 other types of criminal sexual victimization each year. (F.B.I. 1973) Shipman (1968: pp. 3–12) reported in his study of 261 college females that 3.4 per cent had been raped, 35 per cent had had to use physical force to prevent being raped, and 31 per cent had encountered sexual violence; while 3.7 per cent of a population of college males admitted to rape. Sorenson's study of 1,000 young females revealed that 6 per cent were raped as their first sexual experience (Sorenson, 1972: p. 105). The newest situation today which is giving rise to rape is female hitchhiking. One study in a large college community indicated that 7 per cent of female hitchhikers are raped and 26 per cent received strongly worded sexual approaches while hitchhiking (Greenley, 1973: p. 79). Another trend noted is a 10 per cent increase in rape from 1960 to 1970 by boys under the age of 15 (Glaser, 1975: p. 157).

PHYSICAL ASPECTS OF RAPE

The medical evaluation and examination must be carried out by a physician who is experienced in his field and who, ideally, has some forensic experience, because the guilt or innocence of the suspect may depend upon the medical findings. While few hospital emergency rooms are staffed with social workers, those that are may require the social worker to report on the emotional state of the victim or to assist the victim through the emergency room process without increasing her psychological trauma. In most cases, the social worker's function begins after the physical examination. There are already many good examination models for rape victims (Enos, 1970). It is the problem of rape's emotional aftermath which social workers' major contribution should be directed toward in terms of direct service.

THE EMOTIONAL AFTERMATH

As the visibility of rape increases (there have been two national TV shows this year on rape and many articles in women's magazines), female citizens believe that they can no longer realistically expect to be safe in public or private space. For many women there is a growing sense that our social order is breaking down. At the same time, it has been made clear to actual rape victims and to potential ones as well that it is their responsibility to protect themselves since neither law enforcement agencies nor passers-by can or will help.

Due to the personal nature of rape and its increased frequency there is a dramatic focus for the fear and anger of women. As a result of the rape experience, the victim is in a position to question her basic assumptions about herself, about others, and about her social space. Most women, as do all of us, assume the environment renders them invulnerable and that most people can be trusted; indeed, these assumptions are necessary in order to carry out one's tasks with psychological ease. One of the primary reactions to rape is for the victim to begin to display an attitude of mistrust in male-female relationships. Bart's study (1975) of 1,070 victims revealed that 50 per cent developed mistrust as the major symptom following rape; Medea and Thompson (1974) reported this symptom in 27 per cent of their cases.

Other emotional and social reactions to rape consist of an attitude of suspicion towards situations and places that others find neutral or innocuous, increased motor activity characterized by moving away from one's home to the suburbs or to a rural area, vacation, unexplained visitation to parents or relatives, a period of sleeplessness with nightmares, loss of appetite, as well as a wide variety of fears, such as fear of being alone, fear of the outdoors, fear of elevators and parking lots, fear of crowds, and fear that one is being followed (Burgess, 1974). Victims may suddenly stop dressing attractively, go through safety rituals, sleep with the lights on, stop their social life, go to places in groups only, or even begin carrying weapons.

Victims report loss of self-respect, independence, fear of males and hostility toward them. Bart's study (1974) reported 16 per cent became depressed and suicidal, while Medea and Thompson (1975) reported these symptoms in 7 per cent of their cases. Most of these symptoms were short-lived and with only moderate dysfunctions which were correctable through rapid crisis intervention tactics by professionals or friends and relatives in the victim's support system network.

Studies have indicated that some victims do not report any immediate aftereffects of the rape incident and that most women are capable of outliving the trauma (Bart, 1974—20%; Burgess & Holmstrom 1974—14%). One of the beneficial effects of the rape for some consisted in their learning self-defense, self-assertion and rugged individualism, and a realistic awareness of the environment. Data on the effect of age are contradictory. Bart (1974) reported that the child and adolescent were most traumatized and Peters (1975) that they are the least traumatized.

All post-rape symptoms were more severe and dysfunctional if there was an intimate relationship established with the rapist before the event and/or a great deal of physical violence was employed during the offense, and in the cases where gang rape occurred. Further compounding of the trauma occurs if the victim is required to repeat the circumstances of the offense several times before police, hospital and court staffs, and has her sexual reputation attacked by authorities and/or if she has a history of past mental or social difficulties.

PROFESSIONALS' ROLES

Since the victim must now begin to maintain a chronic level of suspicion to avoid future rape, she must use up a high degree of the psychic energy ordinarily used in normal life tasks. This loss may have to be made up by others significant in her environment. How much of this suspicion has real survival value and how much is dysfunctional can only be assessed by each victim's individual circumstances.

The victim will carry out a search for information, clues, feedback and interpretation that will help her, and those she will interact with, to reconstruct the social reality that has been ruptured. In this way others give the rape event meaning which in turn may help or hinder the victim's adjustment. The social worker may need to correct distortions here.

The primary treatment method for rape victims is crisis intervention. It was used by social workers with rape victims as early as 1966 (Fox, 1974), and since then has been employed in emergency rooms and rape crisis centers across the nation (Burgess & Holstrom, 1974a), and has recently been employed with robbery victims and others (Cohn, 1974; Burgess, 1975).

Crisis intervention is a social-work technique which aims at preventing the stabilization of nonadaptive or regressive response patterns due to the crisis experience. No effort is made to revive the past. The post crisis situation accelerates treatment processes. Negative transference is retarded and the negative feelings are worked through.

Basic assumptions for crisis intervention with victims include:

1. The offense is a crisis and disrupted her life-style sufficiently to present problems for her or for others close to her.

2. The victim should be viewed as normal before the rape, unless other information contradicts this.

3. Treatment priority is the "here and now," with ventilating time devoted to talking out the "nearness of death" feelings, and offering an opportunity to experience a warm human encounter through which the assortment of feelings can be recognized.

4. Aggressive intervention is taken with contacts in person or by phone or letter as soon as possible after the rape, toward acute management of the environment.

Details and styles of crisis intervention techniques are highly adaptable to various problems, and effectiveness as a social work method is well established. Crisis intervention may not be appropriate for all types of victims, particularly the ghetto or rural victim, when there is a dearth of resources.

The rape victim may pass through three phases. The *first phase* is an acute reaction characterized by feelings of shock, disbelief, followed by fear and anxiety. Much will depend on reactions to the rape on the part of the victim's spouse, relatives and friends. They should allow regression to occur with reinforcement of the gradual return to normal functioning. The *second phase* is characterized by outward adjustment with denial of affect and rationalization, and a sagging interest in seeking help. The victim may seek solitude and a self-denying style of living. Not much more than encouragement to return for help if needed can be done at this time. And lastly, the *third phase* consists of integration of the experience in such a way that the victim can handle reality. If this phase extends beyond 4 to 6 weeks, referral to a therapist may be indicated. Just the knowledge that help is available if needed is sometimes all that is required from both professionals and friends.

Another area in which social workers can be of great value to the rape victim occurs when the victim decides to prosecute her assailant and to testify in open court. Today, more women feel a civic responsibility to the potential pool of victims to rid the community of the rapist. Social-work tasks consist of preparing the victim for the testifying procedure so that trauma can be controlled. Occasionally the trauma produced by testifying is greater than the rape itself. Social workers need to have a knowledge of court processes and the adversary nature of trials, along with knowledge of styles of victim interrogation on the witness stand.

They should be familiar with the series of often embarrassing questions that will be put to the victim in an abrasive and unnerving fashion (Bailey & Rothblatt, 1973). Trauma can thus be reduced through pretrial role-playing and behavioral rehearsal technique.

RAPE-INDUCED SEXUAL DYSFUNCTION

The data on this aspect of rape are sparse. Masters and Johnson (1970: p. 136) report rape-based etiology in sexual dysfunction, particularly if the rape occurred in adolescence. Bart reported that 33 per cent of her sample of rape victims experienced sexual dysfunction (Bart, 1975), and Medea and Thompson (1974: p. 143) reported a 28 per cent rate of post-rape sexual dysfunction, but did not indicate the length of time the dysfunction persisted. Russell's intensive study of 15 victims indicated that some return to normal sexual response rapidly (Russell, 1975). Occasionally, the husband or lover of the victim may be the first to seek out professional help for their marriage problems when his own efforts to handle the problem have failed. The role of the male in rape counseling or post-rape adjustment has received only scant attention (Gregg, 1975). Treatment success here depends greatly upon the couple's previous sex education, previous sexual responses and their adequacy, husband/lover's reaction to the rape incident and how it affects their view of each other, and to what extent the couple's pre-rape sexual responses resemble the rape incident, particularly if coerced fellatio is involved. Marked clinical effort by the social worker should be directed to degeneralization of fear of all men and all sex response to its appropriate and proper boundaries. The standard methods of sexual therapy can be employed if the sex dysfunction persists beyond a few months, ideally with a team of female and male co-therapists if resources allow (Hoxworth, 1973).

REQUIRED SKILL AREAS

Needed social action, provision and service for the rape problem are not very much different from any other social problem. The problem of rape must compete with other social problems for resources, time, interest and attention, and it may be more productive in the long run to more democratically distribute skills to handle the problem among all existing related agencies, rather than in special rape crisis centers. The skills required are:

1. Community organization planning; coordination and development of all services, programs and policy related to the rape victim.

2. Policy analysis of law, statute, and institutional or agency practice, including all points of contact the victim makes, with political action toward appropriate amending and change.

3. Massive educational efforts in school, church and family toward reducing sexism and the use of violence in sexual relationships. This includes sex education in schools, assertive training for women, consciousness-raising men's groups, and Men against Rape groups.

4. Developing and employing rape crisis techniques, the use of paraprofessionals and volunteers, the development of outreach technique, more effective use of male and female counselors, and advocates who can steer the victims through the victimization follow-up as constructively as possible.

5. More research on causes and control of rape, with the best methods of intervention, and developing ways of generating money for grant research.

6. Development of effective treatment methods for rapists, including the use of women as therapists for rapists.

7. We need skill in developing and implementing massive sex education programs for men and women in schools, jails, prisons, and mental hospitals, with their related agencies.

REFERENCES AND RECOMMENDED READINGS

BAILEY, F., and H. ROTHBLATT. *Crimes of Violence: Rape.* New York: Lawyers Cooperative Publishing Company, 1973.

BART, P. "Rape Doesn't End in a Kiss," *Viva*, Vol. 2, No. 9 (1975).

BURGESS, A., and L. HOLMSTROM. "Rape Trauma Syndrome," *America Journal of Psychiatry*, Vol. 139, No. 9 (1974).

————. *Rape: Victims of Crisis.* Bowie, Maryland: Prentice-Hall, 1974a.

BURTON, L. *Vulnerable Children.* New York: Schocken Books, 1968, pp. 87–161.

COHN, Y. "Crisis Intervention and the Robbery Victim." In *Victimology: A New Focus*, Vol. 2 (1974). A Burgess. "Family Reaction to Homicide," *American Journal of Orthopsychiatry*, Vol. 45, No. 3, (1975), pp. 391–398.

ENOS, W., *et al.* "The Medical Examination of Cases of Rape." In L. Schultz, *op. cit.*, pp. 221–231. J. Massey, *et al.* "Management of the Sexually Assaulted Female." *Obstetrics and Gynecology*, Vol. 38 (1971), pp. 29–36. American College of Obstetrics and Gynecology. *Suspected Rape*, 1970.

Federal Bureau of Investigation. *1972 Uniform Crime Report*, Washington, D.C., 1973.

FEIGAN, G. "Morbidity Caused by Anal Intercourse," *Medical Aspects of Human Sexuality*, June 1974, pp. 177–186. J. Olsen. *The Man With the Candy.* New York: Simon and Schuster, 1974. A. Scacco. "Rape in Prison." Charles C. Thomas. Springfield, Ill., 1975.

FOX, S., and D. SCHERL. "Crisis Intervention with Rape Victims." In L. Schultz, *op. cit.*

GAGNON, H. "Female Child Victims of Sexual Offenses," *Social Problems*, Vol. 13, (1965).

GLASER, DANIEL. "Strategic Criminal Justice Planning," N.I.M.H. GPO, 1975, p. 157.

GREENLEY, J., and D. RICE. "Female Hitchhiking: Strain, Control and Subcultural Approaches," *Sociological Focus*, Vol. 7, No. 1 (1973/74), pp. 81–100.

GREGG, B. "The Use of the Male in Rape Crisis Counseling" Mimeographed. School of Social Work, West Virginia University, 1975.

HAYMAN, C., et al. "Rape in the District of Columbia," *American Journal of Obstetrics and Gynecology*, Vol. 113, No. 1 (1972).

HOXWORTH, D. "A Case Presentation of the Treatment of Dyspareienia," *Clinical Social Work Journal*, Vol. 1 (1973), pp. 251–256.

KINSEY, A. *Sexual Behavior in the Human Female*. New York: Pocket Books, 1953.

LIBAI, D. "The Protection of the Child Victim of a Sexual Offense in the Criminal Justice System." In L. Schultz, *Rape Victimology*, Springfield, Illinois: Charles C Thomas, Publishers, 1975.

MASTERS, W., and V. JOHNSON. *Human Sexual Inadequacy*. Boston: Little Brown and Company, 1970. W. Hartman and M. Fithian, *Treatment of Sexual Dysfunction*, Long Beach, California: Center for Marital and Sexual Studies, 1972, p. 136.

MEDEA, A., and K. THOMPSON. *Against Rape*. New York: Farrar, Straus and Giroux, 1974.

PETERS, J. "The Philadelphia Rape Study." In I. Drapkin and E. Viano, *Victimology*, Vol. 3. Lexington, Massachusetts: D. C. Heath and Company, 1975.

RUSSELL, D. *The Politics of Rape*. New York: Stein and Day, 1975.

SCHULTZ, L. "The Social Worker and the Treatment of the Sex Victim." In *Human Sexuality and Social Work*, edited by H. Gochros and L. Schultz. New York: Association Press, 1972.

SGROI, S. "Sexual Molestation of Children," *Children Today*, Vol. 4, No. 3 (1975), pp. 19–21, 44.

SHIPMAN, G. "The Psychodynamics of Sex Education," *The Family Coordinator*, Vol. 17, No. 1 (1968), pp. 3-12.

SORENSON, R. *Adolescent Sexuality and Contemporary America*. New York: World Books, 1972, p. 105.

ADDITIONAL RECOMMENDED READINGS

For Children

BEIGAL, H. "Children Who Seduce Adults," *Sexology*, Vol. 40, No. 7 (1974), pp. 30–34.

HOGAN, W. "Brief Guide to Office Counseling: The Raped Child," *Medical Aspects of Human Sexuality*, Vol. 8, No. 11 (1974), pp. 129–130.

MC CAGHY, C. "Child Molesting," *Sexual Behavior*, Vol. 1, No. 5 (August 1971), pp. 16–24.

TEN BENSEL, R. *Trauma: Clinical and Biological Aspects.* New York: Plenum Medical Books, 1975, pp. 249–272.

TRAINER, R. *The Lolita Complex.* New York: Citadel Press, 1966.

YORUKOGLY, A., and J. KEMPH. "Children Not Severely Damaged by Incest with Parent," *Journal of the American Academy of Child Psychiatry,* Vol. 5 (1966), pp. 111–124.

For Adults

BAUR, R., and J. STEIN. "Sex Counseling on Campus," *American Journal of Orthopsychiatry,* Vol. 43 (1973), pp. 824–836.

BROWNMILLER, S. *Against Our Will.* New York: Simon and Schuster, 1975.

BURGESS, A., and L. HOLMSTRON. *Rape: Victims of Crisis.* Bowie, Maryland: Prentice Hall, 1974.

CRUM, R. "Counseling Rape Victims," *Journal of Pastoral Care,* Vol. 28, No. 2 (1974), pp. 112–121.

RUSSELL, D. *The Politics of Rape.* New York: Stein and Day, 1975.

SCHULTZ, L. *Rape Victimology.* Springfield, Illinois: Charles C Thomas, Publishers, 1975.

IV.
THE
HOMOSEXUALLY
ORIENTED

It may well be that the homosexually oriented will, in some ways, become the blacks of the 1970's. Their problems have been ignored or misunderstood and their rights denied for too long. They are substantial in number: an estimated eight million men and women are exclusively homosexual, and untold millions live in the twilight zone between exclusive heterosexuality and exclusive homosexuality. As a group only a relatively small number are noticeably different in appearance or behavior from those who are, to a greater or lesser extent, "straight." The vast majority remain invisible, preferring to keep their homosexual wishes and/or behavior unknown to others in their environment.

It is this very invisibility which creates many of the problems of the homosexually oriented. Few people who are black, blind, or aged have to tell others of their minority status—it is obvious. But the homosexually oriented person almost always has the choice of appearing straight simply by his silence (we tend to assume that people who don't say they are gay are straight) or confessing his/her deviant status, and subjecting himself or herself to the possibly unpleasant consequences of such a revelation. If the homosexually oriented person decides that his or her integrity demands that the revelation be made, then a series of questions present themselves: who to tell (parents, straight friends, neighbors, employers, *brothers and sisters, and so on)? when and in what manner? How, too, should he/she handle any disgust, stereotype, hostility, bias, or rejection that might be encountered?*

Even should gays seek professional help, for whatever reason, they cannot necessarily anticipate a positive response. Many in the helping professions—including psychotherapists, physicians and the clergy— approach the homosexually oriented person with the goal of "conversion." That is, regardless of the nature of the presenting problem, the helper wants the person to change their sexual orientation to heterosexuality. Whether or not such a change is therapeutically probable, the fact remains that many, if not most, homosexually oriented adults do not choose to switch, and resent this bias on the part of the counselor. They also resent the still prevalent idea that homosexuality is, per se, a sickness, an idea repeatedly refuted by studies of the general adjustment and social functioning of overtly gay men and women.

The situation is changing, however, partly as a result of society's growing acceptance of diverse life-styles and partly from the efforts of the often-militant gay organizations as well as overtly gay individuals who are providing models to other, hidden gays. In the last few years, Merle Miller, a well-known journalist who had previously hidden his gay orientation, revealed his agony in a New York Times *article and subsequently in his book* On Being Different; *recently Laura Hobson presented a fictionalized account of her and her husband's reaction and ultimate acceptance of their son's homosexuality in* Consenting Adult. *As this is being written, a divorced lesbian is fighting for her right to maintain custody of her son, while Leonard Matlovich, a U.S. Air Force sergeant with a Bronze Star is insisting on his right to stay in the service despite his homosexuality. Perhaps most significant, Elaine Noble was elected to the Massachusetts State Legislature despite (or, to some extent, because of?) her open homosexual orientation.*

At the same time, some significant changes are occurring in the more oppressive sanctions against homosexuals. The governor of Pennsylvania has championed the rights of gays to equal opportunities in state employment. The Federal civil service has similarly banned discrimination in hiring. A growing number of states have decriminalized homosexual behavior. Even organized religion shows evidence of a changing stance on homosexuality: the Vatican has recently suggested "understanding" of "incurable" (sic) homosexuals, while the Methodist Church now welcomes the openly gay into membership.

But major problems still exist. The chapters in this section explore many of these problems still confronting homosexually oriented women and men, and offer some possible remedies. Huggins and Forrester, who have pioneered in the development of a community education and ser-

vice program for sexual minorities called Personal Adjustment Center (PERSAD Inc., Pittsburgh, Pa.) discuss some of the common problems encountered by homosexually oriented men.

Two points of view are presented on the problems of lesbians. Brown vigorously attacks the oppression and some broad social problems related to lesbians, while Goodman addresses some of the common individual problems encountered by these women. Finally, Kelly presents his study of an oppressed minority within an oppressed minority: the aging gay male. His findings challenge many of the misconceptions about this group, including the old adage that "no one loves you when you're old and gay!"

CHAPTER 9

THE
GAY
MALE

James Huggins and Randal G. Forrester

Our society has some rather strong attitudes regarding homosexuality. From the perspective of most gay men, these attitudes are, by and large, negatively skewed. Eugene E. Levitt and Albert D. Klassen, Jr., in their paper titled "Public Attitudes Toward Homosexuality" (1974), review their findings based on interviews with a nationwide probability sample of 3,018 American adults during 1970 and find that the public holds these fundamental beliefs about the causes, cures, and nature of homosexuality:

— homosexuals act like the opposite sex (68.8%),
— homosexuality is a sickness that can be cured (61.9%),
— homosexuals have unusually strong sex drives (58.5%),
— homosexuals are afraid of the opposite sex (55.7%),
— young homosexuals become that way because of older homosexuals (42.5%). (This is the most popular of four causational beliefs surveyed, including inheritance, lack of attraction to the opposite sex, and parental rearing.)

Such negative attitudes are encountered at all levels of our society. In the spring of 1976, for example, the United States Supreme Court upheld a state's right to legislate against homosexual expression. Our society then uses these beliefs as the foundation for a series of attitudes as follows:

— sex acts between same-sex persons are wrong if they don't have a special affection for each other (86.1%),

— homosexuality is obscene and vulgar (83.8%),

—sex acts between same-sex persons are wrong even if they love each other (78.6%),

— homosexuals are dangerous as teachers or youth leaders because they try to get sexually involved with children (73.5%),

— homosexuals try to play sexually with children if they cannot get an adult partner (71.1%),

— homosexuals are a high security risk for government jobs (58.9%).

The public then endorses several forms of social sanctioning in an attempt to inhibit or extinguish the perceived danger and detriment to the society. These sanctions include:

— they wouldn't associate with gays if they could help it (80.9%),

— homosexuals should not be allowed to dance with each other in public places (72.9%),

— homosexuals should not be regarded as any other group (52.3%),

— homosexuals should be denied employment as

(a) court judges (77.2%)

(b) schoolteachers (76.9%)

(c) ministers (76.6%)

(d) medical doctors (67.7%)

(e) government officials (67.4%),

— homosexuals should be permitted employment as

(a) florists (86.8%)

(b) musicians (85.2%)

(c) artists (84.5%)

(d) beauticians (71.1%).

It is these attitudes and the lack of knowledge which encourages their continuation that are the fundamental reasons for the problems of homosexual men.

The process is one of (a) first holding certain beliefs to be true and factual, (b) establishing certain attitudes based on those perceived facts which, in this case, lead to a perception of danger, and then (c) initiating action to protect the society from the perceived danger. It is obvious that if the first set of beliefs held to be facts are not actually factual, then the resultant perceived danger and sanctions against that danger are in reality based on misconceptions.

Since our purpose is to review some of the problems faced by gay men and some possible solutions to those problems, we will not examine the mythology and fact of sexual/social theory. Suffice it to say that a review of the contemporary literature shows that most gay men do not act like the opposite sex, that homosexuality is not a sickness for which there is a cure, that gay men do not have unusually strong sex drives, that most gay men are not afraid of the opposite sex, that homosexuality is not caused by the seduction of an older gay man, and that most gay men have absolutely no interest in sexual contact with young boys.

Because the society believes these to be true, however, gay men do have to cope with society's sanctioning systems. Let us now examine a few of these systems in order to better understand the problems with which gay men must cope.

SOCIAL SANCTIONING SYSTEMS

One of the most overt of these sanctioning systems is the legislative/ judicial system. We might call it the governmental sanctioning system, since it involves all three branches of government: the legislature (which writes and passes the law), the executive (which endorses the law), and the judicial branch (which enforces the law).

Some of the most significant of the legal sanctions are the sodomy laws. These laws prohibit oral and/or anal intercourse and are mainly classified as misdemeanors or felonies. Penalties most often include a stiff fine and/or a significant jail term. While the language of these laws does not specifically refer to homosexuality, in application heterosexuals are generally exempted from their enforcement (with the possible exception of heterosexual prostitution). Some states specifically exempt married persons from the law's jurisdiction. Since gay marriages are clearly not legal in any state, gay relationships are thus never exempted.

Obviously, it is difficult to enforce the sodomy laws when sodomy is committed by consenting adults in the privacy of their home. However, many homosexual men are arrested for solicitation to commit sodomy. The solicitation law makes it a crime to ask someone to commit sodomy. Using the solicitation law, plainclothes police can frequent a gay cruising area, wait to be solicited and then arrest the solicitor. The judicial system has been so unprotective of the rights of homosexuals that an invitation from one man to another to some home for a drink has sometimes been regarded as a solicitation to commit sodomy. Often the penalty for solicitation is as great as the penalty for sodomy.

While some states have repealed their sodomy laws (and consequently, the solicitation-to-commit-sodomy laws), police and courts still find ways to harass gay men. Laws against lewd behavior, disturbing the peace, disorderly conduct and even loitering are used for harassment purposes. Granted, the penalties are rarely as severe as for sodomy, but the process of arrest and the ensuing court procedure is always unpleasant.

These laws and the use made of them constitute an attempt to define what is permissible sexual behavior between consenting adults. The effect is to criminalize a whole class of people. While the "crimes" are victimless, the law makes the "criminal" the victim.

Having criminalized gay men, the law then uses that criminal status in order to justify the denial of civil rights. Though the area of civil rights protection for homosexual persons is presently in a state of fairly rapid change, at this writing neither the Federal Government nor any state has a civil rights act which protects them. (A number of local municipalities have passed such acts.) Consequently, gay men can be discriminated against in a number of ways. They can be denied employment, housing and public accommodation. They can be denied credit and insurance because they are considered to be a "moral risk." As previously noted, they are denied the right to marry, and consequently to such benefits of marriage as tax benefits, joint insurance policies, mutual property and rights of a surviving spouse—for example, the right to control the remains of a deceased spouse and inheritance rights. Gay men are usually prevented from adopting children and are often denied the custody of their natural children. Even visitation rights are sometimes denied. Homosexuals can be prevented from entering the armed services and if their sexual orientation is discovered while in the service they can be dishonorably discharged. They can be prevented from emigrating to the United States, can be denied U.S. citizenship and can be deported. The whole sanctioning system is designed to eliminate, or at least suppress, homosexuality from our society through the use of the legislative/judicial system.

In addition to the "criminal" label, our society also has applied the "sick" label. This has been accomplished through the psychiatric/mental health system. Though this situation has changed somewhat in the past few years, what occurred before the American Psychiatric Association Diagnostic Nomenclature change bears review. In essence, the processes that were operating which resulted in homosexuality being defined as mental illness were processes that bore no relationship to scientific knowledge. Thomas S. Szasz, M.D., in his book *The Manufacture of Madness*, traces the development of the "homosexuality as sick" label from the earlier "homosexuality as witchery" label which preceded it. Szasz sees this as directly related to the general social trend away from theology and toward science in the late eighteenth and early nineteenth centuries. Having established the "sickness" label, the scientific community did not really begin to require a significant defense of that label until the twentieth century (Szasz, 1970).

What was the methodology that psychiatric researchers used to "prove" homosexuality was, in fact, a mental illness? They proceeded to gain research data from homosexuals who were in mental institutions and in psychiatric practice. These findings were then generalized to the entire gay population. If a researcher wanted to discover the nature of heterosexuality and attempted to do so through research using subjects who were confined to mental institutions or in private psychiatric practice, that researcher would be laughed out of the scientific community. Certainly, no one would pay any attention when he announced that he had proved that heterosexuality was a mental illness. And yet this is precisely how the sickness label was perpetuated and defended.

Finally, from 1973 to 1974 the American Psychiatric Association did attempt to correct previous errors by removing homosexuality from its Manual of Diagnostic Nomenclature on the basis of a vote by its members. Unfortunately, the damage created by the "sickness" label has not been eliminated. The public at large still views this entire minority group as sick. Many gay men perceive themselves as sick and in a self-fulfilling prophecy process, they become sick. The sickness label has been, and is, used by some legislators also as the reason for denying civil rights to homosexuals.

Mental health workers of all disciplines have been the chief reinforcers of the sickness label. They incorporated the mental illness theory into their practice and offered a cure for a disease that doesn't even exist, much like the traveling medicine peddlers of the Old West. They have reinforced stereotypic notions about gay men and engaged in the quackery of claiming expertise with little or no actual knowledge. Even though some changes have been made to correct these situations, it is still very difficult for a homosexual to obtain competent unbiased and adequate mental health service. Consequently, most of them will avoid contact with traditional therapists.

Another major social sanctioning system is that of organized religion. The history of discrimination in Western Judeo-Christian tradition is measured in millennia rather than in centuries. Suffice it to say that the roots of the discrimination seem to be based on three major historical factors: One factor was the Jewish culture's reaction to the Hellenic Greek culture in which homosexual love was prized as the expression of Eros, or manly love. While the Greek man was expected to have a wife and produce children, he was also expected to have a male lover. The second major factor was the Jewish culture's reaction to the Canaanite practice of *quedishim*, or homosexual temple prostitution. The practice is essentially one in which the Canaanite man had sexual relations with the temple priest in order to gain holy blessings. Both the Greek and Canaanite practices were regarded as idolatry by the Jewish religious fathers. The third major factor was the ancient Jewish and early Christian view that sex for any purpose other than procreation is sinful. These factors affected the attitudes of the writers of the Old and New Testaments of the Bible and continue to haunt us to the present day.

Most Western religions continue to see homosexuality as sinful. The options most often given to a gay man by the Church is either to reverse his sexual orientation and become heterosexual or to be a celibate homosexual. Clearly, few heterosexuals would accept either of these options if heterosexuality were seen as sinful. Likewise, few gay persons can accept these options, and most are forced either to continue viewing themselves as sinners, to compromise their acceptance of church doctrine, to leave the church entirely or to start a church of their own.

Through these three major sanctioning systems, our society labels homosexuals as criminal, sick and sinful. In the past it has used the full power of its institutional systems in an attempt to eradicate homosexuality. Though this attempt failed, the effects on gay men are nevertheless present.

COMMON PROBLEMS AFFECTING GAY MEN

Aside from the problems which relate directly to the three major social sanctioning systems, there are also a number of problems which result from the composite effect of these systems. One of the common problems is the deciphering of one's own sexual identity. Because our society has such right and wrong, good and evil, healthy and sick attitudes about sexual orientation, people are viewed as either heterosexual or homosexual. The fact that most studies show that every person has both some heterosexual and homosexual potential does not affect society's perception. The fact that over one-third of the men in this country have had at least one incidental adult homosexual experience—Kinsey (1948) reports 37 per cent—does not seem to alter this perception. For the gay man who may find himself occasionally sexually attracted to a woman or who may have had from incidental to considerable overt heterosexual experience, this either/or system is extremely confusing. Even though his major preference is homosexual, the occasional heterosexual experience keeps alive the hope that somehow his homosexuality is a passing phase and that someday he will be "normal." Since sexual preference does not change drastically in adult life, this is a cruel trick which is often reinforced by the mental health sanctioning system.

The difficulty in deciphering sexual identity is often further complicated by the stereotypes of what a gay man is supposed to be. Since most gay men do not fit these stereotypes, many a homosexual initially doubts his sexual preference. He may wonder, "How can I be homosexual if I'm not limp wristed, lisping or effeminate?" or he may wonder, "Do I have to become like the stereotype in order to get along in the gay world?" He may often suffer from considerable guilt, shame and feelings that he is not like everyone else. This is often the most isolated and loneliest time in a homosexual's life.

In order to end this feeling of isolation, this feeling that he is truly alone in his homosexual feelings, the homosexual person must make some attempt to share those feelings with other people. But in order to do this he must make decisions about how and when and with whom to share.

What at first might seem to be a real advantage is the fact that the great majority of gay men are able to hide their sexuality from society's view. In a society which assumes that everyone is heterosexual unless identified otherwise, passing as heterosexual is rather easy. All a man has to do is to allow people to assume that he's straight. Unfortunately, allowing this assumption also means that he must give up the opportunity to share a significant part of his life with those people he cares about.

How honest he will be about his homosexuality affects every major decision that he must make about his life. Where will he live? in a large city where there are more gay people or in a small town? Where will he work? Will he choose a job where he can be freer about his sexuality or one in which he must be very careful that his sexual orientation is not discovered? Will he tell his parents and friends and risk rejection and loss of their love? Will he lead a double life, being honest with some people and dishonest with others? Will he choose to be open and honest about his sexuality with everyone, thus enjoying the freedom of personal honesty but risking the oppression of society? These and many other decisions will not be easy to make, but are necessary for the successful adjustment of a homosexual to a homophobic society.

If a gay man decides to "come out" to his parents, usually considerable stress is created in the family relationship. A look at typical reactions and feelings of parents will demonstrate some of these stresses.

Our society tends to blame parents, especially mothers, for the homosexuality of their sons, since it has been assumed that parents have the strongest influence upon the sexual development of their offspring. Since homosexuality is generally not seen as valuable in our society, parents may experience a great deal of guilt and shame because of their son's sexual orientation.

Parents usually expect that their children will grow up, get married and eventually have children of their own. They may be quite disappointed when they learn that their son will not father any children.

If there are other children in the family, the parents may be concerned that they will somehow be "contaminated" by the gay son; this is especially true if there are younger sons in the family. Parents will often try to isolate their gay son. This may take a mild form such as asking their son not to tell the other children or it may take a more extreme form such as asking him to leave the home.

If siblings know about their brother's sexual orientation, they may be afraid that they too will be gay, since they have the same parents and have been raised in the same environment.

Parents are subject to the same cultural conditionings as the rest of society. They may have stereotypic expectations about how their son will act. They may stop treating him as they always have and begin to treat him as a "homosexual." They may worry about what other people will think about the fact that their son is gay. Will their friends, neighbors and extended family accept their son? Decisions must be made about who outside the immediate family should know.

Also, the parents may have an honest concern about the mental health of their son and wonder whether it is possible for him to be happy leading a homosexual life-style. If they believe that he cannot be happy, much of their disapproval may stem from this belief.

There may be considerable concern about how to integrate their son and his friends or lover (spouse) into the family system. Can the family accept their son's lover in the same way they would have accepted his wife?

In telling his parents, a gay man risks rejection and loss of their love. It is not unusual for parents to demand that a psychiatric "cure" be sought, to withdraw financial support from their son, or even to disown him. Fortunately, it is also not unusual for families to make an honest attempt to understand and be supportive of their homosexual son.

Many of these same risks are involved in "coming out" to friends. Friends, like family, have been culturalized to believe the stereotypes about gay men, and consequently have stereotypic expectations of them. If the friend is a man, he may worry about the motivation of his gay friend. He may wonder if his gay friend is sexually attracted to him, and may not be sure how to deal with it if he is. He may wonder if his gay friend thinks *he's* gay; he may find himself questioning his own sexual orientation. He may be frightened that others will think he is gay because he has a friend who is gay. Unfortunately, this friend may begin to see his gay friend as a totally different person.

If the friend is a woman, she may have some romantic or preromantic ideas crushed. She may have difficulty redefining the relationship. If she sees her friend's homosexuality as an abnormality to be cured, she may attempt to seduce him so that she can teach him how much better heterosexuality is. If she succeeds in the seduction, but finds that her friend still prefers same-sex partners, her pride may be hurt; she may feel that she has failed as a woman.

Fortunately, friends of both sexes often have no difficulty in accepting their friend's sexual orientation. Their open support can be of great value to their friend.

The motivation of a gay man to tell his family and friends comes from a desire to share a portion of his life previously hidden from them. He can end his burdensome double life-style through his demonstration of trust in them. Obviously, he must trust that the answer will be Yes when he asks, "Will you still love me when you find out that I am gay?"

This question looms heavily on a gay man when he is heterosexually married. There are no adequate statistics of the number of gay persons who are heterosexually married. Suffice it to say that some homosexuals are married and consequently must deal with the problems that result from their choice. If his wife does not already know, the homosexual man must decide whether or not to tell her that he is gay. He may want to remain married and fears that his wife will divorce him if she learns of his sexual orientation. As with other close relationships, he risks possible rejection, loss of love, and the possibility of being depersonalized. For these reasons, he may choose not to tell his wife. If this is his choice, he then must deal with his homosexual feelings without her knowledge and possible understanding and support. He may choose to have extramarital homosexual contact. He may attempt to keep these relationships casual so that they do not interfere with his primary marital relationship. If, however, he becomes more than casually involved, then he is faced with the difficult task of balancing his time between the two relationships in such a way so as not to arouse the suspicions of his wife. This is an extremely difficult task and he may well find himself finally forced to make a choice between the two relationships.

Some wives know of their husband's homosexuality when they get married or learn of it soon after they are married. Many wives experience difficulty in adjusting to that knowledge. A wife may feel that she needs to compete for her husband's affection. While she may feel comfortable about her attractiveness in relation to other women, she may doubt her husband's attraction to her as compared to men. She may wonder, "If I were only more attractive or if I were a better wife, would he be more attracted to me?" As a corollary of this, a gay man who is married may feel guilty and ashamed about his sexual orientation. He may want desperately to be heterosexual, and he may feel that he is inadequate as a husband.

Some couples who openly deal with the husband's homosexuality attempt to integrate both life-styles into their relationship. They may choose to contract with each other for an "open marriage" with each partner free to have relationships with other people. Other couples may choose to be sexually faithful to each other and treat the husband's homosexual attractions as they would if he were heterosexual and attracted to other women. However they choose to structure their relationship, both partners must deal with the fears and frustrations concerning their different sexual orientations.

When the couple have a child, they may be concerned about the effect that the father's homosexuality will have on the child. Will the child be gay because his father is? Should the child be told about his father's homosexuality? How will he feel about it? What will other people think about the child of a gay father? Both partners may be confused and in conflict about these questions and this may create added stress in their relationship.

There is a prevalent stereotype that homosexuals cannot form lasting intimate relationships. The stereotype is so strongly entrenched that a great many gay men also believe it. Since there are no adequate statistics to debunk the stereotype, it is difficult to empirically prove that it is unfounded. However, the fact is that a significant number of gay men do form lasting intimate relationships. It is perhaps because of the added difficulties which plague gay marriages that they seem insurmountably difficult.

There are few, if any, cultural sanctions for a gay marriage. If we look at a typical heterosexual relationship, perhaps the lack of cultural sanctions will be clearer. A heterosexual marriage is endorsed, supported and sanctioned by family, friends, the church, the state, and by the community at large. A gay marriage usually has little or none of these endorsements, supports or sanctions. Instead, most homosexual men must hide their relationship with another man. They must be careful not to allow people to discover the true nature of their relationship with their "roommate." For fear of rejection, a gay couple may not tell their straight friends and their respective families about the relationship. For them, the option for a legal union with all its benefits simply does not exist.

The gay subculture may be the only place where a gay couple can get support for their relationship. Even there, however, problems may arise. The subculture mores for gay men include the expectation that they will be sexually active with a number of partners. Gay men in a one-to-one relationship are not really expected to be sexually faithful. This expectation may create many difficulties for a couple who wish to be sexually faithful. As previously mentioned, many gay men believe that lasting gay relationships do not work. If both partners believe this, they may not try very hard to make their marriage work.

Some mention needs to be made about the strengths of homosexual relationships. Since this chapter is devoted to the problems that homosexual men may face, there is little emphasis on discussing the advantages of a gay life-style for a gay man. Suffice it to say that many homosexual men are re-evaluating the whole issue of relationships and have stopped evaluating their success in heterosexual terms. They are finding that homosexual relationships can afford them the opportunity for personal growth unhampered by oppressive heterosexual sex roles or promises of monogamy.

SYSTEMATIC SOLUTIONS

Since discrimination, lack of knowledge and prejudice about homosexuality have been systematized into our society through both individuals and institutions, the solutions to these problems must also be systematized both individually and institutionally. Any other approach is purely hit or miss and will generally be ineffective. Therefore, we would like to examine four proposed systems.

1. The *learner system* is a prerequisite to the other three systems. It is the system in which both individuals and institutions examine their biases and seek answers to their questions. When they find that the answer is unknown, research is begun in order to find the answer. It is this system which puts an end to ignorance and bigotry and lays a foundation of knowledge, instead. Each individual has the responsibility for her or his own "learner system." It is quite easy for all of us to continue to relate to gay men stereotypically. But if we are concerned with change, we will begin a systematic learning or relearning process.

Much of the discomfort experienced by the family and friends of homosexual men is a result of the lack of knowledge about homosexuality and its life-styles. It thus becomes necessary for the family and friends of a gay man to seek out factual knowledge to help them deal with their acculturated stereotypes and biases. Professional mental health workers also need to seek out information. More and more unbiased research is being published and more books are being written by men who are openly homosexual. It is ludicrous for mental health practitioners to ignore this new knowledge just because it may challenge popular theories. The mental health system (which includes social agencies as well as psychiatric facilities) must begin a systematic learning process. Many of the existing mental health programs have no relevancy to gay men because they were promulgated out of the medical "sickness/cure" model. The mental health system must learn what the problems of homosexual men are so that programs can be implemented to ameliorate these problems.

Clergymen must begin to educate themselves about gay men. Several theologians have researched the origins of the concept of "homosexuality as sinful," local clergy should seek out this information and use it to help others. Commissions to study the theological and Biblical interpretations of homosexuality may need to be formed. These commissions could relate new information to the tradition of the church and help both clergy and parishioners to learn more about the religious implication of homosexuality.

Elected officials and lawmakers have a responsibility to learn more about homosexuality. Many of our laws and public policies are based upon fallacious assumptions. Government commissions may be needed to study the problems of homosexuals and to inform legislators of needed law changes.

Throughout this discussion of the learner system we have talked about the need for the acquisition of knowledge. This is impossible unless there is unbiased research about questions for which we as yet have no answers.

2. The next system to be considered is the *advocate system*, in which both individuals and institutions share the information they have gathered in the learner system and begin to advocate for change. It is this system which puts to use the attitudinal, value and knowledge changes which have come about as a result of the learner system. On an individual basis, each of us, whether we are a mental health practitioner, a member of the clergy, public official, friend or relative of a homosexual man, can begin to advocate for change on his behalf.

All of us can attempt to influence our legislators to repeal the oppressive sodomy laws and to include the phrase "sexual or affectional preference" in civil rights legislation. Positive legislators can certainly influence other legislators as well as sponsoring progressive legislation.

Mental health workers can advocate change with the mental health system, to provide programs more relevant to the needs of gay men. They can also provide consultation to professionals in other fields, to help them re-examine their beliefs and feelings about gay men.

Professionals in all fields should use their influence to affect public opinion. Institutions such as the church, mental health agencies, and the Federal Government should use their resources to disseminate information about homosexuality as widely as possible.

Professional organizations and unions can advocate the rights of homosexual employees. They can use their huge communication networks to encourage their members to examine the issues involved. They can use their power to force the institutions to change.

Clergymen can also be advocates for social change by encouraging theological changes regarding homosexuality, supporting the ordination of openly gay clergy, providing information, or even acting as an advocate, for gay parishioners.

All of us, professional and lay person alike, can advocate better sex education in the schools that will include a positive view of homosexuality. We can demand that professionals be knowledgeable about gay life-styles in order to offer an alternative to the charlatans who promise cures.

3. The third system to be considered is the *helper system*. It is within this system that both individuals and institutions provide direct help to homosexual men. It is this system that helps these men deal with their oppression. Earlier we outlined some of the problems faced by a homosexual man in our society. But where is he to go for help with these problems, especially since the very people and institutions that are supposed to be the helpers have often been the source of his problems? He may choose to seek help from his family or friends. He may seek help from the clergy. He may choose to enter therapy with a mental health professional or he may need the help of an attorney. No matter what helper he seeks out, he will need a person who is non-judgmental about his sexual orientation, a person who is so comfortable with his/her own sexuality that he/she won't be threatened by the fact that the person seeking help is gay, who is unbiased enough to treat him as an individual rather than as a stereotype, and who will help him think through his problem and allow him to make his own decisions.

Institutions, too, can be helpers. The mental health institution can set up such services as gay marriage counseling, gay assertiveness training, and gay growth groups. In more urban areas, demand might justify establishing specialized agencies. Mental health institutions can also help by hiring openly gay mental health professionals. This would allow a gay man the choice of a homosexual or straight counselor (a practice not uncommon with other minority groups) and would have the side benefit of helping the agency continue its learning process through the firsthand experience of the gay professional.

The religious institution can help by welcoming gay men into its congregation with full acceptance of their sexual orientation. Special Bible study courses might be run to help both gay and straight parishioners.

The governmental institution can help by repealing oppressive laws, enacting new civil rights legislation, establishing complaint centers, and appointing gay men as aides to legislators, judges or commissioners on regulatory boards, without bias. Grants can be made for research in the area of homosexuality.

Every person and every institution has the opportunity to be a helper; if they have dealt with the "learner system" and the "advocate system" they ought to easily adapt to the "helper system."

4. The last system is the *supporter system*, in which individuals and institutions provide support to homosexuals trying to help themselves. It is the "supporter system" which helps the gay community organize for effective social and political change and to establish services for its own use. It is this system, then, which helps to develop the gay community.

Individually, we may choose to be supportive in many different ways. We may give money to gay organizations or agencies or we may volunteer our time, our car, or perhaps our house for meetings. As a friend or a relative of a homosexual, we may choose to become actively involved in a gay rights organization or we may be personally supportive to him so that he may have the strength and freedom to carry out his own struggle.

Some mental health workers, especially social workers, have considerable skills in community organization which could be utilized by gay organizations and groups. Likewise, some clergymen may be able to provide political support for legislative changes. Positive legislators may provide considerable support and expertise, especially about how legislative bodies work and where political pressure would be most effective.

Since institutional change is one of the goals of gay liberation, workers within the institutions can provide valuable information about the best way to approach their institution and can even aid in that process.

Institutions can provide time, money and person power to the gay community to help it grow and become stronger. For example, in the Commonwealth of Pennsylvania, the governor has not only established a Commission on Sexual Minorities but also has committed his administration to the goal of ending discrimination on the basis of sexual and affectional preference. The impact of this kind of action on the strength of the gay community in the state is immeasurable.

Change also needs to come within the gay community itself. The gay community in many, if not most, areas of the country is primarily oriented around the gay bar. Additional social and recreational alternatives need to be developed. Community centers may be needed where a variety of ongoing social and recreational programs—such as rap groups, coffeehouses and sports activities—are available. Also, permanent meeting places for gay organizations need to be found. However the gay community may choose to organize and develop itself, it will need the active help of the "supporter system."

What are the solutions as here presented? The solutions are to be a learner, an advocate, a helper and a supporter. These are processes and systems that can be applied to every individual and institution in the United States. It will be only through this systematic approach that meaningful change will take place.

A NOTE ABOUT GAY WOMEN

Much of what we have said in this chapter also applies to homosexual women. We say this with caution, however, because too often in the past authors have said that they were writing about both women and men when they were, in reality, dealing only with the problems of men. We have written mostly about the problems of being a homosexual in a homophobic society from a male perspective; but we have not written about the difficulties of being female in a sexist society where gay women are oppressed both for being gay and for being female. Our comments, then, relate only to their *gay* oppression, and we leave it to women themselves, in another chapter, to discuss more fully their own problems.

REFERENCES AND RECOMMENDED READINGS

KINSEY, ALFRED C., WARDELL B. POMEROY, and CLYDE E. MARTIN. *Sexual Behavior in the Human Male*. Philadelphia: W. B. Saunders Company, 1948.

LEVITT, EUGENE E., and ALBERT D. KLASSEN, "Public Attitudes Toward Homosexuality: Part of the 1970 National Survey by the Institute for Sex Research," *Journal of Homosexuality*, Vol. 1 (Fall, 1974), pp. 29-43.

SZASZ, THOMAS S. *The Manufacture of Madness*. New York: Harper and Row, Publishers, Inc., 1970.

CHAPTER 10

THE LESBIAN WOMAN: TWO POINTS OF VIEW

THE PROBLEMS OF LESBIANS
Bernice Goodman

It is difficult to present a definitive history and cultural study of the lesbian in society because of the veil of secrecy that surrounds her. She is usually a productive, creative member of society, but generally has to zealously guard her lesbianism.

THE LESBIAN MILIEU

Prior to the Gay Movement that began in the Sixties, lesbians were invisible in their sexuality and moved through society into gay bars like dark shadows. Bars were run by the Mafia. The atmosphere was hostile. Lesbians were hustled to buy drinks and pay door fees in order to stay lonely and frozen to a bar stool, hoping desperately someone would talk first. Police raids were always a possibility. The sterile heterosexual model of male behavior (aggressive) and female behavior (passive) was expressed in the role playing of "butch" and "femme." In the larger cities, several gay bars existed and tended to be divided along class and ethnic lines. The "blazer dykes" went to the fancy high-class places which featured a piano player—a façade of elegance was the image. The lower-class bars were dark, poorly furnished, and with an atmosphere that was anxious, hostile, and depressing.

[145]

The rest of the lesbians' social life was at parties in friends' homes. Tight cliques stayed together bound by fear of loneliness and the undercurrent of self-hate because of being a lesbian, an outcast from society. In small towns and rural settings, the sense of loneliness was equaled by an environmental reality of isolation. If a lesbian was lucky enough to find a sister or gay brother, it seemed a miracle.

Many older lesbians in both urban and rural settings had a similar "coming out" experience, feeling that they were the only women in the world who loved women. This may seem an impossible assumption today, but it is the reality of women who are in their forties and fifties.

An additional cultural problem facing lesbians that homosexual men have not had to face is the general oppression of women in our society. The lesbian was particularly affected by this because a woman's only status in society depended on her relation to her man-through-marriage as a wife and mother of his children. Since lesbians in general did not fit in this format, the accepted societal sanction of *woman* was denied her.

The rich history and brilliant work of lesbian women in this country and in the world was unavailable to the young women of yesterday. Even today, this problem continues to plague the lesbian community as well as women in general. All over the country, however, lesbians are meeting, talking, loving, and recording their culture for future days so that the problem of invisibility can be eliminated.

PROBLEMS IN BEING A LESBIAN

Problems facing lesbians are both general in nature (applying to all women) and specific (applicable only to lesbians). General problems center around the oppressed position of women in the heterosexual model of human relationships. This model is supported by all the institutions of society such as religion, law, education, communication media, psychiatry, and medicine. The tenets of this model require women to be socialized in specific ways and they are expected to play preconceived roles in society. These tenets are as follows:

1. Women should be kept separate from one another and should distrust other women.

2. The only acceptable way for women to relate to each other is through men (in couples) and around the care of children.

3. Women should accept graciously the economic and institutional discrimination in society which is used to "keep them in their place."

4. Sexual relations can occur with men only and are connected to monogomy and childbearing.

5. Women have no self-sexuality and are only women when related

sexually to men. A woman is not to explore and love her body as a separate entity. She is to deny her aggressive sexual needs.

6. A woman's self is never complete and separate. She must stay "off center" and available to a man who will stabilize her.

7. Aggressive drives such as anger are to be suppressed and therefore can only be turned on herself or on other women or children.

Lesbians, together with all other women, are subject to these socializing patterns. Variations will occur, depending on individual circumstances, but the general direction and tenets of the heterosexual model of "sameness" is rampant throughout the structures of our society.

In addition to these general problems of being a woman, the lesbian has additional specific problems to face. Some of these problems create a sense of self-hate, the force of which tears many lesbians apart. But within these very problems lies strength along with the solutions. In addition, the inherent advantages of being a lesbian that are not available to other women facilitate the solution of problems.

Some of the specific problems that lesbians face are as follows:

1. The introjection of the dominant heterosexual model and its oppressive attitude about women. This is often translated into self-hate, doubt, and guilt.

2. The awareness of positive sexual and emotional feelings for women, while simultaneously feeling the hostility and disaproval of society toward these feelings.

3. The lack of institutionalized positive role models as lesbians in society.

4. The stereotyping by society: lesbians, according to such stereotypes, are ugly, mannish, just need a good man, can't get a man so must settle for a woman, queer, sick, and so on.

5. A paucity of places (other than the Mafia bars) in which to meet and socialize with other lesbians.

6. Sexual dysfunctioning related to fear and shame about their own bodies, and therefore bodies of other women. Taboos about masturbation can be inhibiting (and may be a basic factor in homophobia).

7. The fact that lesbians differ widely regarding class, culture, race and ethnicity, and therefore do not have a common base for relationships with each other. Society has classified lesbians as a specific entity. This is not true and the only common base is the oppression by society.

8. Negative impact on growth of self is related to the fact that many lesbians pass as "straight" women in our society. The energy spent in such deception is not available to the lesbian for use in a positive nurturing of herself; hence the longer a lesbian "passes," the more damaging and corrosive it is to her feeling of being a self-actualized person.

9. Isolation from self and from other lesbians and constantly being

defined by outside forces alienates the lesbian from herself and tends to immobilize and infantilize her.

10. The lack of a positive body image interferes with full expression of eroticism, sensuality and sexuality.

These problems are extensive and pervasive. When lesbians of all persuasions are free to participate fully in society, we will have a more adequate picture of the dimensions of their life-style.

POSSIBLE SOLUTION TO THE PROBLEMS

As stated earlier, many of the solutions are rooted in the problems as presented. The alienation and "difference" of the lesbian is her greatest asset and a distinct advantage. Because of her different sexual orientation and the strong feeling generated by this, the lesbian has a more vested interest in protesting society's definition of her. She does not look to men for sexual satisfaction and therefore does not have to pretend she likes being oppressed or enjoys her unequal status as a way of maintaining contact with men. Freed from her guilt of not being normal or a "real woman" she can redirect her anger and mobilize all her energy toward changing the prejudices of society that allow her to be discriminated against at all levels of societal interaction. Self-love, instead of self-hate, can change the flow of energy toward resolution of problems rather than perpetuating the feeling of being helpless, a victim, and needing a man to take care of her. Within this ambiance of self-love, and in the celebration of being a lesbian, the solution of all problems feels possible.

More specific suggestions to enable lesbians to move toward solutions of problems are as follows:

PERSONAL GROUP EXPERIENCES

Participation in small groups where an intensive sense of self-worth is experienced is a vital first step to be taken. The group form could range from a consciousness-raising experience to a therapy interaction. Many lesbians can engage in several modes of group self-expression simultaneously. The helping professions should be more active in establishing, supporting, and leading such groups.

COMING OUT

This process of telling one's parents, friends and children about one's lesbianism is the most difficult, most important, and most freeing experience. The ability to "come out," to be self-defined as the first step to self-actualization is an exhilarating process. To own one's total identity, including one's sexuality, regardless of what others may feel or how they respond, is to be truly free. This coming-out process is not necessary for heterosexuals and thus many never connect with their inner selves as different from everyone else. The lesbian, in coming out, is forced to confront herself and others in order to be herself. This experience releases great sources of emotional and psychic power within the lesbian woman, and here, too, social workers, psychologists, and other professionals could be more helpful in both making the decision to come out, and in dealing with the problems that may occur.

AFFILIATION WITH INSTITUTIONAL GROUPS IN SOCIETY

Lesbians can (and many do) participate in movements and political groups such as the Gay Academic Union, National Gay Task Force, Lesbian Feminist Liberation, National Association of Women, Older Women's Liberation, Lesbian Mothers' Union, and the regular political machinery of society. In addition, many people are working toward getting a truly representative picture of gay people on radio, television, and the communication media in general. This is a specific task of the gay media groups. Lesbians can participate in local activities of all these groups. Again, the helping professions should do more to promote and engage in such activities.

RELATIONSHIPS WITH LOVERS

Because society has not institutionalized the lesbian relationship, the right to do this has been left to those involved in the relationship. This puts great pressure on the individual to explore her own needs and levels of emotional capacities in relating to another woman or women. The heterosexual model of monogamy was the first stance of many lesbians. As lesbians are freeing themselves from the tyranny of this attitude, other forms of relationships are emerging, with some women developing open relationships and series of relationships, primary and secondary, that may meet more of the natural needs of women.

CREATION OF A LESBIAN COMMUNITY

In order to facilitate the individual growth of each lesbian, a nurturing connection with other lesbians is essential. This has been done through organizations, coffeehouses, and social contacts. Also needed are development of community priorities and the establishment of positive programs that all lesbians can relate to and work for. For example, we need to work closely with lesbian mothers and their children, as well as with gay fathers, in order to nurture a future generation free of oppressive heterosexual values. These are our children and they should be nurtured in an open, supportive, caring, "difference" modality, and not a hostile, competitive, "sameness" model. A necessary part of creating this community is to support all legislation, both local and national, that will end discrimination against lesbians and homosexual people in general.

Each lesbian and group of lesbians must define and create a strategy for survival. We must begin with getting in touch with our anger and hate related to the system that is our oppressor. But we cannot afford to stay at that level. To survive and prosper, we must articulate goals and act from positions of positive action. We must declare and pursue what we each want, not concentrate on what we are not getting. Our uniqueness as lesbians gives us great power and strength. We are learning to use this to create a positive and nurturing environment for ourselves and for others. We can be the strongest advocates of the life force in our society today if we are allowed—and allow ourselves—to connect and function from our inner capacities, our inner selves, our identity.

REFERENCES AND RECOMMENDED READINGS

Amazon Poetry: An Anthology. Joan Larkin and Elly Bulkin, eds. Brooklyn, N.Y.: Out & Out Books.

LESBIAN HERSTORY ARCHIVES, P. O. Box 1258, New York, N.Y. 10001

GINA COVINA and LAUREL GALANA, eds. *The Lesbian Reader.* Oakland, Calif.: Amazon Press.

JONATHAN KATZ, ed. Lesbians and Gay Men in Society History and Literature. (A collection of 54 books and 2 periodicals.) New York: Arno Press.

Lesbian Women and Therapy—Two papers by Bernice Goodman
1. "The Lesbian Mother," presented at the American Orthopsychiatric Association, 1972.
2. Therapy with 45 Lesbians ("The Homosexual in Society—A Force for Positive Social Change"), presented at Practice Symposium, National Association of Social Workers, 1975.

Out & Out Books, 44 Seventh Avenue, Brooklyn, N.Y. 11217.

ABBOTT, SIDNEY, and BARBARA LOVE. *Sappho Was a Right-On Woman.* New York: Stein & Day, 1972.

MARTIN, DEL, and PHYLLIS LYON. *Lesbian Woman.* New York: Bantam, 1972.

MORGAN, CLAIRE. *The Price of Salt,* New York: Macfadden, 1969.

RULE, JANE. *Lesbian Images,* Garden City: Doubleday & Co., 1975.

SIMPSON, RUTH. *From the Closet to the Courts*, New York: Viking Press, 1975.

WEINBERG, MARTIN, and ALAN BELL. *Homosexuality: An Annotated Bibliography*. New York: Harper & Row, 1972.

WYSOR, BETTIE. *The Lesbian Myth*, New York: Random House, 1974.

A WOMAN'S PLACE IS WHEREVER
SHE WANTS IT TO BE

Rita Mae Brown

Sex preoccupies Americans. Our obsession with the how's, what's, where's and with whom's reveals to older, if not wiser, cultures the dangerous adolescence of this nation's character. There comes a time in the lives of individuals and nations when maturity—or at the very least, old age—sets in. On our 200th anniversary we show signs of neither, as we rush into theaters to see genitals in living color, rush to play with gaudy vibrators, missiles and blenders, trampling whoever happens to be in the way.

But just who is this *we*? Do you think you're preoccupied with sex? If not, then why are you reading this book? You say you're in the mental health profession and it's your job to familiarize yourself with sexual oppression. Well, that's as good an excuse as any.

It's fair to ask why I should write for a book with sexual oppression as its theme. Because I was asked. Am I obsessed with sex? No, I find all discussions of sex and sexuality tedious in the extreme. Then why write at all? Surely, the honorarium can't be that tempting? I write this because I am forced to consider sex whether I like such topics or not, for I am a member of the sexually oppressed. I am a lesbian to my great personal joy and to my public calamity.

The calamities are legion; but the worst is that I am not beheld as a person, but, rather, as a category. Oppressors don't grant individuality to the oppressed. In order to dehumanize people, it's necessary to prove them different (read: inferior) and faceless. Thus all blacks are either lazy, shiftless and dumb or wronged, courageous and morally pure—depending on one's brand of whiteness. The latter, on the surface, appears better, but the effect is the same as the former obvious prejudice: to reduce millions of complex, undefinable people into a tidy racial package.

Dehumanization techniques are the same whether the victims are race, class, age, sex or sex-preference victims. There's something deeply infuriating about being lumped with a woman who votes for Ronald Reagan and who has nothing in common with me, other than that we both choose to love a woman rather than a non-woman. There's something wildly ludicrous about being treated as the leather butch out of a heterosexual male porno fantasy, and being lumped together with gay men is an insulting form of annihilation. I face such drivel every day of my life. Fortunately I possess a good sense of humor. I need it.

Now I would need not face any of the above if I would conveniently lie, although I'd still face woman and class oppression. But what does that say about our culture? What does it mean if we reward people for lying? Well, Watergate is one fine example. And it is a grievous lie for me to pretend to be something I am not. Heterosexuality is assumed, cast upon one at birth. I don't find the assumption flattering. I don't find any assumption about anything advisable; perhaps that comes from my training as a journalist. If I lie to you the reader, and say I am straight—or, better yet, say nothing at all—what does that mean about my relationship to you? It means I consider you as narrow-minded as the Sexual Ku Klux Klan; so why tell you the truth? That hardly seems like a firm foundation upon which to base a friendship. Lying isn't a firm foundation for one's own identity, either. What does it say about me if I am willing to deny an integral part of my own complex character? If I'm willing to deny something, then either I think it's wrong or I haven't got the courage to fight for myself in the face of a hostile environment. Obviously I harbor no such socially respectable notions and if I lack intelligence, I don't lack fortitude. So I tell the truth about myself, not just on a one-dimensional sexual level but on as many levels as I can perceive. Life is too short for me to undermine myself and weaken important relationships with other humans. If I am to grow, I must tell the truth.

You might be surprised at this article so far. Did you secretly hope I would open the door to my bedroom? There, you see, lesbianism is viewed as a sexual issue—and so it is up to a point, but that point is quickly passed. I refuse to participate in this culture's brutal infringement on individual privacy. Now we get bizarre rewards for making public what should remain private. Some things are too dear to be cast into the maw of a devouring public. I am no gladiator in America's sexual colosseum. But I am a warrior trying to survive a decaying nation and living to fight for a better place, a more humane environment. So, for me, lesbianism is part of that battle. It is incidentally a matter of sexuality, and crucially a matter of personal freedom and personal integrity. And now I not only have my own integrity to defend, but that of thousands upon thousands of other women who at long last are standing up and fighting back, fighting to define themselves according to their own needs and not to someone else's needs. It matters little to me with whom they sleep; what matters is that they are taking great risks and telling the truth as they know it. How can I lie and weaken our numbers by one? Faith develops when many individuals reach across the breach in the face of fire and grasp the hands of others. The loss of one is not insignificant. I cannot, I will not, let go.

Individual freedom is not just my concern. It must be your concern also. At some point in life, I would hope a person would ask this question: "Why is it proper to kill human beings on the orders of one's government, but not proper to love human beings under the laws of that same government?" Underpinning the issue of personal freedom rests the issue of personal responsibility for moral decisions. Can any of us ever again take for granted that we should kill anyone on the orders of our government? Can we take for granted that love is to be commanded or condemned on the word of authority? By whose authority? Not mine. I protested against the war in Viet Nam and I protest against the war in American streets, kitchens and bedrooms. Sometimes, if the laws of one nation are unfair, a person can emigrate to another country where the judicial climate is better. For a lesbian or for any woman, no such haven exists. For the last ten thousand years laws have been made and enforced by men for male well-being—most especially the well-being of a very few males; but, for reasons still unclear to me, millions of other men went along with this ghastly injustice to themselves, their sisters, daughters, friends. The dynamic of patriarchy is to get the little man to identify with the big man, bask in his reflected light and do his bidding. Ten thousand years of history prove that such a rip-off is highly effective. Note that the key is to identify with the big man, never with your oppressed brother— and never, ever, with your sister. The worst thing imaginable to a man is to be a woman, to identify with his mother's life or with my life. We aren't to have independent lives. Our lives belong to men. It is a running joke in the feminist movement that the woman who is not the private property of one man is the public property of all men. If you doubt this shibboleth is still in effect, watch what happens to two women walking past a construction site and watch what happens when a woman and a

man walk by. In this system of distorted values, material power determines who does what to whom and when. Cut off from male money via
marriage and possibly by inheritance (homosexuals regularly get disin-
herited by parents whose love is conditional: "Be heterosexual or else!").
The lesbian is far down on the power totem pole. As a woman, she is often
denied the better jobs. And this is true in every country on the face of
the earth, for every country is ruled by a few, select men for their own
benefit, perhaps the benefit of other men, rarely women and never for
the benefit of lesbians. So there is no haven.

None of the above, however, explains the particular hatred the lesbian endures. Why do men and some women hate her so much? What is
she doing that gets in their way? She's not jacking up oil prices to gouge
them. All she's doing is living her own life in her own way.

Well, patriarchy has a peculiar quirk. It is based on vertical relationships: men over women, white over black, rich over poor. The farther
down a man is in this system of vertical relationships, the more dissatisfied he is likely to be, for identification with "Mr. Big" can only go so far.
But every man, no matter how far down he is, has one person below him,
a woman of his own race and class. Hence, "small" men sold out their
sisters and made a bond with the "Big" man. It happened again as
recently as 200 years ago in the South when poor whites and poor blacks
had common cause and the rich white planters defused this threatening
alliance by literally buying off the poor whites. (For a refresher course in
this sordid tactic read Edmund S. Morgan's *American Slavery, American
Freedom*, published in 1975 by W.W. Norton & Co.) In the system of
vertical relationships there's relish in knowing someone is below you, no
matter how low you are. Women's betrayal at the hands of their brothers
happened so long ago, in the thick mists of prehistory, that such injustice
is declared the natural order of things. That's why reading of such a
tactic in more recent times has greater emotional impact; the rape has
not set for so long and is therefore not unquestioned.

Who disrupts this "natural order" but me? I disrupt it by loving. I
blow up no buildings, I slit no throats. I throw no monkey wrenches into
a rusty economy. But I am treated as though I did all the above. I offer
the ultimate insult to the patriarch and his flunkies because I ignore him
and go about my business. But we all know the business of women is men
and sequentially children. Not for me, thank you very much. I have
mountains to climb, rivers to ford and, to borrow from Robert Frost,
miles to go before I sleep. I am innocent but I am dangerous, as dangerous in my way as Nat Turner and Harriet Tubman were in their way. I
will not passively comply with a system of injustice, a system that robs
me of choices.

I do not wish to rob my brother; so why does he insist on stealing from me? Until the "small" men learn that I am their sister, until those men see themselves in me (and me in themselves), until they disengage from the "big" man, I have to fight them. But it hurts to fight a blind man, and the small man is just that, intellectually. He would take away from me, from my freedom, to secure his place in the vertical scale. I must also fight women who feed into that injustice as mightily as I fight the blind men. While men have sought to solve problems using genitals as a guideline, I can't.

Just because a person is a woman doesn't make her a creature of beauty, truth and light. She sucks up to "Mr. Big," too. No wonder so many heterosexual women turn on lesbians. To make friends with a woman like me (I said *friend*, not *lover*) might mean she loses the house, loses the car, loses her child, for such things can happen when a woman transgresses without male approval. If women share in the patriarchal prejudices, they certainly reap the rewards unequally. The psychological price of deferring to another or trying to work your will through another (now the man is the victim of his own supremacy!) is high. We could point to nervous breakdown, alcoholism, drug addiction, and so on, but that's not the worst price. The worst price is that these women live and die and never really know who they are or what they want. I'd rather be the outcast I am than pay that.

In the system of vertical relationships I've briefly outlined, a woman is half a man; by the same token a lesbian must be half of a woman or double a woman, depending on one's madness. Either way, the oppression multiplies. Following are examples of things that happen every day to myself and to my friends who are lesbians:

If a lesbian is raped, it is because she is a lesbian and not because the man is sick with woman hatred. If a lesbian is hauled into court by an irate husband battling over child custody, she loses the child because she's unfit to be a mother. Never mind what *he* does. By virtue of a choice the woman has now made regarding her body and her emotional life, she can lose her children. If a lesbian is fired from a job she'll hear every reason but the real reason. What legal recourse does that leave her to protest? What court could she trust for a hearing, anyway—on any issue? The laws were made by men, not women. If a lesbian is beautiful, then she's a lesbian because she can have any man she wants and therefore she's bored with men. If a lesbian is not beautiful, then she's a lesbian because no man will have her. If a lesbian is talented, she's compensating. If she's not talented; well, it's because she's a lesbian, of course. If a lesbian is fascinating company, it's because she's more like a man than a woman. If she's dull, it's because she's too much like a woman and not enough like a man. If she separates from her lover, it's because they're lesbians and not because love takes patience, understanding and imagination for any person. If her relationship lasts, she's lucky. If she has male friends, it's because women really can't do without men in their lives. If she doesn't have male friends, it's because she's a man-hating bitch and wants to cut their balls off. If she loves children, she's secretly heterosexual. If she doesn't love children, she's a monster. If she cries, it's because she's a lesbian and even more emotional than the "average" woman. If she doesn't cry, it's because she's a lesbian, not like a woman at all, hard as nails.

In other words, she is damned if she does and damned if she doesn't. Always the definition of the lesbian is in relation to male perceptions and male needs. (This can be, and often is, echoed by women who never questioned patriarchy.) The definition of a lesbian's life is her own. Her life, my life, has little to do with patriarchal conceptions of who or what I should be . . . but has everything to do with what I think I should be and do. I am I and that's all. You are you and that's all. How would you like it if I sat you down and played a psychological Sherlock Holmes, showing you how you came to be what you are? Even if any human being could perform this homage to the past successfully, would I know you any better today? How dare I presume to intrude on your life in this way? How dare you presume to intrude on mine? Equality is not based on mutual insensitivity.

And what have I to show after suffering most of the above-mentioned societal afflictions? Why would anyone put up with this? You put up with it as well as I do; perhaps the paradox isn't as clear or the punishment as severe, but we all suffer from human irrationality, including our own. Many humans, wounded somewhere in the deep recesses of their brains, rip and tear at whatever gets in their path. I'm an easier target than you, but irrationality can't be counted on to be discriminating in its choice of victims. It's an old phrase but true: misery loves company. Look around you. How many truly happy people do you know? Watch out because the unhappy one will come after you when he's done with me. And if you turn your back on me and do not fight for my rights, the rights of all women, of people of all races and classes and ages—and then you are swept away by prejudice or outright murder, how can I be there to defend you? Whether you like it or not, we are all members of the human race and must defend one another. When we do not defend one another, the evil flowers of Auschwitz bloom. The flesh burning could as easily be yours as mine.

So I pick my way through the societal debris as cleverly as I can. And if my path is somewhat more littered than yours, so be it. Within all the irrationalities, the cruelties, the enforced ignorance, we each have a thin, ever so thin, line of will. We have some choices. I chose my way because, for all the troubles, it gives me joy. What fool would make a choice based entirely on pain? If I've told you of my troubles, I ought to share my joys:

I know who I am. I know what I can't do and what I can do. I know the heterosexual way of life, for we are all raised to be heterosexual. I have the added advantage of knowing the lesbian way of life. I have both eyes open instead of only one. My friends are my friends, whoever they are and wherever they came from, because they've been tried and found true. People-who-love-me love *me*, not some convenient charade. If I know my friends, I also know my enemies and, believe me, that's a comfort. I know Western thought left great gaps in our learning. I no longer believe there is right or wrong, black or white, male or female, "straight" or "gay." Nothing is quite that simple. Polarization is the sign of an immature intellect as surely as a preoccupation with sex is the sign of immature emotional development. There is wrong in right and right in wrong, female in male and male in female, and so forth. Life is a continuum and everything exists simultaneously, within us and without us. I discovered this my way; I hope you find it in your way. Perhaps then we won't need these embarrassing labels, sexual or otherwise, and we can just *be*.

A word about the mental health professions. Organizations of psychiatrists and psychologists must purge themselves of members who are destructive to women or lesbians by reaffirming damaging stereotypes. People within these bodies must re-educate their peers and give them every chance to learn. As a matter of fact, I know this is already in progress. If this surprises you, allow me to quote from Kurt Tucholsky, a brilliant writer and also a Jew, who tried to warn the German citizens during the Weimar Republic years. "Collective judgements are always unjust but useful. A critic of society has the right to regard the lowest type in a group as representative of it, for the group tolerates that type, does not exclude it, and thus positively incorporates it into the group spirit."

REFERENCES AND RECOMMENDED READINGS

BROWN, RITA MAE. *In Her Day*, Plainfield, Vt.: Daughters Press, 1975.
———. *Rubyfruit Jungle*. Plainfield, Vt.: Daughters Press, 1973.
JAY, KARLA, and ALLEN YOUNG, eds. *After You're Out*. Los Angeles: Links Books, 1975.
———. *Out of the Closets: Voices of Gay Liberation*. New York: Pyramid, 1974.
LOVE, BARBARA, and SYDNEY ABBOTT. *Sappho Was a Right-On Woman*. New York: Stein and Day, 1972.

LYON, PHYLLIS, and DEL MARTIN. *Lesbian Woman.* New York: Bantam, 1972.
RULE, JANE. *Lesbian Images.* Garden City, N.Y.: Doubleday & Co., 1975.

A MUSICAL BIBLIOGRAPHY (there are many ways to learn)
CHRISTIAN, MEG. *I Know You Know.*
WILLIAMSON, CHRIS. *The Changer and the Changed.*
  Both records are available from Olivia Records
                      P.O. Box 70237
                      Los Angeles, Calif. 90070

CHAPTER 11

THE
AGING
MALE
HOMOSEXUAL

James Kelly

In recent years many social policies oppressive to gay[1] people have been publicly questioned and several have been overturned. Homosexuality is now no longer considered a psychiatric disorder by the American Psychiatric Association. Several major corporations have revised their hiring policies to permit the employment of openly gay men and women. Sodomy laws have been repealed by a dozen state legislatures. Candidates supporting gay rights have won in several elections. But despite these gay rights victories, a recently published survey by the Institute for Sex Research indicates that most Americans continue to hold negative stereotypes about homosexuality (Sage, 1975: p. 23). In this connection, the increasingly balanced accounts of gay life-styles which are beginning to appear in popular publications and other media presentations may eventually influence the public's thinking. The emphasis in these reports, however, is almost always on the young gay person. In fact, the life-style and problems of older homosexuals have been so little examined that many young gays repeat popular stereotypes or say they don't know when they are asked what aging is like in their own subculture. Consequently, older gays are oppressed not only by discriminatory practices but by the kind of pervasive mythology and stigma which grows up around the unknown. Some of the linkages between stigma, the problems which sexually oppress older gays, and their adaptations to these problems will be outlined here, in the following discussion of some of the findings of a recent study of 241 gay men between the ages of 16 and 79 in the Los Angeles metropolitan area.[2] While the original study examined the attitudes, stereotypes and characteristics of these men in reference to aging, focus here is on the characteristics which older[3] gay men in the study group have in comparison to specific popular myths and on the problems encountered by these men. Data was collected through questionnaire, interview and participant observation techniques over the two-year period of 1973 to 1974. One hundred and ninety-three questionnaires and 48 interviews were analyzed. Sixteen of the men interviewed were over age 65; five were between ages 75 and 79. (All interview material quoted in this article, however, comes from conversations with men over age 65.)

As there are no accurate accounts of the racial, age, or socioeconomic parameters of the American gay subgroup, probability sampling techniques thus become virtually impossible to employ. This study therefore must be considered as an exploratory account, its findings are not meant to be generalizable to all aging gay men.[4]

STEREOTYPES

The old in general are often stereotyped. A number of myths, stigmas, negative societal beliefs and definitions tend to be attached to older persons. However, while the elderly have been generalized to be "politically conservative," "senile," "fanatically religious," and "incapable of sexual activity or interest" (Bengtson, 1973: p. 27), older gay men have repeatedly been singled out as particularly pathetic figures.

Stereotyping, in fact, is not uncommon in supposedly scientific literature. Allen (1961) writes in *The Third Sex*: "The aging homosexual tends to become distinctly odd . . ." (p. 95). Stearn (1961) elaborates on the oddities of older gays in *The Sixth Man*, where he represents the unaffluent older gay as living "in the Bowery, seeking oblivion in handouts and cheap wine" and "regress(ing) to a point where he preys on small children" (pp. 258–259). Esther Newton in her 1972 research defines gay men as "old" at age thirty (p. 27).

Even within the gay subculture the older man is often stigmatized. The "Faggot's Faggot" was the phrase chosen by a columnist in the *Pittsburgh Gay News* recently in an article deploring the Pittsburgh subculture's stigmatization of older gays. Just as gay people in general form a predominantly "secret" society within the larger society, columnist Kochera (1973) describes these groups of older gays as the symbolically stigmatized "unseen victims of ignorance and oppression" about which a hazy folklore seems to exist within the gay community as a whole. In this hazy folklore there are myths and stereotypes and assumptions about the participation of older gay men in subculture activities, about their interpersonal association with other gay men, about their self-identifications as gay people, and about their sexuality. These may be summed up in one composite stereotype of the supposed characteristics and activities of the aging gay man. He no longer goes to bars, having lost his physical attractiveness along with his sexual appeal to the young men he craves. He is oversexed, but his sex life is very unsatisfactory. He has been unable to form a lasting relationship with a sexual partner, and he is seldom active sexually any more. When he does have sex it is usually in a "tea room" (public toilet). He has disengaged from the gay world and his acquaintances in it. He is retreating further and further into the "closet"—fearful of disclosure of his "perversion." Most of his associations now are increasingly with heterosexuals. In a bizarre and deviant world centered around age he is labeled "an old queen," as he has become quite effeminate.

The aging gay men in this study bear little resemblance to this stereotyped composite image of their socially inferred characteristics. In contrast to the mythical man, the "composite" older man in the study group does not frequent "tea rooms," but occasionally goes out to bars, particularly those that serve his peer group. Only 4 per cent of the questionnaire sample and one interviewee mentioned having been in a "tea room" in the past six months. Of the 4 per cent participating in "tea-room" activity, over half (53.7 per cent) were "younger," i.e., under age 36. However, 63 per cent of those between ages 56 and 65 described themselves as bar-goers.

In the study group, the extent of the typical older man's participation in the gay world is based largely on his individual desires. Of the gay people who completed questionnaires for this project, most seem to feel that their level of participation in the gay world's round of activities is low (30 per cent) to moderate (52 per cent). However, no one over age 65 indicated that he had disengaged from activities in the gay world.

The composite older man in the study group says his concern about disclosure of his sexual orientation is related to his many years of working in a profession where known gays are not tolerated. Sixty-three per cent of the gay men over age 36 who responded to the questionnaire expressed "high concern" over disclosure of sexual orientation. However, many respondents indicated that they were merely "concerned," and in some cases concerned *only* about *occupational* disclosure. One retired interviewee, for example, expressed relief:

> Indifferent now, but I used to be concerned about it when I was in industry. I wouldn't want it disclosed. I don't want to be labeled." (*from an interview*)

The representative aging gay man studied has many gay friends but fewer heterosexual friends. The majority of the gay men studied here, of all ages, ranked their degree of social association with other gay people as "moderate" (44 per cent) to "high" (42 per cent), with the overwhelming majority of interviewees (23) rating their association as "high." The youngest and oldest respondents were lower in the extent of their association with gays. However, few respondents indicated low association with gays to begin with, and percentages on the low association item are widely dispersed across the age categories. Association with heterosexuals was found to decrease dramatically with increasing age. While 42 per cent of those under age 26 ranked social association with heterosexuals high, the combined percentages of the oldest three age brackets equals only 36 per cent.

The sex life of the older man in the Los Angeles study is, characteristically, quite satisfactory and he desires sexual contact with adult men, especially those near his own age. He is not, however, currently involved in a gay liaison.[5] Fifty per cent of those in the 50–65 age bracket reported satisfactory sex lives; 83 per cent of the respondents over age 65 report being sexually satisfied. Content analysis of interviews with older gays indicates that the majority of older interviewees are sexually interested and satisfied in relationships with, or are attracted toward, adult men—oftentimes men in their own age cohort. The number of persons involved in liaisons seems to increase with age, peaking with 59 per cent of those 46 to 55 years old being members of gay partnerships. After this apex, partnerships decrease to almost none. Two reasons for this decline often mentioned by older gays were the death of the loved one and the rejection of the notion of having a single lifelong lover.

The typical older man in this study neither considers himself effeminate nor likes to define himself in terms of gay age labels, but he remembers the terms that were commonly applied to "older gays" when he was younger. Only twelve men over age 30 in the questionnaire and interview samples combined defined themselves with feminine self-identifications such as "closet queen," "nelly," and so on.

PROBLEMS FACED BY OLDER GAYS

While these older gay men do not seem to fit the stereotypes which mark them as lonely, sexually frustrated and unhappy, they are not without problems and potential problems. Aging gays face the same problems of stigmatization of "age," loss of people emotionally important to them, and fear of institutionalization encountered by many other older Americans:

I saw a guy, I know of a guy 75, who keeps himself in good shape, you know. When you talk to him, you never think of talking to an old man.

He is very sexy appearing and he doesn't talk and act like, quote, "old man," unquote. You know there is a certain stereotype we have in the whole of our society. You act as if you're a housewife, or you are this. . . . There is a certain repertoire that we sort of force on all the people that they got to act, got to move slow, they got to do a whole lot of crap, dress certainly, but they have to have certain attitudes; they can't be too vivacious. (*from an interview*)

I have no fear of growing old except that you face more loneliness than you do when you're young. I lost my lover when we looked forward to spending our retirement years together, going places, doing things together. Couldn't do it when we were working and then to have it all wiped away overnight. It left me with nobody and not much chance of finding anybody at this age. (*from an interview*)

I hope that I don't end up going to a nursing home. I don't live too far from one now. I walk by there and I see some of these poor old devils, male and female, stuck there on chairs, and so on. Nobody gives a damn. (*from an interview*)

In addition to these problems of aging, older gays face unique discriminations related to the stigmatization of their sexual identity. The discriminatory impact of many practices, laws, rules and conventions seems to increase for the gay man as he ages. For example, several life insurance companies have allegedly refused to insure persons after uncovering evidence of their sexual orientation (Teal, 1971: p. 236).

Also, while the emotional, economic and physical security children can provide for aging parents is a common theme of heterosexual society, only very recently has the concept of gay adoptive parents gained an audience (Altman, 1971: p. 65). Perhaps among the most chillingly tragic and painful discriminatory barriers gays may face are hospital visiting regulations:

A report in the *London Times* referred to a lesbian dying in a hospital who was only allowed visits from her immediate family, and her partner of twenty years was excluded. (Altman, 1971: p. 50)

When a lover dies, his gay companion faces possible legal discrimination. If no will is involved and there are no children from the marriage, the surviving spouse of a heterosexual couple can inherit the other's property automatically. When one party of a gay union dies without a will, however, his property goes to the deceased's family. Even if a will has been drawn up in which a gay person leaves all his property to his lover, his family may contest and break the will on the grounds of "undue influence." Also, while a heterosexual spouse can inherit through the deceased partner, this right is not legally provided for the gay spouse. "A gay person cannot inherit his deceased lover's grandmother's estate under any circumstances." (Baker in Teal, 1971: p. 285)

Property ownership also can become a legal problem for the surviving spouse in a gay relationship:

> In some states . . . there is a form of ownership of property that is reserved solely to married couples. It's called "tenancy by the entirety." It guarantees that the property will go to the surviving spouse despite claims of creditors. Gay people can hold property in "joint tenancy," *i.e.*, as co-owners, but creditors can get to the property and thus there is no guarantee the surviving "spouse" will end up with it. (Baker in Teal, 1971: p. 285)

In addition, only the surviving spouse of a legal marriage can sue a third party for "wrongful death" through malpractice or other negligence. Therefore, this redress is not open to gay couples whose bonds are not legally binding. (Baker in Teal, 1971: p. 285)

And when a lover dies, his gay companion may also be subjected to the personal, sometimes overt, sometimes subtle, prejudice of his loved one's family. Isherwood evokes the memory of such an experience in his aging gay protagonist, George:

> But how very strange to sit here . . . and remember that night when the long distance call came through from Ohio. An uncle of Jim's whom he'd never met—trying to be sympathetic, even admitting George's right to a small honorary share in the sacred family grief . . . (Isherwood, p. 106).

ADAPTATION TO STIGMA

Most of the older gay men who participated in this study have shown strength and resiliency in adjusting to societally defined "inferiority." The comment of one older man supports the hypothesis (Weinberg, 1970; Simon and Gagnon, 1969; Tripp, 1971) that the gay man tends to adapt well to aging, at least partially because he usually faces the crisis of accepting his stigmatized identity early in life.

> I used to feel depressed, but it's a social approval thing. Everybody wants to have self-esteem. They want people to look up to them and be proud. I found out that when I was going to college, people would always walk by and say, "Oh, he's gay." I think all gay persons have to go through that shit, you know. "Oh, he's gay; he's a Pollock; he's a faggot; he's a freak." He has to go through all that change. It takes a while to get used to that. I find one time, if I'm in the mood when I hear that, I'm ready to fight. But

I try to overcome it. When a person says that, they are not aware of you. They want to learn, but they don't want to be obvious about it. So they try to condemn you. But that social approval is a bitch at times. Especially being gay. (*from an interview*)

Strength through mastery of crisis, however, is neither an excuse nor an antidote for the stigmatization faced by older gay people and the problems that stigmatization brings. There may, in fact, be a relationship between stigmatization and discrimination. A theme repeated, in some form or other, by over half of the gays interviewed over age 65 was that "most other older gays have difficulty adapting while I do not," as witness the following extracts from several interviews.

INTERVIEWER: How do you feel about growing older?
INTERVIEWEE: I don't mind it at all. I'm having a good time, so why apologize?
INTERVIEWER: How do you think most gays feel about growing old?
INTERVIEWEE: They dread it.
INTERVIEWER: Any reason why you say that?
INTERVIEWEE: Yes, because it offends their egos. It disturbs ego, I should say.

INTERVIEWER: What happens to old gays?
INTERVIEWEE: They get lonely and desperate. And they just kind of waste away. I have noticed an awful lot of them. Most of them that I know get desperately lonely.

INTERVIEWEE: No, I don't think I'll ever grow old. And I don't fear growing old. So I mean: if I do grow old I'll have a companion whatever. There'll always be gay people growing old with me, so we'll always be together.

INTERVIEWER: Do you believe there are any specific problems that gays have in relation to aging?
INTERVIEWEE: Growing old. Gay people are going to get old and be left alone. Who are they going to turn to?

This outlook may provide the individual with a source of emotional strength, as he feels he has conceptually overcome self-stigmatization. However, while he realizes that his own life doesn't fit the stereotyped pattern, he seems still somewhat indoctrinated in that he does not question the stereotype itself; instead, he believes that he must simply be uniquely well adjusted.

SOCIAL CHANGE AND THE PROBLEM OF STIGMA

It seems obvious that there are laws to change and discriminatory institutional regulations to be challenged. Social situations and institutions, however, may be easier to change than individual prejudicial attitudes. It

has been suggested, in fact, that the popular depiction of gays as pathetic and troubled fulfills an ethnocentric need among the liberal elements of current society:

> Most liberal opinion is horrified by persecution of homosexuals and supportive of abolishing the antihomosexual laws, without really accepting homosexuality as a full and satisfying form of sexual and emotional behavior. Such tolerance of homosexuality can co-exist with considerable suspicion of and hostility toward it, and this hostility is reinforced in all sorts of ways within our society . . . (Altman, 1971: p. 51).

Hostility is reinforced by those psychotherapists who according to Dr. Clarence A. Tripp, director of Psychological Research Associates, Inc., are "frightening the [gay] patient with the image of the aging, lonely homosexual" (Debate, 1971: p. 49). Hostility is also reinforced by social science researchers who continue to fuel the myths about older gays. One very recent example of this is the British report "Campaign for Homosexual Equality" (1974) which suggestively features this quotation on its cover:

> Retired and retiring gay, bereft of mate of 31 years, fanatically sincere, needs an understanding pal desperately (over 21). London/Northarts. Box 12.

And hostility is reinforced, too, by all those educators, scientists and authors who continue to simply ignore homosexuality as a viable life-style for older people. This excerpt from the gerontological literature on sexuality is a classic example of this type of oversight:

> . . . the widespread ignorance about sex and the high frequency in our society of excessive inhibition with respect to behavior that can lead to gratifying heterosexual relationships and the relief of sexual tensions make sexual problems one of the most common causes of helpless feelings among the aging. (Goldfarb, in Berezin, 1969: p. 133)

In terms of making progress in the direction of alleviating many of the problems faced by the older homosexual, let us briefly review them and evaluate avenues of possible change. The stereotyping of the aging gay as an oversexed, unsatisfied, nonappealing unattractive child molester who is unable to form lasting relationships can only be countered by educating both the gay and straight world to the truth. For example, as noted, 59 per cent of the gay men interviewed who were between 46 and 59 years of age had lasting gay relationships. There is a need for role models to be identified and more realistic media coverage.

In addition, the insensitivity of the gay community at large to the older gay population is a real problem. In a subculture which stresses youth and sexual appeal, the aging homosexual is often beyond the pale of his own peer group. Perhaps gay organizations need to address themselves to this predicament by providing social outlets for their senior citizens.

Another significant inconsistency faced by the older gay (especially one in a gay relationship) is his inferior legal status. He has neither the rights of a living nor dead spouse, and in most states cannot file a joint tax return to obtain the same advantages available to a heterosexual couple. There is a great need for much adoptive legislation to deal with these discriminatory practices.

Although the research findings reported in this article are based on a nonprobability sample of one community, there seems to be *no further rationale* for the application of certain "blanket" stereotypes about aging gay men, as these men, at least, are living proof that such assertions are not always accurate. There is little evidence in this study to suggest that being gay causes problems in old age, but there is a great deal of evidence to suggest that societal stigma causes problems *for* aging gays. Only when society becomes aware of, and accepts, this important distinction can full acceptance and equality for older gay people become a real possibility.

NOTES

1. *Gay* is the widely preferred subculture term for those who engage primarily in homosexual relations. Judd Marmor's interpretation of the term *homosexual* appears to be one of the most definitive: "One who is motivated in adult life, by a definite preferential erotic attraction to members of the same sex and who usually (but not necessarily) engages in overt sexual relations with them (1965: p. 4)."

2. The highest concentration of individuals is in the 20 to 34 age range for the large questionnaire group, the age range for this group is 60 years, with a mean age of 33 years. In the interview groups the age distribution is purposively bimodal with seven scores in the 20–24 bracket and eight in the 65–69 age interval. The rest of the frequencies for the interviewers tend to be distributed more evenly although no interviewees were in their fifties.

3. Except when used in a context such as "men older than 25," the term "older" is defined by the majority responses of the men themselves. Most saw age 50 as the end of middle age and the beginning of old age.

4. Because significant differences may exist between gay men's and gay women's communities, only gay males are included in this analysis. Review of several articles (Simon and Gagnon, 1967; Saghir and Robins, 1973; Saghir,

et al., 1969) indicates that "many of the sexual behaviors of adult homosexual men differ from those of adult homosexual women" (Saghir, *et al.*, 1969: p. 229).

5. *Liaison* refers here to an emotional and sexual relationship of one year's duration, or longer.

REFERENCES AND RECOMMENDED READINGS

ALLEN, CLIFFORD. "The Aging Homosexual." In *The Third Sex*, edited by Isadore Rubin. New York: New Book Co., 1961.

ALTMAN, DENIS. *Homosexual Oppression and Liberation*. New York: Avon Books, 1971.

BENGTSON, VERN L. *The Social Psychology of Aging*. New York: Bobbs-Merrill Co., Inc., 1973.

BERETIN, MARTIN A. "Sex and Old Age: A Review of the Literature," *Journal of Geriatric Psychiatry* 9, No. 2 (Spring, 1969): pp. 131–149.

"Campaign for Homosexual Equality." Monograph. London: London West End Group 1974.

ISHERWOOD, CHRISTOPHER. *A Single Man*. London: Methuen & Co., 1961.

KOCHERA, BRIAN. "The faggot's faggot . . . gay senior citizens and gay S & M," *Pittsburgh Gay News* 1, No. 5 (September 1), p. 6, 1973.

MARMOR, JUDD. *Sexual Inversion: The Multiple Roots of Homosexuality*. New York: Basic Books, 1965.

NEWTON, ESTHER. *Mother Camp: Female Impersonators in America*. Englewood Cliffs, N.J.; Prentice-Hall, 1972.

SAGE, WAYNE. "Inside the Colossal Closet," *Human Behavior*, August, 1975 pp. 16–23.

SAGHIR, MARCIL T., *et al.* "Homosexuality II: Sexual Behavior of the Male Homosexual," *Archives of General Psychiatry* 21 (August, 1969), pp. 219–229.

——— and ELI ROBINS. *Male and Female Homosexuality*. Baltimore: Williams and Wilkins Co., 1973.

SIMON, WILLIAM, and JOHN H. GAGNON. "Femininity in the lesbian community," *Social Problems* 15, No. 2 (Fall, 1967), pp. 212–221.

———. "Homosexuality: The Formulation of a Sociological Perspective." In *The Same Sex*, edited by Ralph W. Weltge. Philadelphia: Pilgrim Press, 1969.

STEARN, JESS. *The Sixth Man*. New York: Doubleday and Co., Inc., 1961.

TEAL, DONN. *The Gay Militants*. New York: Stein and Day, 1971.

TRIPP, CLARENCE A. "Debate: Can Homosexuals Change with Psychotherapy?" *Sexual Behavior*, July, 1971, pp. 42–49.

WEINBERG, MARTIN S. "The Male Homosexual: Age-related Variations in Social and Psychological Characteristics," *Social Problems* 17, No. 4 (Spring, 1970), pp. 527–537.

V.
RACIAL
AND
ECONOMIC
MINORITIES

It is often difficult to distinguish between socioeconomic and ethnic factors, since they not only overlap but are also interwoven with problems of discrimination. Taking this into account, this section attempts to explore the difficulties faced by those in such ambiguous categories. We do not mind too much, for instance, if a rich movie star is sexually active with a succession of men or even has a baby outside wedlock, but we do indeed mind if a woman on welfare, particularly if black, indulges in similar behavior.

Chilman tackles the problems facing the poor, who are indeed prevented by our attitudes toward them, the subculture of poverty, and the lack of opportunity associated with financial deprivation, from enjoying responsible and satisfying sexuality.

Johnson traces the effects of discrimination on black attitudes of today, pointing out problems still imposed from without, problems consequently created from within, and the acute problems subsequently now facing black women.

Ogawa discusses the problems of the Asian American accruing from conflict between cultural values (and nowhere is there so much ethnocentrism as in sexual attitudes), the broad range of attitudes in a subculture within a more dominant culture, and the differences between the

Hawaiian experience and the Mainland experience (perhaps by implication suggesting some solutions).

The fact that Asian Americans have been selected for discussion rather than those of Puerto Rican, Mexican, or Italian descent is probably a reflection of nothing more significant than the editor's address (i.e., Hawaii). To some extent, the problems are similar no matter which group is discussed; yet it bears repeating that more understanding must be given to both the problems of ethnic minorities in general, and to the values and unique experiences of each particular group.

CHAPTER 12

BLACKS

Leanor Boulin Johnson

The close affinity of sex and racial oppression has been well illustrated by a number of writers (Hernton, 1965; West, 1967; Cleaver, 1968; Day, 1972; Fanon, 1963; Staples, 1974). This enigmatic duality is echoed in America's history of castrating enslaved Africans (a legal practice unprecedented in any other slave society), denying marriage contracts to slave couples and the arbitrary separation of them by profit-seeking slave masters, lynching and electrocuting of black males for alleged sexual assaults on white women (an example, Emmett Till), antimiscegenation laws (not until 1967 did the Supreme Court declare them unconstitutional), permitting white males to have illicit relations with black females, but forbidding black males to have the same with white females, and, most recently, involuntary sterilization of naive black welfare clients, a procedure only precedented by the goal of eugenics in Hitler's Germany (Alexander, 1973). This paper discusses the rationalizations given for these oppressive acts, gives some specific examples of the role of the U.S. welfare, legal, and health systems in this oppression and reports

My special thanks to Robert Hall, Jim Roberts and Elizabeth Piccard for their suggestions on sources of data that might be important to consider. My thanks also to Australia Henderson, Waldra Lowry, and Bill Johnson for reviewing earlier drafts of this manuscript. The interpretations and recommendations, however, are solely my own.

data which suggest that perhaps blacks have been deceived by the myths surrounding their sexuality and adversely affected by the imbalanced sex ratio.

WHITE MAN'S BURDEN—THE BLACK BODY

The catalyst for the oppressive acts against black sexuality has been the cultural belief that blacks are sexually liberated to the point of obscenity. Although the current sexual revolution is serving to legitimize the more liberal sexual norms of blacks, the insidious shackles of the black super-sexuality myth, which are rooted in America's early history, have not been shaken. For instance, President Jefferson passed on several notions which had preceded him. Negroes, he contended, "are more ardent after their females: but love seems with them to be more an eager desire, than a tender delicate mixture of sentiment and sensation" (Jordan, 1974: p. 182). Also, Jefferson not only accepted the popular belief that Negroes desired sexual relations with whites but he believed in a "beastly copula-tion" associated with blacks—the copulation of black women with orang-outangs. The Negro-ape association had eighteenth-century scientific value, for it was a recognition of a crucial link in the "Chain of Being." If male apes are closest to the black race, then it is natural that they be aggressive to the females of the next evolutionary step.

In 1901 these notions were still being articulated. A leading scholar at that time wrote:

> Soberly speaking, negro nature is so craven and sensuous in every fibre of its being that negro manhood with decent respect for chaste womanhood does not exist. . . . Women unresistingly betray their wifely honor to satisfy a bestial instinct . . . so deeply rooted in immorality are our negro people that they turn in aversion from any sexual relation which does not invite sensuous embraces. . . . Negro social conditions will, however, be but dimly understood, even in their more conspicuous phases, unless we are prepared to realize at every step in our investigation that physical excitation is the chief and foremost craving of the freedman's nature. (Thomas, 1901: pp. 187, 189).

One of the penalties paid for this assumed bestial instinct was racial segregation and political disfranchisement.

Almost seventy years later Schulz (1969), and others continued to imply that black sexuality is guided by "bestial instinct." Schulz, in his case study of ten black families who resided in one of the most deprived housing projects in America, interprets the absorption of children into the grandmother's home as a "greed for babies" which reinforces their daugh-ters' illicit behavior. In describing the abundance of drawings on the stairway walls, he reiterates the sentiment of Thomas in 1901: ". . . the many verbal ejaculations in lipstick and crayon, announce to all passersby that sex is very much a central concern of those who live here." These observations are underscored by the preoccupation of scholars with the higher rate of divorce, separation, and out-of-wedlock births among blacks as compared to whites. Few have given meaningful attention to understanding these facts within the framework of an oppressive society. For example, until 1961 families with an unemployed father present could not receive allowances from the Aid to Families with Dependent Children (AFDC) program. Thus, an unemployed or underemployed father would find it necessary to desert in order to provide for his family. It should be noted that only a little over half of the states have adopted the 1962 amendment to the Social Security Act which allows aid to the family with an unemployed father present. This aid is still not available for the underemployed father living with his family (Miller, 1966; Kadushin, 1974).

Secondly, black sexuality has been debased by America's legal system. The most ancient and disabling legal classification which taints mother and child (social norms shield the father) is the label "illegitimate" for children born out of wedlock. This label works a particular disadvantage on blacks, who are disproportionately located in the lower class. Common-law marriages are more pervasive in this class and children from these unions are legally defined as illegitimate, thereby increasing the black illegitimacy rate. "Illegitimate" children are denied many rights "legitimate" children take for granted. Not until recently did Northern and Southern law enforcers move to compel black fathers to financially support their children. However, their primary concern was not for the children, but for the increasing tax burden created by the rising cost of aid to black families. It is important to note that such legal measures have not been taken against white fathers of mulatto children. Furthermore, the racist interpretation of illegitimacy statistics which is congruent with the blood theory of Nazis and white supremacists, relegates out-of-wedlock children to the black population when the mother is black and the father is white as well as when the mother is white and the father is black. Current comparison practice, then, lumps all blacks together and contrasts their illegitimacy rate against all whites—in effect black lower-class rates are measured against that of white middle- and upper-class (Miller, 1966). Without considering such factors as the higher use of abortions, adoption, and contraceptives by whites as compared with blacks (Gebhard, 1958; Pope and Knudsen, 1965; Furstenberg, 1970), it is no great wonder that the black illegitimacy rate is substantially higher than that of the whites.

Nothing better highlights the high rate of illegitimacy among blacks

than the double standard of academic literature. It is indeed striking that
the question of illegitimacy is almost never raised when the issue is lower
sexual standards in a non-lower-class milieu. Such terms as "illicit relations," "common-law marriage," and "illegitimacy" are replaced with "Sex
and the Single Girl," "Sex in Suburbia," "Sex in the Office," "living together," and "love child." The focus is given to the psychodynamic impact of the sexual revolution on the relationship of males to females.
However, in the context of the black society, illegitimacy is always discussed and never seen as an adjustment to a social, political, or economic
revolution or evolution, but rather to the lower-class culture of poverty
which promotes promiscuity and a childbearing syndrome (Hill and
Jaffe, 1967).

Although blacks generally do not attach social stigma to children
born out of wedlock, white legislators have made illegitimacy a crime. In
1960 Louisiana legislators disfranchised males and females who had an
"illegitimate" child or a common-law marriage. The legislators were can-
did in stating that this law was intended for blacks. A few states have
even enacted laws curtailing assistance to mothers who have a second
child out of wedlock, and twenty-five states have sterilization laws which
affect welfare recipients. In an effort to help save these mothers and their
children from themselves, some "compassionate" welfare workers have
manipulated them into sterilization. A recent study conducted by a health
research branch of Ralph Nader's Public Citizen, Inc., reported that in a
number of cities some patients, most of them poor and black, were subjected to surgical sterilization without an explanation of either the potential hazards or alternative methods of birth control. It was clear to the
researchers that these operations were sold to the public in a manner not
unlike many other deceptive marketing practices. Yet, can it be said that
sterilization is simply another "deceptive market practice"? When it is
realized that as an eighteenth-century legal punishment for all blacks
free or enslaved, castration was peculiarly American, then it appears that
sterilization of modern-day black women is tantamount to the earlier
castration of black male slaves. This underlines how much of the white
man's insecurity about blacks is fundamentally sexual (Jordan, 1974). In
spite of the fact that Congress intended family planning services to be
voluntary in nature rather than manipulative and coercive, these cruel
practices provide support for the worst fears of genocide sensed by
blacks. Welfare clients who need and desire family planning services are
now faced with the question: "Are birth control and abortion tantamount
to Black Genocide?" (Rutledge, 1973: p. 36).

Thirdly, much has been made of the imbalanced black sex ratio
which has increased the probability of black females being sexually exploited by black males; yet, no one has linked this imbalance to the very

nature of American health-care institutions. Medical science has shown that males are more susceptible to spontaneous abortions, birth defects, and disease than are females. The poorer the prenatal care of the mother the less likely she will be to bear a male child or a healthy one. Poor Afro-Americans suffer from both inferior medical care and inferior health. For example, the sixteen poverty areas in New York City in 1963 showed the percentage of mothers receiving late or no prenatal care to be 2.8 times higher than the rest of the city and an infant mortality rate 1.6 times higher. In the last twenty years, the gap between black and white infant mortality has widened substantially and it is no surprise that during this same time the imbalance in the black sex ratio has also worsened. In spite of their ostensible goal of providing health care to all Americans, discrimination and racism are endemic to the organization of American health institutions. The series of complex independent health institutions and the lack of systemic uniformity has precluded any single official governing body which could hold ultimate responsibility for health planning. Each of these independent units is directed by a closed panel of professionals who do not represent all their clientele; thus ignorance and bigotry prevail at the decision-making level. These governors have largely neglected the self-analysis needed to discover whether medical practice is in line with their philosophy of health care for all citizens. Most available data have been collected by civil rights groups who were alarmed at the poor health of minority people. A cursory analysis reveals that there are basically two health-care systems—one for patients who pay for services directly or through purchased insurance and another for patients who receive public assistance. The latter system is definitely inferior to the former and is especially discriminatory against the large number of blacks who are poor. Unless this dichotomous health system is dissolved, it will continue its contribution to the imbalanced black sex ratio and the disproportionate amount of infant mortality among blacks (Miller, 1966; Jackson, 1972; Zelnick and Kantner, 1972; Rutledge, 1973).

How does the ruling class justify these oppressive acts? For it is they who have the greatest power to determine and give meaning to a situation. It is they who, in baptizing black sexuality in racism, have transformed it into four-letter words and who, in christening white sexuality, have elevated it to the highest standard of morality. Eldridge Cleaver responds:

Haven't you ever wondered why the white man genuinely applauds a black man who achieves excellence with his body in the field of sports, while he hates to see a black man achieve excellence with his brain? The mechanics of the myth demand that the brain and the body, like east and west, must never meet—especially in competition on the same level. When it comes to the mechanics of the myth, the brain and the body are mutually exclusive. There can be no true competition between superiors and inferiors (1968: p. 163).

While Cleaver perceives black sexuality as part of a psychological division of labor in a colonial society, others point to psychoanalytical and normative theories. Psychoanalysts suggest that since whites are alienated from their bodies, they are simultaneously threatened and attracted to what they perceive to be the uninhibited and guilt-free sexuality of blacks. The unacceptable sexual feelings whites hold are easily projected onto defenseless blacks. Thus, white males who fear that black males will rape white women may really be interested in raping black women (Bell, 1968). Williams (1972) states that when ego defenses (e.g., projection) break down, the repressed desires may be acted out. Blacks then become the object of violent irrational acts. However, to relegate "the sexualization of racism" to extreme personality types is to abort the legitimate child—the social situation which either constrains or fosters to the point of normalcy such personalities.

Van den Berghe (1967) and McCandless and Holloway (1955) discovered that there is a definite relationship between personality type and a particular social context. Frustrated personality types are usually manifested in socially approved forms of domination and oppression. Scapegoating and depersonalization are natural responses in a racist society, for they represent conformity to normative prejudice. It is interesting to note that in a highly racist society (e.g., the United States, especially the Southern regions), regardless of personality types, most dominant-group individuals manifest prejudice and discrimination, while in societies low on racism, personality factors are related to discrimination and prejudicial attitudes. Within the above framework, it is not surprising that the whites in Myrdal's study (1944) freely expressed their belief that blacks desired sexual intercourse with whites above political, economic, and social justice. It is also to be expected that the most severe punishment is reserved for black males accused of raping white females. It must be noted here that although most rapes are intra-racial and 50 per cent of Southern rapists have been white males, 90 per cent of those executed in the South for this crime have been black. No one, black or white, has been executed for raping a black female (Lester, 1965; Bowers, 1974; Staples, 1975). The crippling effect this irrational psychodynamic process and normative prejudice has on white sexuality and black-white relations is obvious and has been handled adequately elsewhere, but less analyzed is its corrosive effect on blacks.

Fanon (1963) reminds us that the ideas generated by the colonizer will affect the colonized. The common-sense belief is that since the oppressed are blocked from obtaining the rewards and pleasures of the bourgeoisie they compensate through becoming connoisseurs of sex. Thus, minorities have a high number of sexual partners, and males as well as females are guilt-free and lack commitment in their sexual relationships. Using cross-cultural research, let us see how these beliefs measure up to empirical evidence and let us examine how the black supersexuality notion perpetrated by the colonizer may be affecting blacks.

SELF-DECEPTION OF THE RIGHTEOUS

ARE COMMITMENT DIFFERENCES ROOTED IN CULTURE?

Researchers' interpretation of comparative figures on black-white illegitimacy rates gives the impression that blacks, especially the females, are grossly indiscriminate in premarital sexual behavior. My research[1] sheds light on how the oppressed are handling the factor of commitment. The relationship between culture and commitment as measured by two items —number of partners and identity of first coital partner—is presented in Table 1.

The Afro-American male shows a trend dramatically different from all other gender-culture groups. For example, a shift from one or two partners to six or more *increases* the number of Afro-American males 88.4 per cent, *decreases* the number of Midwestern males 29.7 per cent, and creates no meaningful change for Scandinavians. Black males are also more likely than any other group to have their first coital experience with a partner to whom they are not committed. Although Afro-American females tend to have more partners than their white female American counterparts, they are virtually identical to them in confining their first premarital coital experience to a steady or fiancé.

Needless to say, black males are following a drummer who is playing a tune that is off-key for all other groups, including black females. This drummer is often referred to as the "super-stud-compensation" theory. For example, Frazier (1961) asserts that the black male frequently uses sex to manifest his masculinity and to overcome his inferior status in the family as well as in the white world (also see Liebow, 1966). A derivation of this same stream of thought is given by Hare and Hare (1970). They contend that 200 years of brainwashing on the myth of black male sexuality has forced the black male to prove his "super-stud" ability. Thus, he is a puppet in a self-fulfilling prophecy. Socialization into the myth begins early. Many are introduced to the marketplace of the flesh before they have had time to formulate any convictions on sex or to acquire proper sex information (in the present sample, blacks, especially the

TABLE 1

COMMITMENT IN PREMARITAL COITAL EXPERIENCE AS RELATED TO CULTURE BY SEX
(AFRO-AMERICAN, MIDWESTERN, AND SCANDINAVIAN, 1968)

	Males			Females		
	Afro-American	Midwestern	Scandinavian	Afro-American	Midwestern	Scandinavian
	%	%	%	%	%	%
	a	b	c	a	b	c
I. Number of Partners						
1–2	2.3	50.0	34.8	75.0	83.8	54.2
3–5	7.0	29.7	31.7	13.9	11.3	27.9
6 or more	90.7	20.3	33.5	11.1	5.0	17.9
	100.0	100.0	100.0	100.0	100.1	100.0
	(43)	(118)	(161)	(72)	(80)	(190)
II. First Premarital Coital Experience Confined to Steady or Fiance(e) *						
Yes	17.0	54.3	46.5	90.0	89.6	77.0
No	83.0	45.7	53.5	10.0	10.4	23.0
	100.0	100.0	100.0	100.0	100.0	100.0
	(47)	(116)	(170)	(80)	(77)	(200)

a, b: dyx ** = 37.3
a, c: dyx = 29.5

a, b: dyx * = .4
c, c: dyx * = 13.0

* Negative feelings include tenseness, remorse, guilt, disgust, fear of others knowing, fear of pregnancy, and fear of religious punishment.

** This coefficient represents a percentage difference, and is used as a measure of association.

males, began their sexual activities earlier than whites). Overcrowded rooms, working parents who lack the means for proper day care for their children, and the lax attitude of police with regard to sexual offenders, allow slum children as young as age 4 to gain sex knowledge by conversation, observation, and participation (Ladner, 1971). Immaturity, lack of information, misinformation, and oppression create fertile grounds for myths and fallacies. The self-deception of the righteous is deeply rooted when myths have utility for both the "unrighteous" (the oppressor) as well as the "righteous" (the oppressed). Grier and Cobbs (1968), black psychiatrists, point out the functionality of the supersexuality myth in the process of becoming a black man:

> The mythology and folklore of black people is filled with tales of sexually prodigious men. Most boys grow up on a steady diet of folk heroes who have distinguished themselves by sexual feats. It is significant that few, if any, of these folk heroes are directing armies or commanding empires. Dreams must in some way reflect reality, and in this country the black man, until quite recently, had not been in positions of power. His wielding of power had been in the privacy of the boudoir. To be sure, black men have sexual problems. They may have impotence, premature ejaculation, and the entire range of pathology which limits and distorts sexual life. Such ailments have the same dynamic origins in men of all races. But where sex is employed as an armament and used as a cautious and deliberate means of defense, it is the black man who chooses this weapon. If he cannot fight the white man openly, he can and does battle him secretly. But currently the pattern evolves of black men using sex as a dagger to be symbolically thrust into the white man (p. 58).

Victimized by the myth, black males begin an early sex life shrouded in misinformation. Parrish (1974) claims that it is the black males' obsession with protecting what he believes is his manhood that keeps him from recognizing and understanding the sexuality of women. Thus, to admit that his woman did not reach orgasm because he did not stimulate her clitoris or do some form of oral sex is to attack the most powerful and mystical black organ—the black penis:

> Just imagine: There he is, the superstud, on his knees, that powerful organ—the most powerful in the world!—tucked meekly between his legs, unable to free those deepest recesses of his woman's sex except with his tongue! . . . All men have tongues. The myth stripped away, [he is], quite simply, no longer unique (Parrish, 1974: p. 95).

To salvage his manhood when sexual performance fails, the black man concludes that if a black female is not satisfied with him she has to be "hung-up" or "uptight" about sex; the best thing to do is to move on to the many other women in the field. When black males behave in this manner, it presents a real problem for the majority of black females. For if black females require commitment (as the present data show) before they can give freely in coitus, the already low number of eligible males is drastically reduced. Furthermore, it appears that the female has not communicated her dissatisfaction to the black male. Perhaps her silence not only lies in the realization that there are plenty of other women who will provide the black male with the ego protection he needs, but also in the fact that naiveté and passivity traditionally have been considered female virtues. The less concern females displayed about sex, the more they were cherished. The price for this deception has been to eliminate grounds for complaining about lack of sexual satisfaction (Staples, 1973; Parrish, 1974).

GUILTY—BLACK OR WHITE, MALE OR FEMALE?

Several sociologists believe that blacks as opposed to whites have a more wholesome attitude toward sex, accepting sex for its own sake. Staples (1971) illustrates the historical conditions which he believes influenced many present-day black women:

> The flagrant violation of the black woman's body during the slavery era served to devalue the worth of virginity to her. What good was it to value something one was not allowed to have? As a consequence the deeply rooted feelings of guilt about sex never became entrenched in the psyche of black women as they did in her white counterpart (p. 120).

Much the same is said of the sexual history of the Afro-American male. However, my research shows some surprising variations (see Table 2). Among the males of the three 1968 cultures, there is little meaningful difference. As one moves from the Afro-American culture to the Midwestern, there is only a 2.8 per cent change between Afro-Americans and Scandinavians. Black females have dramatically more negative feelings than all gender-culture groups. By 1973 black females appeared to be less guilt-ridden; however, they still held more negative feelings than any other group (1973 data were not available for Scandinavians). The historical explanation of sexual exploitations does not appear to be relevant here. Perhaps the greater adverse consequences among Afro-American females may be associated with the imbalance in the sex ratio which forces them to go against their own sexual code in lieu of losing their partner to more permissive females. The consequences and nature of the first premarital coitus also must be considered. To begin with, the end result of recreational sex is more likely to be pregnancy for blacks than

TABLE 2

NEGATIVE FEELINGS ACCOMPANYING FIRST PREMARITAL COITUS AS RELATED TO TIME, BY SEX

	Afro-American		Midwestern		Scandinavian	
	%	N	%	N	%	N
I. Males Negative feelings following first premarital coital experience°						
1968	21.3	(10)	18.5	(22)	23.5	(40)
1973	5.2	(3)	16.0	(28)	° ° °	
dyx ° °	16.1		2.5			
II. Females Negative feelings following first premarital coital experience°						
1968	53.2	(42)	39.0	(30)	25.0	(50)
1973	40.2	(35)	34.9	(54)	° ° °	
dyx	13.0		4.1			

° Negative feelings include tenseness, remorse, guilt, disgust, fear of others knowing, fear of pregnancy, and fear of religious punishment.
° ° This coefficient represents a percentage difference, and is used as a measure of association.
° ° ° Data were not available for 1973.

for whites. Some black males have convinced black women that the condom is unnatural and should not be used. Since the pill is more difficult to obtain, the likelihood of contraceptives being used is reduced. Second, Staples (1973) contends that the first premarital sexual experience for many black females is likely to be painful, brutal, or in essence a rape that results from a misfired attempt at seduction. Given these two observations, the greater degree of negative feelings among black females is understandable.

It is of interest to note in Table 2 that gender rather than culture is most important in differentiating negative and positive feelings following first premarital coitus. Within each culture, for both years, males had fewer negative feelings than did females. The differences were striking in the American groups, especially among Afro-Americans, and minimal among the Scandinavians. Apparently, the American double standard has suppressed the ability of females, both black and white, to fully enjoy premarital sex. It has allowed a broader range of socially acceptable premarital sexual behavior for males. Thus, when the male violates his own sexual code, he has greater justification for his actions, for society's code is probably more liberal than his own standards. This double standard, more pervasive in America than in Scandinavia, is reflected in the greater male-female incongruence in the former country. In short, what may be reflected here is the tendency for sexism to be more oppressive of sexual behavior than racism.

Reinhold Niebuhr warned that "the chief engine of injustice in this world is the self-deception of the righteous." My research suggests that black males, certified by the supersexuality myth, have acted to create a self-fulfilling prophecy that has adversely affected black females. Blacks have, in a real sense, aided in their own sexual oppression. This is not to negate the necessity of ending the oppressive acts by the ruling class. But it is to suggest that blacks can aid in their own sexual liberation. Black males must trade the myth for the reality if they are to become the lovers they are said to be, and black females must begin to communicate their dissatisfaction and concerns if they are to become guilt-free. The self-deception of the Righteous is, at present, merely an extension of the White Man's Burden—The Black Body.

PRACTICAL CONSIDERATIONS

In the above discussion we have linked the sexual oppression of blacks to the very nature of our American cultural, legal, and health system; a system which generates exploitive, dysfunctional and superficial forms of sexual attitudes and behavior for a great number of both blacks and whites. Present indications are that significant proportions of Americans are attempting to improve their sexual lives. Swinging clubs, contemporary orgies, and sex-therapy clinics are indicative of the earnest and seemingly desperate search of individuals to realize their own sexual potentials, needs, desires, and styles. Although sexual therapy appears to be the most rational approach, it is still in its infancy and in need of refinement. The motivational patterns, sexual histories, and sexual values of those involved in these experiments have yet to be fully explored (Smith and Smith, 1974). One obvious observation is that there are few blacks participating. Sensing that whites are not the only group in need of sexual therapy, a number of clinics have conducted extensive publicity campaigns in the black community. This effort has resulted in a few middle-class black clients. Social scientists and family practitioners, however, should not be too quick to judge low black involvement in sex-therapy clinics as a manifestation of a healthy sex life. After all, few blacks participate in the current Women's Liberation Movement; yet black women's social and economic status is below that of their white counterparts. Similar to the women's movement, sexual clinics are perhaps seen as a white middle-class activity, the suburban housewife's escape from the mundane chores of family living, or even a self-actualization desire of whites—a luxury for those blacks who are simply trying to survive. The white middle-class orientation is sufficient grounds for many blacks to dismiss such clinics and sexual experimentation as totally irrelevant to the black experience. Some blacks may also find comfort in the belief that blacks' historical and generally relaxed attitude toward premarital coitus has protected them from extreme sexual experimentation and the sexual "shrink" doctor. Although this may be true, our data have shown that at least among black females, all is not well. If some argue that black males' low guilt and high coital experience are indicative of both true sexual freedom and lack of sexual dysfunctions, there is still something to be said about improving an already good sex life.

A movement toward improving the quality of sexual experience is developing within the black community itself. There is at least one established clinic in the United States which is owned and directed by blacks —the Institute for Marriage Enrichment and Sexual Studies in Columbia, Maryland. This institute was established by Dr. Richard Tyson, a black physician, who was concerned over the number of sexual problems that he encountered in his private medical practice. It is important to note that this clinic is located in a middle-class black suburban area. Because of the greater number of cost and efficiency problems in the ghetto, sex or health clinics and the offices of private physicians are not likely to be found there (Knowles and Prewitt, 1969). The black lower class is simply not being reached. Thus, as professionals are re-examining and further developing therapeutic programs, they need to investigate the needs of lower-class black people, the specific reasons for their lack of participation in current sex-therapy clinics, and the means by which health services can be delivered to them.

Since it is apparent that a significant increase in black sex therapists, physicians, and representation in American health systems will be a slow process, family-life professionals need to search for short-term solutions. For example, in order to reach the lower-class black community, it may be necessary to establish a mobile health unit (similar to a bookmobile). This unit would not only provide premarital and marital counseling, sex education material, a rape-crisis center, prenatal care and contraceptives for the community but also would operate at convenient times and eliminate transportation expenses of indigent clients. The effectiveness of this healthmobile might be increased if it were staffed by black professionals, local people, and key leaders in the community. The latter personnel is extremely important. A few black counselors have noted that blacks who need help are generally disinclined toward self-disclosure and have a basic distrust of having nonsignificant others regulate their personal lives. Thus, it may be well to have a local minister on the staff. The few reports that are available reveal that black ministers are asked more often than are the professionals in health clinics to solve the marital and sexual problems of their parishioners. Dr. Grant Shockly, president of the Inter-denominational Theological Center (a major source of black ministers), observed that the church has seen an increase in the number of couples seeking help and has been more supportive than dysfunctional in helping them to work through their problems (Morton, 1976). The popularity of pastoral counseling is perhaps due to the minister's frequent contact with the people, his consultation-without-charge policy, and his spiritual role which connects him to the intimate sectors of people's lives. As educators are institutionalizing human sexuality workshops in black medical schools, attention should also be given to the need for them in black theological centers.

As currently practiced, sexual therapy ends when freedom of sexual expression and orgasm or regular orgasm begins. This scope is too limited for blacks (whites as well), particularly the males. There are, no doubt, those who suffer from sexual dysfunctions. However, many black males and females are finding difficulties in establishing interpersonal relationships, not sexual relations. Clearly, sexual fulfillment is not measured merely by the intensity of an orgasm or its frequency, but rather by both the sexual act and the context in which it occurs. Therapeutic goals which promote creative change, interpersonal communication skills, sensitivity, trust, and an awareness of sex-role expectations are needed.

Of course, the best preventive measure is early sex education. Professional and community organizations should work earnestly to influence public policy to provide sound educational programs for children. Such education needs to start earlier than is usually done for most children white or black. However, as the aforementioned discussion revealed, early education is, at this point, even more important for black children than for their white counterparts. Children as young as four years would not be so crudely exposed to coital activities if there were well staffed day-care centers available to low-income working parents, with a sex education program, created in part by parents, an important aspect of these centers. It has been found that black teen-agers are more knowledgeable about the sex act and sex organs than are lower-class whites (Rosenberg and Bensman, 1968), but they gain information concerning menstruation, fertilization, and pregnancy later than their white counterparts. Thus, the nature of sex education should be tailored to the specific needs of black children.

Concomitant with health services and sex education should be public action against egregious oppressive practices. Organizations, such as the Sex Information and Education Council of the U.S. (SIECUS) and the National Organization for Women (NOW) should lobby against the legal label of "illegitimate." It seems advisable for them to press for greater social support to teen-age unwed parents through (1) lobbying for policies which ensure their right to family counseling and medical care without undue adult intervention, (2) providing facilities for continuing education, (3) establishing high-school consciousness-raising seminars where they can learn the art of responsibility and meet others with similar experiences (cf. Mead, 1971), and (4) lobbying for national policies which require the unwed father as well as the unwed mother to take responsibility for the welfare of the child (black or mulatto).

Finally, care should be taken in presenting a proper attitude and perspective on black sexuality. Public-school teachers and social workers who deal with the social aspect of human sexuality should be especially sensitive to condescending, paternalistic, and threatening approaches. The birth-control question, as we have seen, is a delicate one, and should be handled as such. If students and teachers differ with regard to social class or race, then it may be necessary to require courses in intergroup relations, black studies, or programs which give appreciation to cultural differences and individualism (Staples, 1972). Likewise, academicians should examine their work so as to avoid pejorative, ethnocentric, and racist statements, as well as the conceptual models which basically categorize black sexual attitudes and behavior as deficient when they differ from middle-class norms. Non-black scholars would avoid many ethnocentric errors if they would integrate into their work the research and publications of black writers, and then move beyond statistical data to the psychodynamic processes within the black subculture.

As human beings—black and white, male and female—our need is to work positively toward the realization of a socio-cultural system which best creates individuals with authentic selfhood and interpersonal relationships devoid of oppressive and exploitive sexual overtones. The above recommendations are a few necessary steps in this direction.

NOTE

1. My research is an extension of work begun by Harold T. Christensen approximately eighteen years ago. His investigations included universities in several cultures, but in this present chapter we are focusing upon his data gathered in 1968 from a Swedish, a Midwestern white American, and a predominantly Afro-American Southern college. His data were gathered in collaboration with Dr. Jan Trost, a Swedish family sociologist, and Dr. Eugene Sherman, a soci-

ologist of a predominantly black college. In 1973, in order to extend and focus the analysis on American blacks, the present writer in collaboration with Dr. Eugene Sherman readministered portions of the 1968 questionnaire to student samples at the same American schools surveyed in 1968. The non-random samples (total = 2008) included in 1968—51 male and 123 female Southern Afro-Americans, 245 male and 238 female Midwestern white Americans, and 206 male and 250 female Scandinavians; and in 1973–72 male and 148 female Southern Afro-Americans, and 322 male and 353 female Midwestern white Americans. I utilized this data in my 1974 doctoral dissertation which was directed by Dr. Harold T. Christensen.

REFERENCES AND RECOMMENDED READINGS

ABERNATHY, GLENN M. *Civil Liberties Under the Constitution.* New York: Dodd, Mead & Co., 1968.

ALEXANDER, DARYL. "A Montgomery Tragedy," *Essence*, Sept. 1973, pp. 42–43, 82, 96.

AMIR, MENACHEM. "Forcible Rape." In *The Sociology of Crime and Delinquency*, 2nd edition. New York: Wiley, 1970, pp. 644–653.

BARATZ, STEVEN & JOAN BARATZ. "Early Childhood Intervention: The Social Science Base of Institutional Racism," *Harvard Educational Review*, 40 (Winter 1970), pp. 29–50.

BELL, ALLAN. "Black Sexuality: Fact and Fancy." Paper presented in Focus: Black America Series. Indiana University, Bloomington, Indiana, Oct. 1968.

BERRY, MARY. *Black Resistance—White Law: A History of Constitutional Racism in America.* New York: Appleton-Century-Croft, 1971.

BOWERS, WM. J. *Executions in America.* Lexington, Mass.: Lexington Books, Div. of D. C. Heath & Co., 1974.

BROWN, THOMAS N. "Sex Education and Life in the Negro Ghetto," *Pastoral Psychology*, Vol. 19, No. 184 (May 1968).

CLEAVER, ELDRIDGE. *Soul on Ice.* New York: Delta Books, 1968.

CLOWARD, RICHARD A. & FRANCES FOX PIVEN. "Migration, Politics, & Welfare," *Saturday Review*, 51 (Nov., 16, 1968), pp. 31–35.

DAY, BETH. *Sexual Life Between Black and White.* New York: World, 1972.

DERBYSHIRE, R. L. "The Uncompleted Negro Family: Suggested Research Regarding the Effect of the Negro's Outcaste Conditions Upon His Own and Other American Sexual Attitudes and Behavior," *Journal of Human Relations*, 15(4) (4th quarter, 1967), pp. 458–468.

FANON, FRANTZ. *The Wretched of the Earth.* New York: Grove Press, 1965.

FRAZIER, E. F. *The Negro Church in the United States.* Liverpool: Liverpool University Press, 1961.

FURSTENBERG, FRANK P. "Premarital Pregnancy Among Black Teenagers," *Trans-Action*, May 1970, pp. 53–55.

GEBHARD, *et al. Pregnancy, Birth, and Abortion.* New York: Harper & Row, 1958.

GRIER, W. H. & P. M. COBBS. *Black Rage*. New York: Basic Books, 1968.

HARE, N. & J. HARE. "Black Women," *Trans-Action*, November 1970, p. 66.

HERNTON, CALVIN C. *Sex and Racism in America*. New York: Doubleday & Co., Inc., 1965.

HILL, ADELAIDE C. & FREDERICK S. JAFFE. "Negro Fertility and Family Size Preferences—Implications for Programming of Health and Social Services." In *The Negro American*, edited by Talcott Parsons & Kenneth Clark. Boston: Beacon Press, 1967.

ISHERWOOD, CHRISTOPHER. *A Single Man*. London: Methuen & Co., Ltd., 1964.

JACKSON, JACQUELYNE. "Where Are the Black Men?" *Ebony* Magazine, March 1972, pp. 99–106.

JORDAN, WINTHROP. *The White Man's Burden*. New York: Oxford University Press, 1974.

KADUSHIN, ALFRED. *Child Welfare Services*. New York: Macmillan, 1974.

KINLOCH, GRAHAM C. *The Dynamics of Race Relations*. New York: McGraw-Hill, 1974.

LADNER, JOYCE. *Tomorrow's Tomorrow*. New York: Doubleday, 1971.

LESTER, ANTHONY. *Justice in the American South*. London: Amnesty International, 1965.

LIEBOW, ELLIOT. *Tally's Corner*. Boston: Little, Brown & Co., 1967.

MC CANDLESS, R. & H. D. HOLLOWAY. "Race Prejudice and Intolerance of Ambiguity in Children," *Journal of Abnormal Social Psychology*, 1955.

MEAD, MARGARET. "Future Family," *Trans-Action*, September 1971.

MILLER, LOREN. "Race, Poverty and the Law." In *The Law and the Poor*, Jacobus TenBroek & California Law Review, eds. San Francisco, Calif.: Chandler Publishing Co., 1966.

MORTON, CAROL. "Mistakes Black Women Make in Relating to Black Men," *Ebony* Magazine, January 1976, pp. 88–93.

MYRDAL, G. *An American Dilemma*. New York: Harper & Row, 1944.

PARRISH, MILTON. "Black Women's Guide to the Black Man," *Essence*, April 1974, pp. 57, 91, 93, 95.

PETTIGREW, T. F. "Personality and Socio-cultural Factors in Intergroup Attitudes: A Cross-National Comparison," *Journal of Conflict Resolution* 2 (1958), pp. 29–42.

POPE, H. and D. KNUDSEN, "Premarital Sexual Norms, the Family, and Social Change." *Journal of Marriage and the Family* 27 (August 1965), pp. 314–323.

POPE, HALLOWELL. "Unwed Mothers and Their Sex Partners," *Journal of Marriage and the Family*, 29 (August 1967), pp. 555–567.

Population Council Report on Abortions by Age and Race. Washington D.C.: U.S. Government Printing Office, 1972.

RAINWATER, LEE. "Crucible of Identity: The Negro Lower-Class Family." In *Selected Studies in Marriage and the Family*, edited by Robert Winch and Louis Goodman. New York: Holt, Rinehart & Winston, Inc., 1968.

————. *Behind Ghetto Walls*. Chicago: Aldine, 1970.

————, "Some Aspects of Lower Class Sexual Behavior," *Journal of Social Issues*, 22 (April 1966), pp. 96–108.

————. *And the Poor Get Children: Sex, Contraception, and Family Planning in the Working Class.* Chicago: Quadrangle Books, 1960, p. 202.

REISS, IRA L. "How and Why America's Sex Standards are Changing," *Trans-Action*, March 1968, pp. 26–32.

ROSENBERG, BERNARD & JOSEPH BENSMAN. "Sexual Patterns in Three Ethnic Subcultures of an American Underclass," *Academy of Political and Social Science*, 84 (1968), pp. 61–65.

RUFFIN, FRANCES. "Birth Control: A Choice—Genocide or Survival?" *Essence*, September 1972, pp. 42–43, 70, 72.

RUTLEDGE, AL. "Is Abortion Black Genocide?" *Essence*, September 1973, pp. 36, 70, 85–86.

SCHULZ, D. A. *Coming Up Black.* New York: Prentice-Hall, 1969.

SLY, DAVID. "Minority Group Status and Fertility: An Extension of Foldschneider & Uhlenberg," *American Journal of Sociology*, 76 (3) (1970), pp. 443–459.

SMITH, JAMES & LYNN SMITH. *Beyond Monogamy.* Baltimore: Johns Hopkins Press, 1974.

STAPLES, ROBERT. "Race and Family Violence: The Internal Colonialism Perspective." A paper presented at the conference on "Crime and Its Impact on the Black Community," Howard University, Washington, D.C., June 4, 1975.

————. "Internal Colonialism and Black Violence: An Analysis of the Political Character of Black Fratricide." A paper presented at the 2nd Venezuelan Meeting on Criminology and Violence, Maracaibo, Venezuela, July 24–August 3, 1974.

————, "The Black Dating Game," *Essence*, October 1973, p. 40.

————, "Research on Black Sexuality: Its Implication for Family Life, Sex Education, and Public Policy," *The Family Coordinator*, 21, No. 2 (1972), pp. 183–187.

————. *The Black Family: Essays and Studies.* Belmont, Calif.: Wadsworth Publishing Co., Inc., 1970.

THOMAS, WILLIAM H. *The American Negro: What He Was, What He Is, and What He May Become.* New York: The Macmillan Co., 1901.

TRIPP, C. A. "Debate: Can a Homosexual Change with Psychotherapy?" *Sexual Behavior*, July 1971, pp. 42–49.

VAN DEN BERGHE, PIERRE LOUIS. *Race and Racism: A Comparative Perspective.* New York: John Wiley & Sons, 1969.

WEST, LOUIS J. "Psychobiology of Racial Violence," *Archives of General Psychiatry*, 16, June 1967.

WILLIAMS, LEON F. "Sex, Racism, and Social Work." In *Human Sexuality and Social Work*, edited by Harvey Gochros and LeRoy Schultz. New York: Association Press, 1972.

WOLFGANG, MARVIN E. *Crime and Race.* New York: Institute on Human Relations Press, 1964.

YOUNG, LOIS J. "Are Black Men Taking Care of Business?" *Essence*, pp. 73, 75, 94.

ZELNICK, M. & J. KANTNER. "Sexuality, Contraception and Pregnancy Among

Young Unwed Females in the U.S.," Commission on Population Growth and American Futures, 1972.

———. "U.S.: Exploratory Studies of Negro Family Formation—Factors Related to Illegitimacy," *Studies in Family Planning*, No. 60 (December 1970.

CHAPTER 13
ASIAN AMERICANS

Dennis Ogawa

Cross-racially and ethnically, most individuals come to share a common notion of what is or isn't sexually arousing. Miss America for many people is blonde, blue-eyed and curvaceous; she is the wholesome, virgin-like goddess that every red-blooded American male would like to get his hands on. Thus, it is unthinkable that a four-foot ten-inch girl weighing 140 pounds could win a beauty contest because of her happy character, quick-witted intellect or musical talent with a tuba. Indeed, among Americans the need to be beautiful and to associate with beautiful people is a primary yardstick for self-evaluation and mate selection. It should come as no great shock, then, that people from New York to Honolulu are preoccupied with notions of physical beauty as typified by Madison Avenue advertisements. What determines our attractiveness as men or women is our new panty hose, or closer shave, our safer deodorant or our more alluring eye shadow. In this striving to become perfect sexual beings, the ideal embodiment of beauty, we are becoming a nation of neurotics. What we are, we are told, is not what we should be. Most people are enshrouded with feelings of physical inadequacy when their bodies are compared with the beautiful women of commercials who have large, well-formed breasts, curved hips and firm buttocks with long legs or the handsome men who are tall, muscular, well-endowed, and who have strong facial features.

If the American concept of physical beauty which places attention on mirrors, stray pimples and double chins is the basis of personal sexual identity, then the Asian American in his creation of a sexual self-image represents no exception to this standard. Indeed, the concern for a beautiful sexual image is very evident in the Asian American community and creates some peculiarly difficult situations. Given that the ideal of beauty which is projected by the media is based on a white measure of physical appearance and stature, the Asian American is often faced with an unattainable goal. Physically, his build and appearance are not conducive to what one imagines as the perfect white beauty. Try as they may, Asian Americans will never be able to alter their racial features or fundamentally change their bones, muscles or even their hair color.

Consequently, between the ideal which the Asian American is seeking in beauty and the reality of what he looks like, frustrations and anxieties can result. A study done at the University of Hawaii, for example, revealed a great discrepancy between what the Japanese American girls seek as an ideal and what they are in reality. The subjects were asked what they would like to be in terms of height and body statistics, and then they were measured. It was found that most girls had indicated that they would like to be about five feet three or four inches tall, even though in actuality they barely reached five feet one inch with their shoes on. Also, they wished to weigh 106 to 110 pounds, when they really weighed 114 pounds and more. In terms of bust size, they wanted to be around thirty-four and one-half inches when in actuality they were less than thirty-two inches.

With the mammarian fascination among American males, it is no wonder that almost any female, especially an Asian American female, should feel so deprived. Big breasts indicate beauty and sexual attractiveness, and the flat-chested Oriental female looks conspicuously immature and boyish. It is difficult to be the ideal woman and have the uplift and support look of firm breasts when one wears a size 32-A brassiere.

Another physical anomaly that Asian American girls lament about concerns their eyes. The slanting eyes of the Oriental female may be a mystical asset in the romantic Far East of best-selling novels, but many girls feel that slanting eyes are ugly when compared to round, well-formed Caucasian eyes. To correct this situation, quite a number of Asian American girls undergo an eye operation to create a double fold of the eyelids or else use Scotch tape to make their eyes appear rounder and fuller.

The concern with physical beauty goes further than just being a worry to the females. Asian American men also find themselves measured against the ideal appearance of a Paul Newman or Chad Everett. One of the most conscious dissatisfactions that the Asian male has is his lack of height. Being short and stocky, with a long torso and short legs, he is a far cry from the dashing figures of the TV screen and the movies. Lacking physical stature, he is therefore rarely if ever viewed in the role of a policeman or a fireman, but almost always is a waiter or a gardener.

Besides the lack of height and body shape, there are other physical pressures which exist for the Asian American. In a typical Japanese American household, for example, one often finds parents telling their children: "You must always pull the bridge of your nose between your thumb and fingers so that you won't grow up with a flat face." Another point that some parents stress is the necessity to be pale and white. A common expression which mothers say to their daughters when they go to the beach is, "Be careful, don't get too dark."

Although Asian Americans have accepted these Caucasian standards of beauty as goals, as have most Americans generally, one cannot quickly conclude that this is the only direction that can be taken by the group. In Hawaii, where a significant portion of the Asian Americans live, there appears to be developing another standard of physical appearance which could be called the "local idea of beauty."

What is happening in Hawaii is the creation of a concept of beauty and sexual attraction among non-whites which uses some measure of white beauty, but intermingles it with the image of the beautiful Oriental and Polynesian. Probably the most striking example of the new image being evolved is in the local advertisements for clothing stores. In these, a couple of Oriental extraction can be seen. The girl's hair is long and straight, her body is petite but not buxom, and her skin deeply tanned. She belongs not solely to the Orient but also to Polynesian Hawaii where wearing bikinis and having dark tans is the norm. Deeply tanned and giving off the image of a "beach boy," the male is not tall and rugged; instead, he is physically well-proportioned and of normal stature. His hair is lengthy, but neatly trimmed; his slant eyes are confident.

In many ways this local image of what is beautiful and sexually attractive appeals to the young Asian American because it is a practical and feasible attainable image. The couple, who typify the young and beautiful people of Hawaii, are not superstars. Their body proportions are not fantastic, their facial features are not unblemished and ideal. Any non-white, with a little effort, can thus create for himself a sexual self-identity which is comfortable and anxiety-free.

Given the environment, physical conditions and interracial mixtures of Hawaii, it is easy to see why the emergence of this local image is possible. But on the mainland the Asian American often feels like a dwarf among giants. His physical differences are painfully evident whenever he leaves his ethnic community and ventures into the world of the Caucasian.

Though the Asian American in Hawaii, through the media, has learned to measure beauty to a large degree by white standards, the reality of day-to-day living, plus the situation of being with and seeing non-whites consistently, has had mitigating effects on this orientation. If someone living in Hawaii were to be asked who are the most beautiful people, the most plausible answer would be *"hapa-haole"*—that is, a person of Filipino-Caucasian, Japanese-Caucasian or Polynesian-Caucasian racial extraction. This, in itself, could be indicative of the blending of sexual images created by the media and the local standards of beauty which have developed in Hawaii.

To appreciate how Asian Americans view sex and their own sexual identity, however, it is necessary to go beyond the level of thought which is afforded when one speaks of idealized sexual images. Encompassing sexual activities is not only an image of what is physically beautiful, but a series of attitudes toward the nature and morality of sex. It is the attitude and sense of morality toward sex that become the guideposts by which an individual maintains and directs his life. In the Asian American community there are several sexual attitudes which must be identified. But before a description of these attitudes can be attempted, one must first have a general understanding of the American attitude toward sex.

Although it might seem that the current sexual revolution exposes an American heritage of open and liberal sex attitudes, the reverse is actually the case. The Puritan tradition which is often blamed for the hard-work ethic and conservative nature of American values can also be blamed for the closed and narrow conception which the silent majority of Americans have toward sex as an activity to be relegated to a darkened bedroom, to be hidden from children and young ladies. Sex in America has commonly been seen as a dirty business necessary to reproduce the race, but certainly not to be openly enjoyed.

Recognizing the Puritanistic tradition of American values, then, is essential. What must also be understood, however, is the fascination and temptation which Americans have always associated with sex. Regardless of the American values which on the surface make sex to be a necessary evil, sex remains a pleasurable drive. Americans from Benjamin Franklin (who cavorted in the palaces of Europe and wrote eloquently of the virtues of a woman's bosom) to Presidents Warren G. Harding and Franklin Roosevelt (each of whom had a mistress while in the White House) have found adequate expressions of their sexual needs. Arising from this conflict between the so-called evils of sex and the fascination with the forbidden, several sexual attitudes have emerged which define the complexity of sexuality in America, and the way that it is viewed by the Asian Americans as well.

LOWER-CLASS SEXUALITY

The first type of sexual attitude which one finds expressed through our culture and typified in the behaviors of many males and females, is the attitude toward Lower-Class Sexuality. To understand Lower-Class Sexuality, one must let his imagination take him back to the 1850's and to a small plantation in Mississippi or Alabama. Ol' Massa, the white plantation owner, is getting into his pajamas while Missis is getting into bed. Snuggling up to his wife, Ol' Massa plants a gentle kiss behind the ear for which he receives a rap on the mouth. "Really, Henry, not tonight," she gently drawls.

Ol' Massa Henry is spending a restless night unable to get to sleep thinking of the gentle and pure lily-white female next to him who is snoring away. Quietly leaving his wife's side, he goes downstairs and sneaks into the dark slave quarters of his favorite kitchenmaid, Caroline. He knows that the black-skinned Caroline is always ready and willing for a little innocent fun since, after all, she is black. Living without the benefits of culture and civilization, she is like an animal, without the morality and careful breeding of his sexually repressed wife. Caroline's promiscuity is linked to her station in life, her race, and her natural depravity.

Now, a little closer to home, where does the frustrated Asian American male go to relieve himself instantly of his sexual anxieties? Does he cruise the streets of the middle-class suburbs? Hardly. He most likely goes downtown to Main Street where the action is fast and cheap. He can supposedly purchase sex, no commitment or intimacies necessary, from dark-skinned prostitutes. Or he can vicariously seek a sexual outlet by viewing a hard-core pornographic film which arouses and titillates. He knows that on Main Street the sexual attitude is not confining, restricting or mundane as it might be at home. Instead, it is animalistic and wildly immoral.

Essentially, then, one can associate the attitude of Lower-Class Sexuality with that area of town where poverty and race have rendered people "loose and degraded" in the minds of middle-class individuals. Blacks and Puerto Ricans, Filipinos and Mexicans are either pimps, bar girls or whores. Sex of this sort can always be found on the Main Streets and hotel streets around the world.

With people having such an attitude of sex being dirty or available from "sluts," it is not surprising that one commonly takes for granted and enjoys activities such as reading graffiti on bathroom walls. After all, where could a person find a more ample place to let out frustrated sexual drives and fantasies than near a toilet? At the University of Hawaii, the most frequent graffiti concerns a young lady with the initials of V.K. Graphic descriptions of her sex life, crude drawings of her anatomy, medical reports on her physical condition, and personal data such as phone number and convenient times of contact adorn the walls. Obviously, this type of sexual attitude is based upon the opposite notion of puritanical sex. Sex is cheap, thrilling and constantly available from V.K. and other lower-class females like her. Women are loose and have large sexual appetites which must be satisfied.

So Lower-Class Sexuality becomes an attitude which the sexually frustrated middle-class male projects on those people who live in poverty, cultural deprivation or carelesss morality. In Hawaii this attitude is expressed when one stereotypically thinks of the streetwalkers in Waikiki or downtown (be they black, white or local), when one sees a boarding-house full of Filipino men who obviously need to have sex, even if it is with ten-year-old girls, or when one sees a carload of ghetto youths cruising in their souped-up car, drinking beer and obviously looking for some poor girl to rape.

The attitude of Lower-Class Sexuality can also be seen in the case of the Japanese Americans. In the past, when they were still impoverished immigrants, the males were viewed as potential rapists, the women, especially picture brides, as whores. Even today, not all Orientals own houses in nice middle-class areas, or live middle-class lives. Some Japanese American youths hang around street corners in the "rough" areas of town, smoking, sniffing glue, acting in a manner which to the outsider must certainly be called sexually promiscuous and socially irreverent. The attitudes which they project represent the same class of attitudes generated by blacks, Filipinos or Puerto Ricans in similar social settings, no matter what city is involved.

UPPER-CLASS SEXUALITY

In addition to an attitude directed at the immoral and illicit sexual activities of lower-class peoples, one also finds in American culture a sexual attitude which is based on extreme wealth and refinement. This attitude is one of Upper-Class Sexuality and is characterized by a large degree of plastic beauty and geniality. Essentially, Upper-Class Sexuality is expressed in its truest form in *Playboy* Magazine. Here one can see women exposing their bodies in suggestive poses, draped in the status symbols of wealthy apartments, clothes, furniture and with possibly plastic surgery and silicone injections. Even if a magnifying glass is used, no blemish or misplaced hairs will be found. Whether they "will" or "will not" is not a relevant question. What decent, respectable young lady would allow herself to be so photographed if she "didn't"?

Obviously the attitude of Upper-Class Sexuality is more attractive to middle-class men than is the image of Lower-Class Sexuality. These beautiful, proper ladies wouldn't have social diseases. Their bodies are immaculately preserved as if they slept in formaldehyde; they would have none of the bruises and wornout features of women of the streets. Although they may be as loose and as wild as other prostitutes, women of *Playboy* Magazine are more of a challenge. They don't ask to be paid outright for sex, but ask, instead, to be impressed with wealth and savoir-faire. And yet, ultimately, they will give the same thrill and satisfaction that would be obtained from women of the lower class.

The counterpart of this allusion of the *Playboy* girl is found in *Cosmopolitan* Magazine. Like the *Playboy* girl, the type of man which this magazine tells its female readers they should seek is the virile, wealthy bachelor who will aggressively and abandonedly sweep them off their feet. The old girl puzzler, "Should I let him kiss me on our first date?" doesn't become a question of time, but of location. No morality is involved, just the pursuit of sexual pleasure and self-gratification.

In a fundamental way, then, the attitudes of Lower- and Upper-Class Sexuality, in which the Asian American clearly participates, is a sublimation and release of tensions from the Puritanical notion of the restricted sexual life. While it is true that most Asian Americans (and most people, for that matter) do not frequent the prostitutes of Main Street or live the life of the *Playboy* girl or the *Cosmopolitan* man, still they look to such images as referents for judging their own life, or even as symbols to secretly dream upon.

MIDDLE-CLASS SEXUALITY

The last sexual attitude to be discussed and one which is especially relevant for the Asian Americans, as they are viewed by others and themselves, is the attitude of Middle-Class Sexuality. This is the attitude of the majority of Americans who are inclined to be neither streetwalkers nor carefree jet setters. In the demanding life of middle-class living, with an emphasis on studying or working hard, keeping the nose to the grindstone, and "keeping out of debt," there is little time or opportunity for an exciting or varied sex life. Morals and values ranging from the newspaper pulp of Ann Landers or Abigail Van Buren to the deep beliefs and highly respected attitudes of religion are the cornerstone of their upbringing and world view.

For many Asian Americans, the middle-class style of living—including the sexual attitude which characterizes such individuals—has become a fundamental way of life. If the Asians are indeed "out-whiting the whites" in their pursuit of middle-class security, the same is true for the clean sexual image they project. Children are made to feel obligated to achieve in the classroom, not in bed. Girls are taught the necessary acts to become a good housewife, not a thrilling lover. Restrictions on the use of the family car, dating practices, curfew hours, and other techniques of family control conform ideally with the virtues of the church, temple, Ms. Landers or Ms. Van Buren.

The result of the perpetuation of the middle-class modes of living has been to cast a stereotype for the Asian American which reflects neither an attitude of Lower-Class Sexuality of Asian whores and rapists, nor an Upper-Class Sexuality attitude of virile, free lovers. On a normal day at any high school attended by Asian Americans, one can observe that the girls and boys are neatly dressed and scrubbed, their hair clean and combed; all in all, they demonstrate the wholesome quality of good, normal children. It is no wonder, then, that the Asian female is a "virgin" in the framework of the attitude of Middle-Class Sexuality. Petite and demure, she is the epitome of the girl next door, the Pollyanna who naively knows nothing nor even hears anything about the world of sex. She is graceful, dainty, sweet, a lotus blossom, and a lover of flower arrangements, tea ceremonies, and baby-sitting the younger children.

The Asian males are sexually immature and therefore also considered "nice." They have had little, if any, experience with women and definitely lack any sort of debonair quality. They are more involved with studying, raising guppies in aquariums or playing basketball with friends than in scoring with girls. They are the lovers of hobbies, flowers and drive-in food.

Yet, captured within this mystique of sexual inadequacy, the Asian American can become frustrated with his middle-class orientation toward love and sex. Seeking the beauty of an idealized and manufactured Playboy Bunny, the Asian American male may chastise the female for not meeting his expectations. Her body is too dumpy or too skinny to please him. "Why can't you be more aggressive like Caucasian girls are?" he asks. "Why don't you do something to make yourself more attractive?"

On the other hand, the Asian American female will downgrade the Asian American male on the premise that he isn't like the virile creatures who are so popular in the movies and television or in the imagination. Some may even say that under no circumstances would they go out with an Asian American male. They prefer going out with Caucasians because they think Caucasians are freer in their attitudes, more relaxed and easier to talk with. The Asian American male is just too nice, too weak, too "mousy." Unlike the Caucasians whom they imagine to have control and finesse, the Asian American male doesn't know what he is doing. Far from being a refined and sexually free artist of love, he is impotent, castrated and generally a dud.

Thus, to fully comprehend the dynamics of sexuality as it is expressed socially and racially, one must recognize the three attitudes of Lower-, Upper- and Middle-Class Sexuality which are shared not only by Asian Americans, but by all individuals in the American culture. It is within the framework of these attitudes that an individual will view himself and others.

Most studies of sex attitudes have concluded that the stereotypes which have been projected for a racial group have been singular in nature: *i.e.*, blacks are virile; Mexicans are loose; Japanese are impotent. But what is evident when one studies ethnic groups and the attitudes with which they view sex is that such a one-dimensional interpretation fails to recognize the various types of feelings which operate in the different communities where they dwell. Rather than differences of sexual attitude based on race, differences in sexual attitudes are based on social class.

Hence, within the framework of Asian cultural mores previously discussed are variations that reflect the whole range of American behaviors and attitudes: the lower-class "toughs" who pick up prostitutes and frequent shady bars; the upper-class, flamboyant singles who are supremely self-confident about their sexuality and maintain a "swinging" life-style; and, between the two extremes, the majority of more conservative middle-class citizens who may often envy the image of freedom in the outer fringes, but who mainly stick to traditional values and behaviors in their sexual life. Wishing they could have a sexual life like others they perceive in both the upper and lower classes, they often become dissatisfied with their sexual partners. "Why," they ask, "are you so much like me?"

While it is in this latter group that many suffer poor self-images in comparing themselves to Hollywood idols, it would be unrealistic to assume that all middle-class Asian American males and females are dissatisfied with each other sexually. In their own way, they are relatively stable and happy, and are not unlike other human beings who have learned to compromise and place in perspective their frustrations, anxieties and disappointments, even when they are of a sexual nature.

REFERENCES AND RECOMMENDED READINGS

ARKOFF, A., G. MEREDITH and J. DONG. "Attitudes of Japanese-American and Caucasian-American Students Toward Marriage Roles," *The Journal of Social Psychology*, 59 (1963), pp. 11–15.

ARKOFF, A. and H. WEAVER. "Body Image and Body Dissatisfaction in Japanese-Americans," *Journal of Social Psychology*, 68 (1966), pp. 323–330.

CHENG, C. K. and D. S. YAMAMURA. "Interracial Marriage and Divorce in Hawaii," *Social Forces*, 36 (1957), pp. 77–84.

KITANO, H. L. *Japanese Americans: The Evolution of a Subculture.* Englewood Cliffs, New Jersey: Prentice Hall, 1969.

OGAWA, D. *From Japs to Japanese: The Evolution of Japanese-American Stereotypes.* Berkeley: McCutchan, 1971.

———. *Jan Ken Po: The World of Hawaii's Japanese Americans.* Honolulu: Japanese American Research Center, 1973.

PAIK, I. *That Oriental Feeling.* In *Roots: An Asian American Reader*, A. Tachiki, E. Wong, F. Odo, and B. Wong (eds.). Los Angeles: Continental Graphics, 1971.

SUE, S. and D. WAGNER. (eds.). *Asian Americans: Psychological Perspectives.* Ben Lomond, Calif.: Science and Behavior Books, 1973.

TACHIKI, A., E. WONG, F. ODO, and B. WONG (eds.). *Roots: An Asian American Reader.* Los Angeles: Continental Graphics, 1971.

WEISS, M. S. "Selective Acculturation and the Dating Process: The Patterning of Chinese-Caucasian Interracial Dating," *Journal of Marriage and the Family*, 32 (1970), pp. 273–278.

CHAPTER 14

THE
POOR

Catherine S. Chilman

Poverty has seriously adverse effects on the lives of people, including their sexuality. Sexuality, as the term is used here, includes biological, social, psychological, and economic components of masculine and feminine human development, feelings, attitudes and behavior. These attitudes, values, and behaviors regarding sexuality tend to vary at differing socioeconomic levels and for differing ethnic and racial groups. These variations are related to the cultural traditions of the groups and even more to the life situation in which the people are living. Poverty (especially extreme and long-term poverty), particularly when racism is added, tends to create adaptive life-styles in respect to sexuality as well as in other facets of life. These life-styles are frequently criticized by the members of majority and more advantaged socioeconomic groups. Thus, life-styles that develop primarily as a response to poverty and discrimination tend to escalate the chances of being both poor *and* excluded from the cultural mainstream. Greater understanding of the causes and conditions of poverty and racism along with the associated and related sexual life-styles can be helpful to human service professionals who seek to work

I must express special thanks to Dr. Robert Washington, Associate Dean, School of Social Welfare, University of Wisconsin at Milwaukee, for his careful and helpful review of this paper.

effectively at policy, program, and treatment levels with low-income oppressed minority-group people.

Poverty has increased with the recent economic recession. Data from the
1970 census as to the extent of poverty in the United States underesti-
mate the extent of the problem. However, since no more recent national
figures are available, 1970 and 1971 census data are mainly used here.
These show that about 10 per cent of whites and 33 per cent of blacks
were below the official (and meager) "low-income" level in 1969. If more
realistic income levels are used (such as set by the U.S. Department of
Labor), the figures rise to about 25 per cent of white families and 50 per
cent of black ones. There are many levels of poverty; 20 per cent of black
families and 7 per cent of white families were in *extreme* poverty in 1969.
Children and youth were over-represented in the poverty population.
Almost half of the poor were under age 24: one-third of this group were
under age 14. Moreover, families with children were especially apt to
have incomes far below the official low-income level.

Families without a male head were far more likely to be poor. Almost 7 per cent of poor black families and 40 per cent of poor white
families lacked a male head. Black children were especially apt to live in
low-income families. Almost half of all black children under age 14 lived
in poverty and one-fourth of all black children lived in low-income families with a female head.* By contrast, "only" 4 per cent of white children
lived in such families.

The U.S. Bureau of the Census puts it this way in its report (1972a).
"The likelihood of being a child in a female-headed family increased for
black children between 1959 and 1971. The rate of breakdown for black
families with children grew markedly (about 40 per cent) during that
time. However, the rate for white families showed little change."

Among the possible reasons for more extensive family breakdown for
blacks are higher unemployment and underemployment rates for black
people, the adverse effects of the huge urban migration of black families
displaced by the mechanization of agriculture, racism, the impact of the
urban ghetto on family life, and AFDC policies that forbid public assistance in many states to families with an able-bodied father present
(Chilman, 1975).

These cold facts may obscure some of the harsher realities of life in
poverty: poor housing, not enough food or clothing, disorganized and

---

* By 1973, this figure had risen to one-third of all black children (U.S. Bureau of the
Census, 1973).

crowded living conditions, poor community services, social rejection, and a personal sense of failure and despair.

EFFECTS OF POVERTY ON HUMAN SEXUALITY

These harsh realities have a corrosive effect on the development of a positive sense of adequacy and significance as a human being for either a male or female. They tend to call forth such adaptive attitudes as fatalism, hostile alienation from the larger society, apathy, distrust of others, magical thinking, nonacceptance of scientific and impersonal information, authoritarianism, impulsivity, and an action rather than a verbal style. Attitudes of these kinds tend to undermine the possibility of long-lasting and mutually rewarding interpersonal family relationships: both parent-child and male-female. These factors (poverty plus resultant life-styles) probably feed into the higher rates of family conflict and family disorganization found among poor people.

Other related life-styles play a part. Men and women in long-term poverty have a higher tendency to live in quite separate social and psychological worlds with little verbal communication, sharing of interests, and role flexibility. Hostile and mutually exploitative attitudes are more likely to occur between the sexes, and both males and females are apt to have limited knowledge about sex, reproduction, contraceptives and childbirth (Komarovsky, 1964; Rainwater & Weinstein, 1960; Rainwater, 1965; Chilman, 1966; Keller, 1966; Ladner, 1971).

Sex relations, both in and out of marriage, are often viewed as proof of one's prowess as a male or female rather than as part of a loving, larger interpersonal relationship. Peer group pressure for both premarital and extramarital relationships is apt to be strong. Sex is often used exploitatively to fill material needs, especially when unemployment is high and wages are low.

Among low-income white families of rural origin strong double-standard attitudes are apt to prevail, with pressures for virginity at marriage and sexual fidelity afterwards being present for females but not for males. Traditional sex-role values are common, with woman's place being seen as at home with the children and her position as inferior to that of males.

Planning for child-spacing and family size is less accepted and less frequently undertaken in a consistent, effective manner until a number of children have been born, even though small families are generally the goal. An attitude of fatalism, lack of male-female communication, distrust of the human services system, lack of hope for the future, plus unpleasant aspects of contraceptive use, difficulties in getting supplies and services (including, in some states, abortion) all contribute to this behavior

(Chilman, 1968). Fears of genocide affect the attitudes of many low-income minority groups who have suffered from the scourge of discrimination.

Although the evidence is not entirely clear, it appears that some low-income males and females are especially apt to seek proof of their masculine or feminine adequacy by having children. Then, too, observation suggests that children may be particularly valued for the comfort, closeness, and sense of personal significance they can bring—especially when they are very young.

Contrary to the popular general impression that low-income people have particularly free and rewarding sex lives, available studies show that their sexual satisfactions are apt to be less on the average than among higher socioeconomic groups. This, in turn, is related to the barriers to open, mutually communicative, equalitarian, trusting relationships; less knowledge about sex; fewer shared activities and interests, tendency for more conservative attitudes toward masturbation, nudity and a variety of sexual behaviors in intercourse (Rainwater, 1964).

Poor children are apt to be exposed to the physical aspects of sexuality and sexual exploitation early in their lives, especially in the disorganized neighborhoods in which so many of them live (Hammond and Ladner, 1969). On the other hand, their parents may take the attitude that sex largely creates trouble and that communication about the subject will increase its likelihood. Warnings are often given in vague terms so that children learn mostly fear and distrust of their own sexuality and that of others.

Kinsey's studies, now over twenty-five years old, showed that low-income males were especially apt to have many premarital sex experiences from their mid-teens onward. College-bound youths were less likely to have early premarital intercourse and were more likely to masturbate. Males with little education were more likely than their more educated brothers to have extramarital affairs during their twenties, but "settled down" in their later years. On the other hand, more highly educated males were apt to restrict their sexual activities to marriage until they reached their forties, when extramarital affairs became more common (Kinsey, 1948).

Shifting patterns of sexual behavior in the incidence of premarital and extramarital sex behavior at all socioeconomic levels probably make these Kinsey findings less true today and the class differences found for males may now be far less.

More specific information about the sexual behavior of young women is available from a recent study of a national probability sample of females between the ages of 15 and 19 (Kantner & Zelnick, 1972, 1973). According to this investigation, premarital intercourse for girls is beginning at younger ages and its extent among teen-agers is increasing. Almost twice as many black teen-agers as white ones have premarital intercourse and begin this experience at a younger age (about 75 per cent of never-married black girls and 40 per cent of the white girls had had intercourse by age 18). Poverty status increases the likelihood of premarital intercourse for black females but not for white. Low educational level of the father or male guardian in black families particularly increases the likelihood that young black (but not white) females will have premarital coitus. Living in a female-headed family makes premarital sex experience much more likely for white girls, only somewhat more likely for black ones. Girls who have lived on farms and moved into cities have the highest rate of premarital intercourse, especially if they live in the central city of a metropolitan area.

Some of these findings are confusing, especially as they relate to racial differences. As Kantner & Zelnick (1972) comment, these differences doubtlessly have a sociological explanation, even though differential rates of premarital intercourse were only slightly reduced when variables such as socioeconomic status and family structure are taken into account. One possible partial explanation, as this author sees it, may relate to the fact that Kantner & Zelnick did not examine differential levels of poverty and differential periods of duration of low-income status. For instance, it is one thing to be unemployed and somewhat poor for a short period of time; it is quite different to be extremely poor and unemployed for a number of years—a situation that is more likely to afflict black familes than white ones and to also affect patterns of sexual behavior.

RACISM, POVERTY & SEXUALITY

Other incompletely known and understood differences in sexual behavior and attitudes apparently exist between low-income racial groups. Available evidence is generally meager; it is far too limited for us to discuss racial and ethnic groups in this country except in reference to black people. Demographic data and a few investigations make a tentative discussion of this topic possible for this latter group.

Many—probably most—black families have needed both males and females to work in order to have enough family income; in a number of instances, only the females could find employment. This may be the basic reason that low-income black people are less likely to hold a double standard of sex roles and sexual behavior than are other racial and social classes.

Although many would argue this, Ladner is one of the scholars who holds that the influence of the African heritage plus the effects of slavery still have an influence on black culture. According to Ladner, these effects may include such values as: equal work roles for women, reproduction as the central feature of a female's adult identity, a high valuation placed on children, closely knit extended kinships networks, acceptance of sexuality as a natural and enjoyable function (Ladner, 1971).

Today, among black people, especially those at poverty level, virginity before marriage tends not to be expected of either males or females, and the sexes are generally seen to have equally strong sex drives (Hammond & Ladner, 1969; Staples, 1972; Rosenberg & Bensman, 1968). Children are highly valued, although illegitimacy is regarded as undesirable; marriages merely in order to legitimize babies are often seen as unacceptable, as are abortions and placement for adoption of children born out-of-wedlock. Moreover in many states both abortion and adoptive placement services are apt to be more limited for blacks than whites.

To many blacks contraceptives are often seen as unacceptable, dangerous, hard to get, "unnatural," and possible genocidal. Then, too, they frequently are unavailable, especially to young teen-agers. Moreover, the parents of these girls frequently have not used contraceptives themselves, know little about them, and are fearful of their use.

We have already seen that black female teen-agers have been found to have a far higher rate of premarital intercourse than do white teen-agers. (However, they tend to have fewer sex partners and engage in intercourse less frequently than their white sisters.) According to census data, the percentage of illegitimate births has increased for both black and white groups. For whites, almost 6 per cent of all births were outside marriage in 1970; for blacks, the percentage was 34.9. These figures have increased from 2 per cent and 16.8 per cent respectively in 1940. In fact, they have risen steadily over the years with generally similar racial differentials at all periods (Glick & Mills, 1974). The attitudes and values discussed above, plus the life situation of poverty combined with racism, probably account for these differences in birth status.

Some studies show that early childbearing outside marriage is apt to present a serious barrier to "escape from poverty." Stable marriages are less likely to occur; education and employment are frequently interrupted; the health of the child may be seriously affected; and later family size is apt to be especially large. Even if marriage occurs, early marriages have a high rate of failure, especially if the woman is pregnant at the time of marriage or already has a child.

Ladner, in her study of girls and women in a St. Louis ghetto, points to the strong influence of peer groups, defeated parents, difficulties at school, racism, poverty, unemployment of both sexes, lack of successful role models, limited opportunities and limited concepts of upward mobility, plus the desire to be a "woman" through childbearing as some of the leading reasons for early pregnancy outside of marriage (Ladner, 1971).

Ladner also confirms earlier findings (Lewis, 1965) that illegitimacy is not regarded as desirable by low-income black families. Marriage is seen as preferable if it offers love, shared responsibilities, and economic security. She also finds, as do others, (Billingsley, 1968; Staples, 1972; Leibow, 1967; Lewis, 1965) that unmarried black fathers (including adolescents) usually feel a considerable responsibility for both the mother and the child. Although their unemployment or meager employment frequently prevents adequate support, these fathers often give what financial aid they can, visit or live with the family, and help in the care of the children. Such arrangements are not peculiar to low-income American black families, however, but are found in many parts of the world in association with intense poverty (Rainwater, 1964; Lewis, 1961).

Programs for pregnant high-school girls have been supported by Federal grants in many parts of the country. Such programs offered multiple services: educational, health (including family planning), child care, personal and vocational counseling. On the average, however, such programs failed to produce anticipated favorable outcomes in terms of higher rates of high-school completion, later economic independence, and subsequent lower birth rates. Desirable as these programs are, they (a) may come too late in a girl's life, (b) select only those girls who are already pregnant, and (c) fail to reach the boys. Also, they cannot provide jobs or long-time follow-up services, and their expenses are high. Probably one of the major contributions of such programs, however, has been the fact that they have tended to change the earlier educational policy that excluded pregnant girls from high school.

Difficult as life may be for many low-income black females, it can be even harsher for many of the males. In numerous black families, especially in the past, the female has tended to hold greater power in some respects than the male. Racism often had—and still has—harsher effects, in many ways, on males than females. There was (and still is) more white fear of the black male because of his greater physical strength and therefore efforts to oppress him have been more severe and harsh. The female has often had to deal with white society both for herself and for her man (Bernard, 1966). The myth of the endlessly potent black stud was probably created by white society as an excuse for the brutality with which black males were kept in their place. This image of racially superior masculine potency on the part of black males appears to linger on; perhaps it is fostered, in part, by the myth victims themselves since so many other sources of power both within and outside the family are still denied them in a racist society.

These complexities of somewhat different sexual standards and power conflicts probably play an important part in the lack of enthusiasm of many black women for the Women's Liberation Movement. Understandably, to many of them racial liberation is by far the more crucial issue. Among other things, they want good jobs for their men so that they can be freed from the heavy burden of family support and be freed as well from the problem of dealing with the rage and powerlessness of their "society-castrated" males.

INTERVENTIVE CONSIDERATIONS: IMPLICATIONS FOR SOCIAL WORK ROLES
AND FUNCTIONS

As we have seen, poverty and racism adversely affect stable, fulfilling relationships between the sexes, a positive sense of gender identity, and effective contraceptive practices. The root cause of the problems lies in the structure of our society and its economy, however, rather than in personal deficits. This implies that human service professionals need to be active on policy levels and join with others in political action aimed at the reduction of these problems. One cannot wait, however, to provide ameliorative services until such basic reforms come about.

At the direct service level, it is important that families and individuals be reached with well-coordinated, knowledgeable health, educational, social welfare (service and income maintenance), vocational and recreational programs that include sensitivity and skills related to human sexuality in its many aspects. Among other things, such programs are needed in order to help people find fulfillment as males and females in ways that are satisfying to themselves within the constraints imposed by such reality factors as their own health, the demands of positive interpersonal relationships, and effective socioeconomic functioning. Programs concerned with the sexual well-being of people should not only take place in such obvious areas as sex education and counseling, contraceptive and abortion services, and prevention and treatment of venereal diseases—important as these may be—but they also should encompass all aspects of family relationships and work- and play-situations that potentially involve the development and maintenance of a positive sense of gender identity, more equalitarian sex-role functioning, enhanced sharing of interests and open communication between the sexes. As a matter of fact, more specific sex education, sex counseling, family planning and related programs are likely to have limited results unless these more general individual and family support services are also available.

At the specific "sexuality" service level, it is important that these programs be shaped to meet the particular concerns, goals and values of the girls and boys, men and women immediately involved. Participation by these people in program design and implementation should help to make the services more useful and acceptable. We have seen that life-styles vary for differing ethnic, racial, age, and socioeconomic groups. The specifics and subtleties of these variations can be only partially known to the human service professional. He or she needs to work, sensitively and nonjudgmentally, in a team relationship with service consumers. Whenever possible, professionals and paraprofessionals from the reference groups to be served should be employed as program personnel, not only because of their probable greater understanding of the situation and life-styles of service consumers but also because of their importance as successful role models.

Programs including elements of advocacy, "systems management," counseling and education need to reach both males and females at many life-cycle stages—grandparents, parents, youth, and young children. All are involved in the expression of their own sexuality and the sexuality of the dynamic interaction system that is the family. For instance, we have seen that low-income black adolescent girls are afraid to use contraceptives partly because their mothers have not used them, do not understand them, and are fearful of their effects.

Throughout these programs, it is important that human service professionals (including social workers) come to thoroughly understand and accept that sexual behaviors, like all behaviors, have their deeply rooted reasons. Their roots lie in the particular life experience and life situation of a person. Partly they rest in his or her cultural patterns. These patterns have deep meaning. They mean home, family, neighborhood, friends. Though all may be ravaged by poverty and frequent failures, they also have provided a measure of love, belongingness, and rewards. They have provided the competencies to deal with life as it is. To question the person's life-style and values is to question his/her identity. Our own biases, inhibitions, moralities are particularly strong in sexual spheres because of our own acculturation. Thus, a particular effort may be needed to develop the kind of knowledge, empathy, and understanding that can help provide more effective services.

Acceptance and understanding of people does not mean we condone all their behavior. This behavior may often be different from what they want for themselves. For instance, most poor people (like others) want a fulfilling, secure marriage and a small number of children whose births are planned. They want affectionate close relationships within the family, advanced education, good health, with steady and well-paying jobs. They want self-respect and respect from others as significant masculine or feminine human beings. Through a wide range of coordinated, sustaining, long-term human services that emphasize working *with* people as individuals and groups in terms of their own goals, we can hope to help them achieve greater fulfillment in the sexual part, as well as in many other aspects, of their lives. Professionals can certainly do a better job of interpreting to the general public the variations in sexual behavior of people in differing socioeconomic, ethnic and racial groups, along with the causes of these variations and their implications for both social reform and improved human services.

REFERENCES AND RECOMMENDED READINGS

BERNARD, JESSIE. *The Negro Family.* New York: Prentice-Hall, 1966.
BILLINGSLEY, ANDREW. *Black Families in White America.* Englewood Cliffs, N.J.: Prentice-Hall, 1968.
CHILMAN, CATHERINE S. "Families in Poverty in the Early 1970's," *Journal of Marriage and the Family,* 37, 1 (February 1975), pp. 49–60.
———. "Fertility & Poverty in the United States: Some Implications for Family Planning Programs, Policy & Research," *Journal of Marriage and the Family,* Vol. 30, No. 2 (May 1968), pp. 207–228.
———. *Growing Up Poor.* Social and Rehabilitation Service, U.S. Dept. of H.E.W. Supt. of Documents, U.S. Government Printing Office, Washington, D.C., 1966.
GLICK, PAUL C., and KAREN M. MILLS. "Black Families: Marriage Patterns and Living Arrangements." Paper prepared for W. E. B. Du Bois Conference on American Blacks, Atlanta, Georgia, 1974.
HAMMOND, BOONE, and JOYCE LADNER. "Life in an Urban Slum Ghetto." In *The Individual, Sex and Society,* Carlfred Broderick & Jessie Bernard, eds. Baltimore: Johns Hopkins University Press, 1969.
HILL, ROBERT. *The Strengths of Black Families,* New York: Emerson-Hall, 1968.
KANTNER, JOHN, and MELVIN ZELNICK. "Sexual Experience of Young Unmarried Women in the United States" and "Adolescent Sex Behavior in the United States," *Family Planning Perspectives,* Vol. 4, No. 4 and Vol. 5, No. 1 (October 1972 and January 1973).
KELLER, SUZANNE. *The American Lower Class Family.* Albany, N.Y.: New York State Division for Youth, 1966.
KINSEY, ALFRED C., *et al. Sexual Behavior in the Human Male.* Philadelphia: W. B. Saunders Co., 1948.
KOMARVOSKY, MIRRA. *Blue Collar Marriage.* New York: Random House, 1964.
LADNER, JOYCE. *Tomorrow's Tomorrow.* New York: Doubleday and Co., 1971.
LEWIS, HYLAN. Agenda Paper No. 5. *The Family: Resources for Change. Planning Session.* White House Conference to Fulfill These Rights. U.S. Government Printing Office, Washington, D.C., 1965.
LEWIS, OSCAR. *Children of Sanchez.* New York: Random House, 1961.
RAINWATER, LEE. "Marital Sexuality in Four Cultures of Poverty," *Journal of Marriage and the Family,* 26, 4 (1964), pp. 457–466.
——— and KAROL WEINSTEIN. *And the Poor Get Children.* Chicago: Quadrangle Books, 1960.

ROSENBERG, BERNARD, and JOSEPH BENSMAN. "Sexual Patterns in Three Ethnic Sub-Cultures of an American Under-Class," *The Annals of the American Academy of Political and Social Science*, 376 (March 1968), pp. 61–75.

STAPLES, ROBERT. "The Sexuality of Black Women," *Sexual Behavior*, June, 1972, pp. 4, 6, 8–11, 14, 15.

U.S. Bureau of the Census. *The Social and Economic Status of the Black Population in the United States, 1971*. Special Studies. Current Population Reports, Series P-24, No. 42. U.S. Government Printing Office, Washington, D.C., 1972.

———. *Characteristics of the Low-Income Population 1971*. Current Populations Reports, Series P-60, No. 86, Washington, D.C.: U.S. Government Printing Office.

———. *Money Income in 1971 of Families and Persons in the United States*. Consumer Income, Series (a) P-60, No. 85, Washington, D.C.: U.S. Government Printing Office.

———, Series P-23, 1973. Washington, D.C.

U.S. Department of Labor, Bureau of Labor Statistics. *Labor Force Developments: First Quarter, 1975*.

VI.
THE
INSTITUTIONALIZED

American society does not like to look at its rejects. We put many of the retarded, adjudicated criminals, incapacitated aged, and diagnosed mentally ill into institutions, and we put the institutions in out-of-the-way places where we don't have to look at them. There may be several reasons we don't want to see these people. Perhaps we feel guilty that they can't have what we have, perhaps we find them unaesthetic, perhaps we even fear them, and perhaps we don't want to be reminded that there, but for the grace of good fortune, go the rest of us.

But there they are, receiving "adequate" to minimal care from people who are charged with the responsibility of not only caring for them but also keeping them under control. Control may be a major task for institutions understaffed as most public institutions are. Residents are therefore reinforced for their conformity. Individuality is rarely a virtue in such an institution. Residents are often therefore stripped of much of their humanness—including their sexuality. Sex is a frivolous—if not evil —luxury which has no place in a well run marginally staffed program. The easiest maintained residents are those who can be treated and who can be trusted to respond as good children. "Be good" (which means be passive and compliant) "and we'll take care of you."

Paradoxical as it may be, however, one of the few pleasures available *to the residents of many overcrowded, poorly funded institutions is the resident's own body. (Indeed, in the last century the almost constant masturbation by many residents of mental hospitals, a product of a lack of other stimulation, led to the common misconception by observers that masturbation causes mental illness.)*

In this section of the book, Ginsberg discusses the sexual problems of the diagnosed mentally ill as an aspect of the violation of their civil rights. The problems he discusses add to the already existing questions about the therapeutic value of confining most diagnosed "mentally ill" persons to institutions.

Prisoners have the added problem that their institutionalization is perceived as a punishment. If one is to be punished, many people reason, one must give up the greatest joy of all, i.e., sexuality. Although sexual deprivation is much on prisoners' minds (both men and women) and is often at the core of prison violence, few rehabilitation programs do much about the sexual life of the prisoners. Penal programs that provide for the sexual needs of prisoners rarely get far in this country. There is, for example, no American prison which even approaches the Mexican system of allowing prisoners' wives and children to live with them in prison at state expense.

The problems posed by the lack of heterosexual opportunities for prisoners and the associated prison rapes and violence confront the prison officials and correctional staff. All too often those who work with prisoners remain silent about sex-related problems which arise in prison while they try to help prisoners adjust to their impossible situation. As long as they keep silent, they contribute, at least indirectly, to the figurative castration of a racially and socioeconomically selected population of American society through enforced celibacy.

The problems of our contemporary prison systems are much broader than just the sexual deprivation of prisoners. The provision of brief, occasional anxiety-ridden conjugal visits or furloughs has its drawbacks, and may in some ways make prison life seem even bleaker when the visits are over. But this innovation could serve as a step toward prison reform.

The Fortune Society has long been interested in the sex-related problems of prisoners. Their motto (by Dostoevski): "The degree of civilization in a society can be judged by entering its prisons," reflects the organization's mission. Rothenberg, the director of that organization, provides a review of the range of sexual oppression encountered by prisoners, along with some ideas on how the system could be improved.

CHAPTER 15

THE INSTITUTIONALIZED MENTALLY DISABLED

Leon H. Ginsberg

The sexual rights of the institutionalized mentally disabled may be addressed in two ways. The first way is to examine the sexual rights of those who are institutionalized because they have been diagnosed or defined as emotionally disturbed, mentally ill, developmentally disabled, mentally retarded, or otherwise handicapped by emotional or intellectual problems. The second approach is to understand that a person's being defined as mentally handicapped is, in some cases, a result of his or her sexual behavior. That is, some persons may find themselves incarcerated in institutions for the mentally ill because they behave in ways that other persons, such as members of their families, teachers, and others who have power over them, consider inappropriate and disturbing. Offensive sexual behavior may well be included.

Let's look first at the sexual rights of those who are institutionalized as being mentally disabled. Those who want to know more about the legal rights of these people who are defined as mentally disabled should understand that a variety of ideas and behaviors are included in that broad term. The consequences of being called "mentally disabled" also vary from situation to situation.

For example, mental disability may include, at one extreme, severe mental retardation (this affects a small proportion of the world's population) through, at the other extreme, neurotic behavior (this affects virtually everyone at one time or another). The behaviors included within the definition of mental disability are of vastly different orders. The behavior of the child or adult with extremely low intelligence obviously differs from that of the physician or attorney whose behavior is occasionally irrational and destructive.

There are also vast differences in the ways mental illness or emotional disturbance is defined. Many specialists distinguish in ways that appear to be scientific among a variety of emotional disorders, such as schizophrenia, compulsive-obsessive behavior, hysterical behavior, and the rest of the mental illness labels that one encounters in the literature and in the practices of mental health agencies and professionals.

It is important to understand, when dealing with the rights of the mentally ill in particular, that there is a large and growing group of experts who doubt the accuracy of those diagnoses and who doubt the existence of illnesses that are mental. Originally developed by Dr. Thomas S. Szasz, this approach to mental illness, which might be termed "libertarian" or "radical," suggests that what is called mental illness throughout much of the world is really not illness at all but is, instead, a series of unpopular or condemned behaviors which are in conflict with accepted customs, as well as some activities which, while not in direct conflict with the law, are so unpopular that society demands something be done about them. And if society as a whole does not make such demands, the families, employers, and neighbors of the person who manifests such behaviors may make such demands, instead.

LIBERTARIAN GROUPS

A variety of groups hold the belief that there is no such thing as mental illness. Some of them are organizations of those who have been defined as mentally ill and formerly incarcerated themselves. Others are public interest law groups which specialize in helping clients who are faced with the loss of liberty because they have been adjudged mentally ill.

This is not to say that such groups doubt the existence of emotional disturbances or personal problems or difficulties in adjusting to the realities of life. Such problems do exist, and it is clear that many people want help, and indeed can be helped by the various programs that have been created and sustained to assist people in resolving their problems. Such service programs include outpatient counseling, day and night hospitals, community mental health centers, and institutions for the mentally ill.

On the other hand, the services available for the mentally retarded are equally vast. One finds private and public institutions, special schools, services within regular schools, sheltered workshops, camps, recreation programs, and various other manifestations of a desire to assist and enhance the lives of the mentally retarded.

ROLE OF INSTITUTIONALIZATION

Within this framework of mental problems and services to help overcome those problems, the basic dichotomy in terms of rights, particularly sexual rights, is whether or not the person is institutionalized. Whether or not a person is institutionalized is the essential issue one must examine in discussing the sexual rights of those with mental handicaps.

In fact, the deprivation of sexual rights rarely results from a mental handicap itself. Rather, the deprivation usually results from institutionalization.

As sociologist Erving Goffman has noted, total institutions are a special kind of entity which thoroughly and totally control their inmates. An institution for the mentally handicapped is always a total institution. The institution watches, monitors, and makes decisions about virtually every inmate's every function, from his or her excretions to his or her sleeping habits. It controls the food they eat, the clothing they wear, the medical treatment they accept or refuse to accept, the words they use, the postures and facial expressions they choose, and the manner in which each patient maintains his or her living quarters. In such a setting, sexual behavior is controlled. Because it is so overt and visible in such a setting it is one of the typical kinds of behaviors controlled by the total institution. As a result, therefore, sexual contact with other inmates is not usually permitted.

SEX IN THE INSTITUTION

The conjugal visit—which is a subject for discussion in American corrections programs as well as being a common practice in some U.S. penitentiaries and in many correctional institutions in other parts of the world —is rarely discussed in relation to mental institutions. If the patient were able to maintain a sex life with a spouse or other sexual partner, he or she would probably not need to be institutionalized in the first place, some would say. The patient is there because of illness. One should not equate, many institutional managers say, conjugal visits for prisoners who are being punished and rehabilitated (and such visits can be used to reward or to maintain normal sexual patterns during a specified sentence) with conjugal visits for mental patients (who are being treated for illnesses). Obviously the solutions follow the definitions. If one believes that what is called mental illness is an illness, such an argument is persuasive. If one does not accept that idea and equates mental patients with prisoners instead of with general hospital patients, the argument is unreasonable.

There are other kinds of limitations that militate against sex in mental institutions. For example, patients are generally segregated by sex. Male wards and female wards are separate and regular contact is not permitted between the sexes. Clearly, sexual behavior between the sexes is not sanctioned. Of course, males and females in mental hospitals who want to have sex with one another will try, and occasionally succeed in finding a way for achieving it.

There may be institutions for the mentally ill which make exceptions to the foregoing and which try to normalize sexual behavior, but this writer is not aware of any such. The writer remembers one young man who was referred to a highly regarded modern institution that was called a "therapeutic community." The man had been acting somewhat unusual. Before entering the institution, he had been saying strange things and acting in strange ways—all of which indicated a break from his former patterns. Much of his behavior reflected more aggressiveness than had been characteristic of him in the past. Through a careful referral process, he was permitted to enter this treatment program, which was residential and affiliated with a respected medical center. It had a small, relatively young male and female population. However, the young man was expelled after only two days and transferred to a large state hospital because he had made overt sexual overtures to some of the female patients and nurses. It appeared that even in that institution, which had a reputation for flexibility, overt sexual behavior was as taboo as it is in more restricted settings.

Solitary sex is also frowned upon. That is, mental institutions do not consider public masturbation acceptable. In fact, it might be used as a basis for diagnosing the onset of new or the continuation of old mental problems. On the other hand, the lack of privacy of inmates in total institutions is such that public masturbation may be the only alternative. It may also be, for some persons, more tranquilizing and less physiologically destructive than the tranquilizing drugs.

DRUG TREATMENT

Drugs, in fact, are an impediment to sexual behavior within total institutions for the emotionally disturbed and the mentally retarded. They are also the most common treatment, particularly in the large public institutions, for the mentally ill and the mentally retarded. Such drugs, when administered in large doses, inhibit the sexual drive along with overcoming other patient tensions and anxieties.

These limitations on sexual expression appear to be equally applicable to hospitals for the mentally ill and institutions for the mentally retarded.

They are better understood as the characteristic controls placed upon inmates by total institutions than as necessary and proven treatment techniques for mental problems. That is, total institutions discourage expressions of sexuality of all kinds—solitary, homosexual, and heterosexual. They do so not because limits on sexual behavior are demanded by the condition of their inmates, but because it is in their nature to thoroughly limit and control every element of the inmates' lives.

It is characteristic of total institutions for the mentally ill and the mentally retarded to restrict all rights and privileges without regard to the specific diagnosis or needs of the patient or inmate. That is, sensitive examination of individual needs is not the forerunner of rights deprivation. Rights are restricted for institutional purposes, and not for patient treatment. One should suppose that the right to use of the telephone and use of the mails without censorship, the right to leave, and other adult liberties would vary with the problems and the behaviors of the patient or inmate involved. But that is not normally the case. Blanket restrictions are commonly enforced against the total population. Sexual rights could vary, as well, but that is not the tendency. Instead, sex is officially denied to all inmates of the institution.

LOSS OF RIGHTS

Being incarcerated in an institution leads to the deprivation of rights even after one leaves. That is because many rights can be denied individuals on the grounds of incompetence. Most states treat mental hospitalization as *prima facie* evidence of incompetence. For example, such rights as voting, holding office, owning property, and driving a car may be denied individuals who are considered incompetent. Although institutions for the mentally ill may release their patients with certificates indicating their mental health has been restored and that their rights should also be restored, former patients may find themselves excluded from the exercise of some of their rights through competency proceedings. This is particularly true of sexual rights. For example, incarceration in a mental hospital can be sufficient grounds for divorce in some states. The right to defend against a divorce may be waived, if a person is institutionalized. A divorce may be granted because one of the partner's hospitalization in a mental institution can be used as proof of mental illness. The right to marry can also be affected by institutionalization. Marriages may be voided for similar reasons.

The right to maintain one's children—and continue being their guardian and legal parent—can be lost by a person who has been in a mental hospital. The laws of many states provide for the removal of children from a family in which one or both parents have been hospitalized for emotional problems. Emotional disturbance or mental retardation may be used as the basis for the removal of a child from his or her home by public authorities as a means of protecting the child. Therefore, the basic sexual rights to marry, divorce, defend against divorce, and to keep one's children may be severely limited for the mentally handicapped.

The physical ability to reproduce may also be limited for those who are diagnosed as mentally ill or mentally retarded. It is legal in some states for hospital superintendents to order the sterilization of mental hospital inmates and inmates of institutions for the retarded, particularly when they are females and there is a danger of their becoming pregnant. Male sexual offenders, however, may face the same treatment.

Institutionalization is not the governing factor in the denial of rights for reasons of incompetence. The non-institutionalized may also find themselves limited in their sexual rights by the law or by authority figures who have power over them. There are marriages annulled, children removed, and divorces achieved without contest among the non-institutionalized mentally disabled. It may be that this is more true of the mentally retarded than it is with the emotionally disturbed. It is technically possible, however, in every jurisdiction, no matter what the laws may say about the rights of the mentally disabled.

Competency is based upon common or case law and these matters are decided on an individual basis. One must be an expert in the cases which govern such regulations and decisions in a given state before making judgments about what will happen to a specific individual under given circumstances.

SEXUAL BEHAVIOR AS A BASIS FOR INSTITUTIONALIZATION

For a variety of reasons and under a number of circumstances, sexual behavior may be used as a basis for incarceration of individuals as mentally disabled. For example, those who work professionally with juveniles indicate that the basis for the incarceration of some young individuals in institutions for the delinquent or the emotionally disturbed results directly from their sexual activities. Promiscuity, or what parents might define as promiscuity in their daughters (less commonly in their sons) can lead to the incarceration of children in special schools and treatment institutions, removed from the sources of temptation.

One will find mental health records, both within and outside such institutions which use sexual behavior as the basis of the diagnosis. In fact, overt sexuality is sometimes the prime indication for a diagnosis of "adolescent reaction." The writer once worked in an institution for emotionally disturbed youngsters and found that some of the patients, particularly the female patients, carried such a diagnosis, primarily because they had become sexually involved with males. The cases of several teen-agers who were challenging their incarceration in a Pennsylvania institu-tion also indicated that sexual activity has been the basis of their hospitalization.

Homosexuality is another kind of sexual behavior that often leads to a diagnosis of mental illness, despite modern understanding of it as sim-ply another kind of sexual preference, rather than a symptom of emo-tional disturbance.

Perhaps the most striking example of the use of a mental health diagnosis in retaliation against sexual behavior was the case of the late Earl Long, who was governor of Louisiana in the late 1950's and early 1960's. His story was told with what appears to be accuracy in an auto-biography by a Baltimore burlesque dancer and bar owner, Blaze Starr, in her biography which she wrote in cooperation with a West Virginia writer and college professor.

Earl Long was part of the famous Louisiana family that has pro-duced another governor, Congressmen, and Senators. He was an afi-cionado of the New Orleans striptease shows and often attended them while he was governor. One day he entered a bar where Blaze Starr's striptease was the featured act and he was immediately struck by her beauty. He spoke with her and they soon became friends. Not long afterwards they entered into an intense love affair. Long was at the time married to Mrs. Blanche Long but, according to Blaze Starr, not happy with his marriage. At any rate, he never appeared mentally ill to Miss Starr. In fact, not many adults would be surprised at an older man—Long was in his fifties at the time—finding himself attracted to and anxious to spend his time with a young woman who was a certified sex symbol, who paid attention to him, and who told him that she loved him.

Mrs. Blanche Long, however, did not stand idly by while her hus-band pursued Blaze Starr. She sent agents to intrude upon them in Miss Starr's apartment, according to the burlesque queen, and ultimately she and other members of the Long family arranged for Earl to be trans-ported to a mental hospital in Texas. Later, he was finally returned to a Louisiana mental hospital, from which he released himself by dismissing the hospital director as well as the state's director of mental health. Long now left his wife and maintained his relationship and residence with Miss Starr while still engaged in politics. After his governorship, he lost a race for lieutenant governor of Louisiana, but soon was nominated on the Democratic ticket for the U.S. Congress. This was, at the time, the equiv-alent of election in Louisiana. He died, however, before he could assume his new post.

During all this, those who opposed his relationship with Miss Starr, as well as the press, reported on his behavior, which was not, according to his lover, unusual for him. The major magazines and the Louisiana newspapers, along with newspapers of many other states, quoted him verbatim. Actually, his speech had always been colorful, according to Miss Starr, and some of his eccentric behavior, such as holding a press conference in his pajamas with his false teeth removed, was a product of press harassment, the difficulty of his circumstances, and not terribly different from his behavior before he had met the burlesque star. Part of his political success had always come from his common touch. That commonness then became the basis for a diagnosis of mental illness, when others found it convenient to define him in that way. Blaze Starr attributes Long's death to harassment because of his sexual behavior. Clearly he suffered from an image of mental incompetence which arose from that behavior.

Long's case is unusual both because of his prominence and because he was a man. According to some authors, such as Phyllis Chesler in her book, *Women and Madness*, women are more likely to be defined as mentally ill and subsequently incarcerated than are men.

CONCLUSIONS

Sexual behavior is among the strongest of instincts and it is surrounded by perhaps more taboos than any other set of behaviors. That may be more true, however, in an industrialized, prosperous country such as the United States than it is in less affluent settings. Therefore, one should not be surprised that Americans are punished, stigmatized, and otherwise mistreated for their sexual behavior.

There also appears to be a direct relationship between sexual behavior and assumptions of mental illness. That is, when people see sexual behavior of which they do not approve, they are inclined to identify it as mentally disturbed behavior not solely because it is disturbed, but also because it is quite different from what their own values permit.

In addition, as human sexuality becomes more open and its various manifestations more acceptable, it is likely that more and more human sexual behavior will be identified as mentally ill. As the legal codes become more permissive, one may find the practices of mental health institutions and practitioners stepping in to take up the slack. The mental health codes and institutions for the mentally disabled have often been used as means of removing from society those whose behavior is considered unacceptable.

If such abuses of sexual rights are to be prevented, certain steps must be taken. For one, sexual behavior between consenting adults must be defined out of the bases for institutionalization for reasons of mental illness.

Institutionalized mentally ill persons should be granted the right to exercise sexual behavior within an institution, so long as they do not infringe upon the rights of others. Unless their condition specifically makes such activity impossible or unwise, there should be no reason why they should not be given opportunity to have sexual relations with consenting partners, masturbate, use sexually stimulating material, or otherwise engage in sex and sex-related activities.

But perhaps the most important solution to this whole problem is to keep people out of institutions, particularly those people who do not choose to enter. Recently, the United States Supreme Court ruled that persons could not be held in institutions for reasons of mental illness unless they were receiving treatment to overcome those emotional problems. Hopefully, the next step will be a court ruling that no one may be incarcerated for reason of mental illness, unless he or she voluntarily enters such an institution.

In essence, it is only de-institutionalization—the making of all institutionalization absolutely voluntary for those who are judged to need mental health services—that will preserve the sexual rights of the mentally ill.

For the mentally retarded, similar goals are apparent. That is, mentally retarded persons should be institutionalized only if they choose to be or (if they are incapable of making such decisions) their guardians choose that they be. It is far better that they receive services in their own communities through the kinds of specialized education, rehabilitative and social services that are well understood.

For those for whom there is no alternative to institutionalization, sexual activity should be permitted, along with sexual training, intercourse and masturbation. Other sexual outlets that do not infringe upon the rights of other inmates should be available to them, as well as to their non-institutionalized counterparts.

In summary, sexual rights should be preserved by the elimination of involuntary institutionalization. When voluntary institutionalization is the only alternative, sexual activity should be built into the program for those who want it, just as other, though less taboo-ridden, activities are. There are few precedents for such programming, but its introduction should not pose excessive technical difficulties. The problems of staff, relatives, and political resistance may be great, but they can and must be overcome, if the sexual rights of the institutionalized mentally disabled are to be preserved.

REFERENCES AND RECOMMENDED READINGS

CHESLER, PHYLLIS. *Women and Madness.* Garden City, New York: Doubleday and Company, Inc., 1972.

ENNIS, BRUCE J. *Prisoners of Psychiatry: Mental Patients, Psychiatrists and the Law.* New York: Avon Books, 1974.

——. *The Rights of Mental Patients.* New York: Richard W. Baron Publishing Company, 1973.

—— and PAUL R. FRIEDMAN. *Legal Rights of the Mentally Handicapped* (three volumes). New York: The Practising Law Institute and the Mental Health Law Project, 1973.

GINSBERG, LEON H. "Civil Rights of the Mentally Ill—A Review of the Issues," *Community Mental Health Journal,* Volume IV (3), 1968.

——, "Stripped of All Rights: The Mentally Committed," *The Nation,* May 25, 1974.

GOFFMAN, ERVING. *Asylums.* New York: Anchor Books, 1961.

KITTRIE, NICHOLAS N. *The Right to Be Different: Deviance and Enforced Therapy.* Baltimore: The Johns Hopkins Press, 1971.

STARR, BLAZE, and HUEY PERRY, *Blaze Starr: My Life as Told to Huey Perry.* New York: Praeger Publishers, 1974.

SZASZ, THOMAS S. *The Myth of Mental Illness.* New York: Hoeber-Harper, Inc., 1961.

——. *Psychiatric Justice.* New York: The Macmillan Company, 1965.

CHAPTER 16

PRISONERS

David Rothenberg

Sex is prison's hidden agenda. Though it has been rarely discussed by prisoners or their keepers, it hovers in the air—ubiquitous, threatening and miscalculated. Sex in an uncaged society has been translated to the public via exploitative novels and lurid films. The larger society's inability to deal openly with sexuality is magnified within a prison context. There has been much information, distortion and self-serving ambivalence about prison sexuality. The prison rape, or rip-off, has been the subject of investigations, essays, films, plays and political cover-ups. Preconceived attitudes tend to obscure the real sexual ambiance of a prison or jail. Subsequently, homosexuality itself becomes the stated horror of prison existence. We hear prison officials, convicts, ex-convicts and media investigators talk of homosexuality as an example of prison's great denigration of its human victims.

Prison sexuality is, of course, homosexuality. The alternatives are masturbation (still punishable by solitary confinement and/or loss of privileges in many institutions) or total abstinence. At this point it is important to note that 90 per cent of the imprisoned population is male and that the sexual mores in men's prisons are quite different from those in female institutions. Sexuality in female institutions will be discussed separately.

It is also important to recognize the inherently oppressive nature of these institutions. Prison officials, generally, need more than a briefing on homosexuality. Sexuality *per se* is a taboo subject among correctional traditionalists. Correction conferences, forums or conventions rarely confront human sexuality as a topic which requires discussion and understanding. Sex is discussed by correction people only when the control of it is the understood common goal.

Correction administrators have not been able to come to terms with the sexuality of the people in their custody. The *modus operandi* of most penal institutions is that prisoners are to check their sexual impulses, along with their watches and wallets, upon entering within the walls. On their way out, years later, they are given back their watches and wallets, but the years of sexual suppression are never given appropriate attention. Ignoring sexual needs doesn't work. Young men and young women who go into prisons are no less sexual because they have been convicted of a felony. Indeed, there is perhaps even more time to fantasize.

Men in prison can participate in homosexual acts and not consider themselves gay or homosexual. The larger society has prepared them for an exercise in rationalization. Institutional blindness about sexual needs also nurtures this self-deception.

It is necessary to understand sexism in our society in any discussion of prison homosexuality. The prevailing attitude is that a sex partner is an "object" rather than a person, and this allows for most of the brutal indulgence connected with institutional sex. It is an area which has produced a tacit understanding between the keepers and the kept—with sexual mores transcending class and color lines.

Acknowledged gay men become the "girls" in the joint. Indeed, they are often forced to role-play beyond their pre-prison homosexual disposition. Many "men" in prison insist that their "girls" sustain and develop their "femininity". A well-defined role-playing environment allows the "man" to believe that he is not a homosexual. In the macho prison social pecking order, the *label* is far more damaging than the *act*.

Many studies and reports on prison sexuality direct themselves to the man who is ostensibly heterosexual. They have been described as circumstantially homosexual—men who maintain their maleness but participate in a sex act because of the geography and single genderness of the population. This self-deception has much more to do with social pressures than with sexual inclinations. The ability to adapt sexually to a prison environment is deeply entrenched in strong traditional social mores. The "men" rule—and some have their "women."

One long-timer reflected to me that "most male love affairs which exist in prison never manifest themselves in sexual expression. Almost everyone who considers himself a 'standup con' has a partner. That's the guy you share with—food, information, dreams, and so on. There is one rule about this friendship: No touching is permitted. This ironclad but unstated rule is so intense that to violate it would mean the termination of a real friendship. That does not say that all close friendships are nonsexual, but it does say that a sexual relationship cannot develop out of a loving relationship."

Several different prison sexual life-styles are maintained. Here are some examples:

— An ex-convict who had done twenty-four years told me that he resented the propaganda that implied that all convicts participated in sex acts with other prisoners. I asked him how he had dealt with feelings and frustrations about sexual needs while spending his formative years behind bars. He quickly responded, "I'd get into a fight. I'd hit somebody."

— Tommy, an ostensibly heterosexual male, told me that he had fallen in love with a younger boy after three years of imprisonment. He explained, "When the criteria for beauty—day in and day out—is expressed in youthful boys with well defined asses, you realize one day, to your amazement, that you're looking and leering and even feeling like those guys who scared you when you first hit the joint. It is conditioning. And I fell in love with this kid. We didn't do anything about it. But I fantasized about him, and if I am honest with myself, I was in love with him."

— A man who grew up in reformatories and prisons came to see me one day. He said he thought he might be a homosexual. He was a macho type who had been out of prison for nearly five years. He told me that he and another man had been living as husband and wife since his release from prison. His institutional indoctrination was so strong that, in his mind, he was a heterosexual and his partner was his "woman." Since meeting him I have met several other ex-cons who are "men" married to "women" who are biologically males.

— Pat, an acknowledged homosexual who did twenty years in prisons all over the country, was clearly the "woman" in a prison relationship. It was important to the men involved with him that, in order to maintain their prestige, the other prisoners clearly understood that they were men who had a "woman." If there was even a hint that they were not performing all the male sexual duties, their place on the inmate pecking order would be lowered. However, Pat revealed that he was a continual accomplice in perpetuating this kind of self-deception. If the man was to fellate Pat, the "man" would accompany the act with the statement "I love eating your swinging pussy." Pat was once given to a group of prisoners as a reward for keeping their dorm in order. He told the keepers of the federally run institution that he would commit suicide if he did not have a private cell.

Thus we see in the prison situation that it is necessary for the "man" to stress his partner's femininity. If the "queen" gave any indications of male behavior there would be rumors that the two men were swapping-out. To swap-out in jailhouse jargon, is to take turns in sexual role-playing. Cons say to each other, "If you like to pitch, you might end up catching."

Rickey, a former prisoner who is also gay, complained that his prison ol' man made him wear eye make-up, fix his hair, and wriggle his hips when he walked. None of these things were natural characteristics of Rickey. He had to do it because his partner was genuinely in love with him and admitted that he was concerned that he might be a homosexual. As long as Rickey sustained "feminine" characteristics, his man's jailhouse sexuality could be socially justified.

This insistent role-playing to maintain status seems to say more about how male prisoners feel about women than how they feel about homosexuality. The label, as I have stated, is much more damaging than the act. The strong anti-homosexual rhetoric heard is clearly anti-female. A frequently heard prison phrase is "my mother sent a son to prison, and she's not getting back a daughter."

The prison rape, which happens more in overcrowded city jails than it does in larger state prisons, has less to do with sexual needs than with feelings of deep anger. The target of the rape is depersonalized (becoming an "object" or a "hole") and the ritualized demasculinization is a release of imprisoned anger.

Perhaps by looking at a single case it will be possible to grasp the system's inability to deal with sexual pressures or even with the existence of sexuality.

Michael Chaytor is a New Jersey prisoner whom I met in 1972. Chaytor was sexually assaulted and offered the traditional prison options given a victim. Here is Chaytor's statement, offered in a notarized affidavit:

I, Michael Chaytor, having been duly sworn according to law, upon my oath, depose and state:

I am an inmate in the New Jersey State Prison at Trenton, New Jersey.

I am assigned to cell number twenty-four (24) on seven (7) tier in the wing listed as 7-Up. This cell is approximately fifty (50) feet from the officer's desk. The following is an account of what happened on the morning of July 11th, 1972:

I was asleep in my cell when the door opened and someone entered my cell. The door closed and the person came at me with a shank (knife).

I was cut slightly across the neck and chest before the person lost the shank. During the fight, the desk, metal locker, and other objects in my cell were turned over. Also, several times I shouted for the officer.

Three times during the fight someone opened the door to permit the person to exit out of the cell. The third time that the door opened, I tried to dive out of it. At this point I was beaten in the face and the back of the head with a blunt object. I partially lost consciousness and at that point I was raped by the person who had entered the cell.

The next time the door opened the person left my cell. After I had gotten up and tried to stop the blood from flowing from my face I called for the officer again. I continued to call and received no answer. At that point I threw a large glass jar out into the tier. After several minutes the officer (Mr. Robert White) came down and asked me what was wrong. I explained and asked him to open the door and permit me to go to the hospital to receive treatment. He replied that he couldn't open the door. And then he left. Finally, Jay Johnson, the nine tier runner, opened the door and I went over to the hospital.

At the hospital they tried to stop my nose from bleeding. They were unable to do so and gave me a piece of gauze to hold under my nose. On the way back to my wing, while I was going through the Center, Sgt. Reynolds stopped me and took me into the back part of the Center. After going over the facts that I have stated above, he stated that I would have to go into Protective Custody while they were looking into the matter. I informed Sgt. Reynolds that I did not wish to enter the P.C. status. At that point he told me that I would have to sign a waiver of examination form or be put into Protective Custody.

After signing the form I was permitted to return to my cell. Before leaving both the hospital and the Center, I was told that if my nose continued to bleed that I should request permission to return to the hospital. After I was in my cell for about thirty minutes, and my nose continued to bleed, I had the tier runner inform Mr. White, the officer on duty, that I wished to return to the hospital. I was refused permission. I then requested a White Hat from the Center. Officer White sent me an interview request form stating that I would have to fill it out first and he would turn it in at the Center and find out whether a White Hat was interested in talking to me about my return to the hospital.

At approximately 12:30 P.M. the wing went out for lunch. At this time I went back down to the Center and asked the officer on the stairs for permission to speak with Sgt. Glover, who was in charge of the Center. I informed him that I had a mirror that the assailant had used to check the tier and signal whoever was opening the doors, and that it had a lot of clear fingerprints on it.

Stg. Glover took me into the back of the Center and asked me to go into 1-Right (P.C.) for at least a few days, since many of the men confined here had seen me in the back of the Center. I explained to Sgt. Glover that it would be very detrimental for me to do so. Sgt. Glover admitted this to be true and stated that he would like me to be admitted into the hospital at least overnight to make sure that there was nothing wrong.

I was admitted into the hospital and given fresh gauze for under my nose which was still giving me some pain. At no time did I receive any medicine or treatment.

The following is what occurred on the night of the 16th of June and the morning of the 17th:

At 7:30 P.M. I had requested the night nurse because my nose was causing me pain. At approximately 7:55 P.M. the nurse arrived at my cell and talked to me, stating that some sort of medicine would be sent to me.

At 9:50 P.M. I had asked the officer on duty to call and find out what had happened to the medicine I was supposed to have received. The officer (Mr. Scott) called the Center and was told that they would send it over. At 10:30 P.M. there was a guard shift change made and I never received any kind of medicine.

As the night guard made his 11:51 rounds, I asked him to check also. He stated that he would also call the Center.

About ten minutes later he came back with a couple of packets of aspirin. This was the limit which the medical treatment consisted of.

On Sunday morning I again called for the nurse. Later, after the wing had gone out to lunch, I spoke to a White Hat in the mess hall and, upon arriving back in the wing, the nurse arrived and took me to the hospital. At the hospital a regular nurse looked at my nose, gave it a twist, and stated that there was nothing wrong. She referred me to regular sick call during the week.

On June 20th I saw the doctor on sick call who referred me to have X-rays taken of my nose. The X-rays were taken on the morning of the 21st and another on the same afternoon.

On June 22nd I was again called for still another X-ray. The inmate attendant stated that there was a fracture and possibly a complete break. Thus another X-ray was needed to tell just how bad it was.

The above is a true and accurate account of what occurred.

The options for Michael Chaytor, in the traditional prison sense, were:

1. To place himself in protective custody (solitary confinement).

2. Get a knife or some other weapon to use on his known assailants, letting the rest of the population know that he would not be victimized without retaliation.

3. Get a knife and commit suicide.

4. Press charges and be known as an institutional "snitch"—a low man on the inmate pecking order—which results invariably in having to be placed in protective custody.

5. Do nothing. In which case it becomes understood that he *is* public property.

Chaytor defied all of these alternatives and surrendered his anonymity as a prison rape victim. Chaytor went public and assumed the
position that the prison and the administrators were accomplices to the
crime and that the enactors of the physical acts against him were also
victims of a system which perpetuates these abuses.

The anonymity of the victim—along with the accompanying shame
and social negation of it—permitted prison officials to use sexual abuses
as a means of inmate division and control.

For pragmatic purposes, many prisons use sexual needs as a means
to maintain institutional control. Since most prison fights and stabbings
are rooted sexually (a betrayed lover, a love triangle, etc.) it often becomes necessary for rules to be adjusted according to sexual demands.

Much of the inmate perspective on prison sexuality in adult institutions is closely akin to attitudes assumed in children's institutions. In
almost any adult male penitentiary a survey would reveal that more than
half of the population did some time in a children's shelter, reformatory,
training school, orphanage, or other dehumanizing, mass building complex. The prevailing sexual mores, as well as many other social attitudes,
were nurtured in impersonal, repressive, institutional settings.

The most passive child will learn violence in the reformatory subculture. More than half of the kids in institutions start out as unwanted or
mischievous youths who have committed no crime. There are two "giv-
ens" in any boys' institution:

1. Learn to suppress your feelings because vulnerability leads to
your exploitation. This is significant and dangerous because many kids
lose contact with their own feelings—and their resultant inability to be
"touched" affects their social attitudes for the rest of their lives—unless,
by chance, someone intervenes.

2. Learn that power provides safety—and sexual exploitation is
power. Every new arrival in a reformatory must be prepared to protect
himself sexually. Those children who are not street-wise quickly become
manipulated and become someone's sexual property.

The play *Fortune and Men's Eyes* is the perfect exposition of such a
situation. In it, the author, John Herbert, reflecting on his own teen-age
reformatory experience, brings a young man into an institutional setting
who quickly becomes a tough guy's sex object. The trade-off, he imagines, is that unless one man protects him, he will be subjected to a ritual
gang-rape. The young protagonist becomes jail-smart and learns that
violence will get him out from under. Like every child who enters a
training school or reformatory, he knows that his fists and a weapon will
be necessary.

How does this shape the individual?

The following story has been told so many times that it has almost become a cliché. I will combine all the ingredients in one person, but be assured that it represents a silent anger in many of the difficult antisocial men in any community.

The teller of the tale is usually a traditional prison tough guy with many years of prison experience. He has been out of prison long enough by now to have an investment in street life and is looking for causes and solutions to his feelings and attitudes. The revelation goes like this:

> When I was eight years old I was put into a children's shelter because my parents didn't want me. I already had an attitude because my father used to beat me a great deal when he was around, but I was usually left to fend for myself. I was in the institution for about two days when I was sent on a work assignment into the basement. A big guy—he must have been 12 or 13 years old—grabbed me and locked me with him in a room and forced me to lower my pants. He screwed me, caused me to bleed, and threatened that if I talked about it, he would get me. He caught me a few more times, but I soon learned how to handle myself. I was filled with shame and hurt and had no one to go to. I promised myself that no one would ever get close to me again. I became a tough guy. I physically trained myself, developed myself physically, and pulled away from people on all other levels. I spent the next twenty years of my life pushing people away who tried to get close. I had no feelings about myself or anyone else. I wanted to hurt people. I ripped off kids in joints, I committed acts of violence on the street and in prisons. I used to entrap and beat up homosexuals in gay bars. I hated them and never knew why. And I blocked out of my mind those childhood sexual assaults.

America has a sexual subculture, cultivated and nurtured within its cages. Young boys reared in uncaring, impersonal institutional settings use sex as an instrument of power. Sexual violence is an indigenous part of this power play.

Women in prison have their own sexual standard—almost a total reverse of the male's ground rules. Sexism is truly apparent when you compare the sexual mores in a female institution to the sexual mores in a male prison. For, in the women's prison the obtrusive homosexual (the "butch," the "man") is at the top of the power structure. The female who most emulates the man becomes the kingpin. Consequently, homosexual relationships do not have the same stigma for women as they do for incarcerated men. The reasons for this are many, complicated, and sometimes contradictory.

— Women, in society, can have a demonstrative friendship, and therefore signs of friendship within an institution are not so severely judged.

— A lesbian relationship is interpreted as only temporary and is considered less threatening. Implicit is the understanding that once a woman is released, and has a man, she will be heterosexual. There is a much greater social fear that once a man is exposed to homosexuality, he will be forever suspect.

— A male-dominated society accepts or understands a "butch" woman (who is socially upgrading herself) more than the "femme" male (who is socially downgrading himself). It is the same reason that cross-dress among females is socially acceptable and cross-dress among males is grounds for arrest.

— Many women in prison have been involved in prostitution, and a sustained relationship with a woman is less demanding and less violent— and therefore is preferred.

The "butch," however, does provide a traditional male "power symbol" and is considered protection within the institution.

Homosexuality is much more acceptable and includes a larger percentage of the population in women's institutions as compared to men's. Many women have told me that it was the need for friendship and for someone to care. The opportunities for actual physical sex vary from prison to prison, but it is not so complicated a need in women's prisons, since many state that they would maintain a love-friendship, openly, with little opportunity for sex.

Interestingly, men in prison who have a tight friendship would be horrified to consider the sexual potential. The women can accept that they were involved in a lesbian relationship which, if the opportunity permitted, would be expressed sexually, with much less trauma attached.

Prison authorities generally accept lesbianism in the joint. In one California prison the warden announced that some political officials would be visiting and "short hair will be covered and no hand-holding would be permitted in the yard." Implicit here was that such acts were known to the officials, but that it would not be advisable for the outside world to witness it. Of course, no such announcement or thinking has ever existed in a men's prison.

Clearly, the prisons and jails in our country are a sexual reflection of the larger society. Because of the intense pressure of prison, all facets of the life are exaggerated extensions of the outside world. The prisoners bring into the institutions all the sexual ambivalence of the streets. The keepers of these men, women and children are no less confused and in their role as keepers become judgmental and oppressive.

Some very strong and realistic education should be going on in our jails and prisons—but, as institutions are traditionally slow to change, it will be a battle.

ARE THERE SOLUTIONS?

Solutions to the existing sexual problems caused by the Neanderthal conditions in most prisons cannot be approached myopically. A prison system which is anachronistic, negative and dehumanizing will of course be sexually repressive. It is naive to think that meaningful solutions can be realized simply by instituting conjugal visits or accelerating furlough programs. There are merits to each approach, however, *if* they are recognized as evolutionary steps rather than as final goals. Within the framework of the current prison system both conjugal visits and furlough programs carry the danger of being used as items to bargain over in a power struggle without paying heed to the basic issues or the suppressed sexual attitudes of the keepers and the kept. Sexual suppression and oppression is the inevitable result of a system which of its very nature is suppressive and oppressive.

Conjugal visits and furloughs should be fully discussed before moving into the larger area of a general restructuring of the criminal justice system. Within the context of the present penal system the furlough program would have to be selected as the most hopeful alternative. Virtually all conjugal visitation programs are arbitrary and dehumanizing. Quick moral judgments, made on the basis of the sexual mores of the community, dictate which prisoners should be permitted to have sexual release. Only the sexual needs of married males are considered. The sexual needs of single men, men with common-law wives, all women, and all homosexual men are completely ignored by the system of conjugal visitation. It is also a dehumanizing exercise for many of the wives. No matter what facilities or conditions are provided for these visits, there is a strong implication that the sum and substance of a relationship is contained within the genitalia.

Furlough programs have the edge in several respects. The marital status of the inmate is a lesser factor in selecting those who will participate in such a program. The furlough approach also allows the prisoner to spend some time in the community, thus offsetting the antisocial influence of imprisonment. The problem with furloughs is that they are usually limited to prisoners with less than two years remaining on their sentence. It is obvious that the absconding rate would be much higher among prisoners who have more time to serve. Also, since so many prisons are located so far from the prisoners' home communities, the practicality of furlough visits is greatly limited by financial considerations.

There is no indication that conjugal visitation programs have been too successful in large penitentiaries located in rural areas or that furlough programs have minimized sexual manipulation. The furlough programs have had some effect in small county institutions where a sexually mature approach has been part of a broader redefinition of the entire tone of the institution. Such smaller county jails as those in Bucks County, Pennsylvania, and Cambridge County, Massachusetts, have initiated substantive changes under enlightened leadership, but not without strenuous resistance from old-guard officials.

The single most important step which can be taken to alleviate the problems of the prisons is to reduce the prison populations. No meaningful changes can be considered for facilities holding thousands of men. Prison populations can be reduced by accelerating parole (with the realization that long sentences increase the probability of danger to the community when the inmate is ultimately released), by retaining within society those persons who have committed victimless crimes, and by sustaining community programs for persons who are not considered to be a violent threat.

Only when the prison populations have been reduced will correction administrators have the opportunity to create an atmosphere which permits people to come to terms with themselves, their own potenital, and their relationship to society as a whole. The healthy exercise of an individual's human sexuality would be an integral part of any such humane and constructive atmosphere.

But it is unwise to seek solutions based on external factors such as furloughs and conjugal visitations. Such programs will only succeed when the inter-actions of the prison population as a whole have improved in ways transcending the implementation of particular programs.

Prison officials and prisoners, equally, must have the opportunity to become enlightened about human sexuality. Mature dialogues and discussions should be an integral part of any institution. First steps first, however. We must first achieve smaller, less repressive institutions in which the atmosphere encourages free and fearless dialogue.

If a legislator wanted a step-by-step simplification of how to proceed in this area, I would suggest the following:

1. Legislative and administrative action to decrease the prison populations.

2. Decrease the pressure in the atmosphere of the jails and prisons. Much of the aggression that manifests itself sexually is the inevitable result of a dehumanized process and environment.

3. Staff and administrators should have the opportunity of understanding various aspects of sexuality. Men particularly should become enlightened about women, about their own feelings, homosexuality, and all aspects of sexual behavior.

4. Furlough programs and conjugal visits could then be considered as an aspect of sexual enlightenment, rather than as a political pacifier which changes nothing.

Before this legislative millennium is achieved, however, families of prisoners should come together (as has a group in Nassau County, N.Y., called Prison Families Anonymous) to discuss all aspects of what happens to the family as well as to the incarcerated member of the family.

REFERENCES AND RECOMMENDED READINGS

HERBERT, JOHN. *Fortune and Men's Eyes.* New York: Grove Press, 1968.

SCACCO, ANTHONY, JR. *Rape in Prison.* Springfield, Ill.: Charles C Thomas Publishers, 1975.

WEISS, CARL, and DAVID J. FRIAR. *Terror in the Prisons.* New York: Bobbs-Merrill Co., 1974.

VII.
THE
HANDICAPPED,
ILL,
AND DYING

With the exception of the retarded, the oppression of the handicapped, ill and dying is as much a result of neglect as it is of deliberate suppression. We automatically tend to assume that people confined to wheelchairs or with some other highly visible physical handicap, who are sick or dying, have neither sexual desire nor ability. Hence we often inadvertently oppress by failing to educate them or to make provision in our society for fulfillment of their unique sexual needs.

Yet even when we recognize the need, our biases and misconceptions still result in deliberate oppression. This is partly because our biases are toward handicaps in general: we are so uncomfortable with physical imperfections and so unnerved by the thought of death that we think of the afflicted as less than human. We fail to perceive their human needs (which may or may not be affected by their handicap) and fail to allow for the possibility that others may not be equally repulsed. Often our misconceptions result in two ideas at polar extremes: either that the person is totally affected by his handicap or that he is totally unaffected. Hence, even when our biases are not negative, they fail to take into account the special sexual problems that may require attention. And, finally, our attitudes again relate to the reproductive bias that excludes people we think are incapable of caring for children, who do not fit our standards of "socially acceptable," and who may not only desire but may actually require sexual stimulation other than intercourse in order to obtain sexual fulfillment.

It is often assumed that the blind are unaffected sexually by their handicap, and hence their special needs are ignored. At the same time, however, society's attitudes prevent them from having the opportunities for sexual expression open to others, or for receiving the information necessary for satisfying and responsible sexuality. They may be hampered by their own insecurities, by basic problems in transportation or in knowing how to dress attractively. Problems in sensing the appearance and responses of a potential sexual partner, and other problems that interfere with their ease in social relationships and in their ability to both have a date and to know what to do with one may be partly due to overprotection. Education, even when given, may neither adequately provide for their learning handicaps nor relate to their special problems. Indeed, the boy who in an earlier chapter complained that his school sex education was inadequate, was himself blind; both his insensitivity to girls and his uncertainty about sex, he felt, was directly related to the fact that his teachers had completely ignored the fact of his blindness when talking about sex.

There are people who are neither dying nor handicapped, but who for various reasons must be in a hospital for weeks or even months. Not only the pleasures of sexuality with others, but even the tension relief that masturbation might bring is denied them. Their problems require more attention than we have given them. Because the kinds of handicaps are so numerous and varied, space permits discussion of only a few general categories. Despite such omissions, however, the chapters that follow give us a glimpse of the kinds of problems facing people with handicaps, no matter what the handicaps might be.

Smith, from her experiences both as a counsellor and a parent, describes the problems of deaf people, with her sometimes humorous, but always sensitive illustrations. Kempton provides insights into the problems created by both the neglect and the deliberate oppression of the retarded. Romano similarly shows us the problems along with the often surprising capabilities of the physically handicapped. Jaffe completes the section by sharing with us much information and some personal perspectives on the sex-related problems of the dying, including the effects of particular symptoms and treatments as well as the profound emotional experiences shared by the dying and their sexual partners.

CHAPTER 17

THE
MENTALLY
RETARDED
PERSON

Winifred Kempton

Many groups of individuals have been, and continue to be, sexually oppressed, vilified or deprived in their efforts to express their sexuality. Some—for example homosexuals and transvestites—are maligned because of their sexual life-style; some, such as senior citizens, because of their age; some, such as those in mental institutions or prisons, because of their living situation. No group of individuals, however, has been more drastically oppressed because of the mere fact that they are *sexual* than those labeled "retarded." Historically the anxiety of parents, professionals, and the general public that a person who is retarded may also be sexual has frequently reached an almost panic state in which reason flies out the window. Practically everyone has been concerned that if the sexuality of the retarded were not suppressed they would prolifically reproduce, or their sexual impulses would emerge in uncontrollable bursts of sexual violence. As a result society has generally imposed rigid and cruel restrictions upon the retarded, often with a kind of hopeful anticipation that they would become desexed. Until recently the sexual rights of the retarded have never been considered; even their sexuality itself has not been dealt with either in the literative or in arrangements for their direct care. In fact, when the author checked on the writings in professional journals published prior to 1970 she found no reference whatever to the sexual behavior of the retarded other than discussions of whether they should marry or have children. Certainly many positive aspects of their sexuality have been totally neglected, and where sexual needs are admitted, only rigid controls have been used. For example, parents usually try desperately by constant surveillance to keep their retarded offspring from having any contact with the opposite sex. As one mother said recently, "I won't allow my daughter to cross the street by herself. Some man may be waiting to have sex with her on the other side." Also, our institutions have routinely treated the retarded as prisoners, strictly segregating the sexes.

FACTORS IN SEXUAL OPPRESSION

It is important that the factors contributing to this harsh suppression be thoroughly examined. Of these factors, the most obvious one is society's determination that the retarded shall not reproduce. At the turn of the century, a study by Peck and Peck indicated that the average IQ of United States citizens would drop if retarded people continued to pro-create at their current rate. This study played a part in the establishment of many state laws that required sterilization of the retarded. Another factor is the wish of the parents, already overburdened with the care of a retarded offspring, that he or she not produce another child who will add to their problems. The concern of these parents is realistic and they have a right to express it. Social agency and institutional personnel have shared the parents' worries over what would happen if the retarded had children. They saw difficulties emerging from several sources: (1) the genetic risk that the mental handicap would be repeated in the offspring, (2) the inability of retarded parents to provide proper health and home care, (3) the likelihood that mental stimulation would be insufficient for the child to develop intellectually (Garber, 1973).

Quite often the only solution these professionals could devise was to deprive the retarded of all heterosexual relationships in order to keep them from becoming parents. Consequently, the professionals frequently worked hand in glove with the parents in committing a retardate to an institution for the chief purpose of preventing procreation, especially when an attractive, seductive young retarded girl reached puberty. In fact, one institution with which the author has been associated bore the subtitle "The Institution for Childbearing Women" and its residents were mainly women of childbearing age who were never permitted to be in the company of any males outside their own families.

Anxiety over their sexuality in one form or another haunts almost everyone concerned with their care. Thus, worry over procreation by the retarded often puts an additional strain on those who care for them and are already unable to deal with their sexuality. Not only were many attractive girls institutionalized to prevent childbearing, but parents kept the others almost as prisoners in their homes. Sterilizations were frequently arranged for children by both parents and professionals, with most of the children not knowing what was happening to them. In institutions some staff members viewed homosexual activity as being more acceptable than heterosexual involvement because there would be no danger of pregnancy (Rosen, 1970: p. 101). For example, a female resident would be harshly punished for the slightest attempt to communicate with the opposite sex, but, at the same time, would be permitted to participate in sexual activity with the same sex uninterrupted. Naturally the retardate would deduce that homosexual behavior was more desirable than heterosexual activity.

Currently one of the most difficult problems facing rehabilitation counselors who are preparing the retarded to re-enter the community is to help orient them as to their true sexual life-style. This is especially difficult for those retarded males who have lived most of their lives in an institution. If, because of lack of opportunity for heterosexual pleasures, homosexual activity is all they have ever known they must have help in sorting out what their true sexual needs are so they can establish their sexual role identity.

Although the prevention of parenthood is perhaps the most obvious and serious reason for the deprivation of sexual rights of the retarded, other attitudes have contributed to this oppression. One is the myth, held by most of society, that retarded men are sexually dangerous; that they automatically lack control of their sexual impulses and will assault strangers, especially little girls. Workers in the retardation field currently attempting to establish group homes find whole communities belligerently opposing them with arguments like: "We won't be able to allow our children to play outside if retarded men live in the neighborhood."

There has been no systematic research to confirm or disprove this belief. There are only the assurances by those who work closely with retarded men that most of these men are timid and gentle people whose most serious fault in this respect is that they lack social skills. When they have approached others inappropriately, it has usually been for want of training in social sexual behavior. Since the retarded are not usually as keenly perceptive of what sexual behavior *is* and *is not* acceptable, they do not learn at an early age what conduct wins social approval and what conduct makes others uncomfortable. For several reasons, such as feelings of guilt or discomfort over their handicap, those who care for them have traditionally been lax in disciplining the retarded so that they behaved appropriately. As a result many retardates lack good manners, and they also often lack social skills or an awareness of others' feelings. It is not uncommon for a retarded man to be overly friendly, perhaps touching a person who does not know him. Not only does this conduct make him socially unacceptable, but at times there can be cause for an involvement with the law. In fact, according to Myerowitz (1971) one-third of the crimes committed by retarded males are sex related. On closely examining these "crimes," however, one finds that they consist of careless and ignorant acts, such as not having properly zippered pants, urinating on the sidewalk because the retardate doesn't know how to find a bathroom, or approaching a stranger for affection or a homosexual act with no judgment or finesse. Thus the outcome is often arrest and booking for sexual perversion when in reality the act was simply due to ignorance and lack of training.

Whatever the cause or the situation, the fact remains that society's fear of the sexual behavior of the retarded male sharply reduces his chances for a normal and happy sexual life. On the one hand, community education is needed to dispel the myths; on the other hand the retarded need to be taught to understand what is appropriate and responsible sexual behavior.

Another serious problem to those who care for them is that often the retarded have amenable characters that make them more sexually exploitable than their nonhandicapped peers. For example, if a child molester has a choice between a retarded female child and a nonretarded female child, he will usually molest the retarded child. Why? Because she is more likely to (1) trust strangers, (2) lack the ability to determine what is appropriate behavior, (3) not know how to judge the motivation for others' behavior, (4) do what she is told, (5) show and receive affection more readily, (6) not have the ability to defend herself, and (7) not be able to communicate or report the incident effectively. Without proper training, an individual often retains these traits throughout life, and it is not unusual for a retarded woman to be sexually exploited by men or for a male retardate to be sexually exploited by male homosexuals.

Realistically, it is important that retarded children be protected from this kind of exploitation, and a certain amount of supervision is called for throughout their lives, especially if they are severely retarded. In too many cases, however, the anxiety over exploitation results in such overprotection that again they are deprived of their sexual rights and freedom. Instead of receiving training and being supervised only when necessary (at some risk perhaps), retarded individuals have been treated as perennial children who will never learn to fend for themselves. A method of teaching them to protect themselves, in which they practice rejecting exploiters through role playing, is currently being used by some sex educators (Kempton, 1975).

Another factor that has caused sexual oppression is the manner in which masturbatory activities have been handled. In promoting the sexual rights of the retarded, one could hardly expect every retarded person to someday find sexual fulfillment with another human being. At least nobody has as yet come up with answers that would make it possible for all retardates to form close mate relationships. For some retarded persons, masturbation may be the best outlet for their sexual impulses and may help them reach some degree of sexual satisfaction. Most of them, however, are not even receiving effective guidance toward this goal. Historically, masturbation was thought to be a causative factor in mental retardation. This belief has been discarded along with other myths, such as the old belief that masturbation causes impotence, mental illness, excessive fatigue, blindness, acne, and hair on the palm of the hands. Nevertheless, the management of masturbation habits is often inconsiderate and even cruel. True, because many of the retarded do not have enough interesting things to do to occupy their time or do not have opportunities for pleasurable social outlets, they may understandably spend more time masturbating than do other people. It is also more likely that they will masturbate publicly because they did not pick up on early signals from parents or others that it is not appropriate to touch one's genitals in the presence of others. But since the exposure of their sexual feelings in this manner does disturb others, the latter often conclude that retardates cannot deal with their sexual impulses and overly stringent methods are then used to control their behavior.

Very often the retardate is at the mercy of the varying attitudes of those who are responsible for his care. He suffers greatly from the inconsistency with which he is treated, especially in an institution. Suppose a boy inmate is seen masturbating by four staff members. One staff member might become angry and punish him soundly, perhaps by beating him or putting boxing gloves on his hands; a second staff member might tease or joke about it as though it were a dirty or funny act; a third staff member, lacking the ability to deal with sexuality directly, might totally disregard the behavior and pretend to be unaware of it, while a fourth staff member might take the opportunity to teach the boy that sexual impulses are normal and good, but should be expressed privately. This kind of inconsistent treatment is destructive to the retarded and can be avoided only when all staff and parents mutually agree on appropriate guidance based on healthy sexual attitudes.

A fourth manner in which the retarded have been oppressed is by depriving them of knowledge about sexuality itself. It is true that in this respect we are all retarded by our basic lack of information about sexuality. But again, because of the nature of their handicap, the retarded have suffered disproportionately. First, it is more difficult for them than for

other people to find out *anything* about sexuality. Most of us when growing up were able to gain bits and pieces of information about sex from
our friends, families, school, films, books, or by making rational deduc-
tions from observing the behavior of others. The retarded person is at a
heavy disadvantage in using these methods of learning. And his inadequacy is compounded by the tendency of most persons purposely to keep
him ignorant. The rationale is: "Don't tell them so they won't do it." Or,
again, "My son just isn't interested in sex, so I don't see why he needs to
know anything about it." The mother may *want* to believe that her son is
nonsexual, but probably the fact is that he has been forced to repress his
sexual feelings so consistently that he really doesn't appear to have any.
This lack of ability on the part of the retarded to pick up sexual information has led to gross lack of knowledge.

A psychologist reports:

> The mother of a retarded girl asked if I would counsel her retarded
> daughter and her husband who were living with her. The mother was
> concerned that the young couple were not having sexual intercourse, that
> after two years of marriage she did not believe they knew what to do to
> consummate it. The mother was too embarrassed to talk to the retarded
> couple about this matter and asked me to help her. Talking with the
> couple, I learned that they did not know that the woman had an opening
> (the vagina), and had no idea how a penis could be used for sexual
> gratification through the act of sexual intercourse. Their concept of mak-
> ing love for these two years had been to get into bed each night and rub
> each other!

Such ignorance is not unusual. There are many reports of retarded couples who married without knowing that sexual intercourse exists. We
have learned from retarded girls that they believed all sexual intercourse
was intended to hurt the woman because they had put up with all kinds
of unpleasant sexual experiences as a result of this lack of knowledge.

Facts about sex and reproduction are sometimes withheld by parents
and some professionals out of fear that the retardate might want to try
sexual intercourse or develop a desire to have babies. Still other persons
say they don't want to discuss sex with retardates because the retardates
could not learn about sex, anyway. Still others say that learning about
sexual activity, marriage, and parenthood (of which they may be deprived) will only add to the retardate's unhappiness and add to the
frustration of knowing they are different. What many people don't realize
is that the average retardate is full of gross misinformation about sex that
causes him guilt and anxiety and literally advertises his mental handicap.
Sex education for the retarded should start at the lowest level; there is no
reason not to give them as much knowledge as they can integrate. Even

the lowest functioning girl should be taught everything her mind is able to grasp.

All these factors have contributed to serious deprivation of the retarded in the past, as they have often been treated as subhuman beings. However, helping the retarded has made great advances in the past twenty years. In fact, the rate of improvement has outrun other related fields. New methods of diagnosis and treatment, education and training are accomplishing goals unattainable only a short time ago. The standard of treatment has risen dramatically, so that what used to be mainly custodial care has given way to some highly specialized efforts to teach and train each retardate as an individual.

NEW APPROACHES

Many involved in the field of retardation and related areas have been revitalized by the development of new experimental projects and training programs. Courses on retardation are being offered in undergraduate and graduate schools of education, social work, and psychology. Even the term *retardation* is being questioned. Some organizations are trying to dispel old attitudes (for example, the Association for Retarded Children is now the Association for Retarded Citizens). The term *developmentally disabled* is used by the Federal Government and is meant to be applied in the field of retardation. Certain groups, resenting the word *retardation*, prefer to put some responsibility outside the retarded by calling them "persons with mental or learning handicaps or disabilities."

New terminology and theoretical concepts have had definite effects on the trends in services and study. The *normalization principle* was first proposed in the Scandinavian countries (NE b Mikkelson, Denmark, BengrNirje, Sweden). Its aim is "to let the mentally retarded obtain an existence as close to the normal as possible. Thus, as we see it, the normalization principle means making available to the Mentally Retarded patterns and conditions of everyday life which are as close as possible to the norms and patterns of the main stream of society" (Nirje, 1969). From this explanation comes the common term used by many: *mainstreaming*.

Here are some precepts from Mr. Nirje's book:

Normalization means:

1. A normal rhythm of day for the retarded.

2. A normal rhythm of life (live and work in different settings).

3. To experience normal rhythm of the year (such as going on a vacation).

4. Opportunity to undergo normal developmental experiences of the

life cycle—from childhood to adolescence—and the opportunities that involve adult experiences.

5. Having choice, wishes, and desires.

6. Living in a *bisexual* world.

Normalization also means living in a bisexual world. Accordingly, facilities should provide for male and female staff members. When it comes to the integration of retarded boys and girls or men and women, the 1967 Stockholm Symposium on "Legislative Aspects of Mental Retardation" of the International League of Societies for the Mentally Handicapped came to the following conclusion: "Being fully mindful of the need to preserve the necessary safeguards in the relations between mentally retarded men and women, the members of the Symposium are of the opinion that the dangers involved have been greatly exaggerated in the past. This has often resulted in the unfortunate segregation of the sexes in an unnatural way and has militated against their interests and proper development.

"Accordingly, the Symposium strongly advocates the mixing of the sexes in a manner as free as is commensurate with normal restraints, not only in day centers and workshops but also in leisuretime activities.

"Experience in some countries indicates the advantage of mixing men and women in hostels and other residential facilities in such a way as is approximate to normal life." (Nirje, 1969).

The impact from the acceptance of the normalization principle on the field of retardation in the United States was tremendous. An essential step in carrying out this principle is de-institutionalization of the mentally retarded, and concerted efforts are now being directed toward discharging the mentally retarded from institutions throughout most of the United States and Europe. The challenge and problems involved in this process cannot be discussed here. However, the principle has a definite bearing on our discussion of the sexual rights of the retarded because, as they are relocated at a concentrated speed into the community—moving into group homes, halfway houses, and even apartments of their own— their social skills are indeed being tested and exposed. Reluctantly or not, society is being forced to admit that sexuality is a part of every individual and is not necessarily limited by a lack of intelligence. The sexual problems and sexual needs of the retarded can no longer be swept under the rug.

The field of retardation has, in fact, happily joined and become a part of the civil rights movement; the mentally retarded are taking their places among the other oppressed minorities. Meanwhile, numerous state laws have been passed that mandate an education for individuals of all levels of intelligence, resulting in the establishment of many more special education classes in public schools. Other civil rights laws automatically include the retarded.

It is important, however, that we see the civil rights movement of the retardates as being unique; it differs from all the other movements because it is not planned and carried on by the retarded themselves. Obviously, because of their limited intellectual and functional abilities, the mentally retarded must depend on others to verbalize their needs for them and to organize and fight their battles for them. Gradually and steadily, championing groups have been mobilizing during the past twenty years. The movement originated mainly through the organization of parents of the retarded—the Association for Retarded Children (now the Association for Retarded Citizens). It was given impetus and national support by the Kennedy family. Little by little, other movements started by earlier agencies enlarged to include county, state, and Federal Government projects. Advocacy volunteer groups have been established, consisting of high-school and college students and senior citizens. They provide active direct services to the retarded themselves while attempting to guard their charges from being deprived of their rights as they see them.

The workers in retardation and other fields are taking on new directions and trying to implement the rights defined by the movement. New thinking and new methods have replaced the old attitude that the retarded remain protected children forever. Professionals are given new knowledge as they work cooperatively with the parents toward definite goals. It has been the philosophy of the helping profession to support movements for justice for those who have been denied their just privileges. It is only fitting that all personnel agree that the retarded receive sexual rights.

What are these sexual rights? With assistance the retarded themselves are now verbalizing them:

1. The right to receive training in social-sexual behavior that will open more doors for social contact with people in the community.

2. The right to all the knowledge about sexuality they can comprehend.

3. The right to enjoy love and be loved by the opposite sex, including sexual fulfillment.

4. The right to the opportunity to express sexual impulses in the same forms that are socially acceptable for others.

5. The right to marry.

6. The right to have a voice in whether or not they should have children.

7. The right for supportive services which involve those rights as they are needed and feasible.

These sexual rights are fair and reasonable and should be a part of the current advance in the field of retardation. However, education, training, and opportunities in areas relating to sexuality always lag behind other programs. Yet, unless the sexual needs of the retarded are looked upon realistically and honestly, the arrests, pregnancies, and failures of the retarded to find social-sexual fulfillment at a feasible level can be directly attributed to the laxness and sexual hangups of those who are responsible for them. Thus in the past few years there has been widespread interest in providing staff training and parental guidance in dealing with the sexuality of the handicapped; both government and private agencies have financially backed these projects. The author has personally been involved in workshops and seminars in thirty different states. Resource materials are beginning to appear and an expanding literature speaks objectively to the problems of the retarded.

This progress is encouraging, but there are countless unmet needs. More research is required, more experiences have to be shared, more attitudes improved, and new resources developed. By no means do we have answers to many of the problems relating to sexuality that are presenting themselves; by no means are the attitudes of all those involved positive and supportive. Myths, conflicts, and negative feelings still exist. Some workers who are helping the retarded become a part of the community continue to want to keep them forever children, not daring to risk the problems that could occur if they are offered adolescent and/or adult activities and responsibilities.

Too many people still think there is no alternative to sterilizing the retarded when they reach puberty. Some people associate sterilization with castration, and believe that the sex drive is lessened by a sterilization operation. Many parents need counseling, along with encouragement and strong supportive services that will guide them to find reasonable solutions about dating, marriage, and parenthood for their young. The professionals need training to do all of this.

SECURING THEIR SEXUAL RIGHTS

Social services to help the retardates move in the community are varied and challenging. Direct services include counseling in mental health and mental retardation centers, the organization and maintenance of halfway houses and group homes, and the providing of socialization and training programs. Those working in the institutions should offer training and counseling in all areas of social skills, especially during the immediate period before the retardate is discharged. Direct education about sexuality must be included. And, of utmost importance, sex education should be a part of all training and education programs.

What do we mean, then, by sex education for the retarded? Obviously the seriously and moderately retarded will not learn facts or discuss feelings about sexuality any more than they will about any other subject. (Although they have been surprising us by integrating more information about sex than we anticipated.) For them sex education means training in appropriate social-sexual behavior, the imparting of positive feelings about their bodies and their sexual role as man or woman. In practical terms, how can we do this when they vary so widely in abilities and levels of functioning? To simplify the procedure, we should try to determine individually (1) the level of understanding that the student can reach, (2) the reason for the teaching and what the goals are, (3) how the material can be most effectively presented. For example: How do we determine the best way to prepare a retarded girl for her first menstrual period? Here, the first thing to be considered is the level at which the girl generally learns or functions. With this as a base, the purpose for the sex education can be identified. The education process would then be carried out with the same methods used in other areas to train that particular girl. If these guidelines are used, it is possible to meet the needs of each retardate without a great deal of confusion or frustration on the part of the teacher or the learner.

ILLUSTRATION: *A girl is developing breasts and pubic hair, so it can be assumed that her first menses will soon occur. What should be the teaching or counseling process for the girl according to her level?*

For the lowest functioning girl the *purpose* would be mainly to prevent her from being frightened at the sight of the menstrual blood emerging from her body. (Girls can be seriously traumatized by this occurrence.) A slightly higher *goal*, but one which should be attempted even for seriously retarded girls, would be to teach her the proper social behavior while menstruating, *i.e.*, not to flaunt the fact that she is menstruating before others; and to teach her the self-care of cleanliness and the proper changing and disposal of the soiled pads. Objectives that can be accomplished for this particular girl might end right there, and one could be assured that proper steps had been taken for her needs.

For the girl of higher learning, *why* one menstruates and some effort to explain the time factor would be the next step in the teaching process. (At this level, information on menstruation should also be presented to the boys.) For girls of still higher learning skills, one could explain the reproductive process still further and attempt to find what more they would be capable of, and interested in, learning. Of course along the way in all cases the teacher or counselor will reassure the girl with positive attitudes and give her a sense of self-esteem in that she, as a woman, possesses a body that functions like everyone else.

Finally, at the highest level, for the borderline retardate, the same information and discussions that are used for any sex-education program would be included, such as the psychological and social factors, implications of menstruation in the entire reproductive process, menopause, the hormonal changes of the body, and so on.

What *methods* are used for teaching menstruation to girls of these various levels? Naturally, they will vary just as they do in the teaching of other information.

The lowest-functioning retardates must *see* or *experience* in order to learn. Thus the girl would have to *see* the soiled pad of someone else (preferably her mother) in order for her to be reassured that menstruation is not dangerous. The girl of higher abilities would need explicit pictures, much repetition, very simple terms, and very short sessions. The dramatic-play technique of *pantomime* (acting out simple procedures or behavior) can be very effective (Kempton, 1975). At the next higher level pictures would still be needed, but with more complicated explanation and a slightly higher language level. Girls at a still more advanced level can carry on a verbal exchange of ideas, but of course the special problems of each individual must be kept in mind.

Obviously there is no age level designated to be considered in sex education for the retarded. The subject matter must always be adapted to the student's intellectual level, stage of development, and particular needs. Specifically, because the higher-functioning retardates may eventually become self-sufficient in the community, their knowledge should cover every aspect of sexuality: the reproductive processes of male and female (including pregnancy); the physical and emotional changes during puberty; proper personal health care; sexuality as part of the total personality; self-image; role identification; social responsibility; values and moral standards; ideal and realistic relationships between students, families, and friends. And always including the feelings and attitudes that are involved in these.

For the more sophisticated older adolescents and adults we add such subjects as the influence of body physiology on sexual behavior, genetics, premarital moral codes, love and intimacy, the meaning of an adjustment to earlier experiences, health care (including prevention of VD, Pap tests, and regular internal examination), sexual intercourse, dating, marriage and family life, childbearing, and how our attitudes toward sex are formed. These topics are identical to the knowledge about sexuality that is needed by the entire population. However, only some of these can be offered to many retardates, and only a very few of these can be offered to the more severely retarded.

SEX EDUCATION AND COUNSELING

Both sex education and counseling on sex-related matters are essential for the retarded. But much of the counseling process must include sex education or training in social-sexual behavior, and much of the sex education must be presented in the counseling. These mandates are currently complicated by a dearth of staff adequately trained to handle them. The problem of understanding the sex language looms large in both sex education and counseling. A chair is a chair, but a penis can be given thirty different names, varying according to the cultural and geographic location of the discussants. Therefore, a common ground of verbal communication must be established at the starting point by both teacher and counselor.

At present few counselors are competent to help retardates cope with sex-related situations. The fact that all counselors need additional training in sexuality has been indicated. Also, unfortunately some counselors don't want to work with slow learners. It is almost impossible to find an agency to which, for example, a retarded couple can be referred for complete premarital counseling. And it must be recognized that extremely difficult issues are involved in providing such counseling for the retarded. Both professionals and parents are highly diversified and confused in their opinions on dating, marriage, and parenthood for the young retarded adult. Some workers emotionally take the stand that all retardates should be given equal opportunity for relationships with the opposite sex. Some, including many parents, take the opposite stand—that marriage and heterosexual relationships should be discouraged for the retarded and that they certainly should not bear children; that otherwise society, the unborn child, the parents, and the couple themselves will all suffer.

Agency and institutional personnel argue constantly on these issues without, unhappily, having sufficient research to back up their opinions. Often they are mainly influenced either by their own attitudes toward sexuality or by a concern over community acceptance. Parents too show ambivalence; some are deeply concerned that they will be burdened with more problems if their retardate becomes involved in sexual activities; a few are afraid that abstinence from sexual intercourse will harm their son (seldom their daughter).

STERILIZATION?

The issue over sterilization causes special controversy among staff and parents. Some who are very closely involved feel that the retarded should be sterilized at puberty; some believe the low-functioning girls who cannot care for themselves during their menstrual period should have hysterectomies. (The sterilization in these cases is done not only to prevent pregnancy but for the convenience of those caring for the girls because of the extra work in keeping them clean. Whose rights are at stake here?) Other professionals take the very strong stand that sterilization under any circumstances is not necessary to prevent pregnancy; that to perform an operation on their bodies if they cannot understand the procedure is denying the rights of young persons; and that such radical means of preventing pregnancy are entirely uncalled for. As one lawyer said, "I do not feel it is necessary to take a uterus out of anyone to prevent pregnancy these days."

In 1974 national awareness of this issue was brought on by the Relf case (USDC, 1974). The poor parents of two young black girls ages fourteen and twelve respectively, one of them retarded, sued a Federally funded social agency for sterilizing their children allegedly without informed consent. The U. S. Department of Health, Education and Welfare reacted to the Relf case by placing a moratorium on the use of Federal funds for sterilizing minors and legally incompetent adults, and by issuing new regulations for such sterilizations as were to be performed. There is now some question as to whether such guidelines, though they may protect the young retarded individual, are not in some cases infringing the rights of the older retarded who *want* to obtain sterilizations!

There are some compelling reasons, however, why the retarded should not be sterilized when they reach puberty. First, with improved methods of training and teaching it is no longer possible to predict accurately as to what level of functioning a retardate will eventually reach. Therefore, if sterilization is done at puberty, who can say that in ten years the retarded person would not be functioning at a much improved level, perhaps being as eligible for parenthood as anyone else?

The sister of a retarded man states: "My mother had to die before my brother had the opportunity to reach his potential. During the first sixteen years of his life, mother kept Bill at home, sacrificing his social and intellectual growth because of her fears of the risks involved in allowing him to take advantage of community services. She would not permit him to join the Nipon Association, a Philadelphia socialization agency, because she was afraid he would get into trouble or cause the family embarrassment. As a result, while my mother lived, Bill did nothing but sit around the house and he had no friends. When mother died, I took over his care and immediately involved him in the Nipon program. After two years of education and training under good supervision he is now working and fairly self-supporting. When the phone rings in our house now the call is as likely to be for Bill as for my father or me." Whether or not Bill would have been a capable parent or not cannot be proved. However, we can be reasonably certain that he would resent any early actions which would have irrevocably prevented him from fathering a child. In a recent study of fifteen married couples, it was found that the seven couples who had been sterilized without having had a part in the decision were bitter about what had been done to them (Andron, 1973).

Another important reason for avoiding early sterilization is that many persons who are labeled retarded are basically suffering from emotional or physical disabilities that hinder them from learning. It is estimated that 25 per cent of the residents of institutions for the retarded are in this category and might well join the "normal" population if the causes of their learning problems were identified and successfully treated. It would be a gross injustice to have such individuals sterilized so that it would be impossible for them to have children in later life.

A third factor with important bearing on this question of sterilization is that usually the radical means of sterilization or imprisonment is no longer necessary to prevent a retarded female from becoming pregnant now that modern methods of birth control are available. The old methods of birth control—condom, diaphragm, foams and jellies, rhythm, withdrawal—require some judgment, control, and intelligence, which the retarded often lack. These characteristics, are not so necessary, however, to the success of birth control pills, the intrauterine device (I.U.D. or coil), or the Depo-Provera injection. All of these are being used effectively by some sexually active retarded women. Furthermore, there is no longer any need to sterilize women because of fear that they will be sexually exploited because, even though many people are still opposed to it, abortion can now be used as a backup for accidental or enforced intercourse. The morning-after pill and very early detection of pregnancy, followed by the use of menstrual extraction, are other alternatives.

COUNSELING SITUATIONS IN SEXUALITY FOR THE RETARDED

To demonstrate present counseling needs, here is a list of some questions that have been brought to the attention of the author in the past year in which expert counseling is required.

1. Parents ask the counselor to help them get their son or daughter (who has just reached puberty) sterilized.

2. A man is constantly manipulating his genitals in the presence of others.

3. A house parent asks help in protecting a retarded resident from pregnancy.

4. A retarded couple want to get married and ask for help.

5. A girl is constantly making very aggressive sexual overtures to a young male staff member.

6. A boy tries to touch his classmates' genitals whenever he gets the opportunity.

7. A couple are constantly making out in the workshop.

8. A very sexually active girl is unsuccessful in taking the pill and cannot tolerate the I.U.D.

9. A retarded client is working as a prostitute, is making a good salary, and apparently enjoys her work.

10. One of the boys is constantly asking staff members about their sex lives.

11. A retarded physically handicapped man confides his deep sorrow that no girl will date him.

12. Parents are harshly whipping their child for masturbating.

13. It is apparent in the workshop setting that a man is constantly rubbing his genitals because he cannot reach a climax.

14. A student reveals to her teacher that she is a victim of incest by her father.

15. A teacher learns that one of her girls is having sexual intercourse with any boy who wishes to use her.

16. There is a love affair going on between two clients of the same sex.

17. A parent expresses his concern that his son is a homosexual because he has no opportunity to be with girls.

18. A parent is concerned because one of her daughters has a crush on the man down the street and says she is going to marry him.

19. One of the girls is constantly saying that she wants to have many children, and it is quite apparent that she would not be able to take care of a child on her own.

20. A house parent learns that one of her residents is a homosexual and is making inappropriate overtures to the other residents.

21. A house parent learns that one of her sixteen-year-old residents is pregnant.

CONCLUSION

What can be done to end the sexual oppression of the retarded? It is much the same whether it be a professional, a parent, or an outside member of the community who undertakes the task. There will be differences in time and energy spent and in the amount of ground that can be covered, but in order to succeed the same basic process must be followed.

As with everything that has to do with sexuality, one must take inventory of one's own personal feelings. Some people say, "It hadn't occurred to us before that we have been depriving the retarded of something that can enrich their lives." In addition, some people who, from anxiety, are overreacting, need reassurance that their fears are based on myths and that positive action can solve many problems.

In other words we must:

1. Accept our own sexuality as being a positive part of ourselves.
2. Believe that this can also be the case for the retarded.
3. Give them as much knowledge as they can integrate.
4. Give them the opportunity to marry with much supportive help.
5. If they are of age and wish to extend a social relationship into a sexual relationship, see that they have the same opportunity to do so as anyone else has.
6. Concentrate on training them to be socially acceptable; help them develop social skills, so they can enjoy the company of both sexes.
7. Help them have fun, travel, enjoy all the adult activities that anyone else can enjoy within their limitations.

We could mention many more possibilities; it should be unnecessary to do so. Sexual oppression of the retarded will have to end if the over-all goals of normalization, de-institutionalization, and "mainstreaming" are to be realized in the not-too-distant future. The writer feels that the progress may be erratic, but that now it has begun we can't turn back. The sexual revolution—whatever we believe that means—just won't allow it.

REFERENCES AND RECOMMENDED READINGS

ANDRON, L., and M. L. STURM. Is "I Do" in the Repertoire of the Retarded? *Mental Retardation*, 11 (1) (1973) pp. 31–34.

GARBER, HOWARD. "The Milwaukee Project: An Experiment in the Prevention of Cultural-Familial Mental Retardation—Intervention at Birth." In *Sexual Rights and Responsibilities of the Mentally Retarded*, Medora Bass and Malvin Gelof, eds. Santa Barbara, Calif.: Channel Lithograph, 1973.

KEMPTON, WINIFRED. *Sex Education for Persons With Disabilities That Hinder Learning: A Teachers Guide*. North Scituate, Mass.: Duxbury Press, 1975, Chapter V.

MEYEROWITZ, JOSEPH. "Sex and the Mentally Retarded," *Medical Aspects of Sexuality*, Nov. 1971.

NIRJE, B. "The Normalization Principle and Its Human Management Implications." In *Changing Patterns in Residential Services for the Mentally Retarded*, R. B. Kugel and Wolfensberger, eds. Washington, D.C.: President's Committee on Mental Retardation, 1969.

REED, ELIZABETH W. "Mental Retardation and Fertility," *Social Biology*, Vol. 18, Supplement, pg. 542.

RELF, *et al.* vs. WEINBERGER, *et al.*, Civil Action Number 73-1557 and National Welfare Rights Organization vs. Weinberger *et al.*, Civil Action Number 74-243, USDC, DC.

ROSEN, MARVIN. "Psychosexual Adjustment of the Mentally Retarded." In Garber, Howard, *op. cit.*

ADDITIONAL RECOMMENDED READINGS

ALCORN, A. "Parental Views on Sexual Development and Education of the Trainable Mentally Retarded," *Journal of Special Education*, Vol. 8, No. 2, Summer, 1974.

BASS, M. S., S. GORDON, and W. KEMPTON. *Love, Sex, and Birth Control for the Mentally Retarded: A Guide for Parents*. Planned Parenthood Association, Philadelphia, Pa., and Family Planning and Population Information Center, Syracuse, N.Y., 1971.

BASS, M. S. and J. LANG. *Sex Education for the Handicapped and an Annotated Bibliography of Selected Resources*. Eugene, Oregon: E. C. Brown Center for Family Studies, 1971.

DE LA CRUZ, F. F. and G. D. LAVECK. eds. *Human Sexuality and the Mentally Retarded*. New York: Brunner/Mazel, 1973.

EDGERTON, R. B. *The Cloak of Competence*. Berkeley: University of California Press, 1967.

FISHER, G. M. "Sexual Identification in Mentally Retarded Male Children and Adults," *American Journal of Mental Deficiency*, 65 (1960), pp. 42–45.

FLOOR, L., M. ROSEN, D. BAXTER, J. HOROWITZ, and C. WEBER. "Socio-Sexual Problems in Mentally Handicapped Females," *Training School Bulletin*, 68 (1971), pp. 106–112.

KEMPTON, W. "Sex Education—A Cooperative Effort of Parent and Teacher," *Exceptional Children*, May, 1975.

———. *Guidelines for Planning a Training Course on Human Sexuality and the Retarded*. Planned Parenthood of Southeastern Pennsylvania, Philadelphia, 1973.

MATTINSON, J. "Marriage and Mental Handicap." In *Human Sexuality and the Mentally Retarded*, F. F. de la Cruz and G. D. LaVeck, eds. New York: Brunner/Mazel, 1973.

MEYEROWITZ, J. H. "Sex and the Mentally Retarded," *Medical Aspects of Human Sexuality*, 5, 11 (1971), pp. 94–118.

MORGENSTERN, M. "The Psychosexual Development of the Retarded." In *Human Sexuality and the Mentally Retarded*, F. F. de la Cruz & G. D. LaVeck, eds. New York: Brunner/Mazel, 1973.

ROSEN, M. "Conditioning Appropriate Heterosexual Behavior in Mentally and Socially Handicapped Populations." *Training School Bulletin*, 66 (1970), pp. 172–177.

CHAPTER 18

THE
PHYSICALLY
HANDICAPPED

Mary D. Romano

When she first saw herself, she tried to scream, but no sound came. She stood watching the horrible face in the mirror trying to scream, the mouth cavernous despite the fact that the lips could barely open. "Help," she cried soundlessly, "help." No one came. The bathroom light seemed to get brighter. The crimson trench where the nose had been gave her face a bloody jack-o'-lantern look. It was worse than she had thought. (Kellogg, 1968)

In ours, as in all societies, there exist sets of prescriptions and proscriptions on expressions of individual sexuality; these regulations are often tacit, but in some states they are also codified into legislation. Thus, for example, society does not expect the pubescent girl to fulfill her biological readiness by becoming pregnant; public masturbation and fornication are forbidden. The accepted model of a sexual object is a young, physically attractive, graceful man or woman who expresses his or her manness or womanness toward someone equally attractive who is of the opposite sex. In our society, sex is often seen as a luxury rather than as an integral part of life, with no heed to the thought that "man cannot live by bread alone."

For the physically disabled, particularly for those with visible stigmata causing or resulting from disability (Goffman, 1963, pp. 4–5) more perhaps than for any other group within our society, there are singularly clearcut prescriptions and proscriptions regarding sexuality. To be disabled is to be asexual, and, in fact, "cripple," the name in common parlance for a handicapped person, is a neuter word totally without gender. For the handicapped, the prescription is clear: at most, one is half a man or woman, and the half that remains is nonsexual. The proscriptions are equally explicit: the handicapped individual "should not" be interested in sexual matters, "should not" present himself as a sexual person, "should not" dare to satisfy his physical and/or emotional needs for intimacy (Goffman, 1963: p. 57). Even noninteractive sexual proclivities, such as fantasy and masturbation, may be forbidden to the disabled individual; particularly with masturbation, the folklore is such that masturbation has been seen historically as activity which can cause disabilities: insanity, blindness, skin eruptions, weakness, hairy palms, warts, and so forth.

Societal attitudes about the sexuality of the handicapped, or lack thereof, have of course a profound effect upon disabled individuals themselves as well as their families. Even in situations where the handicapped person has experienced extreme social isolation, with attendant lack of opportunities to develop a repertoire of social skills, the societal norms and expectations regarding sexuality and disability have often been internalized so that the handicapped person himself feels unattractive, undesirable, and sexually neutered (Goffman, 1963: 7). He may deprive himself of sexualized thoughts or actions in the belief that these are inappropriate for him as a disabled person; he may deny his own sexuality and often cannot imagine himself being a sexual object to anyone else. In other words, the handicapped individual's belief that he is ugly, contemptible, physically incompetent, and socially inappropriate is as great an internal barrier to satisfying sexuality (no matter what the mode) as are the real external barriers to the achievement of these satisfactions, such as social isolation, lack of recreational opportunities, and architectural and attitudinal barriers.

> Example 1: Mr. G., a 55-year-old single accountant, became disabled in childhood by polio. He sought help for his feelings of self-loathing and despair which he saw as related to his inability to express himself sexually. Although physically and financially independent, he lived with his parents who intruded in all aspects of his life to the extent that he had little privacy even to masturbate. He repeatedly expressed the conviction that he had nothing to offer in relationships and that no woman would want him because of his disability.

In speaking of sexuality, we are not referring solely to explicit physical acts between two adults of opposite sexes but, rather, to a broad range of behaviors from smiling to orgasm and to a set of attitudes within the individual that serve to express manness or womanness. Thus, sexuality involves series of transactions between people, transactions which involve social skills in the presentation of oneself. It is difficult, if not impossible, to separate fully these behaviors and attitudes, for they are well integrated so that social/sexual effectiveness behaviorally enhances one's feelings of self-worth and personal competence, and vice versa. Too often, however, the handicapped individual sees himself as disabled first, and as a man or woman second. In so doing, he is deprived of the opportunity for using his sexuality not only as a means of establishing and reinforcing relationships in a psychological and/or physical oneness but also depriving himself of the other transactional uses of sexuality so frequently employed by the non-disabled population: sex as a tool for communication, recreation, procreation; sex as punishment or reward; sex as power (Hohman, 1972; Romano, 1973).

> *Example 2:* Mr. T., a married man with two young children, was 33-years-old when he became totally quadriplegic as the result of an industrial accident. Although dependent upon his wife for all of his care, he was capable of functioning sexually despite his immobility. His wife was eager for physical intimacy with him, but he refused even to kiss her because he could no longer be the "dominant partner" sexually as he had been before his injury. Although his wife would willingly have initiated and assisted him with sexual contacts, he saw this as emasculating to him.

> *Example 3:* Before his spinal injury, Mr. F. and his wife had enjoyed an active, varied sexual relationship; they had frequently used sexual intercourse as a way of making up after fights, and they both readily admitted that they used to fight a lot, mostly for the fun of making up afterward. While hospitalized for rehabilitation following his injury, Mr. F. received no sexual counseling, nor did his wife. Once he was discharged and sent home, he and his wife continued to fight frequently, but—as they assumed that sex was no longer possible for them—they never made up after these fights; their conflict escalated to the point where Mr. F. had to be rehospitalized to prevent him and his wife from killing one another.

This situation often produces a curious combination of vulnerability and invulnerability, in which the handicapped individual does not have the skills to engage selectively in satisfying adult-adult relationships, nor the information which would enable him to choose whether or not to do so, nor societal permission to interact in these ways—all this can make the disabled particularly open to the depredations of others who, for their own needs, *use* the disabled as sexual objects. There are some, for example, who take amputees as their sexual objects in a somewhat fetishistic manner. It is the absence of a limb or limbs, rather than the person herself, which makes for the basis of the sexual relationship (Cummings, 1973). Similarly, there are "brace freaks" who become aroused by the presence of braces against their bodies, and able-bodied men and women who derive titillation only from engaging in or hearing about sexual contacts with the wheelchair-bound (Perkins, 1974).

The presence of disability not only has effects upon the sexuality of the disabled individual but on the family as well; disability can mean many changes in family functioning, including such important things as housing and employment, along with financial problems, possible pro-longed separation while the handicapped person is in hospital, and changes in roles within the family structure commensurate with the disabled person's limitations. Certainly, when a married adult becomes disabled, the disability can be seen as an unwanted interruption in the tacit contract upon which the marriage is based (e.g., husband works and is breadwinner; wife keeps house and raises the children) and in the homeostasis of patterned behaviors for conjoint living which develop in marital relationships. Depending, of course, upon the severity of the disability, the able-bodied spouse may need to assume a variety of care-taking behaviors with the handicapped partner. Also, for many spouses, it can be difficult to retain sexual feelings toward the handicapped partner due to role confusion, e.g., nurse as well as lover, patient as well as sexual object. In such circumstances, it is not uncommon for a husband-wife relationship to be modified into a parent-child or nurse-patient relation-ship. Coupled with these behavioral and attitudinal changes within the marriage are changes in the ways with which the spouses handle their feelings; the able-bodied spouse may feel great anger at the disabled partner for becoming sick or disabled, and these angry feelings can be directly—occasionally sadistically—expressed or may, due to guilt, be suppressed or redirected into infantilizing, overprotective insistence upon the handicapped partner's dependency. The disabled partner may, in turn, fear expressing his or her feelings, particularly if functionally de-pendent, because his or her survival directly depends upon remaining in the good graces of the able-bodied partner. Intense, but covert, marital conflict can result, often focusing on the sexual relationship between husband and wife. Learning to deal appropriately with the range of human feelings, along with the capacity to forgive, becomes, for these couples especially, essential for the maintenance of the marriage rela-tionship.

Example 4: Mrs. Y., brain-injured early in her marriage as the result of an accident, recovered sufficiently to perform her own self-care, converse in a socially acceptable manner, and travel extensively with her husband. Nonetheless, Mr. Y. insisted upon treating his wife as if she were a young and helpless child. He did tasks for her that she was capable of doing for herself, frequently reproved her in public when she expressed her thoughts or opinions, and scoffed at her desires for sexual intimacy. At Mr. Y.'s insistence, the couple slept in separate beds and had sexual relations, at most, only once or twice a year. When Mrs. Y. sought marital counseling, Mr. Y. himself refused to cooperate, and consistently sabotaged his wife's treatment.

When the disabled family member is a child, families face somewhat different problems. To the extent that a child represents the parents' desires for immortality and a vehicle for the parents' hopes and dreams, a disabled child can represent a narcissistic blow to parental egos. The parent hurts for himself as well as for the child, and his feelings, again, can be expressed directly toward the child in angry rejection, toward the other parent (e.g., "It's your bad genes that caused this!"), or the feelings may be transmogrified through guilt into overprotectiveness and dependency-inducement. Realistically, too many parents of disabled children have little idea of what they can hope for or expect from these children, and, hurt as they are, they do not want to build false expectations in themselves or in the disabled child. Thus, when the child begins to show interest in exploring his body, the parent may act to discourage this, perhaps fearing that the child will damage himself or that the child will learn pleasures that the parents fear can never be heterosexually consummated. Parents of handicapped children can also be reluctant to verbalize the possibility of future sociosexual events to the disabled child; a mother may tell her able-bodied daughter, "When you grow up, you will get married and be a mommy, and I will be a grandma," but this kind of message is frequently not given to disabled children. This can result in disabled children remaining children sociosexually, past the point when this is appropriate. In other words, for a variety of reasons, families may not do all that is possible to help their handicapped children reach for and master the social and sexual tasks that are developmentally appropriate. Within the boundaries of the child's physical limitations, the parents must help the child to explore and master his environment; for the handicapped child whose mobility is limited, this may mean bringing the environment to the child or, conversely, physically assisting the child in exploration. As the handicapped child grows older, parental assistance must extend to help prepare the child to master social situations, including potentially awkward interactions in which the child must deal with strangers who stare at him and ask questions about the causation of the disability, other children's cruelties, and similar common occurrences. Mastery of these kinds of social situations will enable the disabled child to build a repertoire of skills that are not only age-appropriate but also allow the child some control over his interactions with others (Goffman, 1963: p. 12ff.). This ability to project a "self" in interactions and to put strangers at ease by clarifying expectations of them is a key in the later establishment of sexualized relationships.

> *Example 5:* Dolores N., a 38-year-old woman with congenital hand anomalies, related to her peers, relatives and to professionals as if she were a little girl of about five years of age. Totally overprotected by her mother, with whom she lived and who called her "Baby," Dolores had never learned to relate to others as an adult. She spoke in simple sentences, could not converse about anything except how she felt at a given moment, and perceived adult messages to her as "scoldings," to which she responded by crying.

> *Example 6:* Johnny R., an engaging 9-year-old boy, was brought to the Amputee Clinic by his parents for evaluation. Johnny had been born with his right hand absent. A good student, active in Cub Scouts, and an avid baseball and basketball player, Johnny extended his left hand when introduced to the doctor in order to shake hands as he had been taught. Johnny politely allowed the clinic staff to examine him, but expressed an eagerness to "hurry up and get home" so that he could play outside with his friends before suppertime. When asked what he would like to be when he grew up, he answered, "an astronaut" and added, "and a daddy."

One of the principal anxiety-producing areas for the parents of handicapped children is that of sex education. The parents of a blind child, for example, may wonder how to teach their child about basic gender differences, which the child cannot see, in a manner that is neither frightening nor overstimulating to the child. Parents may have little actual information about the physiologic effects of their child's disability on his sexual function; parents in this difficult situation will wonder whether it is best to tell the child about the sexual function of the non-disabled, to say nothing, or to discuss moral rather than factual issues, saying such things as, "God works in strange ways" or "Where there's a will, there's a way" (Gordon, 1974).

It is not only the parents of handicapped children who lack a factual appreciation of the effects of a specific disability on sexual functioning but disabled adults, and even sometimes the professionals working with them, often lack this information. Without this information to serve as a base of reality, it can be difficult, if not impossible, for the handicapped individual to figure out ways actually to be intimate. A given person may have loss of sensation in the genital or other areas; be unable to move his legs, arms, pelvis; suffer from bowel or bladder incontinence; have involuntary spastic movements of the extremities. He may have chronic pain and an inability to move certain joints such as the hips. He may be unable to have an erection, or the erection may last only a short time: again, he may be unable to ejaculate. Each one of these physiological phenomena implies that the handicapped person and his sexual partner may have to consider changing the timing of their sexual intimacy, the positions they can use, the type of sexual activities in which they can engage successfully, their means of contraception, and the nature of their communication around sexual activities. In order for the handicapped person to decide whether or not to engage in sexual activities (and, if so, how), he or she must know what is possible physiologically and logistically. The individual can then integrate facts with feelings about specific activities to arrive at an informed choice.

> *Example 7:* Mrs. A., a severely involved rheumatoid arthritic, complained that her husband rarely approached her sexually and seemed afraid even to hug her. When Mr. and Mrs. A. discussed their sexual relationship with the social worker, it became clear that each time Mr. A. tried to get close to his wife, she would loudly express fear that he would hurt her, and this quickly dampened Mr. A.'s ardor. The social worker helped the A.'s to see this pattern and to modify it by changing verbal communication from punishing to rewarding and by altering the timing of their sexual activity to an hour when Mrs. A. would have less pain and stiffness in her joints.

Within the professional literature, there is a substantial and growing body of information about the effects of specific disabilities on sexual function and about specific techniques for dealing with these changes. This includes material on arthritis, brain injury, endocrine disorders including diabetes, facial disfigurement, heart disease, cerebral palsy, amputation, neurological disorders including epilepsy and multiple sclerosis, and spinal cord injury (V.A. Hospital, 1974; Ehrlich, 1973; Lachniet and Onder, 1973; Lachniet, Onder and Becker; Romano, 1974; Weinstein, 1974; Kupperman and Vaughn, 1974; Rubin and Babbott, 1958; Brenton, 1968; Shearer, 1972; Bors and Comarr, 1960; Bregman and Hadley; Eisenberg and Rustad, 1974; Money, 1970; Romano and Lassiter, 1972). The great majority of this work has been published within the past fifteen years, but as striking as its recent orign is its lack of dissemination to professionals and to the consumers of professionals' services, the handicapped themselves.

Perhaps as a result of increased societal openness in talking about sex, and surely as a result of consumer pressure on professionals, there has been some increase in sexual re-education and counseling for the handicapped; certainly professionals are coming to recognize the importance of sexuality as part of life and to examine their own attitudes and feelings toward the handicapped as sexual beings (Johnson and Matek, 1974). Social workers are in a unique position here, for their training broadly prepares them to conceptualize and deal not only with intrapsychic and interpersonal problems but also to recognize the implications of these problems on the total social functioning of the population. The social worker has skills as a facilitator or enabler, as an educator, and as an advocate, and it is the social worker, as much as any professional, who can differentially employ these skills in direct work with handicapped consumers and their families, with administrators of service programs and institutions, and with other professionals.

There are, of course, a variety of modalities available for responding to the concerns and needs of the handicapped regarding their sexuality. One approach in use is the Sexual Attitude Reassessment (SAR); this method employs intensive, time-limited sex education and counseling for handicapped adults and health-care professionals, in which a multimedia presentation of explicit sexual activities is coupled with periods of small-group discussions. The goals are to desensitize and then resensitize the participants toward an acceptance of the sexual potential of the disabled and to encourage an accepting, experimental attitude toward sexual activity. The SAR model also serves to open up discussion between professionals and consumers on sexual issues and, in so doing, alters the relationship between professional and consumer to a more collegial relationship (Cole, Chilgren, and Rosenberg, 1973).

Of the more traditional approaches, direct one-to-one counseling seems to be the most prevalent; here the counselor, often a physician, talks directly with a disabled individual about his or her questions and problems. The proponents of this method indicate that it has the advantage of offering highly personalized attention to the individual disabled person's needs; on the other hand, however, this method is (a) time-consuming, (b) may not reach a large population, and (c) depends for its efficacy on the consumer's ability to articulate fully his concerns and the professional's ability to perceive both the latent and manifest content of these concerns, their implications for total functioning, and to respond accurately and comfortably without moralizing or temporizing (Hohmann, 1972). Related to this method are the ones in which a disabled person and his or her sexual partner are seen conjointly by a counselor or, using the Masters and Johnson method (1970), by a pair of counselors (Tomko, 1974: pp. 15–17). While this approach can be valuable in that it deals with the sexual concerns of both the handicapped individual and the partner, it, too, is (a) time-consuming, (b) reaches a relatively small population, and (c) *may not respond to the disabled individual without a sexual partner whose sexual concerns relate to the problems of making sociosexual contacts as well as knowing what to do in sexual situations.*

Yet another modality for dealing with these problems is the use of groups as the means and context for sex education and counseling. Typically, these groups involve people with similar disabilities who come together to share their concerns in a problem-solving milieu (Eisenberg, 1973; Romano, 1973a). The group approach can have advantages, including (a) economy of time, (b) familiarity (most people have had some "bull-session" experience in talking about sexual matters), (c) safety in that no participant is forced to reveal himself until he is ready to do so, (d) an opportunity for modeling adaptive behavior, and (e) the establishment of norms and expectations around discussion of sexual concerns and problem-solving to resolve them. The disadvantages in the use of the group method can be (a) that in a particular locale there are not enough handicapped people with a common bond to form a group, (b) that a leader trained in group dynamics and leadership skills is not available, or (c) that the group may become didactic rather than cooperative if the leader becomes a teacher and the consumers become students.

Responding to the sexual problems of the handicapped can, and often must, take place indirectly as well as directly. By this we mean that there must be administrative change in the institutions and agencies serving the handicapped. If an administration does not recognize sexuality as a part of life, if it prohibits all forms of sexual expression, including masturbation and fantasy, if it does not recognize and provide for an individual's need for privacy—then direct counseling for the consumer offers little but an empty promise. Administrative legitimation for dealing with the sexual problems of the handicapped should underlie any counseling program regardless of the modality employed. Sometimes, the obstacle to this sanction is administrative fear that such programs will not be acceptable to the community or to contributors of unencumbered funds upon which a good deal of agency or institutional program may rest. There may also be fear that if a mandate for open attention to sexual problems is given, then rampant licentiousness will result. With apprehensions such as these, the social worker or other professional can use his entire stock of skills to bring administration to the point of view that rehabilitation cannot be complete without giving the disabled an opportunity to choose the ways in which they will deal with their sexuality.

In summary, we have reviewed the range of problematic implications that physical handicaps have on sexuality and sexual function. These problems include intrapsychic feelings of unworthiness, internal and external barriers to the development of relationship skills, physiological changes in sexual function with related logistical problems, and professionals' feelings about accepting the handicapped as sexual people coupled with professionals' knowledge gaps about what is possible. These problems are an integral part of the day-to-day life of the handicapped and their families, and they know these problems well. If we, too, can know them and can open ourselves to sharing them, then together we can use our communication skills and our humanness to resolve them.

REFERENCES AND RECOMMENDED READINGS

BORS, E., and A. COMARR. "Neurological Disturbances of Sexual Function with Special Reference to 529 Patients with Spinal Cord Injury," *Urological Survey*, vol. 10 (December, 1960).

BREGMAN, S., and R. HADLEY. "Behaviors Relating to Feminine Attractiveness and Sexual Adjustment Among Women with Spinal Cord Injury" (unpublished thesis abstract).

BENTON, M. *Sex and Your Heart*. New York: Coward-McCann, 1968.

COLE, T., R. CHILGREN and P. ROSENBERG. "A New Programme of Sex Education and Counselling for Spinal-Cord-Injured Adults and Health Care Professionals," *Paraplegia*, vol. 11 (August 1973).

CUMMINGS, V. "Sexual Problems of the Amputee," presented at the American Congress of Rehabilitation Medicine, 50th Annual Session, Washington, D.C., October 24, 1973.

EHRLICH, G. "Sexual Problems of the Arthritic Patient." In *Total Management of the Arthritic Patient*, G. Ehrlich, ed. Philadelphia: Lippincott, 1973, pp. 193–208.

EISENBERG, M. "Psycho-Social Rehabilitation on a Spinal-Cord-Injury Service" (film), Cleveland: Veterans Administration Hospital, 1973.

EISENBERG, M., and L. RUSTAD. *Sex and the Spinal-Cord-Injured*. Washington: United States Government Printing Office, 1974.

GOFFMAN, E. *Stigma*. Englewood Cliffs: Prentice-Hall, 1963.

GORDON, S. *Sexual Rights for the People . . . Who Happen to Be Handicapped*. Syracuse: Center on Human Policy, 1974.

HOHMANN, G. "Sex and the Spinal-Cord-Injured Male," *Rehabilitation Psychology*, vol. 19, no. 2 (Summer, 1972).

JOHNSON, J., and O. MATEK. "Critical Issues in Teaching Human Sexuality to Graduate Social Work Students," *Journal of Education for Social Work*, vol. 10, no. 3 (Fall, 1974).

KELLOGG, M. *Tell Me That You Love Me, Junie Moon*. New York: Popular Library, 1968, pp. 25–6.

KUPPERMAN, H., and C. VAUGHAN. "Impotence in Nondiabetic Endocrine Disease," *Medical Aspects of Human Sexuality*, vol. 8, no. 11 (November, 1974).

LACHNIET, D., and ONDER, J. "Sex and Arthritis and Women," Department of Social Work, University of Michigan Medical Center, 1973.

LACHNIET, D., J. ONDER, and M. BECKER. "Sexual Counseling, Arthritis and Women," Department of Social Work, University of Michigan Medical Center (unpublished).

MASTERS, W., and V. JOHNSON. *Human Sexual Inadequacy.* Boston: Little, Brown, and Company, 1970.

MONEY, J. "Phantom Orgasm in Paraplegics," *Medical Aspects of Human Sexuality,* vol. 4, no. 1 (January, 1970).

ROMANO, M., and R. LASSITER. "Sexual Counseling with the Spinal-Cord-Injured," *Archives of Physical Medicine and Rehabilitation,* vol. 53, no. 12, (December, 1972).

ROMANO, M. "Sexual Counseling in Groups," *Journal of Sex Research,* Vol. 9, no. 1 (February, 1973a).

ROMANO, M. "Sexuality and the Disabled Female," *Accent on Living,* vol. 18, no. 2 (Winter, 1973b).

ROMANO, M. "Family Response to Traumatic Head Injury," *Scandinavian Journal of Rehabilitation Medicine,* vol. 6, no. 1, (Spring, 1974).

RUBIN, A., and D. BABBOTT. "Impotence and Diabetes Mellitus," *Journal of the American Medical Association,* vol. 168: 498 (1958).

Sex and the Handicapped: A Selected Bibliography (1927–1973), Cleveland: Veterans Administration Hospital, 1974.

SHEARER, A. *A Right to Love?* London: The Spastics Society, 1972.

TOMKO, M. "Facility Role Models." In *Sex: Rehabilitation's Stepchild.* Chicago: National Paraplegia Foundation, 1974, pp. 15–17.

WEINSTEIN, E. "Sexual Disturbance After Brain Injury," *Medical Aspects of Human Sexuality,* vol. 8, no. 10 (October, 1974).

CHAPTER 19

THE
DEAF

Mary Sweeney Smith

When I started to write this chapter I intended to cover problems encountered by the blind as well as by the deaf, but I find there is no meeting ground between these two groups, even in print. There is no more similarity between these two groups than there would be between the problems of a shy girl and a "life-of-the-party" girl. All one can say is that both groups have problems. Although, as I say, there are no real similarities between deaf people and blind people, they are frequently lumped together. I have been working with deaf people for twenty years, and I cannot number the times I've been asked, "Oh, do you read Braille?" But, of course, that's from people who are not expected to know the difference. Many of them have never known a blind person, and few of them would recognize a deaf person if they saw one. It is the professionals in the field of teaching and working with deaf people and blind people whose naiveté amazes me. All over the United States—including Hawaii, where I live and work—the deaf children and the blind children are together in schools usually called, "The School for the Deaf and the Blind." As an illustration of the difference between the two groups, consider the following incident. Several years ago, I went on a field trip with a class of deaf students and a class of blind students. We all went to the zoo. We stopped at the lion cage and watched for a while. Finally the lion became bored with watching us and yawned a tremendous yawn. The deaf children were very excited and said, "Wow, the lion roared." The blind children looked confused and one little boy said, "I didn't hear him."

COMMUNICATION

Deaf people have a difficult time communicating with anyone, but it is utterly impossible for them to communicate with a blind person, since what communication the deaf do have is based on an ability to see.

An anonymous person once wrote "Blindness creates a barrier between people and things, while deafness creates a barrier between people and people, and people are more important than things." And what is sexuality other than relations between people and people? One can see where the deaf stand in that area, right from the beginning.

Deaf people communicate with their hands. The American Sign Language is a very beautiful language to use and there are ways of saying important things using American Sign Language. However, many of the subtleties and nuances are left out of the language. Abstractions are left out. Where a hearing boy knows how to say things like "Your body really sends me, let's go somewhere and get acquainted," a deaf boy would probably say "I want to fuck you." A deaf girl would probably understand that because her own language is just as limited, but a hearing girl might react by slapping his face or calling the cops.

Hence the bugaboo of communication haunts the deaf in every area of their lives and also interferes with their sexuality. When all of your communication depends on freedom to move your hands, every area of your life is affected. If you are eating a meal and your dinner partner says something you really want to respond to, and you, at the same time, are halfway to your mouth with a spoonful of soup, the spoon goes back to the bowl and you respond to the question. Your partner must then put down his spoon and respond to you. In this process, eating a meal gets pretty tedious and the food gets cold. Then the waitress gives you a dirty look because you are taking too much time. Now switch this scene to bedtime. The lights are out and you and your partner are snuggled up together. Half the fun of foreplay is the murmured words of endearment, and you just get an urge to tell your partner how beautiful she is or how much you love her, or how the shape of her ear turns you on, or how much you are enjoying the particular caress she is giving you—so on goes the light, and your hands must stop the enjoyable thing you were doing and, instead, form patterns in the air to convey your thoughts. Hence, deaf people don't convey all those lovely thoughts; they keep the thoughts to themselves, and their isolation grows stronger. Is it to be wondered at, therefore, that there are not many successful marriages among deaf people and that the percentage of divorce is much higher than among the hearing population?

In years gone by, all children were taught that sex is dirty. The world has moved a few steps from that position and today most children are not taught that sex is dirty. Deaf people, however, are still taught in the old way. Not because their parents and teachers want to teach that way, but simply because there is no in-between for *them*! They have to say "No." Parents of deaf children are usually "hearing" people. They cannot communicate with their children in any depth, so they instill fear of sex, rather than an understanding of it. Most teachers of the deaf are also "hearing." One often finds a mash note that a cute little 14-year-old girl is cherishing from an equally cute 15-year-old boy, which says things like: "I want to see naked you. I like fuck you. Fuck is good. You like french kiss." Usually such notes are accompanied by very explicit drawings or, if the boy has no talent, he cuts pictures out of hard-core pornographic magazines and sends them with his mash note. The teacher or administrator or counselor finding such notes is shocked! No matter how reasonable such an authority tries to be, the shock and disgust come through as another lesson in "sex is bad" or even "loving is bad." I'm still not sure I've found an answer to that. As a counselor to students I have found myself saying, "Fucking is not bad, but you just can't do it at school," and maybe that's a cop-out, too. Since their parents are telling them it's bad at home, where can they go? In the end, all the things you and I and the rest of the "hearing" people consider to be so important are reduced from tenderness and loving and that wonderful excited feeling you get from holding hands and hugging the right person to "fucking." Every deaf child knows that the middle-finger sign which gets everyone into such trouble for using it is a bad sign. But that is also sign language for intercourse (or "fuck.") So, all those marvelous feelings, then, mean "fuck," and fuck is bad—so those feelings are bad, also.

DEFINITIONS

It is important when talking about deaf people that one start off with a definition. When I first became acquainted with "the deaf" I was a college graduate, having a degree in psychology and elementary education. I wanted to adopt a child and the social service agency told me of a little deaf boy who needed an adoptive home. I had never heard of a child being deaf! I thought deafness was an ailment of old age and was only something that happened to old people. I adopted the child while still holding that attitude. Put into words, it would have gone something like this: "What's so wrong with that? There's nothing wrong with him, except he can't hear!" And then I gradually learned that deafness is not just a little defect. It may well be the worst handicap an individual can be born with. Almost all our learning comes through our ears. By the time a "hearing" child starts to school, he has all the tools he needs to learn to read. He sits and sounds out his letters, and once they make sense to him by sound, he recognizes that sound. Take a word like *under*. Phonetically the child can pronounce that. He knows *un-der* and then he says it aloud. Immediately the image of himself under an umbrella, under a table, under a myriad of objects comes to his mind. When a deaf child learns to pronounce the word *under* from the written page, he has just that— pronunciation! The teacher shows him the picture of a child under a table. He doesn't know if this is a way to say "boy," "girl," "table," "floor," or maybe "vase" of flowers which are on the table. So it takes many pictures and many times of crawling under all the things the teacher rigs up for him to crawl under, before the meaning becomes clear. *Under* is an easy word to teach and to learn because it can be acted out and pictures can be shown; as the concepts and words become more complex, however, it takes longer and longer for the child to grasp the meanings. How about words like "truth," "beauty," "honesty," "understanding," "compassion," "love," "adoration," "emotion," and so on? In sad truth, most of them are never fully understood. And "acting-out" sexual terminology becomes problematic.

I have sat in courtrooms where deaf people were asked: "Guilty or not guilty?" When the interpreter repeated this to them, they would stare blankly. Finally the interpreter would say: "Were you bad?" How many of us on being asked that question would know what to say? "Were you bad?" When? Where? In whose eyes? Most deaf children grow up thinking they are bad, anyway; just for not being able to hear. Somehow not hearing is an offense against the speaker. Just remember how you feel when you have to repeat a statement. Somewhere in your viscera, there is a conviction that the listener chose not to hear you. And that feeling does not go away when you know the person is deaf. Our highly verbal society is constantly reinforcing the deaf person's feeling of being bad. This, in turn, reinforces his guilt about sex. All teen-agers struggle with feelings of guilt over their sexual thoughts and behavior; but, in the case of an adolescent with such little ability to discuss fantasies, masturbation, and so on, guilt and fear can be expected in the extreme.

O.K., back to definitions. There are deaf people who are born without hearing—usually, these days, because of maternal rubella or the baby's prematurity. There are still a few children who lose their hearing during the first two or three years of life, and these, even though they were able to hear for a short time, eventually function similarly to those who were born deaf. There are a few children who lose their hearing after they have developed the ability to speak well and to understand language, and their problems are very different from those who were born deaf. There are all degrees of deafness to differentiate, as well. Thus, some people have no hearing, some have a little, and some are merely "hard of hearing." Again, hearing aids can help some deaf people, but can do very little or nothing for others. There are deaf adults who grew up as "hearing" individuals. Then they became ill as adults and either gradually or abruptly lost their hearing.

Therefore, it becomes extremely difficult to lump all deaf people together and say that they have certain kinds of problems because they are deaf. Deafness is different from any other handicap. If an individual loses an arm or a leg, or if he is born with an arm or leg missing, naturally his attitude toward the loss is different and his self-image is also different; but his ability to learn to read and think is unaffected by his loss, *i.e.*, only his mobility is impaired. But in the case of a deaf person the exact opposite is true. For him, every aspect of his life, except his mobility, is affected by his deafness.

A DEMOGRAPHY OF THE DEAF

Within the past twenty years, there has been a great shift in the deaf population. Previously, most deaf adults were people who had lost their hearing due to illness well after speech had become developed. Today, due to medical advances in the treatment of diseases, schools for the deaf are mostly filled with children who were born deaf, and the adult deaf population of the future will be made up of those without language or lip-reading skills. Formerly, children without these skills lived in institutions, where they were isolated from the "hearing" population, and where neither family living skills nor sex information was acquired. Whereas recent trends in having such deaf students live in their own homes as much as possible has helped to alleviate their isolation and has allowed them to grow up in a family atmosphere that provides more sexual information, the fact remains that they still live very isolated lives. Most of the parents and siblings do not learn sign language; but each family does develop a gesture language which suffices for ordinary commands and instructions. In those families where one member of the family does learn to communicate with the deaf child, it is usually the mother. Therefore all instruction, including that about sex, comes from the mother, regardless of the sex of the child. The usual pattern in such families is that the hearing part of the family sits around having a discussion, and suddenly the mother remembers that the deaf child is not being included. She takes a moment or two out of the discussion to say, "We're talking about Aunt Helen and Uncle Joe." The deaf child now knows that the discussion is not about him, but he still is not included in the discussion. If the father is needed to have a discussion with his son or daughter about behavior or discipline, the mother must be there to interpret for both of them. Therefore, what the deaf child does see of family life is distorted and different from the life his "hearing" siblings see and hear. Thus, whether they have been raised in the protective environment of an institution or they have been raised at home and attended a day school, most deaf adults have not learned the necessary give-and-take of family life.

PSYCHOLOGICAL MAKE-UP

When observing deaf people, one sees them primarily as paranoid and selfish. They have a tendency to feel that "hearing" people are talking about them. In that connection, I have had several experiences of my own that have made me aware that they are not always wrong about that. For instance, one night I went to a bar with two friends and we each ordered a drink. After receiving the drinks, we started talking in sign language (all of us were "hearing"). At first it was just for practice, but after we had motioned to the bartender to refill the glasses and he had looked so perplexed about how he was going to collect from us, we kept it up as a good joke on him. In the meantime, some other people came in and sat down at the bar. Since we were at a table, they had to keep turning around to look at us. This they did, in a very hostile way. Finally we heard one of the women say, "Look at them. They always do that, even in church. They sit behind me and talk about me all the time." It is easy to see that paranoia goes both ways, but since there are much fewer deaf people and many, many more "hearing" people, it is easier to point at the deaf as the paranoid ones.

Many deaf people can read lips. If they once or twice catch a phrase that lets them know they are being talked about, they are then likely to believe that they are always being talked about. Even though many times it could be a favorable remark, one is prone to be suspicious of anyone talking behind his back. Although this paranoia and suspiciousness in deaf people may have its inception in fact, it frequently becomes a part of the deaf person's personality and, of course, does not lead to a good solid relationship with other people.

The stereotype of selfishness is also, I think, partly true. A deaf person will frequently ask "hearing" people to make telephone calls for him, and at the same time not give them enough information about the reason for the call, not give them the telephone number, and apparently expect not just the favor of making the call, but actually putting a burden on the "hearing" person. I must say, however, that I think this is based on the deaf person's lack of knowledge about using the telephone. To a deaf person, the telephone is a mysterious object that was made to torture the deaf because it puts them at such a disadvantage. The deaf person doesn't realize that the friend he has asked to make the call may view getting information over the phone as a nuisance and that using the phone book may be torture for someone who doesn't see too well. It is a selfish attitude, but it is based on ignorance, not malice.

I need to further explain why the deaf person sees the telephone as something invented to torture him, especially when it comes to sexual matters. When a deaf person wants to make a date, he cannot just pick up the phone and ask the girl for a date. Instead, he must either have a "hearing" person make the call for him or go by car or bus to see the girl whom he wants to date. The more people that are involved in the date, the more complicated the procedure becomes. If it is a double date and a last-minute change in arrangements is necessary, the deaf person has to go to see three people. The telephone may simplify life for all the rest of us, but it does nothing for the deaf person.

The other aspect of their selfishness or unconcern for the feelings of others comes when they write notes. Many deaf people have been fired from their job or have lost friends simply because they sometimes write notes that are inadvertently impolite. Because of their lack of understanding of word order, they may say, "You will give me a raise," rather than, "Please consider giving me a raise." Or "You will love me," when they want to say, "Please show me that you love me."

On the other hand, deaf people have a very good sense of humor, but it is very different from that of "hearing" people. Everything must be more specific for the deaf, including humor. They do not understand subtle jokes or jokes which are a play on words. They are prone to slapstick and playing practical jokes. My deaf son once served "Cat Chow" to my guests, and then watched very politely and with great amusement as everyone sat munching little fish-flavored stars. Most "hearing" people are not greatly amused at such antics and this builds another wall of isolation. Most "hearing" girls would not think it funny to have a chair pulled out from under them as they prepared to seat themselves in a restaurant. In this same context, most deaf girls would not sit down without making sure the chair was there if they were out with a deaf date.

MARRIAGE

Most deaf people marry other deaf people. A great deal of study and research is needed for the genetic problems this entails. Most of the deaf people who have been interviewed about whether they want "hearing" or deaf children tell the interviewers they want "hearing" children. On the other hand, many of the deaf couples I know have told me that they would enjoy having at least one deaf child who would understand them. Sometimes deaf people marry "hearing" people, but such marriages are usually fraught with difficulty. After the first great blush of excitement wears off in any marriage and the honeymoon is over a couple has to settle down to learning to live together. The problems are multiplied when one member of the unit is deaf and one is "hearing." One "hearing" woman I know told me about her romance and engagement to a deaf young man. They were so much in love that no obstacle seemed to be too great. The deaf young man had a very wise mother, however, who tried to tell the girl what hardships she would encounter, but of course the girl could not accept such reality. The mother insisted that the girl spend the summer with the deaf man's family in order to find out what it was like to live with a deaf person and his problems. The young man and the girl found that trying to live with someone so different as a "hearing" person and a deaf person are to each other was not so easy as they had believed it would be, and they broke off their engagement.

Most of the people working with deaf people are women. This is true whether we're talking about teachers, social workers, rehabilitation counselors, or interpreters. Therefore, there is more opportunity for deaf men to meet, date, and marry hearing women than there is for deaf women to do the same. There is a far larger percentage of deaf women who never marry than there are hearing women who never marry.

WHAT OF THE FUTURE?

Not until 1966 was the appalling truth about the lack of services to the deaf revealed. Since that time there have been many efforts to increase the availability of post-secondary education and training for deaf people. Other areas which lack proper services are still far too prevalent even though there are the beginnings of a movement to offer mental health services to the deaf, along with counseling services in areas like marriage, genetics, family living, and consumer protection. As these services are offered to the deaf, more data will become available on the ways in which the "hearing" population puts barriers in the way of deaf sexuality and also the ways in which deafness itself is at fault. Even today, the deaf live in the equivalent of a small town wherever they live. There is a lot of gossip and a lot of genuine concern for each other in their small-town society, but there is a great need for them to join the mainstream of society.

REFERENCES AND RECOMMENDED READINGS

MINDEL, EUGENE D., and VERNON MC CAY. *They Grow in Silence.* Silver Spring, Maryland: National Association of the Deaf, 1971.

RAINER, JOHN D., KENNETH Z. ALTSHULER, and FRANZ J. KALLMANN. *Family and Mental Health Problems in a Deaf Population.* New York: Columbia University, 1963.

RAINER, JOHN D. and KENNETH Z. ALTSHULER. *Psychiatry and the Deaf: A Report of the Workshop for Psychiatrists on Extending Mental Health Services to the Deaf,* sponsored by the New York State Psychiatric Institute and the New York University Center for Research and Training in Deafness Rehabilitation, April 7–8, 1967.

CHAPTER 20

THE TERMINALLY ILL

Lois Jaffe

Our relationship now is more that of strangers because of hospital separation. His sexual desires have diminished because our thoughts are dominated by the cancer and his impending death. The disease, however, is not
repulsive to me. I've had no urge to escape from his touch as other wives
have talked about. We still enjoyed sex until he was unable to perform.
This was a major frustration to him and made him feel less a man and
more the invalid. The frustrations in our lives caused by his illness I'm
sure would be eased if we were still sexually bound and still "one."
Knowing I could ease his tensions of the day at the office by loving him
sexually is such a contrast with knowing I can do nothing now to ease his
frustrations when he is dying. He now feels we are on opposite sides of the
fence. I'm sure it's because I cannot convince him by words or actions
here in the hospital. He feels his masculinity is gone and our "one-ness" is
gone. For thirty-three years I took our loving for granted and assumed it
would always be there. . . . It may sound like we were forever in bed, but
sex is so much more than physical. Even talking on the phone, sitting
across from each other reading, being in a crowd, even being hundreds of
miles apart, we felt the union.

These are the words of a wife of a long-term patient hospitalized with
brain cancer. She is a member of the group I conduct weekly at a local
oncology unit for cancer and leukemia patients and their families. These

encounters provide an opportunity for sharing feelings of anger, sadness, frustration and fear, and for learning from one another how better to cope with facing death. Her description captures the essence of the sexual problems facing the terminally ill and their loved ones.

I myself have been an acute leukemia patient for the last twenty-eight months of my forty-seven years of life. In my work as death educator and family therapist, as well as in my role as patient, I have become convinced that the area of sexual problems with regard to the terminally ill constitutes a "double whammy," and thus has been enveloped in silence. There is little discussion in the literature about the fact that sexual expression is generally denied or severely compromised in situations involving terminal illness and impending interpersonal loss (Barton, 1972; Davis, 1974).

Death arouses the basic underlying anxiety that every human being must face. The fear of the unknown is paralleled only by the fear of being cut off from life before fulfilling one's potential. Death anxiety is exacerbated by the invisibility of personal dying in our society. Eighty per cent of us die in institutions, and thus we are unrehearsed in ways of interacting with those facing death or with those who are left behind. Confronting death generates more anguish and fear than in any other area of human behavior. Care-givers are no different from anyone else; facing a dying person means facing one's own mortality—a realization which can make even the hardiest of souls begin to twitch. Sexuality is the only other area to engender a comparable degree of discomfort, confusion and resistance, particularly when it must be handled by clinicians. This combination of sexuality with terminality constitutes a double-barreled taboo.

Since sexuality and death represent the beginning and end points of life itself, anxiety is understandably heightened by their interface. For the dying patient and his loved ones, aspects of confronting death can be a classical "double-bind." In a double-bind situation, a person is faced with contradictory messages which are often concealed or transmitted on different levels. As a result of this invisibility, the individual cannot escape or effectively comment on the paradoxes which confront him (Erickson and Hyerstay, 1974). Preparing for impending death by either partner in the relationship involves accommodation to an ending, a "deadline." Sexuality, on the other hand, represents a moving forward, a perpetuation of vitality, the quintessence of the life force. Yet, despite this contrast, both experiences share a kind of "letting go." As Keleman (1974) has written: "Dying generates excitement, unformedness, unconnectedness, unknowingness. . . . Excitement is the force that connects sex and dying" (p. 27).

For the healthy spouse, the vitality of sexuality is often experienced as a direct contradiction to the finality of death. As the spouse struggles to stop thinking of the relationship as having a future, he is confronted with the dissonance between sex (a moving forward into the future) and death (an end in the present). Rather than face this clash, the healthy partner may choose not to interact sexually with the patient, and may possibly seek sexual activity with a new partner as an antidote to loss and death. Either way, there is a tendency to move away sexually and emotionally from the dying patient.

For the terminally ill patient, there is the reverse of the double-bind to confront. While the healthy partner may be avoiding sex with the patient, the patient may now desire increased sexual activity with the spouse to counter death anxiety. Sexuality, as Keleman (1974) points out, is almost a training for dying—an intensification of the dying process and a rehearsal for the dying event.

> The orgastic state that produces feelings of ecstasy is a surrendering to the involuntary and to the unknown. Orgasm requires giving ourselves over to what is occurring in us. . . . The orgastic state also produces feelings of dying, raises fears of dying, because the social awareness may be threatened by the involuntary (p. 119).

The terminally ill patient holds in his possession a double-edged sword. He can either become revitalized by the intensity that comes with confronting death, thus making him more sexually aware and responsive, or he can become so frightened by the prospect of death that any stirring up of that anxiety, as in an orgasmic "letting go," may move him into an "asexual" state. It is my belief that the direction a patient chooses is largely determined by (1) his previous experiences with sex and death, (2) the presence or absence of pain, (3) his treatment as "one of the living" rather than as a dying patient, and (4) his perception of hope for being able to live a full and meaningful life in whatever time he has left.

Given this conceptual framework for viewing the sexual problems of the terminally ill patient and his significant others, let us now examine the predisposing, precipitating and perpetuating factors which make this content area so necessary and vital for intervention. By using this primary prevention approach, recommendations can then be made for therapeutic strategies.

PREDISPOSING FACTORS

If one looks at the meaning of death developmentally, it is easy to understand why people are predisposed to inordinate anxiety when handling the interface between sex and death. Psychologist Maria Nagy, studying Hungarian children in the late 1940's, described three phases in the child's awareness of personal mortality as reflected in drawings and words. In Stage One, the preschool child usually does not recognize the irreversibility of death, and regards it as sleep or departure. In Stage Two, between the ages of about five and nine, he tends to personify death as a separate figure, such as an angel or a frightening skeleton, who usually makes his rounds at night. In this second stage, death seems to be understood as final. However, an important protective feature remains: personal death can be avoided if you run faster than the Death Man, lock the door, hide from him, or trick him. Death is still external, and not general. In Stage Three, beginning around age nine or ten, death is recognized not only as final but also as inevitable for all (Nagy, 1959).

Given a child's concept of avoiding death by running away from the death figure, it is no wonder that many adults harbor a primitive fear that they can "catch death" from being too close to their terminally ill partner. Preconsciously, people associate death with night. Consequently, whether to sleep with a terminally ill spouse often arises as an initial conflict for the healthy partner. Case histories point to the number of spouses, who, "out of the blue," pick up and leave home after a long-term hospitalized patient finally goes into remission and/or returns home.

Reinforcing this psychological fear is the well-publicized medical research pointing to viral infection as a probable causal factor in some leukemias and other malignancies. Fear of physical transmission of the disease then compounds the spouse's anxiety. Indeed, patients with many types of malignancies, with unusually low resistance, or who are being treated with steroids, are prone to secondary infections which ordinarily would not affect them. These infections can be potential hazards to people in close contact with the patient (Beeson and McDermott, 1975). Thus, the primitive fear of "catching death" is concretized by publicity regarding possible viral etiology of malignancies, as well as the reality factor of transmissible secondary infections.

Another predisposing factor to inordinate anxiety regarding sex and death is the manner in which parents have handled these topics during the patient's childhood. When parents have been dishonest or evasive in dealing with sex and/or death, "closed communication" around the issue results. When terminal illness occurs—a time when openness is so necessary to avoid isolation and abandonment—the pre-established "conspiracy of silence" is only exacerbated (Zeligs, 1967). Also, if a woman is socialized to believe that sexuality is unimportant, "wrong," useful only for procreation, then she may experience relief at being "exempted" from this felt burden. Obviously, the quality of one's sexuality prior to terminality determines the quality as well as the quantity of sex after diagnosis.

PRECIPITATING FACTORS

Even if a patient has not been predisposed by noxious developmental experiences related to sex and death, the triggering event of the terminal illness and its concomitants invariably precipitates sexual adjustments. These associated factors include numerous drugs, including severe chemotherapy, radiation, body changes and body disability. Yet, when it comes to treating the whole person, the medical team has devoted little or no attention to how a patient's sexuality may be altered or denied during the acute or chronic phase of terminal illness. Drugs, procedures and conditions that can modify the physical or emotional aspects of sexuality are seldom, if ever, discussed with patients, their spouses, or families (Jacobson, 1974).

MEDICAL ASPECTS

Sexual dysfunction can result from many types of physical disorders along with the emotional reactions associated with illness (Masters and Johnson, 1970). It is important to distinguish anatomic and physiological changes from the related psychosocial effects.

Certain hematologic diseases, such as acute and chronic leukemia and Hodgkin's disease, or their treatment, can in and of themselves cause sexual impotence. Other organic conditions associated with malignancies may decrease sexual function. These include diseases of the nervous system, surgery of the pelvic region and endocrine disorders. None of these conditions, however, regularly destroys all sexual function.

Nervous system malignancies: With regard to brain and spinal cord tumors, sexual function is more vulnerable than are the other autonomic functions of urination and defecation. In the male, orgasm and ejaculation are almost always destroyed by a complete upper motor neuron lesion, although erection is preserved. With a complete lower motor neuron lesion, erections are less frequent, but ejaculation and orgasm may occur. With incomplete lesions, whether upper or lower, erection occurs in over 90 per cent, and ejaculation and orgasm may be preserved in 32 to 70 per cent of patients (Bors and Comarr, 1960). They conclude that interest in the other sex and desire for intercourse (or regret of impotence) are present in all male patients with spinal cord lesions. There has been much less research on the sexual behavior of women with neurologic disorders. In these cases, women's libido seems to depend on various psychodynamic factors, as well as their age, and appears to be less constant than in males (Ford and Orfirer, 1967).

Diseases that mutilate: Diseases such as cancer of the rectum and colon not only cause deterioration in bodily processes, but also result in the mutilation and deformation of the body. Consequently, the usual forms of sexual functioning may be diminished or destroyed. Radical surgery employed to prolong life may cause sexual impotence in the male, because the nerves of erection are particularly vulnerable to trauma in the dissection of the rectum and the prostate. The average incidence of this dysfunction is 76 per cent (Jacobson, 1974). Regardless of age, men scheduled to undergo such surgery should be apprised of the possibility of impotence afterwards. The availability of a willing and able sexual partner is the most important consideration in continuing sexual activity before and after surgery. Amputation of the penis as treatment for carcinoma is also sexually disabling; yet patients have reported satisfactory sexual lives following plastic surgical reconstruction of the penis (Barton, 1972).

The female cancer patient also presents special needs. An operation on her genitals, breasts or reproductive organs can be an emotionally traumatic experience. Surgery in these areas often threatens a woman's self-image, making her feel a less-than-complete female, and symbolically signifying the end of all sexual sensation. Sexual dysfunction in these cases appears to be primarily psychologically based. Women who had radical vulvectomies performed, with total removal of the clitoris, were repeatedly orgastic in coitus, and felt that their sexual responsiveness was existent to the same degree as before surgery (Daly, 1971).

Endocrine disorders: The main endocrine disorder associated with sexual dysfunction is diabetes mellitus. The incidence of erectile impotence in men of all ages with this disorder is two to five times higher than in the general population (Ford and Orfirer, 1967). Retrograde ejaculation is also not uncommon in diabetes. Diabetes is sometimes a secondary reaction to severe physiological stress that is often a concomitant of various malignancies, and to prolonged steroid treatment sometimes used in cancer therapy. It is interesting to note that in a textbook on diabetes, the authors state: "Libido usually persists. . . . Effective therapy includes a sympathetic understanding on the part of the physician and a highly individualized approach to each patient" (Ellenberg and Rifkin, 1962; p. 337).

Effects of drugs: The effects of drugs on sexuality are generally better documented and understood for males than for females. This is partly due to the fact that the male response of erection and ejaculation is more visible and quantifiable than the lubrication and swelling in the female.

Central nervous system depressants, including alcohol, barbiturates and sedatives do not have a specific effect on the sex centers. However, small doses of sedatives may temporarily remove sexual inhibitions, while larger doses depress all behavior, including sex. Chronic abuse of sedatives seems to generally diminish sexual functioning. Narcotics, used to control pain, seem to reduce the sex drive specifically. However, this finding is based more upon anecdotal report than on systematically controlled study (Kaplan, 1974).

Firmer evidence supports the finding that androgens, often used in treating breast cancer, stimulate sex centers in both males and females. When phenothiazines are used to control nausea induced by chemotherapy, they can cause "dry" ejaculation to occur. This phenomenon is due to the peripheral autonomic action on the internal vesical sphincter which causes semen to empty into the bladder instead of the urethra. Antianxiety drugs which are also muscle relaxants probably have no direct sexual effects, but sexual interest may increase as a reflection of diminished anxiety. Muscle-relaxing effects may account for the rare orgasm disturbances which are reported (Kaplan, 1974).

Effects of body changes: Body changes which alter appearance and functioning will influence feelings of self-worth, and consequently exert a profound effect on sexual behavior. Extreme weight loss is generally a concomitant of malignancy. Chemotherapy frequently causes hair loss, a devastating blow to the patient's self-image, as well as a traumatizing symbol of pervasive impending losses. Such changes in the patient's appearance can be repugnant to the spouse, causing a further spiraling downward of sexual interest. Patients may use sex to deny their illness. In order to ward off feelings of loss and "asexuality," they may make sexual demands on the spouse which are quite inconsistent with former patterns in their relationship. This attempted overcompensation often meets with failure, which then triggers even more frantic efforts at denial.

Loss of sexual function due to medical factors in terminal illness is less extensive than is often assumed (Ford and Orfirer, 1967). Nonetheless, a self-fulfilling prophecy persists on the part of the patient, spouse and care-giver: a terminally ill individual will neither be interested nor able to function effectively in sex. This assumption may have evolved from people's association of cancer with pain, such that significant others try to spare their loved ones any additional discomfort. Yet this belief is not necessarily valid, for severe pain occurs in less than 15 per cent of cancer patients (Exton-Smith, 1961). Thus, emotional reactions of the patient, family, and care-giver are as important in precipitating sexual dysfunction as is the illness itself (Ford and Orfirer, 1967).

ANTICIPATORY GRIEF

An important aspect of terminal illness is designated "anticipatory grief" —any grief occurring prior to rather than at the time of or following the loss (Aldrich, 1955; Schoenberg, Carr, Peretz, Kutscher and Goldberg, 1974). One might expect a natural disengagement to occur at the same pace on the part of both the patient and spouse. As the former readies himself to "let go," the latter not only is preparing to "let go" of the patient, but may also be seeking new attachments and investments for the future. While this parallel disengagement generally occurs, the patient and his mate are frequently "out of sync" with regard to their individual experiencing of the stages of dying (Kubler-Ross, 1969). Continual confrontation in his hospital environment with the reality of impending death facilitates the patient's move toward acceptance, a part of anticipatory grief. Meanwhile, the healthy spouse may insist on denying reality, and consequently feel betrayed and resentful when the patient does not embrace his own hope for a miracle. This reaction often occurs when couples have been fused in their relationship, continually presenting a "united front" and unable to tolerate any differences between them. Being "out of sync" in the dying process can then cause an irreparable rift between them.

Clinical observations indicate that overt anticipatory grief does not consistently accelerate in degree as the loss approaches. As a matter of fact, the longer a patient is in remission, leading a normal life, the harder it is for the patient and spouse to "keep in touch" with the reality of impending death. The constant balance and flow between denial (forestalling anticipatory grief work) and acceptance (facilitating anticipatory grief work) may prevent a linear acceleration of anticipatory grief over time (Aldrich, 1974).

Long-term hospitalization, generally accompanied by sexual deprivation, may precipitate problems for either partner. The terminally ill patient generally believes that his mate is understanding and accepting of the imposed abstinence. To the contrary, however, the spouse often experiences lowered self-esteem and depression. Anger may be engendered, and expressed directly as chronic irritability or indirectly in the form of seductive behavior toward others. Forced resignation and hopelessness may characterize some situations (Barton, 1972). Ill health may also be a concomitant of separation for the spouse. A recent study (Chester, 1973) indicates that continuing absence of a husband, as well as loss of a husband, appears to precipitate ill health in 85 per cent of women who were studied in a state of psychosocial transition. Other researchers (Murray-Parkes, 1964, 1971; Marsden, 1969; Berkman, 1969) confirm this proneness to ill health during periods of anticipatory grief and bereavement. These findings point to the need for society to furnish such individuals with social support systems.

Severe relationship problems may occur if a patient who has been considered terminally ill does not die as predicted. Paradoxically, both partners may experience a sense of letdown with the shift in prognosis. As Peretz (1970) has pointed out: "Even the loss of an old, familiar symptom as a result of medical intervention can result in unpleasant feeling states when the symptom has provided degrees of secondary gain and control over aspects of the environment" (p. 5). In particular, the healthy spouse may be angry. Having worked through his anticipatory grief, and emotionally buried the person, he lacks the reserves to begin the relationship again. Or he may fear getting close because of the threat of having to endure pain of anticipated loss once again. The former patient must shift his role identity from that of a terminally ill to a healthy individual. Whatever sexual estrangement may have occurred in the course of the illness may now be compounded by these major adjustments (Fellner, 1973).

DOUBLE-BIND COMMUNICATION

As well as the dissonance between sexuality and death, the terminally ill patient is confronted by double-bind communication patterns regarding his impending death. All too often, people significant to the patient emit incongruent verbal and nonverbal messages in their attempts to conceal the patient's terminal status from him. These efforts are futile and misguided: managing a host of contradictory cues is virtually impossible, especially since most dying patients suspect and/or want to know the truth (Avorn, 1973; Feifel, 1963; Glaser and Strauss, 1965; Kelley and Frieson, 1950; Kubler-Ross, 1969). The double-bind process triggers a brutal set of social interactions which can be destructive to the patient in all areas of his life, including sexual function (Erickson and Hyerstay, 1974).

Going along with the charade will cost the patient as much psychological energy as it does his significant others. The dissonance between what the patient hears and what he senses leads him to question his own perception of reality. Cut off from access to valid information concerning his condition, he fills in the gaps with his own fantasies and fears. As a result of his own helplessness and frustration in the double-bind situation, the patient may respond to others with misinterpretations, and exhibit little empathy for them. His constricted and inappropriate emotional behavior serves to estrange him even further from his partner.

This "death dishonesty" is often an overlay of the sexual dishonesty which comprises many couples' *modus vivendi*. When communication patterns have been closed in general, and have been deceptive with regard to sexuality, then dishonesty about death will compound the emotional estrangement. Regardless of the quality of communication before the illness, a patient will withdraw into apathy if he realizes that trusted family members have contributed to the deception concerning his impending death (Strauss and Glaser, 1965).

PERPETUATING FACTORS

The hospital environment is pivotal in perpetuating the sexual problems of the terminally ill. At a time when intimate human relationships are most necessary, the typical hospital design deters any nurturing of bonds between mates. Rarely is there a private room for patients to share intimacies with loved ones. The demand for conjugal visits for prisoners has been voiced more strongly than the same rights for long-term hospitalized individuals. As a human being with basic needs, the patient is certainly entitled to private, tranquil conditions for lovemaking when he is able and desirous.

Diminished sexuality can be considered as a category of loss, with the potential concomitants of depression, grief and process of adaptation which may include suicide. Clinical impressions indicate that as one's sexuality is perceived to decline, the incidence of suicidal ideation, suicide attempt and suicide itself increases (Leviton, 1973). A recent study found that as suicidal ideation shifted to an actual attempt, body-image and sexual self-concept worsened. Case histories of suicidal patients indicated no sexual expression for months prior to their attempt (Henderson, 1971). These findings accord with Farber's (1968) theory of suicide as a "disease of failed hope." In his conceptualization, suicide is a function of vulnerability of the personality (low state of competence) and a deprivation (threat to acceptable life condition).

Emotional withdrawal is a facet of anticipatory grief. Its manifestation by the patient reinforces the commonly held expectation of patient, spouse and care-giver that the sexual life of the terminal patient ends with illness. Furthermore, the patient and spouse may consider it indulgent or inappropriate to seek pleasure during this period, and both will often refrain from making sexual overtures. The healthy spouse in particular may experience guilt over having sexual desires at this time, and the lack of gratification of these needs can lead to depression. An absence of sexual feelings then derives from the grief and depression, resulting in a decreased sense of femininity or masculinity, in turn a threat to self-esteem. A vicious circle culminates in sexual dysfunction. It is not surprising that mates who become intensely depressed during the stage of anticipatory grief, and lack the comfort of a fulfilling sexual relationship are among those who commonly commit suicide. Ironically, the availability of sedatives and tranquilizers from the patient's doctor, prescribed to assuage grief, often adds to the suicide potential (Danto, 1974).

A patient's sexual fantasies and feelings of sexual attachment often transfer to his primary care-giver, in many ways replacing the spouse as love object. The patient's feeling of dependency leads him to perceive the doctor as an all-powerful soother of ills. This emotional investment is reinforced by the fact that during hospitalization, a patient's body is constantly touched and tended by doctors and nurses. Touching in this framework is exempt from the usual boundaries and taboos: even children carry out sexual exploration under the guise of "playing doctor" (Frankfort, 1972). If a woman has been taught that access to her body is only permitted if love is involved, she may reduce dissonance by developing a romantic attachment to her doctor. The same process may apply to men in relation to female doctors and nurses. Thus, the care-giver's use of tactile comfort to minimize the patient's fear and isolation strengthens that attachment. In contrast, the common fear of a spouse to touch a terminally ill patient leads to a weakening of their bond. The efforts of the care-giver are experienced in juxtaposition with the reluctance of the spouse, and thus the parallel disengagement process is reinforced.

RECOMMENDATIONS FOR THERAPEUTIC INTERVENTION

I will now offer recommendations for intervention, based upon the aforementioned factors which can predispose, precipitate and perpetuate sexual problems for the terminally ill and their significant others.

1. Honest and open communication regarding sex and death must begin in early childhood in order to change dysfunctional societal attitudes around both issues. In terms of death experience, small losses and griefs can prepare a child for facing larger ones. For example, instead of immediately replacing a pet that has died, parents should encourage a child's expressions of grief and his reminiscences, including a burial ritual. When a death occurs in the family, its cause should be explained to the child, and its finality differentiated from the temporary nature of sleep. The open sharing of sorrow can include funeral attendance for the child should he so desire. A similar candor should characterize the topic of sexuality. Hopefully, honest communication in the home could transfer to a hospital setting, obviating the need for people to maintain an often unwanted charade, ultimately so destructive to intimate relationships. If double-bind communication is considered to be causal in precipitating schizophrenia (Weakland, 1966), then it would certainly appear to trigger fear, rage and withdrawal in the terminally ill.

2. Sexual interest and activity continue to be important in the lives of a great many long-term patients. In one study of fifty-five male and female patients, over half indicated that they would have liked to discuss sexual problems prior to discharge, preferably with a like-sexed physician (Sadoughi, Leshner and Fine, 1971). Most helping-profession schools give only cursory attention to the areas of sexuality and terminality. As a result, care-givers are poorly prepared to undertake frank discussions with patients and spouses about sexual problems and practices, much less about facing death. Until these anxiety-laden subjects can be comfortably handled as part of one's ongoing education, it would seem crucial to provide separate courses on sexuality and terminality at this point in curriculum development. The courses should be offered early in the curriculum, and not as a mere afterthought for in-service training. This early exposure would facilitate students' specialization and competence in the areas. Furthermore, a combined didactic-experiential approach would enable individuals to work through their own discomfort, confusion, resistance and biases. A combined course on sexuality and terminality could synthesize these phenomena as integral parts of the natural life cycle, rather than as subjects ridden with pathology and taboos.

3. The hospital environment must be arranged to encourage ongoing intimacy for patient and spouse at a time when abandonment is so feared. It is an ironic juxtaposition that there is isolation in hospitalization, but virtually no privacy. In any case, the privacy of a regular hospital room could be self-defeating, since it is associated with so much pain and anxiety. A "Quiet Room" furnished with couch, carpet, soft lights and music is needed to counteract the usual cold hardware of hospital rooms. Such a room could replicate the home ambience which patients miss so badly, and might be used for family and conjugal visits, as well as for group counseling sessions. To further create "home connectedness" as an antidote to disengagement, patients could bring objects from home reminiscent of shared joys, including their own bed linens. A reclining lounge chair should be available in the room of every terminally ill patient, so that a loved one can rest comfortably near a critically ill mate who needs the reassurance of a continued loving presence. Whenever possible, live-in arrangements for spouses should be made which are not contingent on wealth as is generally the case. The therapeutic effects of maintaining one's personal appearance are well-known. The accessibility of a hairdresser in a hospital setting would do much to refurbish the patient's sense of looking as well as possible. Recreation also provides a means of breaking the monotony, as well as furnishing a valuable mode for social interaction. Play, like sex, is intimately related to health and life, and should be encouraged by having a recreation facility for the terminally ill patient and others who are meaningful to him.

4. Individual and group counselling related to sexual issues must be an ongoing part of total patient care. Any medical workup should include an evaluation of sexual functioning, determined by a sexual history as developed by Wahl (1967). Because the spouse is so often ignored in the treatment process, yet is so vital in giving support to the patient, total care should embrace the patient, spouse and family from the beginning. Consequently, in the early stages of the illness, sexual problems may be touched upon briefly, in the form of anticipatory guidance, by indicating how sexual drive or performance may be temporarily reduced by drugs, fatigue or other factors.

Once the patient is over the acute stage of the illness and able to return home, if only for short visits, the clinician should include sexuality in the list of other topics (such as return to work, living arrangements, and so on) to be discussed with the patient. Later, he may ease the way for the patient and/or spouse to disclose any concerns by making some such comment as, "Now that you're home, I expect that you are finding your relationship somewhat different." This statement also reduces threat by implying that the problem is not unique. A most important task for the practitioner is to ascertain the meaning of sexuality in both personal and interpersonal terms for the patient and spouse. If sexuality has played a major role in the person's over-all identity, more difficulties can be anticipated, especially if impairment or deprivation of sexual function is involved. Loss of a sexual outlet often precipitates a reactive depression, which is then exacerbated by avoidance of the topic. A further area of avoidance is that of counseling the elderly about sexuality. An individual over sixty-five years of age, terminally ill and having sexual concerns, is a victim of a "triple whammy." Age is no barrier to a continued sexual life, and when all intimacy is denied the elderly, inappropriate sexual expression may occur (Weinberg, 1971).

As I have implied throughout this article, a team approach to handling the issues of sexuality and terminality is almost mandatory. Much loneliness is engendered by hospitalization, particularly at night. Thus, care-givers, whether they be doctors, nurses, clergy or social workers, should be interchangeably available to the patient and spouse as anxiety rises. Also, instead of becoming surrogates for the spouse, practitioners should encourage mates to touch the patient frequently.

Group counseling is particularly effective in eliciting patient-spouse concerns. It should be a regular, ongoing group, where feelings can be ventilated, information shared and clarified, and coping behavior modeled. The gamut of behavioral approaches to sexual counseling that have been researched and documented could be utilized. These include the therapeutic use of masturbation ("self-exploration"), fantasies, and the regenerating use of the vibrator for women (Annon, 1973). Counseling can also focus on techniques to remediate sexual dysfunction (Masters and Johnson, 1970; Kaplan, 1974), and coital positions which are more comfortable for the disabled (Goldberg, 1960; Romano, 1973). Groups are settings conducive for discussing sex, since most people have had some experience in peer-group disclosure on the topic (Romano, 1973). Thus, groups can be enabling and educational, providing an opportunity for the modeling of desirable behaviors within a nonthreatening context. The support of other individuals facing similar problems engenders hope for being able to live a full, meaningful life in whatever time is left.

CONCLUSION

Terminal illness and impending loss can lead to an intensification of life and serve as a stimulus for a new and richer phase of development. Certainly the common assumption that the sexual life of the terminally ill patient ends with the diagnosis is not borne out by research or clinical observation. Although this attitude is rarely verbalized, its existence is reflected in care-givers' avoidance of the subject. The available literature, however, indicates that sexuality continues as an important part of many patients' lives, although their drive and rate of performance may be reduced. Today, such patients survive longer and with better functional capacity than ever before. Once past the acute stage of illness, they begin to search for a new equilibrium not centered on sickness or disability. It seems both appropriate and necessary therefore to facilitate life-promoting sexual relationships as a factor in any treatment program. As Arnold Toynbee has so poignantly written: "Love cannot save life from death, but it can fulfil life's purpose."

REFERENCES AND RECOMMENDED READINGS

ALDRICH, C. "Some Dynamics of Anticipatory Grief." In Schoenberg et al., Anticipatory Grief, 1974.

ANNON, J. "The Therapeutic Use of Masturbation in the Treatment of Sexual Disorders." In Rubin, R., J. Brody, and J. Henderson, eds. Advances in Behavior Therapy. New York: Academic Press, 1973.

AVORN, J. "Beyond Dying," Harper's, March 1973, pp. 56–64.

BARTON, D. "Sexually Deprived Individuals," Medical Aspects of Human Sexuality. February 1972, pp. 88–97.

BEESON, P., and W. MC DERMOTT. Textbook of Medicine. Philadelphia: W. B. Saunders, 1975.

BERKMAN, P. "Spouseless Motherhood, Psychological Stress and Physical Morbidity," Journal of Health and Social Behavior, 1969, p. 10.

BORS, E., and A. COMARR. "Neurological Disturbances of Sexual Function with Special Reference to 529 Patients with Spinal-Cord Injury," *Urol. Survey*, 10 (1960), pp. 191–222.

CHESTER, R. "Health and Marital Breakdown: Some Implications for Doctors," *Journal of Psychosomatic Research*, 1973, pp. 317–321.

DALY, M. "The Clitoris as Related to Human Sexuality," *Medical Aspects of Human Sexuality*, 5 (1971), p. 80.

DANTO, B. "Drug Ingestion and Suicide During Anticipatory Grief." In *Anticipatory Grief*, Schoenberg et al., eds.

DAVIS, E. "Eros and Thanatos: The Not So Benign Neglect." *Texas Report on Biology and Medicine*, 1974, pp. 32, 43–48.

ELLENBERG, M. and H. RIFKIN. *Clinical Diabetes Mellitus*. New York: McGraw-Hill, 1962.

ERICKSON, R. and M. HYERSTAY. "The Dying Patient and the Double-Bind Hypothesis," *Omega*, 5 (1974), pp. 287–298.

EXTON-SMITH, A. "Terminal Illness in the Aged," *Lancet*, 2 (1961), p. 305.

FARBER, M. *Theory of Suicide*. New York: Funk and Wagnalls, 1968.

FEIFEL, H. "Death," in N. Faberow, ed. *Taboo Topics*. New York: Atherton Press, 1963.

FELLNER, C. "Family Disruption After Cancer Cure," *American Family Physician*, 8 (1973), pp. 169–172.

FORD, A. and A. ORFIRER. "Sexual Behavior and the Chronically Ill Patient," *Medical Aspects of Human Sexuality*, 1967, pp. 51–61.

FRANKFORT, E. *Vaginal Politics*. New York: Bantam Books, 1972.

GLASER, B. and A. STRAUSS. *Awareness of Dying*. Chicago: Aldine, 1965.

GOLDBERG, M. "What Do You Tell Patients Who Ask About Coital Positions?" *Medical Aspects of Human Sexuality*, 1960, pp. 43–48.

HENDERSON, J. "Competence, Threat, Hope and Self-Destructive Behavior: Suicide." Unpublished dissertation. College Park: University of Maryland, 1971.

JACOBSON, L. "Illness and Human Sexuality," *Nursing Outlook*, 22 (1974), pp. 1, 50–53.

KAPLAN, H. *The New Sex Therapy*. New York: Brunner/Mazel, 1974.

KELEMAN, S. *Living Your Dying*. New York: Random House, 1974.

KELLY, W. and J. FRIESEN. "Do Cancer Patients Want to Be Told?" *Surgery*, 27 (1950), pp. 822–826.

KUBLER-ROSS, E. *On Death and Dying*. New York: Macmillan, 1969.

LEVITON, D. "The Significance of Sexuality as a Deterrent to Suicide Among the Aged," *Omega*, 4, No. 2 (1973), pp. 163–174.

MARSDEN, D. *Mothers Alone*. London: Allen Lane, 1969.

MASTERS, W. and V. JOHNSON. *Human Sexual Inadequacy*. Boston: Little, Brown and Co., 1970.

MURRAY-PARKES, C. "Psycho-Social Transitions: A Field for Study," *Social Science and Medicine*, 1971, p. 5.

———. "Effects of Bereavement on Physical and Mental Health—A Study of the Medical Records of Widows," *British Medical Journal*, 1964, pp. 2, 274.

NAGY, M. "The Child's View of Death." In *The Meaning of Death*, H. Feifel, ed. New York: McGraw-Hill, 1959.

PERETZ, D. "Development, Object-Relationships and Loss." In *Loss and Grief*, Schoenberg *et al.*, eds.

ROMANO, M. "Sexual Counseling in Groups," *The Journal of Sex Research*, 9, No. 1 (1973), pp. 69–78.

———. "Sexuality and the Disabled Female," *Accent on Living*, 1973, pp. 27–35.

SADOUGHI, W., M. LESHNER, and H. FINE. "Sexual Adjustment in a Chronically Ill and Physically Disabled Population: A Pilot Study," *Arch of Phys. Med. and Rehab.*, 1971, pp. 311–317.

SCHOENBERG, B., A. CARR, A. KUTSCHER, D. PERETZ, and I. GOLDBERG, eds. *Anticipatory Grief*. New York: Columbia University Press, 1974.

SCHOENBERG, B., A. CARR, D. PERETZ, and A. KUTSCHER. *Loss and Grief*. New York: Columbia University Press, 1970.

WAHL, C. "Psychiatric Techniques in the Taking of a Sexual History." In *Sexual Problems: Diagnosis and Treatment in Medical Practice*, C. Wahl, ed. New York: Free Press, 1967.

WEINBERG, J. "Sexuality in Later Life," *Medical Aspects of Human Sexuality*. 1971, pp. 216–227.

WEAKLAND, J. "The Double-Bind Hypothesis of Schizophrenia and Three-Party Interaction." In *The Etiology of Schizophrenia*, D. Jackson ed., New York: Basic Books, 1960.

ZELIGS, R. "Children's Attitudes Toward Death," *Mental Hygiene*, 51 (1967), pp. 393–396.

ABOUT
THE
CONTRIBUTORS

RITA MAE BROWN, Ph.D. is the author of *Rubyfruit Jungle, In Her Day, Songs to a Handsome Woman,* and *The Hand That Cradles the Rock.* Her political articles have appeared in numerous publications. Ms. Brown has been an organizer in the feminist and gay movements for the last ten years.

CATHERINE S. CHILMAN, M.S.W., Ph.D., is Professor and Director of Family Development Institute, Center for Advanced Studies, School of Social Welfare, University of Wisconsin—Milwaukee. Her major research and publication activities are in the fields of adolescent sexuality, parent-child satisfactions and dissatisfactions, poverty and the family, population and family planning. She was formerly Chief of Research Development and Utilization Branch, Welfare Administrator, U.S. Department of Health, Education, and Welfare. She is the author of *Growing Up Poor, Your Child: Six to Twelve,* and numerous articles in professional journals.

RANDAL G. FORRESTER, Executive Director, Persad Center, Inc.; Appointee, Pennsylvania Governor's Council for Sexual Minorities; Appointee, Task Force for Sexual Minorities, Department of Welfare, Commonwealth of Pennsylvania. Mr. Forrester is a cofounder of Persad Center, a comprehensive out-patient mental health center for sexual minorities. He has had extensive clinical experience working with gay women and men as well as wide experience in lecturing about problems affecting sexual minorities. He is actively involved as an advocate within the state government of Pennsylvania.

[293]

LEON H. GINSBERG, A.C.S.W., Ph.D., is Dean and Professor at the School of Social Work, West Virginia University, Morgantown, West Virginia. He has written a number of articles on the civil rights of mentally ill and mentally retarded people.

JEAN S. GOCHROS, M.S.W., is a social worker in private practice specializing in family and sexual counseling in Honolulu, Hawaii. She is the author of many articles in the lay and professional literature. Her articles "From a Family Counselor's Notebook" appear in the *American Baby Magazine*. She has conducted numerous workshops and classes in human sexuality in Hawaii and on the mainland. She is currently completing a book on sex education for parents and teachers.

BERNICE GOODMAN, M.S., A.C.S.W., C.S.W., is in private practice in New York City. She is a lesbian-feminist psychotherapist, who has a large practice composed mostly of lesbians and lesbian mothers. She is cofounder and chairperson of the Board of Directors of the Institute for Human Identity, an organization offering therapeutic services to the gay and bisexual community of Greater New York. She has taught courses and given professional papers on Homosexuality, Lesbians, and Lesbian Mothers.

RUTH R. GOSSETT, M.S.W., A.C.S.W., is the Director of Special Student Services at Syracuse University, School of Social Work. Her article in this book is a result of research conducted to meet requirements for a Ph.D. in Social Sciences, Maxwell School of Citizenship, Syracuse, New York. She has led workshops on topics relating to youthful black widows at the National Conference on Black Families in Louisville, Kentucky, for Delta Sigma Theta Inc., Eastern Regional Conference, Washington, D.C., National Convention, Seattle, Washington, and for New York City and Syracuse Alumnae Chapters.

ERWIN J. HAEBERLE, Ph.D., has studied literature, philosophy and sociology at Cornell, Glasgow, and Heidelberg Universities. He has written several scholarly publications in various fields and is the co-author (with Martin Goldstein, M.D.) of *The Sex Book, A Modern Pictorial Encyclopedia*. At present he is working on *The Sex Atlas, a New Illustrated Guide*.

JAMES HUGGINS, M.S.W., Director of Education, Persad Center, Inc.; Board Member, Greater Pittsburgh Sexuality Council; Member of the Social Work Advisory Committee, Planned Parenthood Center of Pittsburgh. Mr. Huggins is a cofounder of Persad Center, a comprehensive out-patient mental health center for sexual minorities. He has been actively involved in the Gay Liberation Movement and has lectured extensively to professional and lay groups on the sociological and psychological issues affecting sexual minority persons.

LOIS JAFFE, M.S.W., is Associate Professor at the Graduate School of Social Work, University of Pittsburgh, and a Psychiatric social worker at the Irene Stacey Mental Health Clinic, Butler, Pennsylvania. Since her diagnosis of acute leukemia in 1973, she has written widely about her experiences from the combined perspective of social worker and patient advocate. She teaches a seminar on intervention with the dying patient, conducts workshops at universities and health centers throughout the country, and works directly with patients and their families. She is married and has four children.

LEANOR BOULIN JOHNSON, Ph.D., has been an Assistant Professor of Sociology at Florida State University since 1974. She has conducted seminars and workshops and published articles on the black family, minorities, and cross-cultural premarital sexual patterns. She is currently gathering data on sex role stereotyping, cohabitation, and sexual patterns of black and white college students and is active in combating racism and sexism in elementary school textbooks in the Tallahassee area of northern Florida.

MYRA T. JOHNSON, M.S.S.W., is a doctoral student at the Florence Heller Graduate School of Advanced Studies in Social Welfare, Brandeis University. She is active in several women's groups and projects in the Boston area and is currently researching the dynamics of feminist therapy.

JAMES KELLY, M.S.S.W., Ph.D., is Assistant Professor of Social Work at the University of Hawaii. He is the chairperson of the Gerontology Specialization in the school and Director of the Cross-National Multi-Disciplinary Summer Institute in Gerontology.

WINIFRED KEMPTON, M.S.W., A.C.S.W., is Director of Education and Community Organization of Planned Parenthood of Southeastern Pennsylvania. A lecturer and training coordinator, she has acted as a consultant and educator on the subject of sex education and family planning for handicapped persons to professionals and parent groups throughout the United States and Canada. She is a co-author of *Love, Sex, and Birth Control for the Mentally Retarded* and *Guidelines for Training in Sexuality and the Mentally Handicapped.* She has authored *Techniques for Leading Group Discussion on Human Sexuality,* and *A Teacher's Guide to Sex Education for Persons with Disabilities that Hinder Learning.*

STUART A. KIRK, D.S.W., is Associate Dean and Associate Professor, School of Social Welfare, University of Wisconsin—Milwaukee. His research and publications have been in the areas of deviant behavior, community mental health and the utilization of research.

LARRY LISTER, D.S.W., is Director of Social Services at Leahi Hospital, Associate Professor of Social Work at the University of Hawaii, and a member of the staff of the Social Work Institute for the Study of Sex at the University of Hawaii. He is the father of two teenage daughters.

MARTIN B. LOEB, A.C.S.W., Ph.D., Professor of Social Work and Director, Faye McBeath Institute on Aging and Adult Life, University of Wisconsin—Madison. Professor Loeb has done considerable research in, as well as writing on, the problems of adults and the aged.

DENNIS M. OGAWA, Ph.D. is an Associate Professor in the American Studies Department at the University of Hawaii and the Director of the Japanese American Research Center (JARC). He has written numerous books and articles in the area of Asian American studies and comparative cultures.

MARY D. ROMANO, M.S.W., A.C.S.W., Supervisor, Social Service Department, Presbyterian Hospital, New York. Mrs. Romano has led numerous workshops and published a number of papers related to the socio-emotional concerns and problems of people with physical handicaps. She is consultant in the area of sexuality with a number of consumer and professional groups serving handicapped persons.

DAVID ROTHENBERG, Executive Director of the Fortune Society, was the founder of this organization, which serves as an advocate for prisoners and ex-convicts. The Fortune Society grew out of a play which Mr. Rothenberg produced in New York in 1967. Since then his work has been with prisoners and former prisoners, helping individuals and attempting to make the prison system accountable to the public. He has served on several Governor's commissions and is on the Board of Directors of numerous groups, including the National Council on Crime and Delinquency and the New York City Legal Aid Society.

LE ROY G. SCHULTZ, A.C.S.W., is Professor of Social Work at West Virginia University. He has had extensive experience with sex victims through both criminal court experience and in private practice. He has written numerous articles, has led workshops on sex victims and their treatment, and teaches a graduate course on sexual victimology. He is the co-editor of the book *Human Sexuality and Social Work*.

MARY SWEENEY SMITH, M.A., received her training to teach deaf children at Pennsylvania State University and later taught deaf students in the Erie public school system. She moved to Hawaii in 1960 and taught at Hawaii School for the Deaf and the Blind. In 1966 she obtained her master's degree in the National Leadership Training Program in the Area of the Deaf at the University of California at Northridge. She then served the school as Counselor and as Supervising Teacher. Ms. Smith is the mother of five adopted sons, one of whom is deaf.

MONA WASOW, M.S.S.W., is Clinical Assistant Professor, School of Social Work, University of Wisconsin—Madison. Head of the Family Planning Field Unit at the School of Social Work, she teaches a course on Human Sexuality, with an emphasis on the sexually excluded, and has led numerous workshops on this topic. She is consultant to the Social Work Institute for the Study of Sex, University of Hawaii.